Moral Education

...It Comes With The Territory

EDITED BY

David Purpel

University of North Carolina
Greensboro

Kevin Ryan

Ohio State University

A Phi Delta Kappa Publication

distributed by

McCutchan Publishing Corporation
2526 Grove Street
Berkeley, California 94704

© 1976 by McCutchan Publishing Corporation
All rights reserved

Library of Congress Catalog Card Number 76-18041
ISBN 0-8211-1516-2

Printed in the United States of America

To our parents:
Sybil and I. W. Purpel
and
Margaret and John Ryan

Contents

Foreword   xi
   Harold G. Shane

Preface   xv

Acknowledgments   xix

PART I. BACKGROUND AND INTRODUCTION   1

Chapter 1. Moral Education: What Is It and Where Are We?   3
   David Purpel and Kevin Ryan

Chapter 2. Forming a Value Curriculum: Two Philosophical
           Issues To Consider   11
   James W. Watkins

Chapter 3. The Moral Content of American Public Education   20
   Israel Scheffler

Chapter 4. Moral Education: Aims and Methods in China, the
           U.S.S.R., the U.S., and England   30
   William F. Connell

Chapter 5. It Comes with the Territory: The Inevitability of
    Moral Education in the Schools   44
  David Purpel and Kevin Ryan

Chapter 6. Moral Education in the Classroom: Some
    Instructional Issues   55
  David Purpel and Kevin Ryan

PART II. THE VALUES CLARIFICATION APPROACH   69

Introduction   71

Chapter 7. Selection from *Values and Teaching*   75
  Louis Raths, Merrill Harmin, and Sidney B. Simon

Chapter 8. Clarifying Values Clarification: Some
    Theoretical Issues   116
  Howard Kirschenbaum

Chapter 9. Values Clarification vs. Indoctrination   126
  Sidney B. Simon

Chapter 10. Problems and Contradictions of Values
    Clarification   136
  John S. Stewart

Chapter 11. A Critical View of Values Clarification   152
  Alan L. Lockwood

PART III. THE COGNITIVE-DEVELOPMENTAL
    APPROACH   171

Introduction   173

Chapter 12. The Cognitive-Developmental Approach to Moral
    Education   176
  Lawrence Kohlberg

Chapter 13. The Moral Atmosphere of the School   196
  Lawrence Kohlberg

Chapter 14. Moral Education in a Canadian Setting   221
  Edmund V. Sullivan and Clive Beck

Chapter 15. A Curriculum in Moral Education for Adolescents   235
  Ralph L. Mosher and Paul Sullivan

Chapter 16. Developmental Psychology as a Guide to Value
      Education: A Review of "Kohlbergian" Programs   252
  James Rest

Chapter 17. Two Approaches to Moral Education   275
  Anne Colby

Chapter 18. Why Doesn't Lawrence Kohlberg Do His
      Homework?   288
  Richard S. Peters

Chapter 19. The Kohlberg Bandwagon: Some Reservations   291
  Jack R. Fraenkel

PART IV. THE COGNITIVE APPROACH   309

Introduction   311

Chapter 20. Cognitive Moral Education   313
  Michael Scriven

Chapter 21. Moral Relativism and Values Education   330
  Gary Wehlage and Alan L. Lockwood

Chapter 22. Moral Education: Is Reasoning Enough?   349
  Donald W. Oliver and Mary Jo Bane

Chapter 23. Moral and Ethical Development in a
      Democratic Society   370
  Irving Kristol

POSTSCRIPT   385

Chapter 24. What Can Be Done?   387
  David Purpel and Kevin Ryan

RESOURCES   397

APPENDIX   403

Moral Education's Muddled Mandate   405
  Kevin Ryan and Michael G. Thompson

INDEX   419

Foreword

My childhood in the 1920s was saturated with the moral values
of a middle class, midwest family—values which the home, school,
church, and total community more or less accepted. Nor was there
ever much doubt as to what was "right" or "wrong" fifty years ago.
What was "right" sometimes was tinged by hypocrisy, however, or
was abused more than honored. I clearly recall, too, that while the
moral precepts on which I was reared failed to kill the urge to engage
in minor "sins" such as smoking behind the barn, they generated
enough guilt to destroy my pleasure in many transgressions!

In the 1950s and 1960s, the winds of change began to dissipate
many verities of my youthful years. Parental permissiveness became
commonplace and a tide of relativism leeched away the clear-cut
black and white moral distinctions and left only a gray shade of
doubt and the frustrations of uncertainty. Indeed, by 1965, many of
the moral conformities that a WASP culture once had taken for
granted began to be ignored—for example, the conduct codes that
determined what a "proper" or "moral" person did or did not do.

During the early 1970s almost none of the old values that dictated moral behaviors continued to be held sacred. This was true, for
instance, with regard to one-time sensitive matters such as modest

modes of dress, the use of drugs, and sexually atypical behaviors. What once sufficed to make one a social outcast scarcely caused a head to turn in 1970, except perhaps for an occasional oldster hiding his head in embarrassment. During this interval many middle-aged parents and some younger ones felt ineffectual and uneasy because many of our children and youth churlishly rejected or vigorously resisted adult direction, direction which from time immemorial human communities had imposed on the young through home, church, and school.

Now, as the 1970s wane, a new morality seems to be making itself felt. This quickened interest in what is of value and what is "moral" lends timeliness to the important contribution which Professors Ryan and Purpel have made in their book. Its significance is further enhanced by the dangerous epidemic of crises through which most of the world's nations are passing. These crises serve to remind us that humanity has precious little time in which to reach a number of value-decisions of great importance to the future. As they are made with wisdom or folly these decisions probably will determine whether our species can begin to achieve dignity, equity, and peace or whether we retrogress into a dangerous rerun of the worst features of the middle ages.

At most, about fifteen years remain in which our species has the opportunity to develop policies and practices that will improve the present outlook for more than four billion people on our increasingly crowded globe. After 1990 or 2000, in the absence of wise, value-oriented decisions, irreversible damage may be done to the biosphere. The energy crisis, hunger that last year resulted in a million deaths and ten million cases of severe malnutrition, danger in the spread of nuclear weaponry, and threats to freedom are but a few of the challenges with which the next decade will abound.

Patently, it is impossible to forecast with any certainty what the moral climate will be like ten years from now. One can only hope for the best. However, if the future is free of major catastrophes, some ingredients of a new "mix" of moral values probably can be identified. Foreshadowing new values is the concern for human rights which surfaced recently in various "lib" movements associated with women, ethnic minorities, and the gay, and in concern for the old, the very young, and the disadvantaged. Another is the phenomenon of environmentalism which led to the unexpected rejection of plans to develop an American SST, the unprecedented drive to clean up our air and water, and legislation limiting the prerogative of free enterprise to exploit or pollute. Searching examinations of business practices and the growth of the consumer protection movement is a third development which ranges from exposing shoddy, unhealthy, or dangerous products to probing unduly high profits.

Fourth, and perhaps the most dramatic dimension of the new moral look, is the appraising public eye presently being cast on big government, big labor, big business, the military, industry, and the dubious bribes paid by multinational corporations. All of these institutions once were deemed to be beyond scrutiny or reproach—even if not above suspicion.

In view of the evidence the recent past provides, it seems reasonable to infer that resource depletion, an over-crowded planet, hunger, the threat of nuclear holocaust, and similar problems have combined to create a new concern with values. We are approaching a decision threshold, where decent choices of importance to the quality of twenty-first century life will be made. This decision threshold, if it is to be crossed with a skill that can quell problems of the late 1970s and 1980s, must be based on a reexamination of moral values. These values will permeate adult leadership in policy making during the crucial decades ahead. They also will—by contagion, precept, and example—permeate the moral education of youth.

Clearly, what we can do today and tomorrow, in the process of schooling, to clarify our values deserves the most careful attention from educators. This book should be of distinct value to those with the courage to base their efforts on moral values that serve human welfare.

Bloomington, Indiana   *Harold G. Shane*
April 2, 1976

Preface

Before you begin this book, we would like to sketch out a few notions that underlie its content. We hope this sketch will give a clear picture of the intentions and hopes that have guided us in the preparation of this manuscript.

Audience. First of all, our book is primarily directed at those who are concerned with *practice*, with what actually happens or should happen in school. We hope that this book will be of value to many other people, but we have tried to keep in mind those who are engaged in or who are about to engage in the actual practice of moral education in the classroom setting. Consequently, most of the theoretical concerns deal less with basic philosophical and metaphysical issues and more with rationales and frameworks for curriculum content, instructional emphasis, and organizational climates for school programs.

Purpose. Our purpose is to present a reasonable representation of the current ideas and practices that seem to have the most promise and that merit serious consideration by those educators reflecting on the questions of moral education. This book is a source and compendium of a number of diverse, serious, and important insights, questions, and programs.

Questions and answers. It is difficult to conceive of an area that has as many controversial, complex, and important questions as moral education. This book raises a number of these questions and offers a number of attempts to deal with them. Other, possibly better, attempts will be formulated in the future. However, we think that the questions will persist long after individual programs and personalities are gone, since we are dealing with an area that has challenged us for centuries. It is our basic purpose, beyond the presentation of serious contemporary thought, to increase our sensitivity to and awareness of the underlying questions. Our expectation is not so much that they can quickly be resolved, but that they will be seriously considered.

Definitions. It is beyond our scope to deal in depth with basic metaphysical and religious questions like the meaning of truth, the definition of justice, and the basic distinctions among words like morality, values, morals, and ethics. Here we will content ourselves with a fairly simple definition of moral education: helping people to deal with questions of right and wrong in the interpersonal realm. There are, of course, values other than moral ones. These include esthetic judgments and personal tastes. But we have tried to keep a sharp focus on questions of what constitutes the good in terms of relationships between people.

The role of the school. Since moral education goes on inevitably in the schools, we should be thoughtful and systematic about the way it is conducted. There is no question that the schools have a legitimate as well as an inevitable role. However, they do not have an exclusive or even the most important role. Indeed, the powers of the state have grown so enormously and the authority of the family diminished so drastically, that one significant function of the school might be to focus on ways in which the impact of powerful institutions and bureaucracies might be lessened. The schools must not, at all costs, become agents for an all-powerful and all-knowing state.

What can the schools do? This book contains general and specific suggestions on what the schools might do. These suggestions are relatively sophisticated and require thoughtful and sensitive instruction. Questions will arise as to what magnitude of training will be necessary so that teachers might meet the requirements. All school personnel need to be aware and knowledgeable of the dimensions of moral education. It is an open question to what degree schools as presently constituted are equipped to deal with moral education in a wise and sensible manner. However, we have a basic faith in education, in this case faith in the value of becoming "better educated" about moral education.

Organization. The book is organized into four parts and concludes with a postscript, followed by an appendix on professional attitudes toward moral education. The selections include both previously published and original materials and have been chosen and written to illuminate the area of moral education in practice. Part I offers general background and attempts to provide a useful contextual framework for the specific approaches to moral education described in Parts II-IV. Part II deals with the values clarification approach, Part III with the cognitive-developmental approach, and Part IV with the cognitive approach. We have tried to present each position clearly and fairly. For this reason we have decided against deleting a number of repetitions, e.g., the Kohlberg scheme is presented several times in different selections. We hope this will be helpful rather than redundant. In the postscript, we try to deal with questions of action and implementation.

We hope you find this book useful and that you will share your reactions with us.

Acknowledgments

The authors wish to acknowledge the special contributions of three individuals:

Rhoda Stockwell,
Katie Barnes, and
Frances Tucker.

In addition to their careful typing of the several drafts, their contributions and encouragement were a major source of support to us.

PART I

Background and Introduction

1

Moral Education: What Is It and Where Are We?

David Purpel and Kevin Ryan

The moral education of children is one of the school's oldest missions and one of our newest fads. Suddenly, moral education has reappeared as a major topic at educational conferences and conventions. The educational editors of our newspapers are giving a good deal of space to feature stories like "The Schools Now Place Value on the Development of Personal Values" and "Moral Education: Are We Going Back to the Old Time Schooling?" Books and articles on the topic have multiplied in recent months. There is an increasing demand for the schools to be a more forceful agent of moral development than they have been in the last two decades. If a vacuum in the area of moral education has developed, the schools, which abhor a vacuum, will undoubtedly move to fill it.

Before we act, or even plan to act, we must realize that while moral education may become the sensitivity training of the 1970s, it is not some new mandate handed down to educators. While moral education may be wrongly implemented or trivialized, it should be clear that it has been the terrain of the educator from the time of the Greek philosophers. American educational thinkers and reformers have consistently given attention to the school's role in moral development. In contrast with many of the radical and romantic critics of

3

the last decade, they saw the school as an active and positive force in the development of the young. John Dewey (1934, p. 85) saw moral education as central to the school's mission: "The child's moral character must develop in a natural, just, and social atmosphere. The school should provide this environment for its part in the child's moral development." It was in this spirit that American schools were founded and in this spirit that they flourished during the colonial period and up through the nineteenth century.

The assertion of nineteenth century English philosopher Herbert Spencer that "education has for its object the formation of character" was a truism on both sides of the Atlantic. However, at the very time Spencer made his statement, the moral principles which the school used as the basis for character formation were being questioned; they soon began to crumble. Industrialization and the advent of new technologies broke down kinship ties and established patterns in many spheres. New values drove out old values. This situation was complicated in the United States by massive immigration during the late nineteenth and early twentieth century. Besides introducing new cultural mores and values, many of the immigrants, being Catholics and Jews, were at odds with the religiously grounded moral principles taught in the public schools. This, of course, was one of the major reasons for the development of parochial schools.

The combined effect, however, of both industrialization and immigration has been to neutralize over time the school's overt role as moral educator. Cultural relativism and a supposed scientific objectivity replaced Protestant moral theology. An explicit, systematic moral code was not taught. When moral issues were dealt with, teachers handled them gingerly. Students were presented with the facts and told to make up their own minds. Over the years, there was erosion of the school's deliberate efforts to promote certain values and to aid children in thinking about moral issues. Certainly, many teachers to this day actively and consciously work to instill in their students a moral perspective on life. However, they are hardly in the majority and frequently receive reprimands from their colleagues or students' parents for dealing with "controversial issues." On the other hand, the great majority of teachers, for a variety of reasons—from inability to excessive caution—avoid serious inquiry into the realm of values and morality.

There are understandable reasons for this avoidance. Human morality is a complex subject. Moral education has been described as a "name for nothing clear" (Wilson, Williams, and Sugarman 1967, p. 11). It is one of those suffocatingly large concepts, like learning, and even more so, like curriculum, that seem to stretch over the entire enterprise of education and seep into discussions of almost every school topic. The term *moral education* also brings together two words, each with its own wide spectrum of meaning.

While surely not satisfying everyone, our definition for moral education is a fairly straightforward one. Moral education is direct and indirect intervention of the school which affects both moral behavior and the capacity to think about issues of right and wrong. Our definition is broad in two directions. First, we wish to encompass not only the direct, overt efforts of the school to help the child become a more moral individual, but also the indirect, covert, or hidden efforts which influence the student as a moral being. Second, we believe the consideration of moral education must take into account both the student's capacity to think about moral problems and the way in which a student actually behaves in situations involving right and wrong behavior. Because moral education deals with such fundamental human concerns and relates to so many details of day-to-day living, it is capable of stirring up deep controversies and of bringing passions to the boiling point.

Moral education, then, covers a vast terrain; much of that terrain is a minefield. While the school, at present, may not be taking a very clear or direct role in moral education, the climate is beginning to change. Recent evidence for this comes from studies involving the membership of the Phi Delta Kappa, a professional fraternity in education. Since the membership of the Phi Delta Kappa is composed of teachers, principals, superintendents, educational researchers, professors of education and of the arts and sciences, and citizens with a special interest in education, these studies reflect a wide spectrum of the educational community. In early 1973 the membership of the Phi Delta Kappa was asked to rank in order of priority eighteen distinctive goals of education (Spears 1973). Third in ranking was "develop good character and self-respect," with these subdivisions: (1) develop moral responsibility and sound ethical and moral behavior; (2) develop capacity for discipline; (3) develop a moral and ethical sense of the values, goals, and processes of a free society; and (4) develop standards of personal character and ideas. This goal was only surpassed by the goals, "develop skills in reading, writing, speaking, and listening" and "develop pride in work and a feeling of self-worth."

In the spring of 1975 a survey was conducted of the Phi Delta Kappa membership on moral education (see appendix). The survey showed that schoolmen are almost unanimous in thinking that the schools should be involved directly in moral education. When offered five choices to identify their own views toward the schools' role in moral education, 88 percent chose as closest to their own overall view the following: "An active program of moral education in the school would be a helpful addition to the efforts of family and church to improve the moral development of children." Only 2 percent chose: "An active program of moral education in the school is simply out of the question." However, while the respondents felt that they had a clear mandate, they did not indicate clearly how that mandate should be executed in the schools. Given the choice of five different programmatic approaches to moral education, no alternative received more than one-third of the vote.

And, indeed, why should there not be confusion in the education profession? Certainly we have all lived through a period of moral confusion and lack of consensus on our values. We have been torn and battered by one jarring event after another. The last dozen years has seen a wave of political assassinations, the violence of the civil rights struggles, the student revolution that polarized young and old, the Vietnam war, and, finally, the agony of Watergate. We are numb from the impact of these events. We have lost faith in many of our institutions. At the same time, our private lives are being played out in a world where the landscape is constantly changing. The fast pace pushes aside values almost as rapidly as styles come and go in the fashion world. For instance, in a relatively short period we have switched from valuing frugality to valuing conspicuous consumption to valuing ecologically oriented frugality again. Now with the recession we are urged to buy cars and keep our consumption high. These changes disorient our private and collective sense of values.

In his recent book, *What Is the Human Prospect?,* Robert Heilbroner (1974, p. 15) suggested that much of the unrest and the unease of the present middle-aged generation is due to its apparent inability to pass on its values to the young. While there is more to moral education than the transmission of one generation's values to the next, even this process is inhibited by a weakened family structure. The modern American family is smaller, more isolated, and more fragmented than its counterpart of fifty years ago. In a home environment where the father and, increasingly, the mother leave for the major part of the day to work, and in which families only come together for one brief meal a day, the opportunity for parents to influence the moral attitudes and thinking of their children is reduced. Even when the family is together, there seems to be a good deal of uncertainty about its values and moral stance. On the other hand, early in grade school a child's peer group begins to play a dominant role. While we do not know the precise effect of these social changes, we surmise that they are contributing to a sense of moral confusion.

The family and the school are not the only institutions whose impact on moral development has diminished. A recent report titled *Religion in America, 1975* (pp. 1-5), issued by the Gallup Poll Index, shows that church attendance has dropped markedly in the last ten years. The same report (pp. 9-13) indicates that people believe churches are losing their influence and teaching authority. In the last seventeen years, the percentage of people who say the church is losing influence has risen from 13 percent to 55 percent. The once fixed moral doctrines of the churches have had to give way on many issues. And they are not being replaced by new dogma. Indeed, many church leaders are more concerned with developing a morally autonomous person who takes a few principles and makes up his own mind than with the consumer of moral dicta. However, the means, institutional or otherwise, to form this religiously and morally autonomous man have yet to be developed, leaving moderns caught in a no man's land between old and new forms of support and guidance.

Science, which has pierced many of the mysteries of our existence and enlightened so much of the modern world, has eroded much of the moral certainty and has offered little to lead us out of our confusion. Indeed, while science has ushered certainty and predictability into many areas of the physical world, it has brought to the conduct of human affairs new problems, with only a flabby relativism to guide us.

Similar criticisms could be offered and like questions could be raised about the influence on the child's moral development of the communications industry and the business community. It would appear that, at a time of great need for strong values and the capacity for moral thought, the institutions traditionally supporting the moral code are in a weakened position.

Leaving aside for a moment the case against the schools as an effective force in the moral education of the young, serious questions can be raised about the appropriateness of the school's taking on a more active role.

The school's pluralistic character raises an obvious problem. Whatever the school's past and present failings in providing access to the children of all Americans, an open and pluralistic stance is fundamental to our public schools. Many religious, racial, ethnic, and even regional groups are distinguished by their values, the philosophical and theological bases for their morality, and their different standards of behavior. For this reason, many parents who believe in tax-supported education are loath to have the school take on a role they see as belonging primarily and sometimes exclusively to church and home. The recent school conflagration in Kanawha County, West Virginia, bears witness to this attitude. Many parents feel strongly that the school should not interfere with their position as moral teachers. To keep faith with their many publics, then, it would appear that the schools should stay out of moral education.

An obvious but important distinction is to be made here. Private and parochial schools have a much clearer role in moral education than the public schools. Because they are often chosen by parents because of the particular values advocated and moral viewpoint stressed, these schools can move in the area of moral education with greater freedom.

Another objection to the schools taking a more active role in moral education is that they are currently failing to provide intellectual education and, therefore, teachers should not go down some new avenue that would distract them from their essential task. There are many potentially important roles for the school to assume according to this view, from career education to year-round recreation, but these would be just further excuses to shirk the school's primary mission.

Some observers also object because they see little evidence that teachers are morally superior or have better values than the average citizen. They also doubt that the present teaching force has any special knowledge or set of skills which will enable it to improve the values and thinking of the young.

Finally, there are those who object because they fear that what will start out as moral education will end up as indoctrination. While indoctrination can undercut educative efforts in many areas, it is particularly offensive where the teacher is inculcating an ideology with dangerous attitudinal and behavioral correlates such as white or black supremacy. There are those, however, who believe that the public schools are incapable of engaging in moral education without indoctrinating the young.

In summary, it would appear that whatever program of moral education the school adopts, it must respect the pluralistic traditions of America, it must not further weaken the present school program, and it must be free of indoctrination.

But there is a prior question. Why not stay out? Why not make a clear affirmation that the public schools, at least, are not going to wade into these treacherous and murky waters. Why not assert that the public schools will concentrate on intellectual and physical development and leave moral development to someone else—presumably the family and the church. Over the centuries the schools have rejected their mandate to teach religion. Why not now reject the mandate to be an agent of moral development?

The answer to this is clear. The schools simply cannot avoid being involved in the moral life of the students. It is inconceivable for the schools to take the child for six or seven hours a day, for 180 days a year, from the time he is six to the time he is eighteen, and not affect the way he thinks about moral issues and the way he behaves. Nor can we divorce the intellectual realm from the moral realm. One can suppress discussion about moral issues and values, but one cannot suppress the development of values and the formation of morals. Moral education goes on all over the school building—in the classrooms, in the disciplinarian's office, in assemblies, in the gym (see chapter 5). It permeates the very fabric of the teacher-student relationship. The school, then, cannot help but be a force for growth or retardation—for good or evil—in the moral life of the student. Moral education is an inevitable role of the schools. For the educator, it comes with the territory.

References

Dewey, John. *A Common Faith.* New Haven, Conn.: Yale University Press, 1934.

Gallup Poll Index. *Religion in America, 1975* (report no. 114). Princeton, N.J.: The Gallup Organization, 1975.

Heilbroner, Robert. *An Inquiry into the Human Prospect.* New York: W. W. Norton, 1974.

Spears, Harold. "Kappans Ponder the Goals of Education." *Phi Delta Kappan* (September 1973): 29-32.

Wilson, John; Williams, Norman; and Sugarman, Barry. *Introduction to Moral Education.* Baltimore: Penguin, 1967.

2

Forming a Value Curriculum: Two Philosophical Issues To Consider

James W. Watkins

Schools have been engaged in some sort of value instruction since their very inception, and most educators would dismiss as undesirable any efforts to end this tradition at a time when other institutions are floundering in the task. Yet there is little, if any, agreement on what sort of instruction in values schools should provide.

My purpose in this essay is not to attempt to solve the problem of what the contents of moral instruction should be. Nor is it to provide my personal answer. Rather I want to point out the importance of resolving two philosophical issues before deciding on the contents of a value curriculum. To do this, I shall first present the major alternative ways to handle moral instruction. Then I shall show how the appropriateness of using any particular alternative depends on how the two philosophical issues are resolved.

1. One way to treat moral instruction in the schools is to ignore it completely. To support this position, it can be argued that no instruction in values can escape the taint of indoctrination. In recent years, educational philosophers have given considerable attention to the question of what makes an act of teaching indoctrinatory. Generally, these analyses conclude that a teacher indoctrinates only when

he aims to close the minds of his pupils. (Some philosophers also demand the utilization of nonrational teaching methods for indoctrination to occur, and still others require the teaching of content that is not generally regarded as accepted truth. See Hare 1964; Atkinson 1967; Wilson 1966.) If an educator believes moral instruction will always possess elements of indoctrination, and if he feels schools should give priority to the avoidance of indoctrination, he can then support having no instruction in values in the schools.

2. A second approach to moral instruction is to use it to provide opportunities for students to clarify and defend their own values. No direct attempt is made here to change the students' moral positions. On the contrary, the aim of these lessons is simply to increase the students' knowledge of themselves—specifically in regard to the values they hold—and ability to act more consistently and confidently on the basis of these values when faced with moral decisions. This has recently become the most commonly discussed and espoused method of conducting moral instruction. (See Raths, Harmin, and Simon 1966; Simon, Howe, and Kirschenbaum 1972.) It is defended on the grounds that it does not assume any absolute values or methods of valuing, yet does make the students more capable interpreters of their personal moral views.

3. Moral instruction can also be conducted in schools by teaching students a specific process to follow when making value decisions. Advocates of this procedural alternative argue that, although there are no universally accepted values, there is one way of making moral decisions that is preferable to other ways. Generally, being reasonable and objective in approaching value situations is regarded as this better way. The aim here is to keep students from handling value situations emotionally and irrationally, or merely patterning their moral behavior after what others suggest or expect.

4. A fourth approach to value instruction is to teach students a given set of values, a method that flourished in American education until recent years. Those who support this approach maintain that (a) some values are generally accepted by reasonable people, or (b) even though no such values exist, students will adjust more successfully to their society if they adopt certain values. The first group would seemingly be satisfied if students simply learned the generally accepted values. The second group would apparently not be content until the students inculcated certain values into their behavioral

pattern. Only then would the pupils be sure to adjust to society. The two groups would then use very different techniques to evaluate their moral instruction, but both would defend conducting this instruction by teaching a given set of values.

Any value instruction framework is arbitrary unless it is based on some philosophical foundation. What overall educational philosophy to adopt as the basis of the school's learning program is therefore an extremely important philosophical issue to consider before forming a value curriculum.

Countless educational philosophies have been formulated. However, in terms of their effect on the contents of moral instruction, these can be placed into three general philosophical approaches to education. Adoption of any of these general philosophical approaches limits educators in their decision as to which of the four alternative methods of handling moral instruction to use.

1. First, educators can decide to adopt the philosophical position of idealism or realism. Though there are many clear distinctions between the two, disciples of both would agree that certain permanent values exist that students could be taught.

Idealism declares that values are absolute and unchanging. . . .
The child should learn to live by permanent values, which put him in harmony with the spiritual whole to which he belongs. . . .
Realists agree that any educational system should be geared to certain well-defined values. . . . Similarly, the moral standards that we teach the child should be influenced as little as possible by the views of the teacher or the preconceptions of the era. (Kneller 1964, pp. 36-37, 43-44)

Given these beliefs, both idealists and realists would most logically select the fourth alternative as the proper way to conduct moral instruction—they would advocate the teaching of certain preselected values. Idealists and realists would also favor the use of logic and reason to discern these values. Teaching a rational process of making value decisions does not appear inconsistent with the concept of permanent values, though it is certainly not as appropriate as teaching these values.

However, the other two major ways to handle moral instruction seem distinctly incompatible with the positions of idealism and

realism. If there are some fixed, eternal values, then it seems useless
to have students spend time clarifying their personal moral beliefs. It
seems equally foolhardy to ignore value instruction altogether when
there are some permanent values available to teach. Idealists and
realists thus appear to be limited to the third and fourth alternatives
for their moral instruction, and would most likely select the fourth,
supporting the teaching of the eternal values they believe exist.

2. Alternatively, educators can opt for the philosophical approach of pragmatism. Pragmatists, such as John Dewey, hold that
moral standards vary from society to society, and that a person
should make value decisions on the basis of what is best for human
welfare in his particular community.

For the pragmatist, values are relative. . . . The values to be taught in schools are
those that advance human welfare. The child should learn how to make difficult
moral decisions, not by falling back on rigidly prescribed principles, but rather
by determining which course of intelligent action is likely to produce the best
results in human, finite terms. (Kneller 1964, p. 50)

Of the alternative ways to conduct moral instruction, teaching a
rational process of making moral decisions seems most consistent
with the pragmatist position. In fact, teaching a valuing process is
exactly what the pragmatists espouse. Presumably some teaching of
values generally accepted by the existing society would be acceptable
under pragmatism, even though these values would not be regarded
as permanent. To do this would help students make a successful adjustment to their society, something in the interest of the total group
welfare. However, pragmatists would prefer that students make value
decisions on the rational basis of what is good for society rather than
on the basis of what aids their own adjustment.

Both the first and second alternatives for handling value education seem out of order when pragmatism is adopted. Pragmatists
would surely not choose to ignore value instruction, for they do
want students' moral behavior to be consistent with the welfare of
society. Also, it seems inappropriate for a pragmatist to champion
the clarification of students' own values when he would not believe
that these personal beliefs should be the basis for value decisions if
they conflicted with the overall interest of human welfare. Hence,
pragmatists would most likely opt for the third alternative, the teaching of a rational process of valuing, though they might support teach-

ing some predetermined values if this helped ensure student adjustment to society.

3. Finally, educators can elect to support an existentialist philosophical position. To an existentialist,

> The only values acceptable to the individual are those that he has freely adopted. . . .
>
> Existentialism does not require the school to condone moral anarchy in its students. But it does assert that the student can no longer be conditioned by his teacher into accepting supposedly timeless moral principles which he must uphold inflexibly whatever their cost in human suffering or their repugnance to himself.
>
> The teacher should bring home vividly to the student that, whatever he does, he can not escape the consequences of his actions. . . . (Kneller 1964, p. 65)

In an existentialist framework, moral instruction should avoid interfering with the individual student's freedom to choose his own values, yet stress his responsibility to face up to the consequences of his moral actions. Existentialists certainly would not countenance the teaching of any given values. In fact, even the teaching of a particular process of valuing appears to interfere with the free choice existentialism demands. If, for example, one is taught to make moral decisions on the basis of what is best for human welfare (the pragmatist position), then one's choices are seriously restricted.

Thus, an existentialist apparently cannot use the third or fourth alternative for his moral instruction pattern. He would, in fact, probably select the second alternative, and provide opportunities for students to clarify and defend their personal values. By doing so, he would allow pupils to keep the values they already hold, yet strengthen their ability to comprehend and uphold these values. Moreover, an individual's responsibility for his moral actions would be made clearer and more acceptable through value clarification and defense.

The emphasis existentialists place on personal responsibility makes it unlikely they would choose to neglect value instruction entirely. They want schools to help students recognize the importance of making value decisions responsibly. Hence, the clarification and defense of one's personal values seems to be the only method of dealing with moral instruction that would be wholly acceptable to existentialists.

The philosophy adopted as the basis for the total educational program has been shown to be a major influence on the way students can be instructed in morals. The handling of moral instruction also appears to be affected by the selection of a particular meta-ethical theory. These theories attempt to explain the nature of value terms and expressions. Meta-ethical thinking tries to make normative concepts as clear and definite as possible, though these terms cannot be clearly defined as terms in mathematics and the sciences can be. Like philosophies of education, innumerable meta-ethical theories have been stated but, in terms of their impact on the contents of moral instruction, they too can be organized generally into three major alternative viewpoints.

1. Naturalism represents one major position on the nature of ethical terms. The central assertion of naturalist meta-ethical theory is that

ethical statements can be confirmed or verified in a way parallel to that in which the statements of the empirical sciences can be confirmed. Naturalists hold that an ethical statement—that is, a statement with words like "wrong" or "undesirable"—is exactly identical in meaning with some other statement in which ethical words do not occur, and which everyone will recognize as a statement that can be confirmed or tested by the methods of science, by appeal to experience. (Brandt 1959, p. 155)

In other words, naturalism holds that an ethical statement is a factual statement. The meaning of ethical terms like "good" and "right" can therefore be determined by using the methods of science, by resort to empirical investigation.

Handling value instruction by disregarding it completely or having students clarify and defend their personal values is inconsistent with the meta-ethical framework of naturalism. Surely if a person believes value terms are objective in nature, he is not going to espouse neglecting value instruction altogether. That would be tantamount to ignoring a whole realm of objective knowledge. Moreover, having students spend their time clarifying and defending their subjective values seems pointless if there are some objective ones.

In the framework of ethical naturalism, moral instruction can apparently center on the teaching of certain values that are verifiable through empirical tests. However, many naturalists do not believe any such values have been ascertained. Although they see value statements as capable of empirical verification, they do not think a successful procedure for determining the correctness of a value statement has yet been discovered. These naturalists would seemingly opt for the third alternative—the teaching of a rational process for making value decisions. Given the absence of any known objective values to teach, the best a naturalist could do is develop the students' empirical and rational abilities so that their value behavior can be patterned as closely to available scientific evidence as possible. Both the third and fourth alternative methods therefore seem consistent with the view that value terms contain objective properties.

2. Emotivism is a second widely held view on the nature of ethical terms. Briefly, the emotivist claims ethical words do not describe facts, as the naturalist holds, but express attitudes. To an emotivist, ethical statements do two things: (1) they report the speaker's attitude, and (2) they have a magnetic effect on the attitudes of others.

The Emotive Theory of Ethics is based on the fact that not all adjectives are used to refer to properties and that the specifically moral meaning of ethical terms is not descriptive at all. (Vivian 1969, p. 91)

Given this position, teaching a rational process of valuing is totally inappropriate. Students would not need to be rational in morals if value terms and expressions do not represent something that is objective and verifiable. Moreover, an emotivist would likely reject conducting moral instruction by having students clarify and defend their personal values. The emotivist moral instructor would believe in his own values, and would not be persuaded that students should learn about their values if they differed from his.

Emotivists might not, in fact, accept any school instruction in values as proper. They might feel indoctrination was something the schools should strictly avoid. When an emotivist makes a value statement, he believes he is magnetically attracting his students to the moral view expressed. And this view cannot be rationally defended, if emotivism is accepted, since it sees value terms as possessing no cognitive content. Emotivist value statements are therefore inherently indoctrinatory, according to the most accepted views on what constitutes indoctrination, for they influence students to accept unverifiable positions. Instruction in values can thus occur under emotivism only if the moral instructor is willing to indoctrinate his students. He will seemingly be willing to do this only to get students to accept his own values, for only by doing this would he feel students could improve in morals. An emotivist is therefore apparently limited to choosing the first or fourth alternative for handling moral instruction. He will choose the first—the complete ignoring of value education—if he gives priority to the avoidance of indoctrination. He will select the fourth if he can accept being an indoctrinator to get his students to improve in morals by adopting his value positions.

3. Prescriptivism represents a third type of meta-ethical theory. The prescriptivist position on the nature of ethical terms can be summarized as follows:

a. The nature of ethical terms is partially cognitive and partially noncognitive.

b. The noncognitive element is the expression of a prescription that is universalizable—that can be applied to all people faced with a given situation, including the speaker.

c. Since ethical statements are universalizable, they contain some elements of descriptive statements.

d. A person arrives at his ethical judgments by using reason to derive them from overriding decisions of principle he has chosen to accept (Brandt 1959, pp. 221-23).

Because prescriptivists believe the use of reason plays an important part in the making of value judgments, they would be likely to use the third alternative—the teaching of a rational method of valuing —in their moral instruction. As students learn to use reason in value situations, they would become more proficient in interpreting their overriding decisions of principle, and therefore improved in morals. In addition, it seems appropriate for prescriptivists to spend some of their moral instruction time having students clarify and defend their own values. By doing so, they would be developing the students' knowledge of what their overriding decisions of principle are, and helping them discover if they are acting consistently with these decisions of principle.

In contrast, it seems inappropriate for certain preselected values to be taught within a prescriptivist meta-ethical framework. Since prescriptivists view ethical statements as partially noncognitive, they do not feel any particular value statements are empirically verifiable. Hence, no "correct" values are available to teach under prescriptivism. Furthermore, prescriptivists would not want to ignore value instruction altogether. They believe that ability in morals can be improved by teaching students to be rational in valuing and to clarify and defend their own values. A prescriptivist therefore is limited to employing the second and third alternative methods in his moral instruction.

My analysis in this essay indicates that no approach to moral instruction is consistent with the holdings of every philosophy of education or every meta-ethical theory. Educators can thus provide sound theoretical support for their value curriculum only if, before forming this curriculum, they decide what overall educational philosophy to adopt and what theory to accept on the nature of value terms and statements. Since the resolution of these two philosophical issues profoundly influences the appropriateness of any approach to moral instruction, educators who fail to consider them when forming a value curriculum can only be severely indicted and their work dismissed as meaningless.

References

Atkinson, R. F. "Instruction and Indoctrination." *Philosophic Problems*, edited by Young Pai and Joseph T. Myers. New York: Lippincott, 1967.

Brandt, Richard B. *Ethical Theory*. Englewood Cliffs, N.J.: Prentice-Hall, 1959.

Hare, Richard. "Adolescents into Adults." *Aims in Education*, edited by T. H. B. Hollins. Manchester, England: Manchester University Press, 1964.

Kneller, George F. *Introduction to the Philosophy of Education*. New York: John Wiley & Sons, 1964.

Raths, Louis; Harmin, Merrill; and Simon, Sidney B. *Values and Teaching*. Columbus, Ohio: Charles E. Merrill, 1966.

Simon, Sidney B.; Howe, L. W.; and Kirschenbaum, Howard. *Values Clarification*. New York: Hart, 1972.

Vivian, Frederick. *Thinking Philosophically*. New York: Basic Books, 1969.

Wilson, John. "Comments on Flew's 'What Is Indoctrination?' " *Studies in Philosophy and Education* (Summer 1966): 390-95.

3

The Moral Content of American Public Education

Israel Scheffler

The title of this essay is to be taken not as a declaration but as a question: What should be the purpose and content of our educational system insofar as it relates to moral concerns? This is a very large question, with many and diverse ramifications. Only its broadest aspects can here be treated, but a broad treatment, though it must ignore detail, may still be useful in orienting our thought and highlighting fundamental distinctions and priorities.

Education in a Democracy

The title refers to education as American. But the latter designation is simply geographical; it provides little in the way of distinguishing criteria relevant to our problem. What is more pertinent is the commitment to the ideal of democracy as an organizing principle of society. This commitment has radical and far-reaching consequences, not only for basic political and legal institutions, but also for the educational conceptions that guide the development of our

Reprinted from *Educational Research: Prospects and Priorities* (Washington, D.C.: U.S. Government Printing Office, 1972).

children. All institutions, indeed, operate through the instrumentality of persons; social arrangements are "mechanisms" only in a misleading metamorphical sense. Insofar as education is considered broadly, as embracing all those processes through which a society's persons are developed, it is thus of fundamental import for all the institutions of society, without exception. A society committed to the democratic ideal is one that makes peculiarly difficult and challenging demands of its members; it accordingly also makes stringent demands of those processes through which its members are educated.

What is the democratic ideal, then, as a principle of social organization? It aims so to structure the arrangements of society as to rest them ultimately upon the freely given consent of its members. Such an aim requires the institutionalization of reasoned procedures for the critical and public review of policy; it demands that judgments of policy be viewed not as the fixed privilege of any class or elite but as the common task of all, and it requires the supplanting of arbitrary and violent alteration of policy with institutionally channeled change ordered by reasoned persuasion and informed consent.

The democratic ideal is that of an open and dynamic society: open, in that there is no antecedent social blueprint which is itself to be taken as a dogma immune to critical evaluation in the public forum; dynamic, in that its fundamental institutions are not designed to arrest change but to order and channel it by exposing it to public scrutiny and resting it ultimately upon the choices of its members. The democratic ideal is antithetical to the notion of a fixed class of rulers, with privileges resting upon social myths which it is forbidden to question. It envisions rather a society which sustains itself not by the indoctrination of myth, but by the reasoned choices of its citizens, who continue to favor it in the light of a critical scrutiny both of it and its alternatives. Choice of the democratic ideal rests upon the hope that this ideal will be sustained and strengthened by critical and responsible inquiry into the truth about social matters. The democratic faith consists not in a dogma, but in a reasonable trust that unfettered inquiry and free choice will themselves be chosen, and chosen again, by free and informed men.

The demands made upon education in accord with the democratic ideal are stringent indeed; yet these demands are not ancillary but essential to it. As Ralph Barton Perry has said,

Education is not merely a boon conferred by democracy, but a condition of its survival and of its becoming that which it undertakes to be. Democracy is that form of social organization which most depends on personal character and moral autonomy. The members of a democratic society cannot be the wards of their betters; for there is no class of betters. . . . Democracy demands of every man what in other forms of social organization is demanded only of a segment of society. . . . Democratic education is therefore a peculiarly ambitious education. It does not educate men for prescribed places in life, shaping them to fit the requirements of a preexisting and rigid division of labor. Its idea is that the social system itself, which determines what places there are to fill, shall be created by the men who fill them. It is true that in order to live and to live effectively men must be adapted to their social environment, but only in order that they may in the long run adapt that environment to themselves. Men are not building materials to be fitted to a preestablished order, but are themselves the architects of order. They are not forced into Procrustean beds, but themselves design the beds in which they lie. Such figures of speech symbolize the underlying moral goal of democracy as a society in which the social whole justifies itself to its personal members. (1954, p. 425)

To see how radical such a vision is in human history, we have only to reflect how differently education has been conceived. In traditional authoritarian societies education has typically been thought to be a process of perpetuating the received lore, considered to embody the central doctrines upon which human arrangements were based. These doctrines were to be inculcated through education; they were not to be questioned. Since, however, a division between the rulers and the ruled was fundamental in such societies, the education of governing elites was sharply differentiated from the training and opinion-formation reserved for the masses. Plato's *Republic*, the chief work of educational philosophy in our ancient literature, outlines an education for the rulers in a hierarchical utopia in which the rest of the members are to be deliberately nourished on myths. And an authoritative contemporary Soviet textbook on *Pedagogy* declares that "Education in the USSR is a weapon for strengthening the Soviet state and the building of a classless society. . . . the work of the school is carried on by specially trained people who are guided by the state" (Yesipov and Goncharov 1946). The school was indeed defined by the party program of March 1919 as "an instrument of the class struggle. It was not only to teach the general principles of communism but 'to transmit the spiritual, organizational, and educative influence of the proletariat to the half- and nonproletarian strata of the working masses' " (Lilge 1968). In nondemocratic societies, education is two faced: it is a weapon or an instrument for shaping the minds of the ruled in accord with the favored and dogmatic myth of the rulers; it is, however, for the latter, an induction into the prerogatives and arts of rule, including the arts of manipulating the opinions of the masses.

To choose the democratic ideal for society is wholly to reject the conception of education as an *instrument* of rule; it is to surrender the idea of shaping or molding the mind of the pupil. The function of education in a democracy is rather to liberate the mind, strengthen its critical powers, inform it with knowledge and the capacity for independent inquiry, engage its human sympathies, and illuminate its moral and practical choices. This function is, further, not to be limited to any given subclass of members, but to be extended, insofar as possible, to all citizens, since all are called upon to take part in processes of debate, criticism, choice, and cooperative effort upon which the common social structure depends. "A democracy which educates for democracy is bound to regard all of its members as heirs who must so far as possible be qualified to enter into their birthright" (Perry 1954).

Implications for Schooling

Education, in its broad sense, is more comprehensive than schooling, since it encompasses all those processes through which a society's members are developed. Indeed, all institutions influence the development of persons working within, or affected by, them. Institutions are complex structures of actions and expectations, and to live within their scope is to order one's own actions and expectations in a manner that is modified, directly or subtly, by that fact. Democratic institutions, in particular, requiring as they do the engagement and active concern of all citizens, constitute profoundly educative resources. It is important to note this fact in connection with our theme, for it suggests that formal agencies of schooling do not, and cannot, carry the whole burden of education in a democratic society, in particular moral and character education. All institutions have an educational side, no matter what their primary functions may be. The question of moral education in a democracy must accordingly be raised not only within the scope of the classroom but also within the several realms of institutional conduct. Are political policies and arrangements genuinely open to rational scrutiny and public control? Do the courts and agencies of government operate fairly? What standards of service and integrity are prevalent in public offices? Does the level of political debate meet appropriate requirements of candor and logical argument? Do journalism and the mass media expose facts and alternatives, or appeal to fads and emotionalism? These and many other allied questions pertain to the status of moral education within a democratic society. To take them seriously is to recognize that moral education presents a challenge not only to the schools, but also to every other institution of society.

Yet the issue must certainly be raised specifically in connection with schools and schooling. What is the province of morality in the school, particularly the democratic school? Can morality conceivably be construed as a *subject*, consisting in a set of maxims of conduct, or an account of current mores, or a list of rules derived from some authoritative source? Is the function of moral education rather to ensure conformity to a certain code of behavior regulating the school? Is it, perhaps, to involve pupils in the activities of student organizations or in discussion of "the problems of democracy"? Or, since morality pertains to the whole of what transpires in school, is the very notion of specific moral schooling altogether misguided?

These questions are very difficult, not only as matters of implementation, but also in theory. For it can hardly be said that there is firm agreement among moralists and educators as to the content and scope of morality. Yet the tradition of moral philosophy reveals a sense of morality as a comprehensive institution over and beyond particular moral codes, which seems to me especially consonant with the democratic ideal, and can, at least in outline, be profitably explored in the context of schooling. What is this sense?

It may perhaps be initially perceived by attention to the language of moral judgment. To say that an action is "right," or that some course "ought" to be followed, is not simply to express one's taste or preference; it is also to make a claim. It is to convey that the judgment is backed by reasons, and it is further to invite discussions of such reasons. It is, finally, to suggest that these reasons will be found compelling when looked at impartially and objectively, that is to say, taking all relevant facts and interests into account and judging the matter as fairly as possible. To make a moral claim is, typically, to rule out the simple expression of feelings, the mere giving of commands, or the mere citation of authorities. It is to commit oneself, at least in principle, to the "moral point of view," that is, to the claim that one's recommended course has a point which can be clearly seen if one takes the trouble to survey the situation comprehensively, with impartial and sympathetic consideration of the interests at stake, and with respect for the persons involved in the issue. The details vary in different philosophical accounts, but the broad outlines are generally acknowledged by contemporary moral theorists. (See, for example, Baier 1958; Frankena 1963; Peters 1967; Scheffler 1966).

If morality can be thus described, as an institution, then it is clear that we err if we confuse our allegiance to any particular code with our commitment to this institution; we err in mistaking our prevalent code for the *moral point of view* itself. Of course, we typically hold our code to be justifiable from the moral point of view. However, if we are truly committed to the latter, we must allow the possibility that further consideration or new information or emergent human conditions may require revision in our code. The situation is perfectly analogous to the case of science education; we err if we confuse our allegiance to the current corpus of scientific doctrines with our commitment to scientific method. Of course we hold our current science to be justifiable by scientific method, but that very method itself commits us to holding contemporary doctrines fallible and revisable in the light of new arguments or new evidence that the future may bring to light. For scientific doctrines are not held simply as a matter of arbitrary preference; they are held for reasons. To affirm them is to invite all who are competent to survey these reasons and to judge the issues comprehensively and fairly on their merits.

Neither in the case of morality nor in that of science is it possible to convey the underlying *point of view* in the abstract. It would make no sense to say "Since our presently held science is likely to be revised for cause in the future, let us just teach scientific method and give up the teaching of content." The content is important in and of itself, and as a basis for further development in the future. Moreover, one who knew nothing about specific materials of science in the concrete could have no conception of the import of an abstract and second-order scientific method. Nevertheless, it certainly does not follow that the method is of no consequence. On the contrary, to teach current science without any sense of the reasons that underlie it, and of the logical criteria by which it may itself be altered in the future, is to prevent its further intelligent development. Analogously, it makes no sense to say that we ought to teach the moral point of view in the abstract since our given practices are likely to call for change in the future. Given practices are indispensable, not only in organizing present energies, but in making future refinements and revisions possible. Moreover, one who had no concrete awareness of a given tradition of practice, who had no conception of what rule-governed conduct was, could hardly be expected to comprehend what the moral point of view might be, as a second-order vantage point on practice. Nevertheless, it does not follow that the latter vantage point is insignificant. Indeed, it is fundamental insofar as we hold our given practices to be reasonable, that is, justifiable in principle upon fair and comprehensive survey of the facts and interests involved.

There is, then, a strong analogy between the moral and the scientific points of view, and it is no accident that we speak of reasons in both cases. We can be reasonable in matters of practice as well as in matters of theory. We can make a fair assessment of the evidence bearing on a hypothesis of fact, as we can make a fair disposition of interests in conflict. In either case, we are called upon to overcome our initial tendencies to self-assertiveness and partiality by a more fundamental allegiance to standards of reasonable judgment comprehensible to all who are competent to investigate the issues. In forming such an allegiance, we commit ourselves to the theoretical possibility that we may need to revise our current beliefs and practices as a consequence of "listening to reason." We reject arbitrariness in principle, and accept the responsibility of critical justification of our current doctrines and rules of conduct.

It is evident, moreover, that there is a close connection between the general concept of *reasonableness* underlying the moral and the scientific points of view, and the democratic ideal. For the latter demands the institutionalization of "appeals to reason" in the sphere of social conduct. In requiring that social policy be subject to open and public review, and institutionally revisable in the light of such review, the democratic ideal rejects the rule of dogma and of arbitrary authority as the ultimate arbiter of social conduct. In fundamental allegiance to channels of open debate, public review, rational persuasion, and orderly change, a democratic society in effect holds its own current practices open to revision in the future. For it considers these practices to be not self-evident, or guaranteed by some fixed and higher authority, or decidable exclusively by some privileged elite, but subject to rational criticism, that is, purporting to sustain themselves in the process of free exchange of reasons in an attempt to reach a fair and comprehensive judgment.

Here, it seems to me, is the central connection between moral, scientific, and democratic education, and it is this central connection that provides, in my opinion, the basic clue for school practice. For what it suggests is that the fundamental trait to be encouraged is that of reasonableness. To cultivate this trait is to liberate the mind from dogmatic adherence to prevalent ideological fashions, as well as from the dictates of authority. For the rational mind is encouraged to go behind such fashions and dictates and to ask for their justifications, whether the issue be factual or practical. In training our students to reason we train them to be critical. We encourage them to ask questions, to look for evidence, to seek and scrutinize alternatives, to be critical of their own ideas as well as those of others. This educational course precludes taking schooling as an instrument for shaping their minds to a preconceived idea. For if they seek reasons, it is their evaluation of such reasons that will determine what ideas they eventually accept.

Such a direction in schooling is fraught with risk, for it means entrusting our current conceptions to the judgment of our pupils. In exposing these conceptions to their rational evaluation we are inviting them to see for themselves whether our conceptions are adequate, proper, fair. Such a risk is central to scientific education, where we deliberately subject our current theories to the test of continuous evaluation by future generations of our student-scientists. It is central also to our moral code, *insofar as* we ourselves take the moral point of view toward this code. And, finally, it is central to the democratic commitment which holds social policies to be continually open to free and public review. In sum, rationality liberates, but there is no liberty without risk.

Let no one, however, suppose that the liberating of minds is equivalent to freeing them from discipline. Laissez-faire is not the opposite of dogma. To be reasonable is a difficult achievement. The habit of reasonableness is not an airy abstract entity that can be

skimmed off the concrete body of thought and practice. Consider
again the case of science: scientific method can be learned only in
and through its corpus of current materials. Reasonableness in science is an aspect or dimension of scientific tradition, and the body of
the tradition is indispensable as a base for grasping this dimension.
Science needs to be taught in such a way as to bring out this dimension as a consequence, but the consequence cannot be taken neat.
Analogously for the art of moral choice: The moral point of view is
attained, if at all, by acquiring a tradition of practice, embodied in
rules and habits of conduct. Without a preliminary immersion in such
a tradition, an appreciation of the import of its rules, obligations,
rights, and demands, the concept of choice of actions and rules for
oneself can hardly be achieved. Yet the prevalent tradition of practice can itself be taught in such a way as to encourage the ultimate
attainment of a superordinate and comprehensive moral point of
view.

The challenge of moral education is the challenge to develop
critical thought in the sphere of practice and it is continuous with
the challenge to develop critical thought in all aspects and phases of
schooling. Moral schooling is not, therefore, a thing apart, something
to be embodied in a list of maxims, something to be reckoned as
simply another subject, or another activity, curricular or extracurricular. It does, indeed, have to pervade the *whole* of the school experience.

Nor is it thereby implied that moral education ought to concern
itself solely with the general structure of this experience, or with the
effectiveness of the total "learning environment" in forming the
child's habits. The critical questions concern the *quality* of the environment: What is the *nature* of the particular school experience,
comprising content as well as structure? Does it liberate the child in
the long run, as he grows to adulthood? Does it encourage respect for
persons, and for the arguments and reasons offered in personal exchanges? Does it open itself to questioning and discussion? Does it
provide the child with fundamental schooling in the traditions of
reason, and the arts that are embodied therein? Does it, for example,
encourage the development of linguistic and mathematical abilities,
the capacity to read a page and follow an argument? Does it provide
an exposure to the range of historical experience and the realms of
personal and social life embodied in literature, the law, and the social

sciences? Does it also provide an exposure to particular domains of scientific work in which the canons of logical reasoning and evidential deliberation may begin to be appreciated? Does it afford opportunity for individual initiative in reflective inquiry and practical projects? Does it provide a stable personal milieu in which the dignity of others and the variation of opinion may be appreciated, but in which a common and overriding love for truth and fairness may begin to be seen as binding oneself and one's fellows in a universal human community?

If the answer is negative, it matters not how effective the environment is in shaping concrete results in conduct. For the point of moral education in a democracy is antithetical to mere shaping. It is rather to liberate.

References

Baier, Kurt. *The Moral Point of View.* Ithaca, N.Y.: Cornell University Press, 1958.

Frankena, William K. *Ethics.* Englewood Cliffs, N.J.: Prentice-Hall, 1963.

Lilge, Frederic. "Lenin and the Politics of Education." *Slavic Review* XXVII, no. 2 (June 1968): 255.

Perry, Ralph Barton. *Realms of Value.* Cambridge, Mass.: Harvard University Press, 1954.

Peters, R. S. *Ethics and Education.* Glenview, Ill.: Scott Foresman, 1967.

Scheffler, I. (ed.). *Philosophy and Education* (second ed.). Boston: Allyn & Bacon, 1966.

Yesipov, B. P., and Goncharov, N. K. *Pedagogy* (third ed., 1946). Quoted in George S. Counts and Nucia P. Lodge, *I Want To Be Like Stalin.* New York: John Day, 1947.

4

Moral Education: Aims and Methods in China, the U.S.S.R., the U.S., and England

William F. Connell

"My father is a worker. My mother is a peasant. My brother is a PLA man. I am a pupil. We live a very happy life. We listen to Chairman Mao and the Party. We all work and study hard for the Revolution."

The above paragraph is taken from a textbook used in the teaching of English in a Chinese secondary school in Tientsin. It illustrates four important facets of the moral education of Chinese boys and girls, each of which is important and distinctively different from the approach used in the U.S. or England. First is an identification with proletarian interests: The family is a three-in-one combination of worker, peasant, and People's Liberation Army, the three fundamental elements of modern Chinese society. To identify with proletarian thinking and feeling and to work for and experience the collective unity of the new society are important ways of developing the new moral spirit. Second, one's behavior is to be reshaped under the guidance of Chairman Mao and the Party. Mao Tse-tung is the great teacher whose life and wise counsel provide the guidelines; the Communist Party is a group of dedicated persons whose activities can be

Reprinted by permission from *Phi Delta Kappan* (June 1975), pp. 702-06.

used as models for the behavior of young people. Third, the aim of good citizenship is clearly stated: to further the Revolution. The Revolution is a continuous process in every aspect of life for the 800 million people of China, as they struggle to reconstruct themselves and their society in radically new ways. Another passage from the textbook puts the situation clearly:

> Chairman Mao,
> You are our great teacher. . . .
> We follow your teachings
> And make revolution forever. (See Connell 1974, p. 25)

Finally, life in the new society requires persons of special character. In particular, it calls for an industriousness that is sustained by cheer-fulness—the enjoyment of hard work with a great purpose.

Moral Education and Politics

Moral education is concerned with developing selected kinds of character traits and forms of behavior preferred by the educator. The basis for selection, in China and the U.S.S.R., is political, and moral education is of crucial importance. "The overall aim of bringing up young people today," wrote Nikolai Lenin, "should be the teaching of Communist morality" (Kairov 1961, p. 4).

In the passages just quoted from Chinese textbooks, politics and education are interwoven. Politics, in fact, is a part of every aspect of Chinese life, and, in Mao Tse-tung's view, should and does call the tune. Moral education and political education are inseparable. The good person is the one with the right political attitude. To be a good soldier, peasant, worker, or scholar, one must first possess the correct political views. Technical knowledge and proficiency are essential for the efficient performance of one's tasks, but having the right political attitude ensures that one's task is directed toward the right ends and carried out in the right spirit.

The importance accorded by Chinese educators to holding the right political views is shared by their counterparts in the U.S.S.R. As collective societies, both are vitally interested in developing collective habits and the socialist morality that underpins them. Some of the best statements of the importance of educating for collective living are to be found in the writings of leading Soviet educators.

Education for the Collective Life

Anton S. Makarenko, who ran several colonies for delinquents in the 1920s and 1930s and from his experiences distilled principles for the conduct of Soviet education, has become the most widely accepted guide to the practice of education in the U.S.S.R. In 1937 he wrote an article in *Izvestia* outlining his ideal Soviet citizen, a concept which has remained sound and acceptable to the teaching profession:

> In the Soviet Union, no individual can live outside the collective and there can be, therefore, no separate personal destiny, no personal course, and no personal happiness that is opposed to the destiny and happiness of the collective. . . .
>   We must send out from our schools energetic members of the socialist society devoted to the collective idea, and capable resolutely at all times of finding at every moment of their life the right standard for their personal actions, and of demanding at the same time the right conduct from others.

Here also, as in China, is a clear expression of the importance of a political idea in determining the kind of character education that teachers would be expected to promote among their pupils. The aim of education is to produce the collective man: a person who identifies himself with the welfare of his group and is honest, upright, and energetic in promoting the interests of his comrades.

The collective is a complicated social organism; to learn how best to serve it involves an extensive experience of its various purposive activities. Teachers, therefore, must spend much time and thought in developing, with great sensitivity, the life of a collective in their classroom. There is a need for efficient organization, mutual consultation and agreement on purposes and methods, acceptance of collective decisions, the allocation of responsibilities for action, and the development of cooperative feeling. Makarenko's *Road to Life*, completed in 1935, describes the way in which the author developed a thoroughgoing collective life in his colonies; it is still widely read and used in teacher training as an inspirational model for future teachers.

The political and collective man in Communist society is paralleled in Western democracy in the ideal of the democratic citizen with a sense of social responsibility, which many schools attempt to cultivate. The degree of emphasis on and the exclusiveness of the

Communist aim, however, make it vitally different. It is conceivable in the U.S. or in England to attribute a high level of morality to a person who is not particularly democratic and whose sense of social responsibility is not highly developed. He may be high-minded but wrong-headed, narrow but honest in his opinions, uninterested in community affairs but with a scrupulous private conscience, and he may well earn a high moral reputation. In China and the U.S.S.R., such a situation would not be possible. In those countries, Communist morality is achievable only by the political and collective man.

The Collective Virtues

Collectives are of various sizes and have various purposes. There is a progression among them, from the small group of peers, the school class, the school, the Party, to the Soviet Union itself. Students belong to or have some connection with each at various times. The behavior associated with the different collectives is different in each case but has the same basic moral elements: honesty, selflessness, industriousness, and responsibility.

Since the collective spirit extends to the Soviet Union as a whole (for most students this represents its widest workable limit), patriotism must be added to the list of collective moral virtues. Both the U.S.S.R. and China have a recent history of foreign invasion repulsed after long and desperate struggle that makes patriotism a pertinent and easy virtue for the schools to teach. In a Moscow ten-year school, for example, there is a room, scrupulously kept by the senior pupils, which is dedicated to the students and alumni who served in the Great Patriotic War of 1940-45. In it one can find the records of their full careers, a collection of personal school exercise books, and the military dress and equipment belonging to each one. In Novosibirsk the children visit the memorial erected to those who died fighting for the Revolution in central Siberia against Kolchak's army in 1919. In China examples of heroism, endurance, and devotion to the Chinese people are taken from the recent war against Japan and the struggle against Chiang Kai-shek. Stories of the heroes of these wars occur frequently in textbooks and children's picture books and are the basis for many stage shows. The modern revolutionary ballet, *The White-Haired Girl*, and the operas, *The Red*

Lantern and *The Red Detachment of Women*, tell the story of heroic deeds by ordinary but dedicated persons during the wars of liberation. They are widely known and much loved.

A further special addition to the list of virtues is that of class consciousness. Among those working for the desired collective state of affairs, the principal obstacles to be overcome include the class interests of various groups in society. There are obvious middle-class and capitalist interests to be circumvented, but there are also more subtle class influences to be fended off in a seemingly proletarian society. Petty ambitions, individual advantage, and avoidance of manual work are the kinds of things a class-conscious society has to guard against. The three-in-one linkage mentioned above in the Chinese school textbook is one way of keeping proletarian class consciousness alive.

Thus the two principal characteristics of moral education in the U.S.S.R. and China are its intimate relationship with politics and, associated with this, its commitment to collective behavior. The person who has thoroughly absorbed and put these characteristics into practice in his life will also be a person of honesty, integrity, industry, patriotism, and class consciousness.

The basis for moral education is the same in both China and the U.S.S.R. There are, however, different emphases. The connection between politics and morals is more openly stressed in China, and so, too, is the need for an active class consciousness. In the U.S.S.R. these are background factors and do not appear in the forefront of educational discussion and practice. There is, nevertheless, a firm belief that the person who is not working in the interests of the collective society is acting immorally. For example, writers whose books may undermine the solidarity of the Soviet Union or cause individualistic dissension within it are regarded as acting improperly.

Methods of Moral Education

Moral education in every country combines both formal and informal teaching. In each country there are subjects, called by different names such as politics, morals, the American Constitution, history of the Communist Party, and social studies, in which ideology is examined and approved forms of behavior are taught. Informal and substantial support is usually given by teachers in other subjects who—for example, in teaching English, Russian, or Chinese literature —may select and emphasize materials that, it is hoped, will deepen the students' devotion to a sense of justice, class consciousness, or individual liberty.

In the U.S.S.R. and China, there is a substantial amount of formal moral education. Both formal and informal teaching are more intense and more visible than in England and the U.S., and techniques of teaching are probably more varied. Techniques tend to be of three kinds: teaching by exhortation, by example, and by experience.

Teaching by Exhortation

A quotation from Lenin, Makarenko, or Mao Tse-tung displayed in the classroom or the school entrance hall exhorts students to look forward to the better tomorrow they are building, or to enter joyfully into their learning tasks, or to learn better how to criticize and improve their own behavior. Posters with similar messages are to be found on notice boards and in many public places. The themes are frequently taken up by teachers in classroom discussions or by parents and neighbors around the home. It is a continual and widespread process, and children are saturated with advice on how best to behave. Teachers in England and the U.S. adopt somewhat similar procedures, depending rather more on opportunities presented for informal classroom discussion and individual counseling.

Teaching by Example

In the U.S.S.R. and in China, models of exemplary behavior are found from many sources, e.g., in heroes of revolutionary wars, in women who have been devoted to revolutionary causes, and in children who have shown courage in adversity. Their deeds are expounded in textbooks, picture books, school plays, songs, and storytelling.

In studying literature, Chinese teachers in several city schools have adopted the practice of taking their students on excursions into different sections of a city to study the language, vocabulary, speech, informal literature, and general activities of the people. The students write accounts of their studies and often compose original stories about interesting people or significant episodes. Thus the students gain a closer appreciation of the qualities of the ordinary person.

In a well-read book titled *The Seeds*, a group of young Chinese students wrote a number of stories about contemporary heroes who work devotedly for the people in a great variety of situations and who demonstrate the way in which peasants, People's Liberation Army, and Party workers can most fruitfully cooperate. For example, there is a vignette of young Liu, who was a member of the Youth League. Interested in developing new rice varieties for the cold areas of northern China, he visited a small mountain village. Steadily, with intelligence and dogged persistence, he managed to improve the quality of the local rice seeds; he also became the deputy head of the District Revolutionary Committee. The story concludes, "He smiles, his eyes shining. I think to myself, 'Isn't he also a seed of special quality?' Our country with its vast land is waiting for the new generation to display such talents."

Inspiration is drawn also from models of a larger scale: The heroic 900-day siege of Leningrad in World War II is the source of a great many moral and patriotic stories, songs, and poems available for use in the schools of the U.S.S.R. In China, the extraordinary progress of the village of Tachai from an unpromising settlement into a modern, highly productive agricultural commune has prompted the widespread slogan, "Learn from Tachai."

Teaching by Experience

Practical experience, the third technique, is a fundamental part of education in China and the U.S.S.R. and is used in various ways and with varying degrees of effectiveness.

In their ordinary school activities, children of all countries, wherever possible, begin to experience appropriate moral behavior. A firm start is usually made at the preschool level. An American or English kindergarten, for example, teaches young children to play together, share their toys, and act as civilized social beings. In the Communist countries, the same virtues and habits of good behavior are taught with an emphasis on collective consciousness; for example, the kindergarten teacher in the U.S.S.R. will say, in introducing doll play, "Children, here is our dolly. Vanya, you give our dolly to Katya; Katya, pass it to Marusya; now Marusya and Petya, swing our dolly together" (Bronfenbrenner 1969, p. xii). And in China the kindergarten children will learn songs and dances about cooperation and the way the peasants, PLA, and workers help each other.

An important aspect of teaching morals by experience is the combination of productive labor with the work of the school. Students of all ages, from kindergarten to university, are given work experience appropriate to their age, at school, in factories, and on farms. The work may occupy as much as a fifth of their time and, where possible, is linked with the theoretical work they may be doing at school. The students' experience of productive work is of moral significance in three ways: It makes them a part of the work force and helps them develop a sense of the importance of work and a feeling of commitment to the reconstruction of their society; it puts them in touch with proletarian habits and attitudes and helps them understand and absorb the class consciousness of the workers; and it puts them into a disciplined productive team and helps them see the necessity for conscious self-discipline.

A second kind of experience, particularly in China, is the use of factory workers and peasants for a variety of educational functions. Some are found on the regular staff of schools, familiarizing the pupils with the attitudes and work of the PLA or the local commune, and some serve on the revolutionary committees that run each school and help keep the schoolwork in touch with the values of the people. Retired workers may supervise extracurricular activities or look after the youngsters of a neighborhood each day between the time school ends and their parents return from work. Retired workers in many cases pass on their experience of the bitter past; they impress upon the children the new dignity and worth of the workingman and the need to struggle to maintain the values of the new society.

Perhaps the most significant experience of all is the responsibility given to peer groups to run many of their own affairs and perform tasks of substantial social importance. Peer groups in the U.S. and England play an important part in the informal education of children and youth. They both compete with and reinforce the influence of parents and teachers. In the U.S.S.R. and in China, the peer groups are not divergent; they accept and work for the same purposes as their society and they feel themselves to be making a recognizable contribution to the development of the society. Educators in the U.S.S.R. and China acknowledge that from time to time some groups of children find themselves differing from their parents on various matters. This is quite healthy and to be expected in a developing society. What is unhealthy is consistent opposition on significant matters, coupled with a persistent in-group solidarity, something like a separate peer-group culture defying the general norms of society. An interesting study in the U.S.S.R. showed that this undesirable situation had a tendency to arise among "children whose relations with teachers and parents were built on the basis of authoritarianism." Where children had responsibility for socially useful activities and their behavior was evaluated by their group and adults together, their relations with one another and with adults displayed more trust, mutual respect, and interest in collective welfare (Dragunova and Elkonin 1965).

Peer-group activities are channelled through a youth organization to which most of the children belong: Young Octobrists, Young Pioneers, and Komsomols in the U.S.S.R., and Little Red Soldiers, Red Guards, and Communist Youth in China. Members of these organizations supervise the behavior and discipline of the pupils at school; their youthful leaders are expected to set an example of diligence, interest in social progress, honesty, and devotion to Communist principles. Youth groups have been organized more comprehensively in the U.S.S.R. They run their own national daily newspaper; have a substantial network of pioneer palaces, centers, and camps; and have built up a long tradition of service to society and courageous determination in helping backward or handicapped communities. The Chinese youth groups, though less extensively organized, have played decisive parts in recent Chinese history, notably in the Cultural Revolution of the late 1960s; they too, therefore, have developed considerable prestige and exercise a strong influence on the behavior of Chinese youth.

In both countries the children's centers are focal points in moral and political education. In the U.S.S.R., where there is no school subject formally and fully devoted to moral and political education until the final school year, they are the principal source of systematic education in this area; in China, where politics and morals appear as a subject in the curriculum for all age groups, the youth center's work is supplementary but nonetheless important.

In these youth centers may be found a microcosm of Communist moral education. By exhortation, by actual example, and by reference to experience, the youth, assembled in their own center and surrounded by evidences of society's commitment to their welfare, are made vitally aware of the merits of patriotism, revolutionary struggle, political consciousness, class consciousness, and the virtues of productive work and collective life in the new and important society that they themselves are building.

English and American Traditions

To what extent do the Western democracies of England and the U.S. accept the same basic views of moral education as China and the U.S.S.R., and in what ways do they differ?

Honesty, integrity, industry, and patriotism—but not class consciousness—are important virtues in the West as in the East, and the schools of England and the United States regard the teaching of them as a serious matter. Working together and being a good team member, too, has traditionally been part of the schools' teaching, emphasized perhaps more in England than in the U.S.

English schools and teachers have tended during the present century to adopt the ideals of English independent public secondary boarding schools. In these schools, the behavior pattern that is taught aims at esprit de corps, service to the community, and the acceptance of subordinate roles, together with a training for cautious, responsible leadership and the informal learning of manners and attitudes which make for smooth community life. Loyalty—doing one's duty, not letting the side down—is the prime virtue. The individualist, though tolerated, has always been uncomfortable in these schools. The English public school is a small, modest, collective society committed to teaching the virtues which preserve its way of life, on the assumption that English society is or ought to be like that of the school. It is remarkably similar to the picture of the behavior expected of young executives in American corporations painted in William H. Whyte's *The Organization Man*. The good executive does not rock the boat. He is loyal to his corporation and builds his life around it.

Loyalty has also been extended to a wider society such as the nation; patriotism has long been an important part of the teaching in all American and English schools. It was particularly stressed in the jingoistic first decade of this century, when manuals of patriotism, flag ceremonials, and selections of patriotic literature were introduced into the schools. English enthusiasm for this kind of teaching waned after World War II, while American insistence on public indications of national loyalty continued and at times was actually intensified in response to various political developments, the most notable of which were the McCarthyism of the Cold War era, and the Vietnam war.

Religion has played a central role in the tradition of moral education. In England the school chapel has been an important influence in the life of the independent public schools, and religious observances and instruction are still maintained throughout the state school system. In the U.S., while the public schools are jealously preserved as secular institutions, moral education is usually justified on the ground that it is actually Christian ethics. It would be widely contended in the teaching profession, in both England and the U.S., that the fundamental beliefs and attitudes which should govern the behavior of individuals and the relationships between them are a part of the Christian heritage and get their warrant from their religious basis.

Since World War II, however, the English have begun to question the traditional public school approach to moral education. Two of the main factors behind the rethinking have been the rise of the Labor Party to power, supported by a wider and less conventional range of interests, and the rapid development of universal secondary education, increasing the number and variety of state secondary schools.

One important result is that teachers are much less sure of what the "best" behavior is and what the ideal student looks like. He is no longer the "public school" type, but elements of that model are still strongly entrenched even in the new comprehensive secondary schools. In this less traditional atmosphere of the expanding school system, English views on character education seem to be increasingly similar to American ideas and practices.

Current Aims in England and the U.S.

Three important characteristics seem to have emerged in moral education in both U.S. and English schools during the last few decades. They are neither new nor universal. They are, however, undoubtedly widespread in the two countries, are incorporated into teaching methods used in most schools, and are frequently explained by educators in articles and speeches as basic to life in a Western democracy.

The person who is objective and uncommitted, who is able to get along pleasantly and helpfully with other people, and who is interested in his own individual development and success is the kind of student that educators in England and the U.S. appear to be trying to produce. Objectivity, social participation, and individual effort might therefore be regarded as the principal characteristics at which moral education aims in England and the United States.

Objectivity and Noncommitment

The approach to social studies best illustrates the first of these qualities. In the courses on government, economics, and social problems which most American high schools offer, the emphasis is on finding the facts, appreciating different points of view, and understanding the problem or process being studied.

One of the best-known social studies programs currently used in England is designed specifically to explore controversial issues. In each unit secondary school students have an opportunity to gather evidence about the issue from various sources and with various techniques. They evaluate the evidence, explore the issue in the light of it, and discuss moral values that may be involved. Thus they develop an understanding of the controversy, and they may form opinions on it. However, there is no commitment to act in any way. And the teacher is required to be impartial to avoid influencing the students' opinions.

This procedure is common in both English and American state schools. It is an effort to keep teaching clear of politics. It embodies the view that the state school and its offerings are neutral and are designed to produce people who are objective and uncommitted. They may get their firm opinions or their prejudices from other sources outside the school. The school's job is to teach students to examine and evaluate. This ideal, of course, is not always reached. It defines a tendency. On some political matters, English and American schools do try to inculcate firm beliefs. Patriotism, for example, is insisted upon and reinforced in many ways at all levels of schooling; parliamentary democracy, though queried in detail, is always seen to be ideal in principle; and the traits of character and moral virtues which help to make and preserve a strong and democratic United States or England are, for that very reason, seen in the schools of each country to be good, proper, and worthy of inculcation.

Social Participation

The foreign observer of American twentieth century secondary schools is always impressed by the facility with which students talk with him and with their fellow students, by the skill they exercise in handling group discussions, and by the poise and responsibility they show in a variety of social situations. Their ability to get along with their fellows is the result of long practice and a continual emphasis from earliest school days on social skills. English schools, though less successful in this area, nevertheless pay increasing attention to it. Consideration for others, tolerance of various attitudes, valuing each individual expression of opinion, and seeking for ways of reaching agreement are the kinds of behavior that are practiced, learned, and approved in these exercises in human relations.

Individual Effort

Almost every statement of educational purpose and every introduction to a course outline that one would care to examine in England and the U.S. would somewhere indicate that one of the main objects was to enable each individual to develop to the full extent of his capacity. Individual effort is encouraged by teaching procedures, counseling, and competitive examinations; and individual excellence is rewarded both by formal grading, placement, and promotion and informally by teacher and parental praise and support. Students are expected to join teams and pull their weight in the various drama, discussion, and sporting groups to which they may belong, but individual success even in group situations tends to be sought. Modest, self-effacing efficiency or self-sacrificing effort is admired when it is perceived, but is seldom imitated or wholeheartedly encouraged.

Western and Communist Comparisons

How do these characteristics differ from those encouraged in China and the U.S.S.R.?

Objectivity is encouraged in the search for facts and the analysis of situations, but involvement and commitment to act in the way agreed upon by the study group is also an important part of moral education in the Communist countries. Action is always in some measure political action. It is taken in order to forward the interests of the proletariat and the Revolution. Students in China and the U.S.S.R. are taught to see that they are part of a society in which the actions of all the members contribute to a common purpose. To act with it is right; to act against it is wrong. Ideal students are those who have learned to be committed to their society's purposes, to participate in the working out of the policies of the collective group to which they belong, and to act according to the determination of the collective. Cooperativeness and skill in social relationships are obviously also important. In England and the U.S., they are balanced by the cultivation of individual interests. In China and the U.S.S.R., they are part of the overwhelming interest in social improvement; individual excellence is encouraged in a student for the contribution that he makes not to his own prestige but to the advancement of his fellow citizens. "We all work very hard for our country and for socialism," says a language textbook in China.

References

Bronfenbrenner, Urie. Preface to *Soviet Preschool Education* (vol. 1), edited by Henry Chauncey. New York: Holt, Rinehart & Winston, 1969.

Connell, William F. *China at School.* Sydney, Australia: Novak, 1974.

Dragunova, T. V., and Elkonin, D. B. "Some Psychological Features of the Adolescent Personality." *Sovetskaya Pedagogika* 6 (1965). Translated in *Soviet Education* 8, no. 2: 28-37.

Kairov, K. A. "Content and Method of Soviet Education in the Schools." *SCR Bulletin* (Spring 1961): 4.

5

It Comes with the Territory:
The Inevitability of Moral Education
in the Schools

David Purpel and Kevin Ryan

A major assumption of this book is that public schools are actively, continuously, and heavily involved in moral education. We will try in this chapter to support this assumption by specifying the various ways in which moral concerns and viewpoints are expressed in the schools. The great bulk of these moral education experiences and activities are very likely *not* considered to be moral education by those involved. However, we are including in our concept of moral education those events and activities that carry with them some explicit or implicit moral concern, position, or orientation. We are convinced that on any given day anyone sensitive to moral issues will find a great deal of moral education going on in any public school in the nation. There is in effect really no point in debating whether there should be moral education in the schools. What needs to be debated is what form this education should take since we believe that moral education, in fact, "comes with the territory."

An important disclaimer needs to be made. To our knowledge there is not very much in the way of systematic, precise data as to just how much and in what ways moral issues are presented in the schools. We are basing this description on our own personal impressions, observations, and experiences as well as those of others. The field very much needs much more precise and detailed information on the moral life of schools, even though we are confident that our impressions have significant bases in reality.

In lieu of hard data, we invite our readers to join us in an imaginary visit to some imaginary schools. As we journey together, we feel confident that some of our observations will seem familiar and that some will not. We urge our readers to augment, correct, or revise our analyses. We are less concerned with convincing our readers that any particular practice does or does not have moral significance than with increasing general sensitivity and understanding of the moral implications of current school experiences.

We will begin our visit by examining and observing the most obvious and most accessible instances, namely those found in the formal curriculum and in the day to day instructional programs.

Moral Education in the Visible Curriculum

An increasing number of schools (no one really knows how many) are involved in curriculum programs that openly and directly deal with moral education. Since they are described and analyzed in Parts II-IV, we will only note their existence here; our analysis will *not* deal with formal programs in moral education but rather with morally laden curriculum that emerges from traditional school practices.

When one visits a school and concentrates on the program of study and the instructional content of classroom activities, he is very likely to encounter a great many instances of morally loaded content in virtually every aspect of the curriculum:

1. A debate on abortion in a biology class raises questions on the value and definition of life.

2. A discussion on the radical nature of the American Revolution in a history class deals with the question of when insurrection and disloyalty are justified.

3. A critical analysis of the values implicit in Huckleberry Finn's relationship to Jim, the runaway slave, in an English class raises questions of the conflict between law and human dignity.

4. A mock trial of Daniel Ellsberg in a civics class raises questions on the meaning of the First Amendment.

5. Any number of moral issues are embedded in discussions of any number of current events, e.g., Watergate, the My Lai massacre, the morality of terrorism.

These activities and others like them can be conducted with explicit and conscious attention to moral issues but often the moral issues inevitably intrude even when not invited. Naturally, there is immense variation among teachers as to how these issues are handled but one thing is evident—moral considerations are involved and moral messages are inevitably conveyed about them, deliberately or not.

What our visitors might note is that this kind of moral education goes on in most schools routinely and unchallenged, as accepted and legitimate elements of the formal curriculum.

As we walk through the school corridors we might come across some less traditional settings where moral issues arise easily and naturally. There are, for example, programs in career education and personal development which provide opportunities for students to directly and systematically reflect on their lives so as to help make more informed decisions. Stress is put on self-knowledge and realistic appraisal of self in relation to society which inevitably involves a whole host of moral questions. For example, students are often asked to deal with such questions as:

1. Should one work for a career that pays well or one that pays not so well but involves considerable opportunities for public service?

2. Should one defer immediate concerns (e.g., playing varsity football) for ones with longer range considerations (e.g., studying for exams)?

3. Should one plan for a career that will increase the possibility of family alienation? For example, a student under pressure from home to work in the family hardware store contemplates a career in marine biology.

We might also chance to visit other discussion activities having such names as town meeting, class gathering, and show-and-tell that center on personal concerns. What these groups all have in common is an opportunity for students to express and examine personal concerns, many of which have significant moral implications. For example, a child's complaint of feeling friendless and rejected can lead to a discussion of the responsibilities of other class members to respond to the child's needs.

Or we might visit a class where an incident or event is being used as a learning situation, e.g., a death in the school community, any number of school disciplinary actions, a field trip, petty thievery, or a plagiarism case.

Or we might see a number of other classroom events in which moral issues either intrude themselves or arise but are apparently not stressed. For example, many stories, myths, and folk tales are told and retold in the schools and they inevitably reveal some moral emphasis or another:

1. George Washington and his fallen cherry tree are often used to extol the virtues of honesty and facing the music.
2. "Three Little Pigs" are often used to point up the value of careful planning and industry.
3. Bible readings (in some schools) are used to illuminate a variety of subjects including the divine bases of authority and goodness.
4. Cinderella is presumably rewarded for her patience, forebearance, modesty, and obedience—or is it because she's good looking?
5. "The Man Without a Country" finds that to reject one's nation is to invite despair and emptiness.
6. The little Dutch boy who saved his community from disaster by plugging up a hole in the dike certainly demonstrates the importance of social responsibility and how every little thing helps.

An extended visit would probably give us an opportunity to hear (and see) a great number of exhortations, proverbs, mottos, homilies, and epigrams carrying with them some moral imperatives:

1. Waste not, want not.
2. Love thy neighbor.
3. You reap what you sow.
4. If at first you don't succeed, try, try, again.
5. Patience is a virtue.
6. Think!
7. Make love not war.

8. To thine own self be true.
9. Have a nice day.
10. Busy hands are happy hands.
    Idle minds are the devil's playground.
11. Fight for dear old P.S. 162.
12. Happiness is anyone or anything at all loved by you.

It's fun (and what's important, very easy) to make such lists. We urge our readers to make their own list of favorite and persistent memories of moral messages received in schools. Here's ours:

1. Patriotic songs like "God Bless America," "America the Beautiful," and "The Battle Hymn of the Republic" said something to us about God's special relationship with the U.S.A.

2. We still remember the Alamo, the Maine, and Pearl Harbor—lest foreign treachery and American bravery and steadfastness be forgotten.

3. King Arthur set on his round table for us a number of vivid instances of loyalty, persistence, dedication, and devotion to God, women, and a set of rules. (Usually *not* included, we found out later, were Arthur's marital difficulties.)

4. We were often reminded of the long-run advantages of the steady persistent pace of the turtle over the erratically brilliant lope of the easily distracted rabbit.

5. Robin Hood shot holes through the notion that stealing is categorically wrong.

6. Abraham Lincoln's childhood of poverty, honesty, and determination seemed to provide the necessary ingredients for a political career of emancipation, charity for all, and martyrdom.

7. The little engine that could prove that stubbornness and willfulness can overcome humility and modesty.

8. Squanto and his fellow Indians' assistance to the Pilgrims in 1620 became early models of: (a) giving technical assistance to underdeveloped nations, (b) assisting the culturally disadvantaged, and (c) Brotherhood Week.

Moral Education in the Hidden Curriculum

Our imaginary visit so far has been mostly limited to an examination of the formal curriculum and to classroom observations. We now need to widen our horizons and to examine those activities which have been labeled the "hidden curriculum." The hidden curriculum has been defined as what students learn that is not in the formal curriculum. It has to do with the relationships among students, teachers, administrators, and staff particularly as they relate to authority, rules, and the quality of interpersonal relations. We will use the term to include some aspects of school which are not really hidden, such as formal rules, as well as to designate the more subtle and informal activities. We shall divide this analysis into four parts: the classroom culture, other formal school activities, the student culture, and the school culture.

The Classroom Culture

In our visit we need to be mindful of how students, teachers, staff, and administrators relate to each other. Lots of very powerful things happen in classrooms that go beyond the formal course of study. Many verbal transactions inevitably involve moral issues. Students, like all institutional citizens, derive notions of fair play, justice, and morality from how they are treated by the institution, its representatives, and fellow constituents. Schools certainly do "teach" about authority, about justice, about what is right and wrong, and about priorities in the myriad of school policies and practices ranging from the trivial to the significant. Think of the moral implications of these school events:

1. An entire class of children is punished because one or a small group has misbehaved.

2. A teacher sets up groups of children to work collaboratively on projects.

3. A pregnant unmarried student is not allowed to attend school.

4. An applicant for the cheerleader squad is blackballed because of "poor citizenship."

5. A student is not allowed to make up an exam because he went on a family trip on the day of the exam.

6. A teacher apologized to a class for having insulted a student during an argument.

7. Some students with a history of trouble making are not allowed to go on a field trip.

8. Some students volunteer to tutor younger children with reading problems.

9. A teacher taunts a child for not being nearly as productive as another sibling.

10. A teacher allows a student fight to continue as a way of settling an issue "once and for all."

11. A civics class decides to work on Saturdays to clean up a local playground.

Further observation might reveal certain patterns that express certain moral views:

1. Teachers hugging, patting heads, and showing affection to kids who have been "good."

2. Students who "misbehave" are chastised, exiled, humiliated, and even beaten.

3. Students who achieve at a certain level are given special privileges like being eligible to participate in varsity sports, work on the school paper, or go on special trips.

4. Students who fight or cheat or argue are, by the same token, often deprived of certain privileges.

5. Students who get all their math problems right often get gold or blue stars on their papers.

6. Students who "try hard" are often singled out and recognized, a policy which often extends to passing any student who shows sufficient effort. In this value system, high achievement/low effort is not as appreciated as low achievement/high effort.

Other Formal School Activities

The school, obviously, formally provides opportunities for learning other than courses and subject matter. There are such functions as the counseling and guidance program, athletic programs, various extracurricular activities such as dramatics, band, or debating society. Any one of these programs provides opportunities for issues with strong moral overtones to be developed (e.g., winning and losing in a program of competitive athletics; or deciding who gets the lead in the major school production, the talented but uncooperative or the modestly talented but even tempered). And just what would be an appropriate topic for the debating society? "Resolved, All Holidays Should be Celebrated on Mondays" or "Resolved, Marijuana Sales Should be Made Legal"?

We could very well see assemblies and pep rallies which attempt to involve students emotionally and experientially in issues with moral content. For example, the purpose of some Memorial Day exercises seems to be to involve participants in grieving for fallen warriors and for reaffirming the validity and majesty of giving one's life for one's country. Pep rallies are designed to generate the kind of enthusiasm, fervor, and identification that will produce deep and abiding support for athletic teams. If our visit were at Christmas time we might see a pageant in which students can be expected to experience piety, awe, and reverence.

Student Culture

The observant visitor will see how students themselves (unwittingly or not) become agents of moral education. Teachers very often cite certain youngsters as models to be emulated and admired for their character. (Within this category is the more specific and for some more vivid phenomenon of comparing a student with a sibling.) In addition, students by themselves and without prompting are affected and influenced by other students and are apt to derive notions of good behavior from those they admire. This is an area where subtle combinations of peer and teacher approval provide powerful reinforcements for modeling certain behaviors. Some examples are:

1. Kids beating up "tattletales."
2. Social cliques ostracizing individuals.
3. Kids taunting "show-offs" or "teacher's pets."
4. Kids developing and enforcing rules in playground games.
5. Kids threatening unruly peers lest all are punished.

The strength and power of the student culture is reflected in the increasing tendency of many teachers, particularly student and beginning teachers, to identify with their students. Many teachers find themselves torn between the traditions and forms of the school and the inclination to respond to students' needs and feelings. Students as a group do affect the quality of school life and their values, be they hedonistic or pietistic, represent another important strand in the moral fabric of the school.

Teachers and administrators often face the opposing values of the school as an institution and the needs of students, individually or collectively. The increasing stress on personal and civil rights has sharply strengthened sensitivity to student concerns and indeed has led to situations where students significantly share decision making responsibilities. This by itself represents a particular set of values, i.e., the values of shared decision making and affording the individual an increased sense of self-worth.

School Culture

The individual school or school system as a whole conveys certain beliefs, attitudes, and tenets that represent moral positions. It is therefore important that as we become aware of the operational principles of the school. We can do this by reading official publications like bulletins, codes, and regulations as well as becoming sensitive to the implicit mores of the school. Some examples:

1. Good "conduct" is as important as good achievement.
2. Punctuality and neatness are good.
3. Cheating is bad.
4. Regular attendance is good.
5. School loyalty is good.
6. Informing on misbehavior is good.
7. Respect for adults is good.
8. Overt aggression is bad.
9. Damaging books is bad.

Although there is no question that moral issues and responses are involved in these policies and practices, there is still considerable disagreement and confusion over whether a school ought to represent or stand for a particular moral orientation. It is one thing to say that moral issues are involved in what the schools do and another to maintain that schools ought to deliberately act as moral institutions, i.e., to indicate their conception of moral behavior and to proceed accordingly. Should the school deliberately set up moral criteria and judge conduct by those criteria?

For example, one sometimes hears teachers and administrators characterize a particular class or subgroup as having unusual attributes. We have in mind such statements as, "this third grade is a particularly rambunctious group" or "this year's graduating class seems more interested in personal rather than school matters." Are such observations expressions of legitimate school concerns? Should the school intervene in such areas? For example, what should teachers do if a graduating class seems to be on the verge of not following the tradition of making a gift to the school? Irving Kristol's article in Part IV indicts the schools on this very point, i.e., for refusing to stand for any intellectual, moral, or social standard.

Conclusion

We have tried in this chapter to accomplish two basic tasks: (1) to make a case for the extensive and pervasive ways in which moral education is willy-nilly going on in our public schools, and (2) to try to increase our sensitivities to moral concerns as expressed in school life. Our intention was not to take any particular position on the policies and practices used as examples but only to point up the inevitability of moral education in the schools. We are not criticizing the schools for being moral agents but rather are asking that they be more aware, systematic, and informed about their moral influence.

In chapter 6, we will deal with some of the broad instructional questions inherent in developing moral education programs. There is, of course, the prior question of whether any intervention is appropriate, since the argument exists that intervention in the realm of values constitutes manipulation and control of a personal and profound nature. However, we have tried to demonstrate that moral education does in fact go on in schools, and that it inevitably goes on even when not desired or intended. It is our view that the professional must not look at the issue as "should we have moral education in the schools?" but rather "to what degree and in what dimensions and areas should we deal with moral education in the schools?" We need to become more aware of the implicit techniques and goals that are used, not so as to eliminate them but so as to provide us with a basis for making reasonable judgments no matter how complex and painful they may be.

The basic professional decisions, then, are in the realm of choosing an approach that approximates general school and community policy on moral education. Obviously, professionals need to participate in this policy making since it is really not possible to separate goals from techniques. However, broad school policy on moral education should emerge from discussions with parents, students, and community representatives. We say this with full knowledge that it creates difficulties, controversies, and conflicts. Professionals, however, have a vital role to play in informing the public on the nature of the issues and the nature of the options.

The age, ability, and background of students affects the nature of the program, and many moral education programs stress verbal and intellectual abilities not found in younger children. Some programs require certain levels of emotional and personal maturity. Some goals of moral education can be reached through teaching specific skills, others may be more a matter of developmental growth and maturity. Some programs will require special understanding or training for teachers. It is to these more technical questions of approaches and programs that chapter 6 is addressed. We will present a number of specific approaches with different theoretical frameworks utilizing combinations of techniques described above. Any one of these approaches is a reasonable response to the requirement for a moral education program that is intellectually valid, pedagogically sound, and consistent with our democratic traditions.

6

Moral Education in the Classroom: Some Instructional Issues

David Purpel and Kevin Ryan

We have already indicated a number of the critical social and educational issues involving moral education. In this chapter we will zero in on a number of important instructional questions. These questions can be seen as largely technical, but they must be viewed within the perspective of the larger, more fundamental dilemmas described in chapter 1. Two of these issues need to be considered as part of the context for examining the pedagogical questions emphasized in this chapter. These are: (1) Does moral education involve indoctrination of ideas and manipulation of students? and (2) What is the theoretical framework that underlies any moral education program?

The Issue of Indoctrination

This issue is perhaps the hottest, the most persistent, and in many ways the most important professional or technical question. The issue is raised in many ways: "Isn't moral education akin to brainwashing?" "The public schools are no place to impose moral standards." "Teachers have no right to manipulate the moral thinking of children." Anyone in the business of discoursing on moral education needs to deal directly with this issue since a great deal of resistance can be traced to concern and confusion over the distinction between education and indoctrination.

In an important sense, this concern is as critical to education in general as it is to moral education. Our educational values clearly rule out indoctrination* and manipulation as a legitimate technique for achieving traditional goals (e.g., the English teacher must take care lest his interpretation of a poem be read by the class as the "right answer"). In like manner, other teachers want students to do their own thinking, exercise independent judgment, and develop personal positions. There are limits, however, and it is these limits that constitute the basic framework of our educational approach, namely, a system of rational, logical, and critical intelligence. One hopes that students will make independent judgments that are *informed* and that have been subjected to rigorous analysis based on well-established and accepted methodological principles. We hope to develop in our students and in ourselves the skills and capacities to deal critically with the onslaught of ideas, notions, hypotheses, assumptions, "facts," etc. that we are all asked to confront, so that we can resist manipulation and indoctrination and make intelligent, independent judgments.

The same general notions apply to moral education, except that the stakes involved are possibly higher and the methods of manipulation are possibly subtler. It is difficult to compare the dangers of "indoctrinating" students to believe that American firepower was the principal factor in the Axis defeat of 1945 and to believe that the use of the atomic bomb was or was not morally justifiable. We simply have to face the idea that the moral aspects of education are of immense significance and therefore must be handled with the greatest care. Anyone interested in balancing the responsibilities of imparting accumulated wisdom and knowledge with those of encouraging independence and individuality faces a continuous struggle and

---

*In chapter 2, James Watkins refers to a number of attributes of indoctrination—teaching that aims at closing minds, use of nonrational methods, and teaching content "not generally regarded as truths." The *Dictionary of Education* (1945) defines indoctrination in this way: "in the broadest sense, the attempt to inculcate beliefs, a possible concomitant of any learning situation; in narrower terms, the attempt to fix in the learning mind any doctrine and in a manner preventing serious comparison and evaluation."

risk. Those struggles and risks are just that much more significant and complicated when moral education is involved.

The answer to dealing with this risk surely cannot be to avoid moral education since, as we have seen, this is a delusion. Nor can it be to ignore the real dangers of indoctrination. The answer would seem to be in making extra efforts to develop informed, independent judgments. This means the further development of the basic intellectual skills of thought, criticism, reflection, and analysis. It means presenting students with a variety of viewpoints as well as their criticisms. Perhaps above all, it means developing an atmosphere of intellectual trust where students and teachers alike can feel free to inquire into, challenge, share, and reflect upon ideas. *What the public schools must do is not "teach morals" but teach appropriate ways of responding to moral issues and concerns. Our basic attitude toward moral education is that it should involve careful and sensitive inquiry into moral questions.*

To say that, however, is to raise the other major theoretical problem that provides the context for discussion of instructional issues. We have presented the problem and risk of indoctrination and have argued that the development of critical intelligence in a trusting environment that fosters free inquiry is a necessary condition for any program in moral education. It is not, however, a sufficient condition. What is also required is some framework for moral education. A moral education program presented openly and critically does not by itself meet the requirement of giving students what we have called "appropriate ways of responding to moral issues and concerns." Of course, there has been enormous controversy over the centuries as to what constitutes "appropriate ways." There are a great number of frameworks, some of which are represented in Parts II-IV of this book. Each framework either implicitly or explicitly reflects some notions on the nature of the universe, man, and the ultimate questions of life. In addition, these frameworks reflect some assumptions on how people learn as well as what people should learn and under what conditions. Considerable effort has gone into welding these assorted beliefs and assumptions into coherent systems that provide philosophic and psychological frameworks for finding meaning and generating theories of moral education.

It is another delusion to think that we can offer education that does not emerge from some framework of assumptions. It is far more profitable to examine one's assumptions and work to make them coherent than to deny them. This is, of course, particularly true of teachers and of extra significance for those involved in moral education.

Moral issues have been examined within a variety of philosophical contexts. These include the Marxist orientation, the cultural relativist position, the pragmatic position, developmental and behaviorist theories, and psychoanalytic theories. There are many sources for moral insight—religious inspiration or revelation, intuition, logical analysis, and emotional release. Chapter 2 provides further insight into the significance of philosophic views for moral education. Our task, then, as educators, is to develop and transmit systematic ways of examining moral issues, remembering that we must do this in a context where students have the intellectual antibodies to ward off the debilitating effects of manipulation.

Direct vs. Indirect Approaches

The Direct Approach

This approach takes the position that, since moral education is needed and goes on one way or another, we should consciously, rationally, and carefully make provision for it. The view is that moral education is sufficiently important and complicated to warrant specific attention, energy, and resources. However, there is a great deal of debate on whether it is better to develop a frontal attack on moral education needs through the development of specialized programs and courses taught by specially trained teachers or whether it is wiser to integrate specific moral content into the existing curriculum in an organic and functional manner. Values clarification (see Part II) has been developed both as a separate program and as a technique that can be adapted and assimilated into traditional courses such as history, English, math, biology, and home economics. The opportunities to integrate moral issues in reading and language programs are obvious and multitudinous. For example, Sullivan and Beck (chapter 14) have developed a course in ethics and Mosher and Sullivan (chapter 15) have developed a course in moral development, both at the high school level.

Subcategories of the direct approach are the programmatic

approach and the integrative approach. We can perhaps gain further insight by looking at each subcategory and examining its advantages and disadvantages.

The Programmatic Approach. This view, consistent with much that has gone on in modern curriculum development, attempts to recognize a specific set of learning goals and organize directly and systematically to achieve them. This means not only specifying goals but developing particular materials, resources, activities, and experiences that are directly related to these goals, in this case moral education. It means having courses in moral education, books and materials on moral education, and instructors with specific expertise in moral education. Those who favor this approach posit a number of possible advantages:

1. It provides a more honest and open approach, since there are fewer opportunities for hidden and implied messages. This allows all concerned to respond to a specific set of principles and practices, which should significantly facilitate and sharpen public and professional dialogue.

2. Since moral education goes on willy-nilly, it is more professional and responsible to be systematic and rigorous in developing the curriculum.

3. Such a curriculum can be more efficient, careful, organized, and focused. Resources and techniques can be better selected and organized when there are specific objectives and goals and when there is less ambiguity about priorities.

4. Such an approach might facilitate meaningful evaluation of its effectiveness and therefore meet the demands of accountability.

5. This approach allows teachers to specialize in this highly sensitive and complex area, which reduces the amount of misinformed and naive teaching.

However, there are potential problems with a programmatic approach:

1. A direct approach might lean toward indoctrination and manipulation.

2. A specific program in moral education might be seen as naive, inappropriate, and far-fetched, since there is no available structure, discipline, or field.

3. Although a course in philosophy or psychology dealing with moral issues is feasible, it would be so academically oriented that it would probably be detached from questions of moral behavior.

4. It seems quite possible that any formal programs, however valid, can be subverted or undermined by incompetent teachers.

The Integrative Approach. The integrative approach accepts the importance of moral education and assumes that moral issues are best dealt with within conventional contexts.

This approach deals directly with those moral issues that are integral parts of larger, broader topics. Sometimes this happens almost unavoidably, as in dealing with the morality of slavery in the course of studying the Civil War, while sometimes teachers will have to introduce moral implications of topics that have been traditionally taught "straight." An example of the latter is conducting a classroom discussion of America's responsibility to share its food supply in connection with a course in nutrition.

The argument is that moral issues will be more meaningful if they emerge out of and are integrated into established, systematic, and well-developed fields and disciplines. For example, a discussion of the social aspects of pollution can easily and naturally flow out of a biology unit on conservation, thus enriching biology and providing a sound intellectual framework for dealing with moral issues. There are a number of possible advantages to the integrative approach:

1. It provides a natural and functional approach that is comprehensible to parents, teachers, and students.

2. Integration of study prevents compartmentalization and fragmentation of thought. Separation of moral issues from the disciplines is arbitrary, misleading, and artificial.

3. It does not require much in the way of special materials and training, nor does it demand a special priority for moral education goals.

4. The discipline framework is a good protection against indoctrination and manipulation as well as sloppy and fuzzy thinking.

On the other hand, several disadvantages of the integrative approach come to mind:

1. Moral education goals can easily be overlooked in a curriculum that emphasizes traditional academic ones.
2. The study of moral education is limited to those issues that come out of a relatively narrow curriculum. It would be better to start with critical moral issues and then look to the disciplines for help in dealing with them.
3. It does not provide an opportunity for teachers to learn in depth the procedures and principles that underlie the study of moral issues. There is a considerable amount of knowledge and a number of critical skills involved in the psychological and philosophical aspects of moral study that are crucial to effective moral education.

In any case, the programmatic and integrative approaches are united in their belief that moral education should go on in schools and that teachers have a responsibility to deliberately provide opportunities for students to deal with moral issues.

The Indirect Approach

This approach accepts the importance of dealing with moral education but holds that a strong, basic education plus a fair and responsive school environment is the best way to help students in this area. The old cliché that moral education is "caught and not taught" summarizes the position that we cannot or should not directly instruct students on moral behavior, but we can provide the intellectual tools and skills that will enable the student to handle these concerns. The view is that a strong school program would make it unnecessary to develop highly specialized programs like sex education, drug education, and moral education. Moral education would come as a consequence of the development of intellectual skills that can be applied to moral issues; the permeating spirit of free inquiry; and the hidden curriculum, i.e., the school environment that determines the quality of interpersonal relations.

The Development of Intellectual Skills. These skills include basic reading and comprehension as well as the more developed skills of logical analysis, reasoning, critical thinking, self-understanding, and ability to cope with a great number of problems and issues. The argument is that the same standards of rational discourse can be applied to moral problems as to any other set of problems. Part of this intellectual process includes identifying and sorting out issues, and a good school program would certainly result in students being able to identify moral issues on both personal and social levels.

In addition to these intellectual skills, the schools also provide, through the basic perspectives of history, science, literature, and mathematics, the broad patterns of human civilization. This broad canvas is the basic framework for our present human condition—our problems and their origins, our traditions, our hopes. Again, if the school has done its job well, students should learn enough from the traditional curriculum to give them a good sense of the fundamental questions, dilemmas, and paradoxes that face us all. The schools then, according to this view, have as their major goals:

1. Teaching students about the nature of civilization.
2. Helping students form the critical questions and problems about civilization.
3. Giving students the tools to enable them to respond to these questions and problems.

These are very powerful arguments but they beg the question of whether the traditional curriculum could not be altered so as to significantly improve the quality of moral education. A very wise man once said that the most critical question to be confronted by curriculum leaders is: "What should be left to chance?" Is specific understanding of and insight into the moral nature of life to be left to chance? Does the homogenized morality of the media and the increasingly ethical neutrality of the schools signal to the child a low priority for questions of morality? Does our existing curriculum and school practice give us confidence that competence in dealing with moral issues is not simply a matter of chance?

The Importance of School Environment. As we tried to show in chapter 5 the hidden curriculum is another powerful, perhaps critical, way in which moral education happens, and to some it is the area of greatest opportunity for intervention. Teachers, administrators, and parents, for example, are made aware every day of the intense interest that children have in the concept of "fairness." Kohlberg (see chapter 13) has said that the best way to teach justice is to have a just society or at least a just school. Unfortunately, a great deal of the hidden curriculum is so hidden as to be unconscious or unconceptualized. School personnel have an urgent responsibility to examine a whole variety of school practices that affect the quality of life in the schools. A simple change in the way lunch is handled, for example, might do a great deal for students' perceptions of what it means to be human. For example, it might be useful to look at lunch in human rather than institutional terms—as an opportunity for tension release, personal interaction, relaxation, and re-energizing rather than a problem that requires getting a large number of people filled with a certain volume of food in the shortest possible time.

By insisting on scrupulous adherence to procedures in a suspension or expulsion case, a school can drive home a point about judicial safeguards more effectively than with a lesson in the civics curriculum. Seating arrangements can signal to students and staff, subliminally, some notions on the authority structure.

In fairness, we need to point out a strong scholarly tradition, seen most often in anthropology and sociology going back to Durkheim, that holds the hidden curriculum to be but another legitimate aspect of the socialization process. Their broad view is that this socialization process represents the unconscious accumulated wisdom of the culture and is designed to preserve and protect the well being of the individual and the society (see chapter 13).

To sum up then, we have dealt with the assumption that those skills and attitudes that derive from a successful traditional school program can indirectly but significantly help people with moral issues. Certainly, this approach avoids many of the sticky and complicated problems inherent in moral education (controversies on indoctrination, public policy, curriculum questions, etc.), but two key questions remain. Is this approach anything more than a way of avoiding difficult questions? Is it realistic to work on the assumption that traditional school programs will be effective enough to make special compensatory programming unnecessary?

Affective Considerations

Inevitably, because moral issues deal with rightness, goodness, justice, and virtue, they are confused with "affective" concerns involving personal feelings and emotions. Example: A man is confronted with the question—should he steal a loaf of bread so that his family might eat? The question of the rightness or wrongness of stealing the bread might be called "moral." The man might have a variety of feelings about stealing—fear, anxiety, excitement, anger. If he steals the bread he might decide that it was morally defensible because human survival is a greater good than personal property, or he might decide to steal it even though he could not justify it morally. His personal reactions to stealing could involve guilt or satisfaction and achievement.

"Moral education" in this case would mean helping the man understand the ethical implications of his actions while "affective education" would mean helping the man become aware of his feelings, their origins, and perhaps how to cope with them. Certainly both could be done together and for some purposes with greater efficacy. However, it is also clear that they *can* be separated. Many proponents of affective education indicate explicitly or implicitly that insight and understanding of moral issues is an important consequence of increased sensitivity of feeling and openness to expression. Indeed, the Values Clarification program represents an attempt not only to mesh personal, cognitive, and moral concerns but seems to say that the latter emerge from the former.

Teachers are very often sensitive to these issues and, as we have said, many try to encourage students to think and reflect upon them in both formal and informal settings—in discussion groups, on the playground, with special materials or without. However, what is critical is whether or not children are given sufficient opportunity to think carefully about *moral* concerns and whether they are encouraged to do anything more than verbalize their feelings. It is one thing to feel and express and another to think, analyze, and reflect carefully upon these feelings.

Many writers feel that role playing, the technique of assuming the posture, attitudes, and feelings of another, is the critical technique for dealing with the intellectual and personal aspects of moral education. Role playing is based on the assumptions that (1) at the heart of moral issues is concern for the implications of what one does for others and (2) the ability to empathize with others is crucial to having access to those concerns. Role playing is both a way of confronting one's feelings and beliefs about an issue and a way of "getting inside" different, perhaps conflicting beliefs. It is a way of complicating, personalizing, and deepening one's views, which often has the effect of easing harsh, egocentric, and simplified judgments. There are any number of illustrations of role playing techniques for moral education in both traditional and atypical settings:

1. Dramatization of plays with significant moral overtones, such as "Diary of Anne Frank" or "The Crucible."

2. Improvisations with suggested premises, such as asking three students to imagine themselves marooned on an island with enough food for only one to survive.

3. Improvisations on issues that emerge out of the classroom, such as a re-enactment of a lunchroom fight or a cheating incident.

4. Role playing events with moral concerns, such as someone needing medical attention, someone being assaulted, or someone wanting "help" with homework.

5. Asking students to assume roles of parents, teachers, or other adults, in order to provide an opportunity for them to deal with issues of authority and fairness.

Developmental Considerations

Another important pedagogical question is that of determining teaching techniques appropriate to students' age or developmental stage. Piaget and Kohlberg have generated sophisticated and specific approaches to moral education based on developmental principles (see Part III). There are, however, a number of key instructional questions related to age that we feel need to be mentioned. The reader will recognize that these issues are similar and parallel to teaching other subjects at different developmental stages.

First, there is the issue of intervention, the question of what kind of interference with development is appropriate. We dealt obliquely with this issue earlier when we talked of the direct vs. the indirect approach to moral education. One could say that moral development is part of a natural maturation process and requires only a reasonable level and quality of environmental stimulus. On the other hand, there is the view that adults have an opportunity to accelerate and deepen the growth rate by providing rich and stimulating activities. A related question has to do with the nature of growth required—cognitive? emotional? social? Kohlberg and Mayer (1972) argue for simultaneous stimulation of psychological, intellectual, and moral development. In effect, they say that psychological and intellectual growth are necessary but not sufficient conditions for moral education.

This raises the question of what kinds of intervention procedures are particularly appropriate for elementary school children. The most common question is: At what age can children deal intellectually with abstract and conceptual questions involved in moral problems? This is a concern not only for the theoreticians and researchers, but for the classroom teachers, who need to make decisions on whether their particular students have the intellectual, social, and emotional readiness to deal with moral issues. In practice, there is a tendency among moral educators to emphasize personal and social development for younger children and defer intellectual discussions of moral issues until children are more able to deal with them at a conceptual level.

Moral education for very young children is a particularly interesting and difficult problem. Although it is rare for elementary school children to deal directly with moral issues or to receive instruction in this area, they are usually getting a great deal of morally loaded instruction (see chapter 5). This is the period, for example, when many traditional fairy tales, myths, legends, songs, etc. are introduced and retold. It is also the time when schools are heavily involved in socialization activities, i.e., the process of learning how to behave in a school, what one's responsibilities are, who is in charge, and what the rules, regulations, and mores of school life are. Perhaps most significantly, it is a time when, for most youngsters, group participation and group values become central concerns. All of these highly significant events happen when children are perhaps most vulnerable to the influence and manipulation of the school, and when their intellectual and emotional capacities to resist dependence and control are at their lowest. If there is a serious concern about moral education as manipulation, it may be most critical for younger students who have not yet developed autonomy and independence.

Conclusion

We have presented a number of technical instructional issues involving moral education. Although these issues are complex and substantial, we must not lose sight of the larger cultural, social, and political context. We have particularly stressed the key importance of two major considerations that must be part of the perspective of all discussions of instructional problems, i.e., the problem of indoctrination and the importance of the theoretical framework. In addition to these concerns, we have discussed the relative merits of direct as opposed to indirect moral education, affective aspects of moral education, and developmental considerations.

References

Good, Carter V. (ed.). *Dictionary of Education*. New York: McGraw-Hill, 1945.

Kohlberg, Lawrence, and Mayer, Rochelle. "Development as the Aim of Education." *Harvard Educational Review* 42 (November 1972): 449-96.

PART II

The Values Clarification Approach

Introduction

Our task is not to discover some elusive road—or rediscover some lost road—to moral education and commence traveling it. As we will reiterate throughout this book, the moral and ethical education of the young is a matter of great complexity and variety. There are, we believe, many roads to the moral education of the young. Parts II-IV provide a rough road map.

There are several problems, however. One deals with the destination: helping the young to deal with moral questions. As indicated earlier, there is a good deal of confusion and outright disagreement about what constitutes morality. Is morality conforming to the laws of the major institutions in a society or responding to one's conscience? Is it showing concern for others, or is it the ability to think clearly about issues of right and wrong?

There is also the question of what we might call the levels of moral activity. Is our concern that the young be emotionally attracted to what is considered to be right and good? Or are we concerned primarily with the cognitive domain, the ability to apply the skills of reasoning to moral questions? Are we primarily concerned with behavior? Or are we hoping to address all three of these levels? Since different approaches to moral education attend to different levels, it is important to keep in mind to what level the individual authors are giving greatest attention.

While this book is primarily concerned with the effect of schooling, we need to remember that the school is but one influence. The school-age child is subjected to many, many influences. While difficult to measure, the child's moral attitudes are influenced by the economic system of which he is a part, the media to which he is exposed, the ethnic group to which he belongs, and his friendship network. It is against this background of complex human and institutional forces that we must look at the interventions of the school.

In recent years, a number of researchers and scholars have given attention to the school as an agent for moral education. Some of these have been philosophers, some psychologists, and some educators seeking to apply insights from other fields. They have, if you will, charted out new and different roads. Many of these roads have different starting points and, while they point in the same general direction, they do not always converge. Some of these roads are clearly marked and well-traveled. Others are interesting, but, as yet, very rough paths. Parts II-IV attempt to pull together some of the most important writing in the field that shed light on how the schools can be a positive force in the moral education of the young.

We have tried to include approaches that directly deal with the issues of moral education in the public schools. Obviously, there are other general orientations, for example, the behaviorists, who are very uncomfortable with the whole concept of moral education and would prefer to deal with these issues from a totally different set of psychological and philosophical assumptions. Still others, particularly those interested in religious education, find it impossible to deal with moral education unless it is within some broader religious and spiritual framework. Our focus in this book is on those educators who accept the validity of the concept of moral education in the public schools and who have responded creatively to the tasks of program development.

We have, perhaps arbitrarily, grouped these articles into three subgroups: the values clarification approach, the cognitive-developmental approach, and the cognitive approach. Where possible, we have tried to present a range of perspectives from the theoretical to the practical. We have also included critiques of the various positions. The intent is not to write a prescription for moral education, but rather to delineate positive alternatives now available. Nor do we find all of these approaches of equal value. We have our biases, too. One of these biases is the belief that the task of entering into the lives of children as a positive moral force is a legitimate and necessary role for the schools. Another is that teachers will probably not be allowed to deal with moral education with the conceptual purity of the articles presented here. Many of the articles were written by researchers and individuals committed to a certain view, rather than those immersed daily in the work of helping children to understand and cope with their needs and problems, moral and otherwise. Our intention, then, is to share with educators some of the most current reports from the territory called "moral education," and to give them some idea of the many roads into it from those who have traveled the roads.

The Values Clarification Approach

Since the publication of *Values in Teaching* ten years ago, the values clarification approach has gained the most attention and has been the most widely practiced in the American school. Its meaning is in the title. The purpose is to clarify one's values. No particular set of values are advocated. No individual or institution's values are held up for emulation. The intention is for the individual to get in touch with his own values, to bring them to the surface, and to reflect upon them.

Values clarification has become popular in schools for a number of reasons. Basically, it is a series of loosely related techniques which are quite easy to learn. The approach is, then, easily accessible to teachers. Besides the pioneering book by Raths, Harmin, and Simon, there is a large and growing number of books of the "how to" variety that supposedly equip teachers to be value clarifiers. Second, teachers have the satisfaction of dealing with very important issues, such as racial attitudes and an individual's life goals. These important issues are dealt with in a seemingly open and honest way. Third, the teacher does not have to be didactic. She does not have to impose her own views on the students. Fourth, teachers widely report that "values clarification works." They feel that it turns kids on in what is otherwise a dreary and largely irrelevant curriculum.

Part II opens with a statement of some of the underlying principles by the major architects of the values clarification movement: Louis Raths, Merrill Harmin, and Sidney B. Simon. Next, Howard Kirschenbaum, a major theorist of the movement, attempts to put values clarification into a theoretical framework. This is followed by a study of values clarification vs. indoctrination by Sidney B. Simon. The attention that has come to values clarification in recent years has also led a number of scholars to raise questions about what values clarification actually accomplishes. In two critical essays by John S. Stewart and Alan L. Lockwood, the major criticisms are analyzed.

As parents, teachers, and administrators search for ways to respond to the reported valuelessness of youth, the values clarification movement is one of the first they encounter. In the following chapters we have attempted to provide a balanced overview of this vital and provocative movement.

7

Selection from Values and Teaching

Louis Raths, Merrill Harmin, and Sidney B. Simon

Persons have experiences; they grow and learn. Out of experiences may come certain general guides to behavior. These guides tend to give direction to life and may be called values. Our values show what we tend to do with our limited time and energy.

Since we see values as growing from a person's experiences, we would expect that different experiences would give rise to different values and that any one person's values would be modified as his experiences accumulate and change. A person in the Antarctic would not be expected to have the same values as a person in Chicago. And a person who has an important change in patterns of experience might be expected to modify his values. Values may not be static if one's relationships to his world are not static. As guides to behavior, values evolve and mature as experiences evolve and mature.

Moreover, because values are a part of living, they operate in very complex circumstances and usually involve more than simple extremes of right and wrong, good or bad, true or false. The conditions under which behavior is guided, in which values work, typically

Reprinted by permission from *Values and Teaching: Working with Values in the Classroom* (Columbus, Ohio: Charles E. Merrill, 1966).

involve conflicting demands, a weighing and a balancing, and finally an action that reflects a multitude of forces. Thus values seldom function in a pure and abstract form. Complicated judgments are involved and what is really valued is reflected in the outcome of life as it is finally lived.

We therefore see values as constantly being related to the experiences that shape them and test them. They are not, for any one person, so much hard and fast verities as they are the results of hammering out a style of life in a certain set of surroundings. After a sufficient amount of hammering, certain patterns of evaluating and behaving tend to develop. Certain things are treated as right, or desirable, or worthy. These tend to become our values. . . .

We shall be less concerned with the particular value outcomes of any one person's experiences than we will with the process that he uses to obtain his values. Because life is different through time and space, we cannot be certain what experiences any one person will have. We therefore cannot be certain what values, what style of life, would be most suitable for any person. We do, however, have some ideas about what *processes* might be most effective for obtaining values. These ideas grow from the assumption that whatever values one obtains should work as effectively as possible to relate one to his world in a satisfying and intelligent way.

From this assumption comes what we call the *process of valuing*. A look at this process may make clear how we define a value. Unless something satisfies *all* seven of the criteria noted below, we do not call it a value. In other words, for a value to result, all of the following seven requirements must apply. Collectively, they describe the process of valuing.

1. *Choosing freely.* If something is in fact to guide one's life whether or not authority is watching, it must be a result of free choice. If there is coercion, the result is not likely to stay with one for long, especially when out of the range of the source of that coercion. Values must be freely selected if they are to be really valued by the individual.

2. *Choosing from among alternatives.* This definition of values is concerned with things that are chosen by the individual and, obviously, there can be no choice if there are no alternatives from which to choose. It makes no sense, for example, to say that one values

eating. One really has no choice in the matter. What one may value is certain types of food or certain forms of eating, but not eating itself. We must all obtain nourishment to exist; there is no room for decision. Only when a choice is possible, when there is more than one alternative from which to choose, do we say a value can result.

3. *Choosing after thoughtful consideration of the consequences of each alternative.* Impulsive or thoughtless choices do not lead to values as we define them. For something intelligently and meaningfully to guide one's life, it must emerge from a weighing and an understanding. Only when the consequences of each of the alternatives are clearly understood can one make intelligent choices. There is an important cognitive factor here. A value can emerge only with thoughtful consideration of the range of the alternatives and consequences in a choice.

4. *Prizing and cherishing.* When we value something, it has a positive tone. We prize it, cherish it, esteem it, respect it, hold it dear. We are happy with our values. A choice, even when we have made it freely and thoughtfully, may be a choice we are not happy to make. We may choose to fight in a war, but be sorry circumstances make that choice reasonable. In our definition, values flow from choices that we are glad to make. We prize and cherish the guides to life that we call values.

5. *Affirming.* When we have chosen something freely, after consideration of the alternatives, and when we are proud of our choice, glad to be associated with it, we are likely to affirm that choice when asked about it. We are willing to publicly affirm our values. We may even be willing to champion them. If we are ashamed of a choice, if we would not make our position known when appropriately asked, we would not be dealing with values but something else.

6. *Acting upon choices.* Where we have a value, it shows up in aspects of our living. We may do some reading about things we value. We are likely to form friendships or to be in organizations in ways that nourish our values. We may spend money on a choice we value. We budget time or energy for our values. In short, for a value to be present, life itself must be affected. Nothing can be a value that does not, in fact, give direction to actual living. The person who talks about something but never does anything about it is dealing with something other than a value.

7. *Repeating.* Where something reaches the stage of a value, it is

very likely to reappear on a number of occasions in the life of the person who holds it. It shows up in several different situations, at several different times. We would not think of something that appeared once in a life and never again as a value. Values tend to have a persistency, tend to make a pattern in a life.

To review this definition, we see values as based on three processes: choosing, prizing, and acting.

Choosing: (1) freely
(2) from alternatives
(3) after thoughtful consideration of the consequences of each alternative

Prizing: (4) cherishing, being happy with the choice
(5) willing to affirm the choice publicly

Acting: (6) doing something with the choice
(7) repeatedly, in some pattern of life

Those processes collectively define valuing. Results of the valuing process are called values.

The reader might pause for a moment and apply the seven criteria for a value to one of his hobbies, be it sewing, skiing, or hi-fi. Is it prized, freely and thoughtfully chosen from alternatives, acted upon, repeated, and publicly known? If so, one might say that you *value* that hobby.

Value Indicators

Obviously not everything is a value, nor need it be. We also have purposes, aspirations, beliefs, and many other things that may not meet all seven of those criteria. However values often do grow from our purposes, aspirations, beliefs, and so on. Let us briefly discuss some things that could indicate the presence of a value but that are different from values. We call these expressions which approach values, but which do not meet all of the criteria, *value indicators.*

1. *Goals or purposes.* To have purposes gives direction to life. If the purpose is important to us, we cherish it and we organize our life

in ways by which we can achieve the purpose. This doesn't mean that every stated purpose is a value. Instead, we should think of a stated purpose as a potential value or a value indicator. If, in our presence, a child should state a purpose, it is, until we inquire further, merely a stated purpose—and we have an opportunity to pursue with him whether or not he prizes it, has freely chosen it, has wanted it for some time, and is willing to do what is necessary to achieve it. Some stated purposes are dropped when these processes are applied. The child finds out that what he said is not what he really wants. He might have had what amounts to a passing interest in the idea, but even brief examination often results in depreciation of the stated purpose. Thus a purpose *may* be a value, but, on the other hand, it may not be.

2. *Aspirations.* We sometimes indicate a purpose that is remote in terms of accomplishment. It is not something that we wish or expect to accomplish today or tomorrow, or within a week or sometimes even a month. The statement of such an aspiration frequently points to the possibility of something that is valued. We shall not know if it is truly a value until we have asked questions which relate to the seven criteria which have been mentioned. When the responses are consistent with those criteria, we can say that we have touched a value.

3. *Attitudes.* Sometimes we give indications that we may have values by expressing attitudes. We say that we are *for* something or *against* something. It is not always a sound practice to infer that such a statement represents a value. Is it really cherished? Has some consideration been given to alternatives? Does it come up again and again? Is it related to the life activities of the person who expresses it? Unless these criteria are met, it may be just so many words. That is, it may just be an attitude and not a value.

4. *Interests.* Very often you hear people say that they are interested in something. Care should be taken, however, in concluding that this means that a value is present. Very often when we say we are interested, we mean little more than that we would like to talk about it or to listen to someone talk about it, or that we might like to read a little more in that area. It isn't a combination of the criteria which have been proposed. It may be a bit more than a passing fancy, but very frequently it does not work out to be a value.

5. *Feelings.* Our personalities are also expressed through our

feelings and through statements about how we feel. Our feelings are sometimes hurt. Sometimes we feel outraged. On other occasions we are glad, sad, depressed, excited; and we experience dozens of other feelings. We cannot always say that a value is present. In terms of a definition of a value, our feelings may be responses which are dissipated by very brief reflection. We should have to ask a number of questions in order to find out if the feeling reflects an underlying value.

6. *Beliefs and convictions.* When we hear someone state what he believes, it is all too easy to accept the statement as a value. A man may believe that there should be discrimination with respect to race, but he may be ashamed of that belief. He may not prize holding it. Moreover, upon examination, he may have doubts about the truth or goodness of his belief. It is the examined belief, the cherished belief, the freely chosen belief, and the belief that pervades life that rises to the stature of a value. The verbal statement provides a pointer, but it is only through careful examination that we get to know whether it represents a value.

7. *Activities.* We sometimes say about a figure in public life, "That's what he says, but what does he do?" We seem to be saying that not until a person does something do we have some idea of what he values. With values, as with other things, actions speak louder than words. Of course, it isn't true that everything we do represents our values. For example, we are pretty sure that going to church does not necessarily mean a commitment to religion. One may go to church for many reasons. One may go often and regularly to bridge parties, all the while wishing that he didn't have to do. One may do a certain kind of work every day without having chosen that work or prizing it very much. In other words, just by observing what people do, we are unable to determine if values are present. We have to know if the individual prizes what he is doing, if he has chosen to do what he is doing, and if it constitutes a pattern in his life, etc. All by themselves, activities do not tell us enough, but they may indicate a value.

8. *Worries, problems, obstacles.* We hear individuals talk about worries that they have, or problems that they have, and we sometimes infer from the context that we know the values that are involved. Here again we may be giving undue importance to verbal statements. If we were to ask questions bearing upon the seven criteria which have been proposed, we might find out that nothing of

great importance is involved; that the statement represented "a conversation piece." Many of us talk a good deal, and we may mention problems or worries only as ways of entering into a conversation. Examining the worry or the problem may reveal that something *is* deeply prized, that a belief *is* being blocked, that one's life *is* being disturbed, and under these circumstances we can be more confident with the judgment that a value is involved.

We have explained something about eight categories of behavior which have a significant relationship to valuing. There is no implication that other categories of behavior may not be just as important. However, these eight categories—goals and purposes, aspirations, feelings, interests, beliefs and convictions, attitudes, activities, and worries—are often revealed in the classroom. We believe it is important that opportunities for revealing these become a vital part of teaching, for the next step—as will be discussed in later chapters—is for the teacher to help those children who choose to do so to raise these value "indicators" to the level of values, that is, to the level on which all seven of the valuing processes operate.

We now want to turn our attention to one of the value processes that seems to have particular importance in our work with children growing up in this confused and complex world, the process of choosing.

The Crucial Criterion of Choice

Because we see choosing as crucial to the process of valuing, it may be useful at this point to expand on the conditions that must exist if a choice is really to be made.

The idea of choosing suggests the notion of alternatives. One chooses something from a group of things. If there is only one possibility, we cannot make a choice and, according to our definition, we cannot have a value in that area. Yet so often we eliminate all but one alternative or we restrict alternatives available to children. For example, we say to a child that he must either sit silently in his chair or stay after school. Or we ask, "Wouldn't you like to learn your multiplication table, John?" If we restrict alternatives, so that the child's preferred choice is not among them, we cannot say that his choice represents a value. It is common practice to give children either-or choices, both of which may be undesirable from his stand-point, then wonder why he does not value his own behavior.

Unless we open up decisions, and include alternatives that a child might really prefer, we may only give the illusion of choice, at least in terms of this value theory. Values must grow from thought-ful, prized choices made from sufficient alternatives.

When we take the lead in presenting alternatives to children, we should also take some care in seeing to it that *the alternatives have meaning* for them. A student may be familiar with only one of the possible choices and may not be aware of what the others involve. We can discover this by asking questions; and if he doesn't know what other choices could mean, we can help him to understand them better. It is useless, therefore, to ask a young child to make choices from among alternatives he doesn't understand, and it is inaccurate to *think* a choice has been made when, for example, a child selects democracy over autocracy without much understanding of either.

We should also help children to see the probable *consequences of a choice* and find out if they are willing to accept the conse-quences which may follow. Where a child has put himself on record as willing to take the consequences, the situation has been clarified, and his choice has some meaning. Without such an understanding of and acceptance of the consequences, we can hardly call the choice meaningful.

Also there is the idea that the child needs to be really *free to choose*. If for many reasons we don't want him to choose a particular alternative, like setting fire to the house, we should let him know that this is not within the realm of choice. We should not try to fool him into thinking that he is a free agent and then disappoint him when we refuse to honor his choice. We should be clear and forceful when we deny choices. Otherwise we subvert the faith of the child in the very process of deciding and choosing. But when we are con-cerned with values, we must be willing to give the child his freedom to choose. In short, we are saying that a coerced choice is no choice at all. It is not likely that values will evolve from a choice imbued with threat or bribery, for example. A condition of choosing that the value theory suggests is freedom to choose. One important implica-tion for teachers is the diminution of the punishment and reward systems so widely used in schools. Choices cannot be considered suf-ficiently free if each one is to be weighed, approved or disapproved, or graded by someone in charge.

Does this mean that the whole world should be open for choice and that we should respect a child's choice no matter what it is? Most teachers, in the light of policies suggested by a school board or school administrators, make quite clear to students that there are areas where choice is not possible. One of these relates to life itself. We do not allow children to engage in activities which might result in serious danger. This is almost always directly stated and carried out without exception. We say to children that in matters like this they cannot choose, that their behavior is restricted; and the reason we give is that the consequences of an unwise choice are not tolerable or that the alternatives can probably not be well enough understood to make a choice meaningful.

Many of us are also against vulgarity in many forms. Profane language, obscene behavior, filth, and dirtiness are matters on which many of us take a stand. We may indicate to children that they may not engage in things of this kind; that the policies for which we stand do not allow such things to go on; that deviations from our standards bother us too much to be tolerated. When an individual reveals this kind of behavior, we may directly intervene and, perhaps privately, talk with the student. Thus may some teachers want to restrict choices in areas that are important to adults.

In almost every culture and in many communities there are areas which are sometimes called "hot" or "very delicate." In some communities it may be matters pertaining to religious issues; in some other communities it may be matters relating to political issues; sex is frequently such an issue. Where these so-called hot issues are matters of civil rights, rights which belong to all individuals, teachers may wish to challenge restrictions or taboos. It is good policy, however, to do this on a professional level, working among colleagues first, and not to take up things with children in a public way which may be against public policy. It is usually wiser to make attempts to clarify public policy and to modify it before involving the children in affairs that might be extremely embarrassing and extremely provoking. Whether children should be encouraged to reflect and choose in a controversial area is not the point. They *must* reflect and choose if values are to emerge. The question is one of what teachers might do first in communities which frown upon opening certain issues.

In summary, we are saying that if children—or adults, for that matter—are to develop values, they must develop them out of personal choices. We are also saying that these choices, if they are possibly to lead to values, must involve alternatives which (1) include ones that are prized by the chooser; (2) have meaning to the chooser, as when the consequences of each are clearly understood; and (3) are freely available for selection.

The Personal Nature of Values

The point has been made that our values tend to be a product of our experiences. They are not just a matter of true or false. One cannot go to an encyclopedia or to a textbook for values. The definition that has been given makes this clear. One has to prize for himself, choose for himself, integrate choices into the pattern of his own life. Information as such doesn't convey this quality of values. Values come out of the flux of life itself.

This means that we are dealing with an area that isn't a matter of proof or consensus. It is a matter of experience. So, if a child says that he likes something, it does not seem appropriate for an older person to say, "You shouldn't like that." Or, if a child should say, "I am interested in that," it does not seem quite right for an older person to say to him, "You shouldn't be interested in things like that." If these things have grown out of a child's experience, they are consistent with his life. When we ask him to deny his own life, we are in effect asking him to be a hypocrite. We seem to be saying in an indirect way, "Yes, this is what your life has taught you, but you shouldn't say so. You should pretend that you had a different life." What are we doing to children when we put them into positions like this? Are we helping them to develop values or are we in effect saying that life is a fraud and that one should learn to live like a fraud very early in life.

We have an alternative approach to values. . . . For now, it is important to note that our definition of values and valuing leads to a conception of these words that is highly personal. It follows that if we are to respect a person's life, we must respect his experience and his right to help in examining it for values.

As a matter of fact, in a society like ours, governed by our Constitution, teachers might well see themselves as obliged to support the idea that every individual is entitled to the views that he has and to the values that he holds, especially where these have been examined and affirmed. Is this not the cornerstone of what we mean by a free society? As teachers, then, we need to be clear that we cannot dictate to children what their values should be since we cannot also dictate what their environments should be and what experiences they will have. We may be authoritative in those areas that deal with truth and falsity. In areas involving aspirations, purposes, attitudes, interests, beliefs, etc., we may raise questions, but we cannot "lay down the law" about what a child's values should be. By definition and by social right, then, values are personal things.

As a matter of cold fact, in the great majority of instances, we really don't know what values an individual child has. We are apt to make inferences which go beyond the available data and to attribute values to children which they do not hold. We probably will be better off if we assume in almost every case that we really don't know. If we are interested in knowing, we might well initiate a process of investigation and inquiry, and more attention will be given to this notion later.

One last point needs to be made before we go on. Some people, when they travel, seem to be much more interested in the motels or hotels at which they stop than in the experiences which they have along the way. Some other people are much more interested in the road than the inn. In what has been said thus far, the reader may see that we associate ourselves with the latter group. We are interested in the processes that are going on. We are not much interested in identifying the values which children hold. We are much more interested in the process because we believe that in a world that is changing as rapidly as ours, each child must develop habits of examining his purposes, aspirations, attitudes, feelings, etc., if he is to find the most intelligent relationship between his life and the surrounding world, and if he is to make a contribution to the creation of a better world.

The development of values is a personal and life-long process. It is not something that is completed by early adulthood. As the world changes, as we change, and as we strive to change the world again, we have many decisions to make and we should be learning how to make these decisions. We should be learning how to value. It is this process that we believe needs to be carried on in the classrooms, and it is at least partly through this process that we think children will learn about themselves and about how to make some sense out of the buzzing confusion of the society around them. . . .

The basic strategy of this approach to value clarifying rests on a specific method of responding to things a student says or does. This basic responding technique is discussed in this chapter.

Fundamentally, the responding strategy is a way of responding to a student that results in his considering what he has chosen, what he prizes, and/or what he is doing. It stimulates him to clarify his thinking and behavior and thus to clarify his values; it encourages him to think about them.

Imagine a student on the way out of class who says, "Miss Jones, I'm going to Washington, D.C., this weekend with my family." How might a teacher respond? Perhaps, "That's nice," or "Have a good time!"

Neither of those responses is likely to stimulate clarifying thought on the part of the student. Consider a teacher responding in a different way, for example: "Going to Washington, are you? Are you glad you're going?" To sense the clarifying power in that response, imagine the student saying, "No, come to think of it, I'm not glad I'm going. I'd rather play in the Little League game." If the teacher were to say nothing else at this point other than perhaps "Well, we'll see you Monday," or some noncommittal equivalent, one might say that the student would be a little more aware of his life; in this case, his doing things that he is not happy about doing. This is not a very big step, and it might be no step at all, but it might contribute to his considering a bit more seriously how much of his life he should involve in things that he does not prize or cherish. We say it is a step toward value clarity.

Or note this example. A student says that he is planning to go to college after high school. A teacher who replies, "Good for you," or "Which college?," or "Well, I hope you make it," is probably going to serve purposes other than value clarity. But were the teacher to respond, "Have you considered any alternatives?," the goal of value clarity may well be advanced. The "alternatives" response is likely to stimulate thinking about the issue and, if he decides to go to college, that decision is likely to be closer to a value than it was before. It may contribute a little toward moving a college student from the position of going because "it's the thing to do" to going because he wants to get something out of it.

Here are two other samples of exchanges using clarifying responses.

Student: I believe that all men are created equal.

Teacher: What do you mean by that?

Student: I guess I mean that all people are equally good and none should have advantages over others.

Teacher: Does this idea suggest that some changes need to be made in our world, even in this school and this town?

Student: Oh, lots of them. Want me to name some?

Teacher: No, we have to get back to our spelling lesson, but I was just wondering if you were working on any of those changes, actually trying to bring them about.

Student: Not yet, but I may soon.

Teacher: I see. Now, back to the spelling list. . . .

Teacher: Bruce, don't you want to go outside and play on the playground?

Student: I dono. I suppose so.

Teacher: Is there something that you would rather do?

Student: I dono. Nothing much.

Teacher: You don't seem much to care, Bruce. Is that right?

Student: I suppose so.

Teacher: And mostly anything we do will be all right with you?

Student: I suppose so. Well, not anything, I guess.

Teacher: Well, Bruce, we had better go out to the playground now with the others. You let me know sometime if you think of something you would like to do.

The reader may already sense some criteria of an effective clarifying response, that is, a response that encourages someone to look at his life and his ideas and to think about them. These are among the essential elements.

1. The clarifying response avoids moralizing, criticizing, giving values, or evaluating. The adult excludes all hints of "good" or "right" or "acceptable," or their opposites, in such responses.

2. It puts the responsibility on the student to look at his behavior or his ideas and to think and decide for himself what it is *he* wants.

3. A clarifying response also entertains the possibility that the student will *not* look or decide or think. It is permissive and stimulating, but not insistent.

4. It does not try to do big things with its small comments. It works more at stimulating thought relative to what a person does or says. It aims at setting a mood. Each clarifying response is only one of many; the effect is cumulative.

5. Clarifying responses are not used for interview purposes. The goal is not to obtain data, but for the student to clarify his ideas and life if he wants to do so.

6. It is usually not an extended discussion. The idea is for the student to think, and he usually does that best alone, without the temptation to justify his thoughts to an adult. Therefore a teacher will be advised to carry on only two or three rounds of dialogue and then offer to break off the conversation with some noncommittal but honest phrase, such as "Nice talking to you," or "I see what you mean better now," or "Got to get to my next class," or "Let's talk about this another time, shall we?," or "Very interesting, thanks." (Of course, there is no reason why a student who desires to talk more should be turned aside, the teacher's time permitting.)

7. Clarifying responses are often for individuals. A topic in which John might need clarification may be of no immediate interest to Mary. An issue that is of general concern, of course, may warrant a general clarifying response, say to the whole class, but even here the *individual* must ultimately do the reflecting for himself. Values are personal things. The teacher often responds to one individual, although others may be listening.

8. The teacher doesn't respond to everything everyone says or does in a classroom. There are other responsibilities he has. . . .

9. Clarifying responses operate in situations in which there are no "right" answers, such as in situations involving feelings, attitudes, beliefs, or purposes. They are *not* appropriate for drawing a student toward a predetermined answer. They are *not* questions to which the teacher has an answer already in hand.

10. Clarifying responses are not mechanical things that carefully follow a formula. They must be used creatively and with insight, but with their purpose in mind: when a response helps a student to clarify his thinking or behavior, it is considered effective.

The ten conditions listed above are very difficult to fulfill for the teacher who has not practiced them. The tendency to use responses to students for the purpose of molding students' thinking is very well established in most of our minds. The idea that a function of a teacher is to help the child clarify some of the confusion and ambiguity already in his head is an unfamiliar one for many of us. After all, most of us became teachers because we wanted to *teach* somebody something. Most of us are all too ready to sell our intellectual wares. The clarifying strategy requires a different orientation; not that of adding to the child's ideas but rather one of stimulating him to clarify the ideas he already has.

Here is another classroom incident illustrating a teacher using clarifying responses, in this case to help a student see that free, thoughtful choices can be made. The situation is a classroom discussion in which a boy has just made it clear that he is a liberal in his political viewpoints.

Teacher: You say, Glenn, that you are a liberal in political matters?

Glenn: Yes, I am.

Teacher: Where did your ideas come from?

Glenn: Well, my parents I guess, mostly.

Teacher: Are you familiar with other positions?

Glenn: Well, sort of.

Teacher: I see, Glenn. Now, class, getting back to the homework for today . . . (returning to the general lesson).

Here is another actual situation. In this incident the clarifying response prods the student to clarify his thinking and to examine his behavior to see if it is consistent with his ideas. It is between lessons and a student has just told a teacher that science is his favorite subject.

Teacher: What exactly do you like about science?

Student: Specifically? Let me see. Gosh, I'm not sure. I guess I just like it in general.

Teacher: Do you do anything outside of school to have fun with science?

Student: No, not really.

Teacher: Thank you, Jim. I must get back to work now.

Notice the brevity of the exchanges. Sometimes we call these exchanges "one-legged conferences" because they often take place while a teacher is on one leg, pausing briefly on his way elsewhere. An extended series of probes might give the student the feeling that he was being cross-examined and might make him defensive. Besides it would give him too much to think about. The idea is, without moralizing, to raise a few questions, leave them hanging in the air, and then move on. The student to whom the questions are addressed, and other students who might overhear, may well ponder the questions later, in a lull in the day or in the quiet moments before falling asleep. Gentle prods, but the effect is to stimulate a student who is ready for it to choose, prize, and act in ways outlined by the value theory. And . . . these one-legged conferences add up to make large differences in some students' lives.

Thirty Clarifying Responses

There are several responses that teachers who have worked with the clarifying approach have found very useful. A list of some of these is presented below. As the reader goes through the list, he might make note of some he would like to try; that is, make his own list. There are too many noted here to keep in mind at one time. It is probably best then, to gather a dozen or so together, ones which sound as if they could be used comfortably, and try them out, perhaps expanding or revising the list as experience dictates.

Be reminded, however, that the responses listed here are recommended as useful clarifying responses only when they are used in accordance with the ten conditions listed earlier. The acid test for any response is whether or not it results in a person reflecting on what he has said or done, clarifying, getting to know himself better, examining his choices, considering what he prizes, looking at patterns in his life, and so on. If the response makes the student defensive, or gets him to say what the adult wants him to say, or gives him the feeling that the adult is nagging at him, it is being used improperly or with poor timing. An accepting, noncommittal attitude on the part of the person making responses is crucial.

The reader might note that some of the responses listed below are geared directly to one or another of the seven valuing components: prizing, searching for alternatives, thinking critically, choosing freely, incorporating choices into behavior, examining patterns of living, and affirming choices. Some other responses stimulate reflection in a more general sense. But, in *all* cases, responses are open-ended—they lead the student to no specific value. No one must deliver a "right" answer to a clarifying response. Each student must be permitted to react in his own personal and individual way.

1. *Is this something that you prize?* To respond in a way that gets the student to consider whether he prizes or cherishes something he has said or done helps him to clarify his values. The response could, of course, be in a different form and have the same intent, e.g., "Are you proud of that?," "Is that something that is very important to you?," "Is that idea very dear to you; do you really cherish it?" The particular situation in which the response is being made, as well as the age of the child to whom it is directed, will help determine the precise wording.

2. *Are you glad about that?* This encourages the student to see whether things he feels, says, or does are things that he is happy about and make him feel good. One could also ask if the student is unhappy about something. Such questions stimulate a child to evaluate his life and to consider changing it if *he* finds it does not bring him satisfactions. Note how different the effect of this response is from the scolding "Aren't you ashamed of that?" Clarifying responses are accepting and illuminating, not rejecting and moralizing.

3. *How did you feel when that happened?* It advances clarification for a person to understand that his feelings are part of his understandings and awareness and that they have to be considered in decision making. He needs to know that feelings are important, that we respect his right to have his own feelings, and that feelings do not have to be suppressed.

4. *Did you consider any alternatives?* Note how this tends to widen, to open up the thinking of children (and adults). With this response, as with *all* the others in this list, teachers will need to accept whatever the student replies without judgment. After he answers the question, leave him with an honest "Oh, now I see," or "I understand," or "You stated your views clearly," or "I appreciate hearing what you say," or some nonjudgmental phrase or gesture.

5. *Have you felt this way for a long time?* Questions that get at the same thing are, "When did you first begin to believe in that idea?" and "How have your ideas or understandings changed since

the time you first considered this notion?" Here the person is pushed to examine the history of his beliefs or attitudes, to look at their origins, and to see if they are really his or if they have been absorbed unthinkingly. Note how the next response might follow after a student replies to this one.

6. *Was that something that you yourself selected or chose?* This reminds persons that they *can* make their own choices, if they want to do so. An affirmative reply to this response might well be followed by response number 7.

7. *Did you have to choose that; was it a free choice?* Here, no matter what the student says, it is probably wise to say no more but to discontinue the conversation with some nonjudgmental closing.

8. *Do you do anything about that idea?* This response helps persons see the responsibility for incorporating choices into actual living. A verbalization that is not lived has little import and is certainly not a value. Another way of saying the same thing: "How does that idea affect your daily life?," or "In what ways do you act upon it?"

9. *Can you give me some examples of that idea?* This helps push generalizations and vague statements of belief toward clarity. Note also the relevance of the next response.

10. *What do you mean by* _____ : *can you define that word?* This also pushes understanding to clarity and helps prevent the mouthing of words students cannot really mean because they do not really understand them.

11. *Where would that idea lead; what would be its consequences?* This encourages the student to study carefully the consequences of ideas. No meaningful choice can be made unless the consequences of alternatives are understood. Therefore, it is often very useful to help children examine the consequences of each available alternative. Accordingly, one could also ask, "What would be the results of each of the alternatives?," or "How would those ideas work out in practice?"

12. *Would you really do that or are you just talking?* Again the encouragement to see the importance of living in accordance with one's choice.

13. *Are you saying that . . . [repeat]?* It is sometimes useful merely to repeat what the student has just said. This has the effect of reflecting his ideas and prompting him to ask himself if he really meant that. It is surprising how many persons seldom hear what they

say. Sometimes the phrase "Did I hear you correctly?" can be used for this purpose.

14. Did you say that . . . [repeat in some distorted way]? Sometimes a teacher does well to purposely twist what a student has said. Will the student attempt to correct the distortion? After trying it, one senses that the effect is much the same as response number 13.

15. Have you thought much about that idea (or behavior)? Of course one accepts whatever reply a student makes to this. It is destructive to the valuing process to attack a negative answer to this question with something like, "Well, in the future it would be wise to think before you speak (or act)." An accepting and nonjudgmental mood is vital for the valuing process.

16. What are some good things about that notion? A simple request for justification of expressed ideas in some such nonjudgmental words often brings dramatic re-evaluation of thinking on the part of students. Many persons rarely realize that there could or should be good, desirable, worthwhile aspects of ideas they hold. The ideas are just there, unexamined and unevaluated.

17. What do we have to assume for things to work out that way? Many persons have neglected to examine the assumptions upon which rest their ideas, aspirations, and activities. This probing helps persons understand better, make choices more wisely, and make valuing more possible. It is sometimes useful, in this context, to suggest an assumption that the student seems to be making and ask him if he has considered it, e.g., "Are you assuming that there was *nothing* good about the depression?"

18. Is what you express consistent with . . . [note something else the person said or did that may point to an inconsistency]? To present such a disconcerting challenge, to note an exception, to relate things with other things, can produce real clarification *if* it is not done with an "I think I have trapped you in an error" tone of voice. The idea is not to slap students down, but to open things up for them so that they can think with new insight, if they want to do so. (Happily, teachers trying this approach seem to find that most students do want to do so.)

19. What other possibilities are there? This raises alternatives to students and thus it aids them in valuing. Sometimes this question is posed to a group and all alternatives are listed on the board, without judgment again. Of course, other students and the teacher, too, can say which alternative *they* prefer, but there is no judging a child because he chooses a different alternative. No teasing or otherwise deriding others' choices is tolerated or else there is no free choice.

20. Is that a personal preference or do you think most people should believe that? To inquire whether a statement is intended as a personal preference or whether it is something that should be generally endorsed is one way of helping to distinguish an attitude or prejudice from a social principle. "Is this idea so good that everyone should go along with it?" is another way to get at this.

21. How can I help you do something about your idea? What seems to be the difficulty? This question reminds the student that *action* is a component of life and intentions are incomplete until acted upon. Sometimes such questions uncover suppressed feelings or misunderstandings. Obviously, they locate real or imagined obstacles, too. Also try: "Where are you stuck?," or "What is holding you up?" (But be prepared to offer help if it's asked for.)

22. Is there a purpose back of this activity? Asking students what, if anything, they are trying to accomplish, where they are headed with ideas or activities, sometimes brings the realization to students—and for the first time—that they might really have purposes and goals and that they might relate their ongoing activities to those purposes and goals.

23. Is that very important to you? This gets students to consider more seriously what is and what is not important to them. It is also often useful to ask students to put several things in order of rank. Assigning priorities is a variation, and a useful one.

24. Do you do this often? "Is there any pattern to your life that incorporates this idea or activity?," one might inquire. The idea here is to help students see what is repeated in their lives and what is not and to leave them with the decision of whether or not to build a pattern.

25. Would you like to tell others about your idea? Inviting a student to explain his ideas to the class or others provides two challenges. It tests to see whether he is committed to his beliefs strongly enough to affirm them in public. It also puts him in the position of thinking through his ideas well enough to explain them, and perhaps justify them, to others.

26. Do you have any reasons for (saying or doing) that? This tests whether or not a choice has been made and to what extent that choice was based on understanding. *Danger:* Avoid using that question to pull up short on a student who is obviously not thinking. If you want to tell a student that you believe that he is not thinking, tell him so. But use the above question when you really want to have a student consider his beliefs or actions.

Incidentally, when a student does (or says) something and the teacher inquires, "Sonny, why did you do that?," the student often hears, "Sonny, now why in the world did you ever do something as foolish as that?" "Why" questions are usually to be avoided when attempting to help students clarify their values. "Why" questions tend to make a student defensive, tend to prod him into making up reasons or excuses when he really has none in mind. Besides, the question "Why did you do that?" carries with it the assumption that the student *knows* why, and that is perhaps the reason he tends to concoct a reason when he has none. It is much more effective, for value clarifying purposes, to ask "Do you *have* a reason?" and then sometimes follow up an affirmative reply with, "Would you mind telling me?"

27. *Would you do the same thing over again?* This helps a student to evaluate things that he has done, to consider why he has done them, and perhaps to affirm the wisdom of doing it in the future. Do not use this question every time someone does something that *you* do not like. That would be an example of not-so-subtle moralizing. Use the question when you want to stimulate thinking, and strive to keep it nonjudgmental.

29. *How do you know it's right?* When a child makes a moral or ethical judgment about something by saying that a thing is right or lovely or good, it is useful to ask how he knows that that judgment is correct. Sometimes we ask how he was able to decide. Note this dialogue.

> *Teacher:* I see you're hard at work on that project, Jimmy.
> *Student:* It's not good to be lazy, you know.
> *Teacher:* How do you know it's not good?
> *Student:* Everybody knows that. My parents always say it.
> *Teacher:* (Walking away) I see.

Thus may a teacher subtly and persistently suggest that one might think about such matters as rightness, or beauty, or goodness if one wants to do so.

29. *Do you value that?* Merely picking out something a student

has said or done and asking "Is that something that you value?" helps to stimulate clarifying thinking. Perhaps such a question could have been added by Jimmy's teacher in the above dialogue, e.g.,

> *Teacher:* I see. Is working something that you value then, Jimmy?
> *Student:* Huh? I suppose so.
> *Teacher:* O.K., Jimmy. Thank you.

30. *Do you think people will always believe that? Or, "Would Chinese peasants and African hunters also believe that?" Or, "Did people long ago believe that?"* Such questions are useful to suggest to a student that his beliefs may be unknowingly influenced by his surroundings, by his social milieu. It helps him gauge the extent to which he may be conforming. See also response number 5.

Note chart 1 for examples of how some of the above clarifying responses, and others, are related to the seven components of the valuing process. Those seven criteria are helpful for thinking of other useful clarifying responses and for keeping in mind the ones above. All clarifying responses in one way or another encourage the student to choose, prize, or act in terms outlined by the value theory.

Chart 1
Clarifying Responses Suggested by the Seven Valuing Processes

1. Choosing freely
   a. Where do you suppose you first got that idea?
   b. How long have you felt that way?
   c. What would people say if you weren't to do what you say you must do?
   d. Are you getting help from anyone? Do you need more help? Can I help?
   e. Are you the only one in your crowd who feels this way?
   f. What do your parents want you to be?
   g. Is there any rebellion in your choice?
   h. How many years will you give to it? What will you do if you're not good enough?
   i. Do you think the idea of having thousands of people cheering when you come out on the field has anything to do with your choice?
2. Choosing from alternatives
   a. What else did you consider before you picked this?
   b. How long did you look around before you decided?
   c. Was it a hard decision? What went into the final decision? Who helped? Do you need any further help?

d. Did you consider another possible alternative?

e. Are there some reasons behind your choice?

f. What choices did you reject before you settled on your present idea or action?

g. What's really good about this choice which makes it stand out from the other possibilities?

3. Choosing thoughtfully and reflectively

a. What would be the consequences of each alternative available?

b. Have you thought about this very much? How did your thinking go?

c. Is this what I understand you to say . . . [interpret his statement]?

d. Are you implying that . . . [distort his statement to see if he is clear enough to correct the distortion]?

e. What assumptions are involved in your choice? Let's examine them.

f. Define the terms you use. Give me an example of the kind of job you can get without a high school diploma.

g. Now if you do this, what will happen to that . . . ?

h. Is what you say consistent with what you said earlier?

i. Just what is good about this choice?

j. Where will it lead?

k. For whom are you doing this?

l. With these other choices, rank them in order of significance.

m. What will you have to do? What are your first steps? Second steps?

n. Whom else did you talk to?

o. Have you really weighed it fully?

4. Prizing and cherishing

a. Are you glad you feel that way?

b. How long have you wanted it?

c. What good is it? What purpose does it serve? What is it important to you?

d. Should everyone do it your way?

e. Is it something you really prize?

f. In what way would life be different without it?

5. Affirming

a. Would you tell the class the way you feel some time?

b. Would you be willing to sign a petition supporting that idea?

c. Are you saying that you believe . . . [repeat the idea]?

d. You don't mean to say that you believe . . . [repeat the idea]?

e. Should a person who believes the way you do speak out?

f. Do people know that you believe that way or that you do that thing?

g. Are you willing to stand up and be counted for that?

6. Acting upon choices

a. I hear what you are for; now, is there anything you can do about it? Can I help?

b. What are your first steps, second steps, etc.?

c. Are you willing to put some of your money behind this idea?

d. Have you examined the consequences of your act?

e. Are there any organizations set up for the same purposes? Will you join?

f. Have you done much reading on the topic? Who has influenced you?

g. Have you made any plans to do more than you already have done?

h. Would you want other people to know you feel this way? What if they disagree with you?

i. Where will this lead you? How far are you willing to go?

j. How has it already affected your life? How will it affect it in the future?

7. Repeating

a. Have you felt this way for some time?

b. Have you done anything already? Do you do this often?

c. What are your plans for doing more of it?

d. Should you get other people interested and involved?

e. Has it been worth the time and money?

f. Are there some other things you can do which are like it?

g. How long do you think you will continue?

h. What did you *not* do when you went to do that? Was that o.k.?

i. How did you decide which had priority?

j. Did you run into any difficulty?

k. Will you do it again?

Topics Ripe for Clarifying Responses

Let us now consider what kinds of student expressions might fruitfully be followed by clarifying responses. One does not follow all student statements and behaviors with clarifying responses. They are not for teaching subject matter, for example. They are for promoting student thought of a particular kind, the kind we call valuing. But when does one use clarifying responses?

We have arrived at five important categories having a relationship to values: *attitudes, aspirations, purposes, interests,* and *activities.* We call these "value-indicators"; and they are just that, they point out that the expression (a statement or an action) indicates something about values. Of course, we save the precious word "value" itself only for those expressions which meet all seven of the valuing criteria outlined in previous chapters. Value indicators are expressions which are *headed* toward values, but they have not yet "arrived." They are, however, ideal matter for value clarifying responses.

The teacher who would help students must learn to listen for the specific comments students make which are in the realm of value indicators. With just a little practice, most teachers can hear these indicators. After a while, they come at a teacher with red flags flying.

Below are some charts showing several value indicators and some examples of the kinds of things students are apt to say which tell a teacher that things are ripe for a clarifying response.

No value indicator operates alone, but suffice it to say that a teacher who listens for those comments from his students that fall in the several categories and who then responds within the framework of the valuing methodology should do much to advance the clarification of values and, in turn, should witness significant behavioral changes. Students who had been listless and apathetic should become more purposeful and self-directed. Students who had been over-conforming should more often stand on their own two feet and come closer to discovering their own identity. So it will be with other students with value-related behavior problems. This is part of the reward for the teacher who begins to work in the area of value clarification.

On Attitudes

As seen in chart 2 people express an *attitude* when they reveal what they are *for* and what they are *against*. Beliefs, opinions, and convictions are often similarly used. In number 1 on chart 2, it is clear that the student is against letting in too many immigrants. In number 2 the student is for the "buyer beware" principle. (We might say that he is against revealing every flaw. Most of the things we are against can be expressed as something we are for and *vice versa*.) In number 3 the student is for giving Negroes more than just equal opportunities. In number 4 we have someone against doll playing, at least for him; and in number 5, an impatience with a particular law. Such statements are ripe for a clarifying response.

Chart 2

Value Indicators: Attitudes

Statements students have made:

1. "If you let in too many immigrants, I believe it just makes it tough for everyone else."

2. "When I sold him my bike, I didn't feel I had to tell him *everything* that was wrong with it."

3. "I think we just have to overcompensate Negroes at this time, because they're so far behind."

4. "You wouldn't catch me playing with dolls."

5. "I don't see why we have to wait until we're eighteen to drive."

Typical keywords that signal the statement of attitudes:
> I'm for . . .
> I'm against . . .
> I feel that . . .
> I think if . . .
> The way I see it . . .
> If you ask me . . .
> In my opinion . . .
> My choice is . . .
> My way of doing it is . . .
> I'm convinced that . . .
> I believe . . .

One useful tool for teachers to work with in the area of attitudes is to listen carefully to what students say and then to mentally "plus" and "minus" their statements. We plus what they are for and minus what they say they are against. This is particularly easy to do in students' written work. . . . We have found that students are not always aware when they have revealed that they are for and against something. They are, of course, quite surprised to see their inconsistencies. We must be careful to avoid making our students feel they will lose face as these things are exposed, however. It is important, terribly important, to maintain that accepting atmosphere and to say over and over again, and mean it, "All of us are inconsistent from time to time, and all of us tend to be confused about certain things that we are for and against. One of the things we hope to learn is how to think about our attitudes and clarify them."

It may be helpful for the reader to try to match up the expression of an attitude, such as those in chart 2, with a reasonable clarifying response, such as from the list of thirty. (Responses 10, 11, and 12, among others, are often suited to expressions of attitudes.) One need not commit this to memory; after trial-and-error practice, a sense of it is likely to emerge, permitting one to improvise freely.

On Aspirations

As seen in chart 3, students express *aspiration* when they reveal some long-range plan or goal. Sadly, without help from sensitive teachers, so many plans never can come to fruition; and when a series of one's hopes goes down the drain, it becomes difficult to continue to aspire. Such is the soil in which grow listlessness, indifference, and apathy. One of the most important things we can do when we deal with aspirations is to bring some of the dreamers face to face with the necessary steps between the first dream and the final achievement, and to do this without throwing cold water on what may be a reality greater than we are able to recognize. It reminds us again that there are no right answers in clarifying. It demands in the clarifier a quiet humility. Nevertheless, one can see how statements of aspirations invite a value clarifying response.

Chart 3
Value Indicator: Aspirations

Statements students have made:
    1. "Someday I'd like to join the Peace Corps."
    2. "If only I were better in math, I'd try for engineering."
    3. "My hope is to someday buy a summer home on a lake and to have my own boat."
    4. "My dream is to someday run a little nursery school of my own."
    5. "We want to have six kids, three boys and three girls, eighteen months apart."

Typical keywords that signal the statement of aspirations:
    In the future . . .
    When I grow up . . .
    Someday, I'm going to . . .
    My long-range plan is . . .
    In about ten years I'm . . .
    If all goes well . . .
    One of these days . . .

On Purposes

As seen in chart 4, students express *purpose* when they reveal some short-range goal or hope. They require planning, sometimes writing letters or making phone calls, getting commitments from others occasionally, and almost always some money (working for it, saving it, borrowing it). When a student has a plan, his excitement often spills out. Plans and goals give a much needed lift to life, and people with many plans (if they don't get frenetic) tend to be zestful and purposeful. The teacher can help students test the consequences of some coming adventure, can pose alternatives for what else might use this energy, time, and money, and can help the student see what else could grow from the coming event. These are legitimate clarifying efforts. Moralizing, preaching, and generating guilt are not.

Chart 4
Value Indicator: Purposes

Statements students have made:
    1. "This weekend we're going to play."
    2. "At the end of the month three of us fellows are going skiing."
    3. "If I can find the right rear end from an old car, I'm going to make a trailer."
    4. "I called my buddy and he's going to write for the appointment to see this man about the summer job."
    5. "When I save up the twenty dollars, I'm going to buy that guitar."

Typical keywords that signal the statement of purposes:
    We're thinking about doing . . .
    On the fifteenth, I'm going . . .
    On the way downtown we're . . .
    I wrote for the plans . . .
    When I get this . . . I'm going to do that . . .
    We're waiting to hear from him . . .
    Boy! Will Saturday ever come?
    I'd like to . . .

On Interests

As seen in chart 5, students express *interest* when they reveal some of the things they like to do in their spare time. Included are those things which excite us, which occupy our minds and hands, and which cause us to spend time, money, and energy on them. Hobbies are the most obvious expressions of interests, but so, too, are our reading and what we go out of our way to see or experience, such as sporting or theatrical events.

One of the interesting side effects for a teacher when he begins to listen and really show an interest in something a student is excited about is that the teacher's own life can take on some added flavor, for students have many delightful and really creative pastimes. Not all of them are values, however, and this is one of the ways we can help students, by getting them to clarify which are those that are merely passing whims or thoughtless behaviors and which are headed well along the road to becoming values.

Chart 5
Value Indicator: Interest

Statements students have made:
    1. "I read everything I can lay my hands on about nursing."

2. "I'd rather listen to Bach than almost anyone else."
3. "I'm saving up to subscribe to this photography magazine."
4. "I'm going to enter this glider into the contest."
5. "No, I won't be home Saturday. I'm going to the town drag strip."

Typical keywords that signal a statement about activities:

I love making [or doing] . . .
My hobby is . . .
Yes, I subscribe to . . .
I really enjoy reading about . . .
If I had my choice I'd take the ticket to . . .
Most weekends I'm over at the . . .
Every night after school I . . .
Boy, nothing makes me feel better than . . .
I got this catalogue on . . .

On Activities

As seen in chart 6, students express *activity* when they reveal how they use time. Actually, the activity category is a part of each of the other value indicators, and that is why we list it last. When one has attitudes, often activities will follow, and so it is with aspirations, purposes, and interests. In short, what we *do* with our waking hours hints at what values we may have. As an ideal, we might strive to value everything we do and to do only what we value.

To merely kill time might be a value for some people, but for most of us the measurement of how we survive the onslaught of time tells much about the values we hold.

It is so prevalent nowadays to mouth the right words but to do very little about them. We must come, more of us, to do more about what we value. A list of our activities tells us more about what we prize and cherish than does an eloquent statement of beliefs. As teachers we do well to hold up a mirror to our students, to help them reflect on what they do with each day's 86,400 seconds, and to help them clarify the issue of the use of time and energy.

To summarize a bit, a teacher learns to spot value indicators and to follow them up, at least part of the time, with clarifying responses, sometimes in brief one-legged conferences, sometimes in written comments in the margins of student papers, and in other ways to be discussed. Expressions, verbal or behavioral, that are value indicators include attitudes, aspirations, purposes, interests, and activities. This list could be expanded to include opinions, convictions, beliefs, feelings, appreciations, and worries. The general intent is clear: Find value indicators, expressions that may not yet meet all seven criteria, and help students use the valuing process to see if they are at the value level or can be raised to the value level.

Chart 6
Value Indicator: Activities

Statements students have made:
1. "I took my dog for a long walk."
2. "I worked five hours Saturday waxing the car."
3. "Friday night we watched the late show and then the late-late show."
4. "These two fellows and I made a hut."
5. "I lay down to take a nap, but just slept right through the night."

Typical keywords that signal a statement about activities:
After school, I usually . . .
Last weekend, we . . .
On my day off, I went . . .
One of the best things we did Halloween . . .
All yesterday afternoon . . .
We just like to play . . .

Some Examples

It might be well now to give some additional examples which show how the clarification process operates. Several cautions might be reiterated first, however. For one thing, there is no set formula for clarifying. It is very personal and individualized, both in the ways clarifiers proceed and in the range of problems that come up for clarification. There is a danger in seeing a clarifying incident in print. It is not to be taken as the only way it could have been done. There are easily a dozen variations on this theme, and all could readily be said to advance clarification.

Another danger occurs to us. Seeing the dialogue in print sometimes makes it seem bland or even silly. We ask you to accept the idea that these conversations are held, on the contrary, with dead earnestness. The person being "clarified" usually senses the power of this methodology and generally does not fritter away an opportunity to get clear on something related to his values. In other words, the dialogues do not print as movingly as they sound. Finally, we might remind the reader that the examples we cite do not stand alone. Clarifying is not a one-shot business. Each incident may stand by itself, but the sensitive teacher is constantly looking for other incidents and, especially if a teacher uses some of the techniques noted in the following chapters, there will be more incidents than can ever be used.

Let us look at this dialogue,

Teacher: You were late again today. Do you like coming to school late?

Student: Well, no.

Teacher: How long have you been coming to school late?

Student: Quite a while. I guess most of the time since I've been coming to school.

Teacher: How do you feel about being tardy?

Student: Well, I feel funny about it sometimes.

Teacher: What do you mean by "funny"?

Student: Well, that I'm different from other kids. I feel embarrassed.

Teacher: As I get it, you feel uncomfortable about being late.

Student: That's right.

Teacher: What can I do to help you get here on time?

Student: Well, my mother usually calls me in the morning—but sometimes she oversleeps.

Teacher: Do you have an alarm clock?

Student: No.

Teacher: Could you get one? I could help you get one if that is what you think you need.

Student: It would be kind of fun. I'll try to get one.

Later in the semester, this student's mother said: "What have you and my son been talking about? He is getting to school on time and he hustles around to get ready. When I asked him what had been happening he said, 'Oh, my teacher and I have been talking' " (Raths 1962, pp. 37-38).

Here is dialogue which grew out of a classroom discussion in a high school social studies class.

John: If you let in too many immigrants it just makes it tough for everyone else.

Teacher: Tough in what way, John?

Here great courage was needed on the part of the teacher not to leap in with the usual chestnuts about "Was not your grandfather once an immigrant?" or "Don't you know that this country was founded by immigrants, that George Washington was an immigrant, etc.?" The sum effect of that kind of question would have been to make John wish he hadn't brought up the topic. This is a most important point; every effort must be made to cull out of our questions those which moralize, get preachy, or back a student into the wall so that what appears to be a question is in reality a statement. Too often a question is asked in a way that tells us that only one right answer is acceptable, i.e., "Don't you think . . . ?," or "Wouldn't you agree . . . ?," "Is it not true that our ancestors were all immigrants?" Instead, this teacher has asked a real clarifying question, "Tough in what way?" It is a clarifying question for several reasons:

1. It keeps open the invitation to dialogue.
2. It talks to the real concern, which is probably more closely related to some problem about money than it is to immigration.
3. It works at making things clearer.

Back to our dialogue.

John: Well, they work so much cheaper that a decent American can't get a job.
Teacher: Can you give me an example of that happening, John?
John: Well, I went to this supermarket which had an advertisement, but this kid with an accent got there first.
Teacher: And he was willing to work cheaper?
John: Well, I don't know that for sure.

Again, the teacher resists the temptation to make John feel like a naughty boy, for he knows that would not advance clarification. Instead he offers a clarifying question.

Teacher: What did you feel when you found out that you didn't get the job?
John: Boy I was mad.
Teacher: Would you have been mad say if Pete over there had gotten the job?

John: I guess I would have been just mad at anybody, because I really need that job.

Teacher: Have you tried any of the other markets? Maybe we could make a list of them together and you could check them out one at a time.

Teacher makes a mental note: Why does John want that job after school? Is he going to buy a car? Does he have one already and must work for it? Big dance coming up? Saving for college? Perhaps explore these in some future clarifying contacts, for money, what we spend it on and what we don't spend it on, is one important bellwether of values.

What about the prejudicial statement about immigrants which John made and which started off this dialogue? Can a teacher, in good conscience, ignore such poor critical thinking? One answer is that a frontal attack is not always the most effective. The teacher in this dialogue worked under the assumption that the statement about immigrants, although obviously not entirely innocent, was triggered more by John's frustration over not getting the job he needed. At another time, in another context, the teacher may well pursue the prejudice expressed.

Here is another example, this time based on an expression of an aspiration.

Clara: Some day I'd like to join the Peace Corps.

Teacher: What are some good things about that, Clara?

Clara: Oh, the chance to be of service excites me and going to faraway places does too.

Teacher: Of those two, which would you put in first place?

Clara: I guess the faraway places part.

Teacher: Are you glad that that one is first?

Clara: No, I guess people would respect me more if the service part was first.

Now, the teacher has some interesting alternatives at this point. Which of the following should he pursue?

1. The area of how important it is for Clara to feel respected.

2. The area of what services she has performed and might perform right now.

3. The area of what other possibilities does she have for getting to faraway places?

4. The teacher also has the possibility of not going forward at all and saying, "Well, it's been interesting talking with you Clara, but I must get back to my papers. Perhaps we can talk about it another time."

In the transcript of the incident above, the teacher did just that. When questioned, the teacher said that he felt that Clara had been a bit embarrassed when she realized what she had been doing and was anxious to terminate the conversation herself. The teacher's sensitivity must always be alert.

Other directions this discussion could have taken might have been equally productive. The reader might want to look back at the list of clarifying responses and think about which of those might have reasonably followed Clara's opening statement.

A teacher may wonder when these conversations take place and where they are held. One obvious place is after school or between lessons. Other conversations occur in the morning before school, or in line in the cafeteria, or before class starts, or when you see students downtown. Often they grow right out of the subject matter during class, as did the incident about immigration mentioned above.

More such dialogues would occur, we feel, if teachers cared more about them and went out of their way to hold them. Students seem to welcome them. Certain teachers have already established such rapport with students that they can talk often and easily with them. We advocate that such talks more often focus upon values via the clarification process. For example, a young teacher was walking down the hall and overhead this snatch of conversation.

Jerry: When I save up the twenty dollars, I'm going to buy that guitar.

The teacher heard the expressed purpose, turned and said that he overheard the comment.

Teacher: Can you play a guitar, Jerry?
Jerry: A little, but I'm going to really learn when I get my own.
Teacher: Is playing the guitar important to you, Jerry?

Jerry: Yes, very.

Teacher: What are the possibilities for making the twenty dollars?

Jerry: Not too good right now, I'm afraid.

Teacher: Any chance of cutting down on what you now spend and saving it?

Jerry: You mean giving up smoking?

Teacher: That's one alternative.

Joe (Jerry's friend): Or staying out of the bowling alley for three weeks.

Teacher: Well, good luck to you, Jerry. See you later.

The school day is really full of opportunities for these "one-legged conferences," for they are not interviews and not therapy. (We do *not* recommend the clarifying technique for the solution of emotional problems.) The clarification methodology is concerned only with values and as such it seems to be a process well within the boundaries of the work of teachers.

Sometimes a student will view a clarifying response to something he has said or done as an intrusion.

Teacher: I see, Vic, that you are still hard at work on that map. Is that something that you are very happy to do?

Victor: (No clear response. Appears to want to avoid a conversation. Continues to work at map.)

Teacher: Just thought I'd ask. See you later, Vic.

This example shows what often happens with clarifying: sometimes some children just do not seem to want to respond and the teacher, ever respectful and permissive about the clarifying process, attempts to let the student off the hook without any embarrassment or pressure. A clarifying teacher encourages the valuing process but does not insist upon it. In fact, the teacher smiles to himself whenever the student shows that he knows he is respected enough to be able to say to a teacher, "I'd rather not talk about it." The wise teacher walks off with something like a "Well, bring it up again someday if you would like," knowing that at least the child has passed the point of total acquiescence.

Two final comments. Although when we deal with values, we

emphasize the need for a nonjudgmental approach, for acceptance, for the student to arrive at his *own* ideas on the basis of his *own* critical thinking and evaluation, we do not mean to suggest that the teacher must remain neutral. The teacher may take a clear position about a value-related issue—but the student must be encouraged to take his own position and to use his knowledge of the teacher's position only as interesting information, perhaps worth considering when he makes up his own mind. If, however, a teacher senses that students are not yet accustomed to critical thinking and taking independent positions, he might well conceal his beliefs and attitudes until they are weaned from this intellectual and moral dependence upon authority. Note this conversation:

Teacher: June, it seems to me that you very seldom talk in class discussions. Does it seem that way to you? (In this case, the teacher was picking up on something that a student did, or failed to do, and working at clarifying it.)

June: Yeah. I suppose so.

Teacher: Is that a pattern in your behavior? I mean are you pretty quiet in other groups and outside of school?

June: Well, maybe. Yes, usually.

Teacher: It seems to me that it would be more fun participating and getting your ideas into the group, but there is nothing wrong with not participating if you want to, either. Have you thought about this?

June: Well, no, not much I guess.

Teacher: Well, I won't interrupt your studying any longer, June. You can get back to your work.

In this exchange, the teacher clearly stated his position—it seemed to him that a lack of participation was not good—but also left open the possibility that others could disagree. The teacher did not leave the student, hopefully, with the feeling that there was a "right" way to behave, but rather left the student with a bit of food for thought. One can almost hear June meditating after this incident: "Now, I usually am quiet aren't I? I wonder why. Should I push myself to talk up and participate? Would Mr. Nelson want me to? I guess he doesn't really care. But what do *I* want?"

Again, if this teacher did not have an open and accepting atmosphere and if the students were not accustomed to hearing the teacher's opinions and knowing that those opinions were only some of many possible ones, it might have been better for the teacher to omit the statement of his position in the above exchange. The conversation could have been exactly the same, except that the sentence preceding "Have you thought about this?" would be omitted.

It seems to us desirable that a teacher's ideas, feelings, and opinions are made known to students. This demonstrates to students that one can talk openly about such things. And this provides alternatives for students to consider when making up their own minds. But if the teacher cannot do this without fear that students will copy those ideas, feelings, or opinions routinely and meekly, they might better be concealed—or even disguised—until the students learn to use the valuing process for themselves.

And lastly, an important word about getting started with this use of clarifying responses. . . . Students are accustomed to having teachers ask questions. The standard recitation lesson is basically a question and answer process. In value-related areas, many teachers also use questions to guide student behavior and thinking, e.g.,

Johnny, didn't I tell you to be quiet?
Don't you think it would be a good idea to wash your hands before lunch?
Why do you tease the girls? When are you going to stop? Do I have to punish you again?
Don't you think it would be good for you to get higher grades?
You know that the way you're going you'll never get into college, don't you?

However, these questions have very little to do with the clarifying approach we are discussing. A clarifying response respects the right of the individual student to make decisions; the above questions are really not questions at all but statements of the teacher's decisions, and one can sense that they are not likely to trigger a clarification process.

Because of this, because many students expect that when a teacher asks them a question it is really a concealed directive, it is wise to begin to use clarifying questions at times when the student knows that you are *not* trying to disapprove of what he is saying or doing. Do not begin the use of clarifying responses by saying "Have you thought of any alternatives to what you are doing?" after a student hits another student—such a question will most likely be interpreted as a rebuke. Rather, when you first try the process, use such a response after a student has *helped* another student, or worked hard to pass a test, or volunteered to do extra work, or done something else he knows that you are not likely to disapprove of. After students become familiar with the use of clarifying responses, you can, of course, use them with little fear that students will view them as disguised criticisms.

The point here, then, is that a teacher would be wise to begin using clarifying responses only in situations that will prevent students from equating those responses with criticism or rebuke. The simplest way to do this is to use clarifying responses, in the beginning, in situations of which you either approve or have no preferences.

Incidentally, after students become familiar with the clarifying responses, they will begin to use them on one another and on other friends, and that is a delightful development. Somehow, persons like to have genuine clarifying responses directed to them. It doesn't threaten, and they know it helps clarify ideas and feelings.

Conclusion

Basic to the use of the approach to values of this book is the clarifying response. The clarifying response is usually aimed at one student at a time, often in brief, informal conversations held in class, in hallways, on the playground, or any place else where the teacher comes in contact with a student who does or says something to trigger such a response.

Especially ripe for clarifying responses are such things as expressions of student attitudes, aspirations, purposes, interests, and activities. These sometimes indicate a value or a potential value and thus we refer to them as value indicators. Also in this category are expressions of student feelings, beliefs, convictions, worries, and opinions. A teacher who is sensitive to these expressions finds many occasions for useful clarifying responses.

The purpose of the clarifying response is to raise questions in the mind of the student, to prod him gently to examine his life, his actions, and his ideas, with the expectation that some will want to use this prodding as an opportunity to clarify their understandings, purposes, feelings, aspirations, attitudes, beliefs, and so on.

Undergoing this, some students may find the thoughtful consistency between words and deeds that characterizes values. But not everything need be a value. Beliefs, problems, attitudes, and all the rest are part of life too, although in most of our lives they might be even clearer and more consistent one to the other.

It may be useful to list some things that a clarifying response is *not*.

1. Clarifying is not therapy.

2. Clarifying is not used on students with serious emotional problems.

3. Clarifying is not a single once-shot effort, but depends on a program consistently applied over a period of time.

4. Clarifying avoids moralizing, preaching, indoctrinating, inculcating, or dogmatizing.

5. Clarifying is not an interview, nor is it done in a formal manner.

6. Clarifying is not meant to replace the teacher's other educational functions.

If clarifying is none of the above, what is it? It is an honest attempt to help a student look at his life and to encourage him to think about it, and to think about it in an atmosphere in which positive acceptance exists. No eyebrows are raised. When a student reveals something before the whole class, he must be protected from snickers from other class members. An environment where searching is highly regarded is essential.

We emphasize that students will probably not enter the perplexing process of clarifying values for themselves if they perceive that the teacher does not respect them. If trust is not communicated—and the senses of students for such matters can be mystifyingly keen—the student may well play the game, pretending to clarify and think and choose and prize, while being as unaffected as by a tiresome morality lecture. This is a difficult and important point, for it is not easy to be certain that one is communicating trust, whether or not one believes he is doing so. (A moot point is whether some persons can communicate a trust that they, in fact, do not have.) One must be chary about concluding that a teacher who says the right words is getting the results desired. There is a spirit, a mood, required that we cannot satisfactorily describe or measure except to say that it seems related to a basic and honest respect for students. It may be fair to say that a teacher who does not communicate this quality will probably obtain only partial results.

For many teachers a mild revolution in their classroom methodology will be demanded if they are to do very much with the clarification of values. For one thing, they will have to do much less talking and listen that much more, and they will have to ask different kinds of questions from the ones they have asked in past years. Teachers usually favor questions that have answers that can be scaled from "right" to "wrong." No such scoring can be applied to answers to clarifying questions.

The rewards for giving up the old patterns may not come right away, but there is mounting evidence that teachers who act "responsively" begin to have small miracles happening in their classrooms. They often see attendance go up, grades rise, and interest and excitement in learning crackle. They witness students who had been classified as apathetic, listless, and indifferent begin to change. In the words of one teacher, "students get their heads off their elbows and use those elbows to wave hands in the air."

In brief, one might see the clarifying response as fitting into the value clarifying method in the following framework:

1. Look and listen for value indicators, statements or actions which suggest that there could be a value issue involved. It is usually wise to pay special attention to students who seem to have particularly unclear values. Note especially children who seem to be very apathetic, or indecisive, or who seem to be very flighty, or who drift from here to there without much reason. Note, also, children who overconform, or who are very inconsistent, or who play-act much of the time.

2. Keep in mind the goal: children who have clear, personal values. The goal, therefore, requires opportunities for children to use

the processes of (a) choosing freely, (b) choosing from alternatives, (c) choosing thoughtfully, (d) prizing and cherishing, (e) affirming, (f) acting upon choices, and (g) examining patterns of living. One does this with the expectation that the results of these processes are better understandings of what one stands for and believes in and more intelligent living.

3. Respond to a value indicator with a clarifying question or comment. This response is designed to help the student use one or more of the seven valuing processes listed above. For example, if you guess that a child doesn't give much consideration to what is important to *him*, you might try a clarifying response that gets at prizing and cherishing. Or the form of the value indicator may suggest the form of the clarifying response. For example, a thoughtless choice suggests responses that get at choosing, and a fine-sounding verbalization suggests responses that get at incorporating choices into behavior.

Reference

Raths, James. "Clarifying Children's Values." *National Elementary Principal* (November 1962): 37-38.

8

Clarifying Values Clarification:
Some Theoretical Issues

Howard Kirschenbaum

Since the publication of *Values and Teaching* in 1966, "values clarification" has become an extremely popular approach in education and other helping professions. Along with its widespread use, there have been criticisms and several misunderstandings about what this approach is and what its goals actually are. Among other criticisms, values clarification has been called "hedonistic," "superficial," "relativistic," "value free," and devoid of any cogent theoretical or research base. Simultaneously, thousands of teachers, parents, counselors, and others report that this same approach has been of significant help to them in their work with students, children, and clients, or in their own personal lives. How do we reconcile these conflicting views? Is values clarification merely a helpful "tool" or educational technique, or does it contain more profound implications about the nature of human growth and development and the process of education?

Perhaps those of us closest to values clarification have contributed to the misunderstandings or criticisms by not taking the time to deal with these issues. As an active writer and trainer in this area, I want to take this occasion to explore tentatively some of the more theoretical issues raised by critics and friends of values clarification alike. After discussing the social context out of which values clarification arises, I will present a somewhat different perspective on what values clarification is. With this background, I can then respond directly to the theoretical issues referred to above.

Confusion and Conflict

How do we help young people (and each other) deal with areas of confusion and conflict in their lives? "Value-rich" areas like:

Politics	Love, sex
Religion	Male-female roles
Family	Race, poverty, energy, etc.
Friends	Health
Work	Money
Leisure	Personal habits

We could *moralize* to them. Gently or forcefully, subtly or harshly, we could tell them what to do, how to think, what is right or wrong, good or bad. Only the teacher down the hall might be telling them something different. So might their parents, their minister, their peer group, the mass media, the movie stars, the sports heroes, the politicians, the advertisements—in fact, already, they are probably being bombarded from all sides with different messages about what values to pursue, what goals to strive for to be successful, to belong, to be popular, to succeed with the other sex. We could add our input, certainly. But, then, how does the young person sort it all out?

Many don't. They grow into adults who are filled with contradictions among their values, inconsistencies between their beliefs and behaviors, an easy prey to the ad man's version of reality, the demagogue's lie, or the peer group's pressure toward complacent mediocrity.

We could *model* a set of values, be a living example of what we believe. Hopefully we will. One of the best ways to teach anything is to present a concrete example of it. And young people today are quick to spot adults who say one thing and do another. Unfortunately, though, the problem remains. There are too many models modeling different values—different goals, life styles, speech patterns, moral codes, orientations toward work and play, life and death. Which models are the real teachers, which the charlatans? How does the young person decide?

We could very well despair of being any help at all. We could take a *laissez faire* stance, throw up our hands, let them go their own way, and hope for the best. It would be a naive hope. Removing a few moralizers or a few models doesn't make growing up any simpler, doesn't turn confusion to clarity, doesn't teach anyone anything—except maybe that we don't care.

If we do care, we will model our values. But we can go a step further. We can teach young people (and each other) a *process* for clarifying and developing values—a process which they can use throughout their lives. We can teach a *set of valuing skills* that will serve our young people long after they are beyond our immediate sphere of influence.

The Seven Processes

For several years, my colleagues and I have attempted to identify such a process or set of valuing skills and, under the name of *values clarification*, have encouraged educators, parents, and helping professionals to become actively involved in helping young people learn the process. Raths, Harmin, and Simon (1966) first explicated this process in *Values and Teaching*, describing seven subprocesses which lead toward value clarity. These were: choosing from alternatives, thoughtfully considering the consequences of alternatives, choosing freely, prizing and cherishing, publicly affirming, acting repeatedly, and acting with a pattern or consistency. The seven subprocesses were also described as "criteria" for a "value." Subsequent publications explored new strategies to teach the seven subprocesses (Simon, Howe, and Kirschenbaum 1972) and ways to combine values clarification with traditional school curricula (Harmin, Kirschenbaum, and Simon 1973). Many other volumes on values clarification have recently been published.

In a sense, the very term "values clarification" has contributed to some misunderstanding, implying to some people the goal of simply clarifying or "being clear" about one's values, and implying to others a hedonistic lack of interest in anyone else's values; to be clear about one's own values is enough. This has never been the case.

Central to the clarifying process has always been a concern for the *consequences* of one's position—both personal and social. And from the beginning, values clarification has never encouraged a static "clarity," but the ongoing *development* of one's values, including acting on them.

Nevertheless, in recent years I have had some misgivings about Raths' conception of seven processes of valuing or criteria for a value. One problem is with the concept of criterion. While useful theoretically, it is not operational. How proud must someone be of a belief before it may be considered a "value"? How many alternatives must be considered before the alternatives criterion is satisfied? How often must action be repeated? And so on. No one can say except the individual, and his concern is to use the valuing processes wherever and whenever appropriate, not to achieve some theoretical goal of an official "value." More importantly, the seven subprocesses seem insufficient to fully comprehend the valuing process—the means by which values are clarified and developed. A more recent formulation of the valuing process (Kirschenbaum 1973) is based on Raths' original seven processes and consistent with them, but goes further in expanding the concept of "valuing."

Expanding the Process

The valuing process, as I understand it today, is a process by which we increase the likelihood that our living in general or a decision in particular will, first, have positive value for us, and second, be constructive in the social context. As I am defining it, the use of the valuing process does not guarantee a good decision for ourselves or society; it merely increases the likelihood.

The valuing process has five *dimensions*, each containing several subprocesses (hereafter referred to as "processes"). The five dimensions are not discrete psychological processes; an individual can be engaged in all of them or some of them at the same time. It is helpful to separate them primarily as a means toward clarity of educational goals. I don't believe that anyone will ever write the definitive list of valuing processes, since we may legitimately choose to describe one part or another or to use different terms. What I will do here is to indicate several processes under each dimension of valuing.

Thinking

One way we can make better value decisions, by our own or society's standards, is to *think*. In this sense, anything we can do to help students learn to think and reason more effectively is a help to them in their value development. Included in this dimension would be the skills of *thinking on various levels* (Bloom et al. 1956), *critical thinking* (Raths 1967), *moral reasoning on the higher levels* (Kohlberg 1968), *divergent or creative thinking* (Parnes 1967), and others. Humanistic approaches to education, in their emphasis on the affective, often forget this dimension. It is an essential dimension of valuing, if students are to learn to control their own lives, to get along in a complex world, to analyze advertising, propaganda and information, and to make crucial value decisions.

Feeling

Feelings can be an aid or an obstacle to effective thinking, deciding, and living. The traditional values clarification process of knowing that we "prize and cherish" is an important part of value development, but only one part of the affective domain. People who feel good about themselves tend to be more effective by almost any criteria (Combs, Avila, and Purkey 1971). People who are aware of their feelings are psychologically more mature and able to achieve their goals more readily (Rogers 1961). When we are not aware of or attempt to deny our feelings, they often come out in surprising ways and interfere with our conscious goals. People who have learned a process of discharging distressing feelings (emotional or physical hurt, anger, fear, embarrassment, etc.) have greater access to their full problem-solving capacity and are freer from the grip of patterned distress (Jackins 1965). So again, anything we can do to help students (and each other, I hasten to add) to strengthen their self-concepts and to deal with their feelings is helping them learn a process that is part of their ongoing values development.

Choosing

"Choosing from alternatives" and "considering the consequences" certainly belong here. A longer menu doesn't ensure we'll find something we like to eat; it just increases the odds. We can't predict the future, but we can make an educated guess and lessen the chance of unexpected and undesirable consequences. *Choosing freely* is another valuing process, which involves distinguishing the pressures and consequences urging us toward certain choices from our own subjective sense of which choice is best. Another choosing process that many teachers have been teaching their students is that of *achievement planning* (Alschuler, Tabor, and McIntyre 1971), a process by which students learn strategies to increase the likelihood of achieving their goals. Luck need not determine what we choose; we can learn skills or processes to become better choosers.

Communicating

Values do not develop in a vacuum, but through an ongoing process of social interaction. Therefore, the ability to *send clear messages* is an important valuing skill or process. To the extent that we can make our own needs, values, or desires known to others, there is that much greater chance they will respond in ways which meet those needs. In addition, appropriately sharing our feelings and thoughts can have a clarifying effect, as we see how others respond and how we respond to our public or private affirmation of our inner world (Jourard 1964). Another valuing process here is empathy, active *listening*, or taking another's frame of reference. It opens us up to new alternatives and decreases the likelihood that our values will rigidify and become self-defeating as a result of excluding the realities of the people and the changing world around us. *Conflict resolution* is a third valuing process under this dimension. Conflicts can end with neither party actualizing his or her values, with one party winning and the other losing, or with both parties achieving a satisfying solution that realizes most of their values. To be clear about our own goals and values is not enough to achieve them—not if we are living among other people. Thomas Gordon's work (1970, 1975) has been particularly helpful in teaching individuals these communication skills and processes.

Acting

As values clarification has traditionally indicated, to act repeatedly upon our beliefs and to act consistently toward our goals increases the likelihood that our living will have positive value to us. To this could be added the process of acting skillfully in the areas in which we do act. To read, to change a tire, to cook a meal, to teach a class, to build a bridge, to clean up a polluted lake—whatever the field of our endeavor, *competence* is going to increase the likelihood that the process and product will be satisfying to us and socially productive.

Based on this expanded conception of the valuing process, values clarification can be defined as *an approach that utilizes questions and activities designed to teach the valuing process and to help people skillfully apply the valuing processes to value-rich areas in their lives.* Now it is possible to respond to some of the misconceptions often associated with values clarification.

Is Values Clarification Value Free?

It is true that in discussing value-rich areas such as those mentioned at the beginning of this article, the teacher accepts all answers and does not try to impose his or her views on the students. In that sense, the approach is "value free." But it should be clear that values clarification definitely values thinking, feeling, choosing, communicating, and acting. Moreover, it values certain types of thinking, feeling, choosing, communicating, and acting. Thinking critically is regarded as better than thinking noncritically. Considering consequences is regarded as better than choosing glibly or thoughtlessly. Choosing freely is considered better than simply yielding to authority or peer pressure.

We can go even a step further, and I think we have erred in not making this explicit. Toward what end are these valuing processes better than their counterparts? Here, again, there are certain value judgments implicit in each process. If we urge critical thinking, then we value *rationality*. If we support moral reasoning, then we value *justice*. If we advocate divergent thinking, then we value *creativity*. If we uphold free choice, then we value autonomy or *freedom*. If we encourage "no-lose" conflict resolution, then we value *equality*. Some of these values are probably "instrumental" values and others "terminal" values (Rokeach 1971), as with the instrumental value of rationality being a means toward the terminal or end value of justice. In any case, all these "larger" values are clearly implicit in the valuing process. Called before the committee, we can only say that values clarification is not and never has been "value free."

Is Values Clarification Relativistic?

On what authority do we propose a system which has as its core the values of justice, equality, freedom, and so forth? These questions generally come from two sources—the church and the cognitive-developmental psychologists.

To the church, we must say, "We don't know." Many advocates of values clarification do believe that there are absolute values, that is, truths about the universe which everyone should hold for reasons which transcend rationality. Others do not believe this. Values clarification does not propose to answer all questions of human existence, including the origin and design of the universe. It does attempt to describe a valuing process and say that if people use the process they will experience more positive value in their living and will be more constructive in the social context.

To the cognitive-developmentalists dealing with moral reasoning, I would say: Simply because your research shows that Kohlberg's sixth stage of moral reasoning is the product of a sequential, irreversible, cross-cultural sequence of human development, this does not prove that justice should be a universal value. What you have shown, and your work is terribly important, is that if we provide certain conditions for people (e.g., moral reasoning at one level beyond their own), they will grow in certain predictable directions. Similarly, a physical educator could tell us that, if we provide the right conditions for children, we could have almost everyone running a five-minute mile. And the behaviorists have demonstrated that if we provide the right conditions of reinforcement, we can get pigeons to play ping pong. This does not mean to me that all pigeons should play ping pong, all people should run the five-minute mile, or all people should reason morally. I think we should teach students how to reason morally because I value justice. I can give you reasons why I value justice, but I can't prove it to you. And neither can you.

Does Values Clarification Have a Theoretical Base?

Considering values clarification as the expanded process I have described (but keeping in mind that this is merely an elaboration on what it always was), it should be clear that values clarification is supported by a significant base of psychological theory and research.

Research and theory in the areas of moral reasoning, critical thinking, creativity and problem-solving, self-concept, psychotherapy, achievement motivation, group dynamics, helping relationships, and skill training, to name a few areas, has burgeoned in the last few decades. We still have an enormous amount to learn, and a separate paper could be written on the research possibilities inherent in this presentation; but the fact remains: whatever research exists to support any of these areas of study also supports values clarification.

Even in the traditional area of values clarification, as defined by the seven processes of Raths, Harmin, and Simon (1966), there is an ever-increasing amount of research that can be cited (Kirschenbaum 1974). An important focus of future studies will be how values clarification experiences can be more effectively sequenced, adapted, and combined with other approaches, based on our increasing knowledge of the nature of human growth and development.

Conclusion

In many ways, I wonder if values clarification, when considered as a separate educational approach, is any longer a useful concept. Many different approaches, both cognitive and affective, have a part to contribute to the goal of fuller value development. In expanding our conception of the valuing process, we begin to develop a picture of a well-rounded person and soon find ourselves asking: What does it mean to be a mature or effective human being? What are humans potentially capable of being and becoming—physically, intellectually, and emotionally? In medicine and psychology, especially, we are discovering each year new areas of human potential, new abilities to extend life, to communicate verbally and nonverbally, to operate on different brain wave levels and perhaps in other psychic realities. One of the oldest philosophical questions—toward what end should we live?—is raised for us anew by these amazing discoveries of what actually is possible.

I would hope that values clarification and all the other approaches devoted to humanizing education will work together in an effort to better understand human growth and development and, on this understanding, create better living and learning environments. Professional jealousy, competition, economic interests, or attitudes of "my approach is better than yours" should not be allowed to interfere with such important work.

References

Alschuler, A. S.; Tabor, D.; and McIntyre, J. *Teaching Achievement Motivation.* Middletown, Conn.: Education Ventures, 1971.

Bloom, B. S., et al. *The Taxonomy of Educational Objectives: Handbook I: The Cognitive Domain.* New York: David McKay, 1956.

Combs, A. W.; Avila, D. L., and Purkey, W. W. *Helping Relationships: Basic Concepts for the Helping Professions.* Boston: Allyn & Bacon, 1971.

Gordon, T. *Parent Effectiveness Training.* New York: Peter Wyden, 1970.

Gordon, T. *Teacher Effectiveness Training.* New York: Peter Wyden, 1975.

Harmin, M.; Kirschenbaum, H.; and Simon, S. B. *Clarifying Values Through Subject Matter.* Minneapolis: Winston Press, 1973.

Jackins, H. *The Human Side of Human Beings.* Seattle: Rational Island Publishers, 1965.

Jourard, S. M. *The Transparent Self.* New York: Van Nostrand, 1964.

Kirschenbaum, H. "Beyond Values Clarification." Upper Jay, N.Y.: National Humanistic Education Center, 1973.

Kirschenbaum, H. "Recent Research in Values Clarification." Upper Jay, N.Y.: National Humanistic Education Center, 1974.

Kohlberg, L. "The Child as a Moral Philosopher." *Psychology Today* (September 1968).

Parnes, S. J. *Creative Behavior Guidebook.* New York: Scribners, 1967.

Raths, L. E.; Harmin, M.; and Simon, S. B. *Values and Teaching.* Columbus, Ohio: Charles E. Merrill, 1966.

Raths, L.; Wasserman, S.; Jonas, A.; and Rothstein, A. M. *Teaching for Thinking.* Columbus, Ohio: Charles E. Merrill, 1967.

Rogers, C. R. *On Becoming a Person.* Boston: Houghton Mifflin, 1961.

Rokeach, M. "Persuasion that Persists." *Psychology Today* (September 1971).

Simon, S. B.; Howe, L.; and Kirschenbaum, H. *Values Clarification: A Handbook of Practical Strategies for Teachers and Students.* New York: Hart Publishing, 1972.

For further information on materials and workshops on values clarification and humanistic education, write: National Humanistic Education Center, 110 Spring St., Saratoga Springs, N.Y. 12866.

9

Values Clarification vs. Indoctrination

Sidney B. Simon

Whatever happened to those good old words we once used when we talked of values? Remember how comfortable it was to say *inculcate*? It was a nice, clean, dignified, closely shaved word if there ever was one. Then there was the old standby, *to instill*—usually followed by "the democratic values of our society." Doesn't anyone instill anymore? And what about the word *foster*? In schools, not so very long ago, we used to "foster" all over the place. But nobody does that much anymore. What has happened to the old familiar jargon of value teaching?

What happened was the realization that all the inculcating, instilling, and fostering added up to indoctrination: and despite our best efforts at doing the indoctrinating, we've come to see that it just didn't take. Most of the people who experienced the inculcation, instillation, and fostering seem not the much better for it. They appear to play just as much hanky-panky with income taxes as anyone else, and concerned letters-to-the-editor are not written by them in any greater profusion. They pollute and defoliate; move to the

Reprinted by permission of the author from *Social Education* (December 1971), pp. 902-05.

suburbs to escape integration; buy convertibles with vinyl tops that collapse in roll-over accidents; fail to wear seat belts; and commit all kinds of sins even while they are saying the very words that have been dutifully inculcated, instilled, and fostered in them. It *is* discouraging.

At this point, one might ask: "Is it all that bad?" "Aren't they also among the good people who go to the polls in November, read the current events weeklies, and pay their BankAmericard charges on time?" Yes, of course. But in these troubled, confused, and conflicted times, we need people who can do much more than that. We desperately need men and women who know who they are, who know what they want out of life, and who can name their names when controversy rages. We need people who know what is significant and what is trash, and who are not so vulnerable to demagoguery, blandness, or safety.

The indoctrination procedures of the past fail to help people grapple with all the confusion and conflict which abound in these baffling days. For example, in values clarification, we apply a strategy which is deceptively simple. We ask students to spend some time listing the brand names in their home medicine cabinets. Just think of your own medicine cabinet as you are sitting reading this. What's in it? How many creams, ointments, and salves have you been sold? Do you use a brand-name, buffered product instead of plain old aspirin? How did you get started on that? What about the spray cans? How many are in your aerosol arsenal? What did you use before the product you now spray? How did all those brand names get there? Who bought them? What was the motivating force? How did you learn what to value as seen in your medicine cabinet? As long as you have the door to your cabinet open, why don't you pull out the cosmetic tray? How vulnerable are you to avoiding the hysteria surrounding all of us about getting a wrinkle? Getting old has become such a negative value. Who are the people who fear it?

In place of indoctrination, my associates and I are substituting a *process* approach to the entire area of dealing with values in the schools, which focuses on the process of valuing, not on the transmission of the "right" set of values. We call this approach *values clarification*, and it is based on the premise that none of us has the "right" set of values to pass on to other people's children. Yes, there may be some things we can all agree upon, and I will grant you some absolutes, but when we begin to operationalize our values, make them show up in how we live our days and spend our nights, then we begin to see the enormous smugness of those people who profess they have the right values for others' children. The issues and hostility generated around hair length and dress and armbands are just the surface absurdity.

More dangerous is the incredible hypocrisy we generate when we live two-faced values and hustle the one right value to children. Think about the hundreds of elementary school teachers who daily stop children from running down the halls. I close my eyes and I see them with their arms outstretched, hands pressing against the chest of kids who put on their "brakes" in order to make the token slow-down until the teacher ducks into the teacher's room for a fast cigarette before all the kids get back to hear the cancer lecture. Think of those teachers preaching to children about the need to take turns and share. "We wait on lines, boys and girls, and we learn to share our crayons and paints in here. And, I don't want to see anybody in my class being a tattletale—except in cases of serious emergency, naturally." The words are all too familiar. I have used them in the old days. I have also seen myself cut into the cafeteria lunch line ahead of third graders. (Take turns? Well, not when we have so few minutes for lunch and always so much to do to get ready for afternoon classes.)

The alternative to indoctrination of values is *not* to do nothing. In this time of the anti-hero, our students need all the help we can give them if they are to make sense of the confusion and conflict inherited from the indoctrinated types. Moreover, we all need help in grappling with the chaos of the international scene, with the polarization of national life—not to mention the right-outside-the-door string of purely local dilemmas.

An approach to this problem is to help students learn a process for the clarification of their values, which is a far cry from indoctrination. The theory behind it can be found in *Values and Teaching* (1966). In the remainder of this article, I will describe some of the strategies we are presently using to help students learn the process of values clarification and begin lifelong searches for the sets of personal values by which to steer their lives.

Five Value-Clarifying Strategies and Their Use

Strategy no. 1—Things I Love to Do

Ask students (teacher does it with them) to number from 1-20 on a paper. Then suggest they list, as rapidly as they can, twenty things in life which they really, *really* love to do. Stress that the papers will not be collected and "corrected," and that there is no right answer about what people *should* like. It should be emphasized that in none of values strategies should students be forced to participate. Each has the right to pass. Students may get strangely quiet; and, at first, they may even be baffled by such an unschoollike task as this. Flow with it, and be certain to allow enough time to list what they really love to do. Remember, at no time must the individual's privacy be invaded, and that the right of an individual to pass is sacrosanct.

When everyone has listed his twenty items, the process of coding responses can be started. Here are some suggested codes which you might ask the students to use:

1. Place the $ sign by any item which costs more than $3, each time you do it.

2. Put an *R* in front of any item which involves some *risk*. The risk might be physical, intellectual, or emotional. (Which things in your own life that are things you love to do require some risk?)

3. Using the code letters *F* and *M*, record which of the items on your list you think your father and mother might have had on their lists if they had been asked to make them at *your* age.

4. Place either the letter *P* or the letter *A* before each item. The *P* to be used for items which you prefer doing with *people*, the *A* for items which you prefer doing *alone*. (Stress again that there is no right answer. It is important to just become aware of which are your preferences.)

5. Place a number 5 in front of any item which you think would not be on your list 5 years from now.

6. Finally go down through your list and place near each item the date when you did it last.

The discussion which follows this exercise argues more eloquently than almost anything else we can say for values clarification.

Strategy no. 2—I Learned That I . . .

This strategy fits in with the one above. After students have listed and coded their twenty items, the teacher might say, "Look at your list as something which tells a lot about you at this time in your life. What did you learn about yourself as you were going through the strategy? Will you please complete one of these sentences and share with us some of the learning you did?"

> I learned that I . . .
> I relearned that I . . .
> I noticed that I . . .
> I was surprised to see that I . . .
> I was disappointed that I . . .
> I was pleased that I . . .
> I realized that I . . .

The teacher must be willing to make some "I learned that I . . ." statements, too. And they must not be platitudinous, either. Every effort is made for the values-clarifying teacher to be as honest and as authentic as possible.

"I learned that I . . ." statements can be used after almost any important value clarifying strategy. It is a way of getting the student to own the process of the search for values. It should be clear how diametrically opposed "I learned that I . . ." statements are from indoctrination, although it is possible to misuse this or any clarification strategy to get kids to give back the party line. On the other hand, using this strategy can begin to build that lifetime search for personal meaning into all of our experiences.

Strategy no. 3—Baker's Dozen

This is a very simple strategy which teaches us something about our personal priorities. The teacher asks each student to list thirteen, a baker's dozen, of his favorite items around the house which use *plugs*, that is, which require electricity.

When the students have made their lists, the teacher says, "Now, please draw a line through the three which you really could do without if there were suddenly to be a serious power shortage. It's not that you don't like them, but that you could, if you had to, live without them. O.K., now circle the three which really mean the most to you and which you would hold onto until the very end."

It should be clear that again there is no right answer as to what "good" people *should* draw lines through and circle. The main thing is for each of us to know what we want and to see it in the perspective of what we like less.

Strategy no. 4—"I Urge" Telegrams

The teacher obtains Western Union telegram blanks. Or simply has students head a piece of paper with the word *Telegram*. He then says, "Each of you should think of someone in your real life to whom you would send a telegram which begins with these words: *I urge you to*. . . . Then finish the telegram and we'll hear some of them."

A great many values issues comes out of this simple strategy. Consider some of these telegrams:

To my sister: "I urge you to get your head together and quit using drugs." Nancy. (All telegrams must be signed. It is our affirmation of the need to name your name and to stand up for what you believe in.)

To my Sunday School teacher: "I urge you to quit thinking that you are the only person to know what God wants." Rodney Phillips.

To my neighbor on the North Side: "I urge you to see that we have no other place to play ball and that you not call the cops so often." Billy Clark.

One of the things that students working with values-clarification learn to do is to find out what they really want. "I urge" telegrams help do that. Just think of the people in your own lives to whom an "I urge" telegram needs to be sent. The second thing students working with values clarification learn to do is to find *alternative* ways of getting what they need and want. Take the case of Billy Clark's neighbor. The class spent some time brainstorming ways of approaching that neighbor. They talked about how to negotiate with a grouch, and how to try to offer alternatives in your drive to get what you want.

"I urge" telegrams are used several times during the semester. The students keep them on file and after they have done five or six, they are spread out on the desk and "I learned" statements made from the pattern of the messages carried by the telegrams.

Students also learn to use the "I urge you to. . . ." model to get messages across between student and student and between student and teacher.

An assignment I like to use, related to the "I urge" telegram, is to have each student get a letter-to-the-editor published in a magazine or newspaper.

Strategy no. 5—Personal Coat of Arms

Each student is asked to draw a shield shape in preparation for making a personal coat of arms. The teacher could go into the historical significance of shields and coats of arms, but the exercise is designed to help us learn more about some of our most strongly held values and to learn the importance of publicly affirming what we

A Personal Coat of Arms

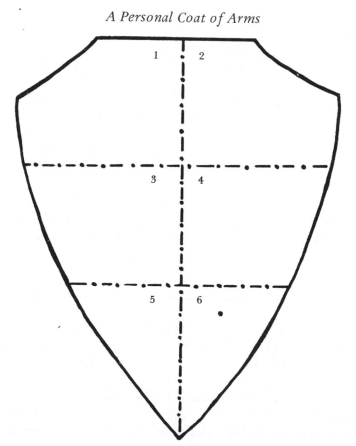

believe, that is, literally wearing our values out front on our shields.

The coat of arms shield is divided into six sections (see figure). The teacher makes it clear that words are to be used only in the sixth block. All the others are to contain pictures. He stresses that it is not an art lesson. Only crude stick figures, etc., need be used. Then he tells what is to go in each of the six sections:

1. Draw two pictures. One to represent something you are very good at and one to show something you *want* to become good at.

2. Make a picture to show one of your values from which you would never budge. This is one about which you feel extremely strong, and which you might never give up.

3. Draw a picture to show a value by which your family lives. Make it one that everyone in your family would probably agree is one of their most important.

4. In this block, imagine that you could achieve anything you wanted, and that whatever you tried to do would be a success. What would you strive to do?

5. Use this block to show one of the values you wished all men would believe, and certainly one in which you believe very deeply.

6. In the last block, you can use words. Use four words which you would like people to say about you behind your back.

The teacher can do several things at this point. He can have the students share among themselves in little trios or quartets. He can also get the pictures hung up on the walls and get people to take each other on gallery tours to share the coats of arms. A game could be played which would involve trying to guess what the pictures represented. The class might try to make a group coat of arms to represent their living together in that classroom. In any case, the value expressions elicited in this nonverbal way are very exciting and lead to discussions which range far and wide. Incidentally, this strategy is a good one to use with parents to illustrate to them the power of the values clarification methodology. It makes a meaningful exercise for an evening PTA meeting.

The coat of arms strategy illustrates quite well some things common to all of the values clarification strategies. The teacher sets up an interesting way of eliciting some value responses. He establishes that there is no right answer. The strategy is open-ended and allows students to take the exploration to whatever level they want to take it. Finally, there is a chance to share with each other some of the alternatives that emerge from our searching. This whole process allows each student to focus on areas where he has some work yet to do in order to keep growing. The coat of arms can be done several times during the school year and the various shields compared and seen as measures of a student's search.

Conclusion

The five strategies used as illustrations of what values clarification is must raise some serious questions in the minds of readers who have more conventional views of what the social studies should be. For one thing, I have used no standard subject-matter content, there is no history, no geography, etc. Yet, if one thinks through what the outcomes of a course will be making use of the five strategies, he will see the student emerging with a deeper sense of who he is, what he wants, what is precious, and what is of most worth in his and others' lives. Has the social studies ever done more than that?

Values clarification demands that we take a new look at what we have been calling the social studies. I feel more and more strongly that the most severe problem facing all of us is *how to get people to look at the lives they are leading.* How can we get fathers and mothers to see that high college-entrance scores are not the end of a high school education? How can we get people to see that getting a high-paying job is not the final reward of a college degree? How can we get men and women to take on some larger share of their personal responsibility for the rampant racism in our nation? Or for allowing a senseless war to continue indefinitely? When will educators make a contribution towards helping people examine the headlong pursuit towards accumulating more and more material possessions and enjoying them less? Or what can we do about keeping our students from making drab and dreary marriages or being trapped into pointless jobs which they hate to go to each morning? It boils down to a concern for values, and yet we must not fall into the trap of believing that if only we could give boys and girls the right set of values to believe, they would avoid the mistakes of the rest of us. Nonsense!

Indoctrination is not the answer. The only thing that indoctrination did for people in the past was to help them postpone the time when they began the hard process of hammering out their own set of values. Values simply can't be given to anyone else. One can't value for other people. Each individual has to find his own values. One can memorize all the platitudes he wants, but when it comes to living and acting on the values, he needs to carve them out of carefully reflected experience. The skills necessary for doing this can be learned in values clarification.

Perhaps when the reader and author acknowledge how little help they received from their own education about making sense out of life, maybe then they will be willing to help other people's children learn the *process*, a lifetime process, of searching for a viable set of values to live by and perhaps even to die for.

The author is convinced that he can leave his own children no greater inheritance than the gift of knowing how to negotiate the lovely banquet of life ahead of them. That is indeed something of value.

Reference

Raths, Louis; Harmin, Merrill; and Simon, Sidney B. *Values and Teaching.* Columbus, Ohio: Charles E. Merrill, 1966.

For further information on materials and workshops on values clarification and humanistic education, write: National Humanistic Education Center, 110 Spring St., Saratoga Springs, N.Y. 12866.

10

Problems and Contradictions of Values Clarification

John S. Stewart

Values clarification is unquestionably one of the most popular and commercially successful educational fads of our generation, and perhaps of all time. Its acceptance has been truly phenomenal not only in extent, however, but also in manner. For that acceptance has been, for the most part, somewhat unreflective, uncritical, and un-clarified—a strange state of affairs for a movement purporting to seek clarification and reflection. Paradoxically and ironically VC has become some kind of sacred cow that is adopted largely on face value on the basis of its own claims with little or no examination of its educational soundness, philosophical justification, or alleged efficacy. As with similar educational fads, however, time, experience, and deeper judgment are beginning to reveal hyperbole in its claims, profound deficiencies in its theoretical base, enormous problems in its moral orientation, and serious questions about its proclaimed achievements. Even some of the most ardent and experienced disciples of VC are beginning to see the problems and recognize the superficiality of this approach. Even the teachers who believe they have used it properly and with some success can be heard to say: "Well, I have used values clarification and I like it, and the kids seem to enjoy it, but I'm not sure what's been accomplished, or what to

An earlier version of this chapter appeared in *Phi Delta Kappan* (June 1975), pp. 684-87. Reprinted by permission of the author.

do next. Where do I go from here?" These teachers will tell you, especially after careful probing about specifics, that VC simply isn't enough, both the teachers and students eventually become bored, and they really don't know quite what they are doing or why. Other teachers, quite frankly, may say they must do something in the area of values or moral education, they don't know what else to do, and values clarification is simple, easy, and readily available. And, in all honesty, most classroom teachers are either too busy or not adequately prepared to evaluate values education methods or approaches. But this area of education is too important to permit any theory or practice to go unexamined and unquestioned.

My analysis of values clarification begins with the claim that it is deceptively and dangerously superficial. One can easily be fooled into believing that many of the VC strategies really lead to an in-depth examination of one's values, when in fact one may have really done little more than look at opinions or feelings, and frequently on relatively trivial matters. One of the dangers involved is the conviction that values or moral education is really taking place in any significant way. The superficiality of values clarification is more important than it may appear at first glance, and grows out of at least four major weaknesses or problems inherent in its basic premises. First, there is the error of reification or hypostatization. The VC authors have converted the abstract idea of "value" into a concrete entity that actually exists. They have made a construct into a thing. Arvid Adell treats this problem in his excellent critique entitled "Values Clarification Revised" (1976). He defines this error as "treating [values] as though they were independent entities existing apart from persons" (p. 436). The result, as Adell makes clear, is that:

The confusion of the values clarification program is its implication that choosing a value is like choosing a vegetable: there are a variety of values to be affirmed, and so long as a person chooses freely, deliberately and purposively, he or she is performing well. But values are *not* like vegetables: they are not objects, entities, things-in-themselves, nouns. Instead, they are indicators, appearances, symptoms of something deeper and more substantial. . . . The mistake is that vegetables tangibly exist and values do not! . . . To reify a value confuses rather than clarifies because it suggests that values are items which can be isolated, diagnosed and then treated, if necessary—and such is not the case. (p. 437)

Now my claim of superficiality parallels Adell's conclusions that follow from the above, namely, that values are not things but indications of one's deeper conceptual systems about the world and life, about good and bad, about right and wrong, and about why one believes as he or she does; and that values clarification fails to "trace values back to the life-understandings which give rise to those values," and therefore, as Adell asserts, "it remains a peripheral operation dealing with shadows and bogus entities" (p. 437).

Second, VC's superficiality in part is related to its overwhelming concentration on what the structural-developmentalists (e.g., Piaget, Kohlberg, Selman, Loevinger, Harvey, Hunt, Schroder, and others) call *content* in distinction to the relatively more important underlying *structure* of one's thinking and valuing. Content refers to "what" one thinks; structure refers to "why" one thinks that way, or the cognitive logic behind the content. My own belief on this matter is that both are important and need to be seen in relationship to each other, and to the action that one takes in conjunction with them. Values clarification strategies not only focus primarily on content and almost completely ignore structure, they largely concentrate on trivial content.

A third source of superficiality grows out of Simon's perpetuation of the *content-process* argument that has needlessly divided educators on curricular and pedagogical issues. As the reader can easily see in chapter 9, Simon confuses the teaching of content with indoctrination, inculcation, and related terms, and in so doing throws out content in favor of process in the false belief that he has thereby eliminated the moralistic dogmatism that has dominated traditional approaches to values, moral, and character education. Simon's error is the failure to differentiate *content* from *a particular content*. He has correctly assessed one of the major problems of traditional moral education, but his proposed solution ignores the deeper problem and commits an equally grievous error. He fails to see, for example, that his own approach contains a very definite, identifiable, and prejudiced content; and that *content* and *process* cannot exist in separation except as a conceptual distinction for limited technical purposes. An educator cannot teach any kind of content without a process, and cannot use any kind of process without some kind of content. Consequently, the VC attempt to isolate and focus on process creates the superficial illusion that this process is devoid of content, and therefore devoid of any moral message. Furthermore, the student does not experience content, process, or teacher in the manner implied, but is involved in the totality of complex transactions in the entire occurrence. The only way the VC teacher can "appear" to use this methodology in the manner prescribed is by avoiding deep and complex moral issues that necessarily have significant content, and using strategies that deal with relatively superficial or trivial issues.

The fourth source of superficiality in values clarification stems from one of its most serious difficulties, the problem for which it probably receives more criticism than any other, namely its ethical relativism. Since this issue will be discussed later, I merely want to say that a relativistic position again leads to remaining at the superficial level in the classroom. After all, if anyone and everyone is ultimately right about anything and everything, then it's strictly a matter of opinion and feelings. The best way to keep classroom debates from getting out of hand from this philosophical stance is to avoid the truly meaningful moral issues and remain at the level of interests, tastes, likes, dislikes, and other matters on which there is no powerful justification for deciding right and wrong or good and bad. A survey of the VC strategies and methods in chapter 9 or the several larger works containing hundreds of similar procedures reveals the superficiality, banality, and triviality, of a great deal of the questions, issues, and activities. And even if the deeper moral issues are raised, where can you go with them? Probably round and round the relativity bush until everyone has justified his or her own position *ad infinitum*, or possibly even *ad nauseam*. Those of us who have been classroom teachers can recite this scenario with ease.

Moving beyond the problem of superficiality, I will now deal with a very serious element in values clarification: the emphasis and reliance on peer pressure and a tendency toward coercion to the mean in many of the recommended activities. In spite of the relativism and individualism that lies at the heart of this approach to values education, and in spite of the statements and caveats about avoiding peer pressure that appear throughout the VC literature, many of the strategies and much of the social orientation of the methodology either overtly rely on peer influence or covertly elicit it as an inherent part of the process. This is particularly true and very important in view of the fact that the major users of values clarification are teachers whose students are especially vulnerable to the powerful pressures that emanate from peer relationships. But, of course, the point is relevant even to adults who are particularly attuned to the judgments of others, such people being in great abundance in our society, according to the research on this subject. The emphasis on frequent public affirmation of positions, for example, carries this danger. Given the social dynamics of a normal group of teen-agers, only the most popular or the strongest dare express their honest opinions and feelings about values/moral issues publicly without fear of ridicule or rejection.

Space permits only one example, but it easily communicates the problem. One of the most frequently used strategies is the "values continuum" (Simon, Howe, and Kirschenbaum 1972), which involves having students take positions on issues presented on a continuum from one extreme to its opposite. One of the items in this strategy asks, "How do you feel about premarital sex?" The two ends of the continuum are (1) Virginal Virginia (sometimes called Gloves Gladys) and (2) Mattress Millie. Virginal Virginia "wears white gloves on every date" and Mattress Millie "wears a mattress strapped to her back." Now consider the very shy, sensitive, and fearful girl in the class as an extreme example—the girl who's tremendously concerned about her standing with the other girls, or the boys, or the teacher. Suppose that her position on this issue is clear, even as the result of having applied the principles of values clarification, and that she truly believes in either one of the two extreme positions. Would she be likely to affirm publicly such a position in this situation? I would think not. The risks would simply be too great. Assuming that she also does not want to run the risk of being judged somehow for passing, one of the legitimate choices in all VC exercises, she might be inclined to express a middle position.

This is what I mean by coercion to the mean, and I see it as a great factor in many of the VC strategies, especially those strategies like the values continuum in which the extreme positions are so value-specific and/or emotionally loaded as to preclude them as legitimate alternatives for public affirmation for many people. Even the middle choice in many cases is equally unacceptable, because of the implications of its wording, e.g., "compulsive moderate." Some of the items in the values continuum offer extreme choices in pejorative terms along with compulsive moderate as a middle choice. What is one to choose in cases like this? Again, given the dynamics of teenage social relationships, the values clarification approach can be harmful, or at least can actually lead to anything but true clarification. The VC creators include many forewarnings about some of these problems, yet tend to minimize them, offer unrealistic and simplistic solutions, or be glib about them. In fact, both in the design of many of the strategies and in the directions given for their use, the biases (values) of the authors are blatantly obvious and enormously influence the way people respond.

A related criticism deals even more directly with the judgmental nature of some aspects of values clarification methodology, in spite of the enormous emphasis the VC authors place on the necessity for being nonjudgmental in clarifying values. One of the so-called "clarifying responses" recommended is worded, "Do you do anything about that idea?" (Raths, Harmin, and Simon 1966, p. 58). The authors say about this, "A verbalization that is not lived has little import and is certainly not a value." This is one of their basic tenets, but I find it highly judgmental, and considering the limitations of life that drastically reduce our opportunities to act on all of our ideas, it may be absurd. But the mere challenge, no matter how ostensibly neutral or nonjudgmental the question asked, carries an implicit threat or implies a judgment. The VC position on this point is an oversimplified generalization, and is also highly moralistic in nature. (And moralizing is even more strongly rejected by the VC creators.) In order to evaluate (not judge) a person's acting or not acting on any given issue, one must know a lot more about the situation, the person's developmental progress, the costs or dangers involved in acting or not acting, and many other factors. But the judgmental nature of values clarification is pervasive. The creators have built a methodology based on their own values, which are frequently in conflict. They claim value neutrality with regard to the content of the methodology, but fail to see that their own values are built into the methodology. As a result, they fail to see how enormously judgmental are many of their questions, techniques, and strategies.

The demand for public affirmation and action which is such an important part of the VC philosophy, in addition to being highly judgmental, is also potentially dangerous, especially when one is working with teen-agers. Research conducted by social psychologists has revealed that when people take public positions or are forced to act they tend to cling to the beliefs or values involved, even if those beliefs or values are tentative or not genuinely held at the time of the commitment or action. Once the stand has been taken and the action completed, there is a tendency to live with it and not risk embarrassment or threat by changing later. To go back on a public affirmation or action is often to lose face. Premature affirmation or action, therefore, can be a very dangerous thing to induce. I have seen many teenagers make premature statements or perform actions they later regretted, but felt obliged to maintain until even they came to believe in what they had said or done. During the important developmental years of adolescence and youth, there is a need for genuine commitment, rational action, and public affirmation. But the risks are also great, and such behaviors should not be artificially induced or prematurely generated.

The values clarification position on action seems to be one-dimensional and stereotypical. Throughout their writings, VC authors dogmatically assert that what is not acted upon is not a value. Action is one of the seven criteria that must be met for the idea to qualify as a value. In fact, mere action is not sufficient; it must be repeated action. Of the VC writers, only Howard Kirschenbaum (1973) acknowledges some of the absurdities in this position. What constitutes action? How many times must one act in order for it to meet the seventh and final criterion of "acting repeatedly, in some pattern of life"? (Raths, Harmin, and Simon 1966, p. 30). This assertion ignores the realities of life and limits most people to a very small number of values. Only martyrs are able to affirm and act consistently and publicly on some of the highest values. Would the values clarification authors be willing to claim that only Martin Luther King and others who were able, for various reasons, to act repeatedly on their beliefs and values about racial justice could claim racial equality as a value? If so, then they are claiming courage and a whole host of other highly questionable factors as criteria for holding values.

Of the criticisms made against values clarification, probably none is made more frequently or more loudly than the charge that it is inadequate, ineffective, and possibly even dangerous because of its basic moral relativism. But to see values clarification as morally or ethically relativistic is to see only half of its very confused philosophy. It purports to believe, on the one hand, that values are personal, situational, individually derived, not amenable to objective evaluation, and relative. It offers, on the other hand, a list of values-based behaviors that are undesirable and objectively inferior and can be cured with values clarification. This list, mentioned frequently in the literature, contains the following: apathy, flightiness, uncertainty, inconsistency, drifting, overconforming, overdissenting, and role playing. Counterbalancing this list of "vices," of course, would be the corresponding and opposite desirable and objectively superior "virtues," to which Simon and Polly deSherbinin (1975) have added purposefulness, productivity, strong beliefs, thoughtfulness, consideration, zestfulness, manageability, and others. The confused philosophy is strikingly revealed in "the bible" of values clarification, *Values and Teaching.* At one point the authors of this text assert:

The point has been made that our values tend to be products of our experiences. They are not just a matter of true or false. One cannot go to an encyclopedia or to a textbook for values. The definition that has been given makes this clear. One has to prize for himself, choose for himself, integrate choices into the pattern of his own life. Information as such doesn't convey this quality of values. Values come out of the flux of life itself.

This means that we are dealing with an area that isn't a matter of proof or consensus. It is a matter of experience (p. 36)

On the following page, they make this important statement:

As teachers, then, we need to be clear that we cannot dictate to children what their values should be, since we cannot also dictate what their environments should be and what experiences they will have. *We may be authoritative in those areas that deal with truth and falsity.* (Italics added)

There are a few problems here that merit discussion. First, both of the above statements make it clear that the authors see values as relative. But the italicized sentence in the second statement completely contradicts the basic relativity premise of values clarification. What are those areas of truth and falsity about which we may be authoritative? And on what basis may we be authoritative? What are the criteria for truth and falsity? Why are these areas, whatever they are, not subject to the same conditions as other areas of experience? And is this statement itself not a values statement of the most absolute order? It is interesting that this most important statement is made in the stream of thought about the relativity and personal nature of values without any discussion, qualification, or elucidation of its meaning.

Some light is shed on the above problem by an examination of other VC writings. It is especially interesting to note that the two statements about to be considered are from articles addressed to religious educators. In "Three Ways To Teach Church School," Simon (1973, pp. 237-40) clearly enunciates the basic VC position: "Values are very complex and very personal; there are no 'right' values." In "Value Clarification: New Mission for Religious Education," Simon and two other writers (1973, pp. 241-46) say:

> But aren't there any absolute values that we can teach our students? Many of our readers undoubtedly ask this question.
>
>   We would allow that *there are certain absolutes* essential to Christian education: belief in God, the Resurrection of Christ, the Holy Spirit, and the veracity of the Ten Commandments, to name a few. *But there are really far fewer immutable and absolute values than most of us realize. What students need most is not a list of values of today but a process for finding new expressions of values that are yet to come. This is what value training is all about.* (Italics added)

And in chapter 9, Simon further contributes to the confusion:

> We call this approach *values clarification*, and it is based on the premise that none of us has the "right" set of values to pass on to other people's children. Yes, there may be some things we can all agree upon, and I will grant you some absolutes, but when we begin to operationalize our values, . . . then we begin to see the enormous smugness of those people who profess they have the right values for others' children.

Unfortunately, Simon never explicitly and directly shares with us the absolutes he grants us and the religious educators. They are, however, implicit throughout his writings.

An examination of the "values" on which Simon rather dogmatically and very judgmentally does take strong positions clearly exemplifies my claims. Simon is opposed to those who "play . . . hanky-panky with income taxes," do not write letters to the editor, "pollute and defoliate," "move to the suburbs to escape integration," "buy convertibles," "fail to wear seat belts," and "commit all kinds of sins even while they are saying the very words that have been dutifully inculcated, instilled, and fostered in them." In the conclusion we find that Simon believes that we should not seek high test scores as an end in themselves, "that getting a high-paying job is not the final reward of a college degree," we should take personal responsibility for racism in our nation, educators should help "people examine the headlong pursuit towards accumulating more and more material possessions and enjoying them less," and that we should try to do something to keep "our students from making drab and dreary marriages or being trapped into pointless jobs."

Now I or anyone else may agree or disagree with Simon on these or any other issues and positions. That is not the point. The point is that Simon not only takes these positions for himself, he clearly abandons his relativist's stance and manifestly implies that *we* should also hold these beliefs. And furthermore we should try to get others—"fathers and mothers," "people," "men and women," "educators," and "our students"—to also adopt them. But shortly after he pleads for *his* values as those we should teach and adopt he declares: ". . . we must not fall into the trap of believing that if only we could give boys and girls the right set of values to believe, they would avoid the mistakes of the rest of us. Nonsense!" Three sentences later he proclaims: "Values simply can't be given to anyone else. One can't value for other people. Each individual has to find his own values." In his presentation of Strategy no. 3 (Baker's Dozen), Simon makes it clear that there are no right answers, and that "The main thing is for each of us to know what we want and to see it in the perspective of what we like less." The directions for Strategy no. 5 (Personal Coat of Arms) stress that the teacher "establishes that there is no right answer."

Now how are we to reconcile these conflicting positions and contradictory directions for values clarification? It should be quite easy for the reader to take any of Simon's declared values that should be adopted generally and relate it to the relativistic directions for VC strategies and see the unresolvable problems. Perhaps it is clear why I have classified values clarification as an exemplar of an ethical position and form of values education that I have labeled *absolute relativism* (Stewart 1974). The basic VC premise can be fairly and concisely presented as: *All values statements are relative— except the following:* (1) this basic statement, (2) those essential for the values clarification theory and methodology, (3) those proclaimed by the VC writers, and (4) those deemed absolute by groups or organizations who want to use values clarification but keep their own values systems intact, e.g., Christian educators, schools, and others. In other words, values are absolutely relative, or perhaps they are relatively absolute. In one article, religious educators are told "there are no 'right' values." In a different article, they are told by the same author that there are some "right" values—"right," that is, if Christians say they are right, but there are fewer of these "immutable and absolute values than most of us realize." Obviously, this ambiguous and self-contradictory position would have to apply to *any* person, group, or organization. Or the values clarification people would have to decide for whom it does or does not apply—which would, of course, make them the absolute judges, a position they do not want to be in—or do they? This unresolved problem in VC shows us how far the old absolute/relative argument can take us. But, it seems to me, the VC leaders need to wrestle with the problem and make a clear and forthright statement of their position—a public affirmation of their values, that is.

Space does not permit me to go into the complex metaethical issues involved in relativism. They are so serious, however, that the reader's own evaluation of values clarification is incomplete without considering them. These matters are covered briefly in the outstanding statement by Adell cited earlier, touched on somewhat by Anne Colby (see chapter 17), and treated at greater length in Alan Lockwood's penetrating analysis of values clarification (see chapters 11 and 21). And, of course, the fundamental problem of moral relativism is treated abundantly in the literature of philosophy. Even a cursory look at some of that literature will reveal the deep structural problems that strike at the very heart of values clarification theory, and reveal the untenability of its basic premises.

Many of the problems presented so far stem from one basic problem: the failure of the creators and leaders of this movement to develop—thoroughly, systematically, and continuously—an integrated conceptual framework, a theory. Except for some of the questions raised by Kirschenbaum and some of his attempts to reformulate the theory, values clarification has accepted, and has remained committed to, an inadequate theory it inherited from Louis Raths—a theory that is philosophically indefensible and psychologically inadequate. To claim, as do Raths and Simon, that the theory is derived from John Dewey's ideas, especially his 1939 *Theory of Valuation*, may be somewhat of an exaggeration. It possibly reflects a misunderstanding of Dewey's thought, and certainly it needs explication not found in the VC literature. Some of Dewey's ideas have been adopted, but unsystematically and without regard for the context or the larger system of Dewey's thought. One significant difference between Dewey and the VC people is that his understanding of democracy was quite different from theirs. They use the same word but mean somewhat different things. Also, Dewey was a contextualist, but he was not an absolute relativist. Furthermore, and of primary importance, the values clarification people have failed to consider adequately or come to grips with either social psychology in general or developmental psychology in particular.

The research offered to support the validity and efficacy of values clarification is weak and seriously flawed, especially the research cited in chapter 10 of the basic VC text, *Values and Teaching*, by Raths, Harmin, and Simon. Many of their statements are nothing more than the subjective claims of the teachers and/or the researchers involved in the studies, and the objective findings are frequently inconclusive. Moreover the research designs have so many problems that even the conclusive findings cannot be taken seriously. Admittedly to conduct research in this field is extremely difficult, but to recognize this would be better than to cite dubious findings and defective designs as research support for the methodology. One of the most serious problems facing researchers in this arena is to control for the Hawthorne effect. Many of the observed outcomes of values clarification may be the result of the increased attention and/or the overall warming of the environment that may be a natural concomitant of this type of activity or of any change from one approach to another. It may be that any, or almost any, humane, open, and more affective approach could generate similar results. But this is an open question that requires a great deal of attention. In the meantime, the values clarification people need to be extremely conservative in their claims for empirical support.

The conceptual and logical contradictions and theoretical inadequacies of values clarification are especially evident in the Raths, Harmin, and Simon book cited earlier as the "bible" of the VC movement, and in the Simon and deSherbinin article also previously mentioned. The latter exemplifies the pervasive theoretical confusion and supports my claim that the VC creators have failed to conceptualize values, valuing, and other fundamental concepts in consistent and defensible terms. In the opening paragraph, Simon and deSherbinin assert: "There's no place to hide from your values. *Everything you do reflects them.* Even denying that *your values show in your every act* is a value indicator" (italics added).

In previous writings, however, VC writers have strongly emphasized that values are extremely rare phenomena reflected and manifested in very specific behaviors that fall under the umbrella defined by the now well-known seven criteria: *choosing*—(1) freely, (2) from alternatives, (3) after reflection; *prizing*—(4) cherishing, being happy with the choice, (5) willing to affirm the choice publicly; *acting*—(6) doing something with the choice, (7) repeatedly, in some pattern of life. Raths, Harmin, and Simon (1966, p. 28) assert emphatically: "Unless something satisfies *all* seven of the criteria . . . , we do not call it a value" (italics in original). And in the same book (p. 32), they make the following statement that directly contradicts the quotation cited above:

Of course, *it isn't true that everything we do represents our values. . . . Just by observing what people do, we are unable to determine if values are present.* We have to know if the individual prizes what he is doing, if he has chosen to do what he is doing, and if it constitutes a pattern in his life, etc. (Italics added)

These few excerpts merely illustrate the kinds of conflicts, ambiguities, and poor scholarship so characteristic of the VC theoretical foundations. But such problems are not necessarily in themselves cause for rejection or lack of credibility. All theories and practices suffer from similar flaws and weaknesses. The difference between defensible theories, sound practices, and solid scholarship, however, and the opposite so characteristic of faddish and superficial movements like values clarification is the degree to which the creators and defenders of the ideas and practices submit their work to public scrutiny and respond to professional criticism. One of the universally recognized hallmarks of true science is the progress made from the seeking and consideration of responsible evaluation by other scholars. Science and scholarship are matters of inquiry, evidence, and corroboration. Feelings and intuition, of course, are part of the evidence given proper consideration, but they are not sufficient in themselves. The basic VC theory, anemic as it is, has been in published form and widely distributed for at least a decade. And it has, for the most part, remained virtually unchanged in spite of enormous evaluation and criticism. Even the attempted reformulation of some aspects of the theory by one of the central figures of the movement,

Howard Kirschenbaum, has had no observable impact on some of the other leaders, especially Sidney Simon, the generally recognized leader of values clarification. In fact, even in chapter 9, Simon refers the reader to the original "bible" published ten years ago for the theory, without so much as a footnote acknowledging the work of his colleagues or others to update the idea base for the movement. Are we safe in concluding that Simon sees no problems with the theory or practice of values clarification? May we also safely conclude that he and most of the other VC leaders feel no need to respond to the frequent and serious criticism of the moral relativism? The indications are rather strong that Simon is quite content with the original theory and is considerably impervious to criticism.

Perhaps the reader and the users of values clarification will be willing to take a critical look at this important and successful movement. And perhaps they will be able to sort out the contradictions and problems from the benefits and strengths. I hope they will be able to look beneath the veneer and see this approach to values education objectively and in proper perspective. I hope they will be able to identify the hidden agenda and moralistic bag of virtues concealed behind the gossamer veil of absolute relativism.

Curiously, the virtues and vices that can be extrapolated from the VC literature are strangely reminiscent of those of the old character education approach used by Sunday school teachers, the Boy Scouts and Girl Scouts, and most traditional schools. It is the preaching, moralizing, and manipulating of these approaches, organizations, and institutions that the values clarification creators and workers have so effectively and so justifiably criticized. One of the greatest contributions of values clarification to the field of values/moral education has been its direct confrontation with traditional-authoritarian education, clearly revealing the inadequacy, inhumanity, and injustice of this approach. For values clarification to fall into the same traps, then, seems inexcusable. In fact, even in their article Simon and deSherbinin make the following claim: "Moralizing offers the illusion of looking like the right way to go, but the whole focus of trying to shape and manipulate people into accepting a given set of values is doomed to failure." The claim in this statement relates to the pragmatic inadequacy of moralizing, shaping, and manipulating. But anyone familiar with the VC literature and people knows that their opposition is more than pragmatic. It is made primarily on moral grounds. Yet the examples of VC research and applications I have already cited clearly reveal the particular values sought and the manipulations used to obtain them. I suggest that Simon and deSherbinin make statements they would disdain if read in connection with some other approach to values/moral education. Take, for example, the following statement, made in a plea to go beyond the traditional modeling approach: "Values clarifiers believe, however, that people who go through the process of deciding what they value will in the end reflect the ways one would hope, in any event, all good teachers would behave." How can these authors, in keeping with their basic premises, make a statement like this? In consideration of Sidney Simon's strident rejection of indoctrination and all related notions, contained in chapter 9, these kinds of declarations seem both preposterous and ludicrous, but boldly illuminating of the tremendously moralistic inner nature of values clarification and some of its leading figures.

I hope that this critique has pointed out some problems and raised some questions that will generate deeper reflection on the extremely important and influential movement known as values clarification. There is no question in my mind that this approach to values/moral education has made some significant contributions. If nothing more, it has increased awareness of the issues and generated an enormous amount of movement away from the restrictive and inhibiting forms of traditional moral education.

My assignment has been to take a look at the problems and weaknesses of values clarification. In spite of its significant and positive influence. I believe that VC has some potentially serious, even dangerous, problems and implications. Unfortunately, in my judgment, the movement is rooted in a confused philosophy of absolute relativism and in an inadequate psychology of instrumental individualism. It carries a mixed and conflicting bag of virtues. Some of its methodology is excellent and highly useful for approaching values/ moral development; but much of its methodology is faulty and some of it creates an illusion of significance that can lead one to think that more is happening than is really happening.

In conclusion, if values clarification is going to fulfill its promise and exceed its past glories, it will have to make some major reformulations and extend itself far beyond its present theoretical and empirical base. More than anything, the values clarification leaders must apply their basic principles to their own work: They must clarify Values Clarification in order to make it possible to choose wisely, publicly affirm a more rational program, and act repeatedly with humanity and justice to improve values/moral education. Otherwise, in the long run it will probably turn out to be one of those great fads that came into the educational world like a meteor, rose to the heights of commercial success and public acceptance, and burned itself out in the confusion of its own energy because it couldn't or wouldn't stop long enough to reflect, evaluate, change, and grow. Unless the present leaders of the movement, or new leaders, can reconstruct the present inadequate and defective foundation of values clarification and cure some of its most serious defects, I suspect that it will eventually fade into oblivion and be viewed in retrospect many years from now as one of those potentially great ideas that turned out to have more hope than substance and was, as Shakespeare said, "full of sound and fury, signifying nothing."

References

Adell, Arvid W. "Values Clarification Revised." *The Christian Century* 93, no. 16 (May 5, 1976): 436.

Kirschenbaum, Howard. "Beyond Values Clarification." *Readings in Values Clarification*, edited by Howard Kirschenbaum and Sidney B. Simon. Minneapolis: Winston Press, 1973.

Raths, Louis; Harmin, Merrill; and Simon, Sidney B. *Values and Teaching.* Columbus, Ohio: Charles E. Merrill, 1966.

Simon, Sidney B. "Three Ways To Teach Church School." *Readings in Values Clarification*, edited by Howard Kirschenbaum and Sidney B. Simon. Minneapolis: Winston Press, 1973.

Simon, Sidney B.; Howe, Leland; and Kirschenbaum, Howard. *Values Clarification: A Handbook of Practical Strategies for Teachers and Students.* New York: Hart, 1972.

Simon, Sidney B.; Daitch, Patricia; and Hartwell, Marie. "Value Clarification: New Mission for Religious Education." *Readings in Values Clarification*, edited by Howard Kirschenbaum and Sidney B. Simon. Minneapolis: Winston Press, 1973.

Simon, Sidney B., and deSherbinin, Polly. "Values Clarification: It Can Start Gently and Grow Deep." *Phi Delta Kappan* (June 1975): 679-83.

Stewart, John S. "Toward a Theory for Values Development Education." Ph.D. dissertation, Michigan State University, 1974.

11
A Critical View of Values Clarification

Alan L. Lockwood

What role, if any, should values play in the school curriculum? One response to this perennial question is embodied in the currently popular values clarification approach developed by Louis Raths, Merrill Harmin, and Sidney Simon (1966). Although their approach is being practiced by many teachers throughout the nation, their theory has not been subjected to systematic, critical scrutiny. This paper attempts to provide such an examination.

In this essay I will discuss three problem areas in values clarification: (1) the definition of value; (2) the characterization of effective treatment; and (3) the moral point of view. Prior to exploring these problem areas, however, I will briefly describe the values clarification approach.

Values Clarification

The theory incorporates the familiar assertion that the nature of technological society is such that a wide range of values impinge

Reprinted by permission from *Teachers College Record* 77, no. 1 (September 1975), pp. 35-50.

upon the consciousness of each citizen. In the face of this potpourri of values, young people are often confused and uncertain about which values to hold. Persons experiencing values confusion ". . . are often identifiable by idiosyncratic behavior patterns—apathy, flightiness, extreme uncertainty, and inconsistency; drift, overconformity, overdissension, and chronic posing, and, frequently, underachievement" (Raths, Harmin, and Simon 1966, p. 8). On the other hand, those who have attained value clarity do not manifest these characteristics but rather are ". . . positive, purposeful, enthusiastic, (and) proud" (p. 5).

Given these conditions, it is the task of each individual to ". . . wrest his own values from the available array" (p. 10). Values clarification is intended to provide a method through which ". . . humans *can* arrive at values by an intelligent process of choosing, prizing, and behaving."

In practice values clarification employs a variety of ingenious teaching techniques which encourage students to state their value preferences. The teacher responds to these initial value choices with questions or statements intended to help the student further clarify his views to determine whether he genuinely holds the values he has expressed. Examples of recommended questions are: Did you freely choose that value? Are you proud that you hold that view? What would be the consequence of that idea? Have you acted on the basis of that value? The reactions to these questions comprise the "clarifying response," the application of which ". . . results in his considering what he has chosen, what he prizes, and/or what he is doing. It stimulates him to clarify his thinking and behavior and thus to clarify his values; it encourages him to think about them" (p. 51).

By necessity this description has been sketchy. A fuller picture of the approach will emerge from the following discussion of three problem areas in values clarification.

The Definition of Value

Among scholars there is no definitional consensus for the term "value." Kurt Baier (1969, pp. 35-36) notes ten of the "more popular" definitions, indicating the variety of conceptions of value among academics. The advocates of values clarification have their own particular definition of value which I will discuss in this section. It is not my intent, given such a lack of definitional consensus, to claim their definition is literally "incorrect," but rather to show how their definition and conception of value reflects certain inadequacies in their theory.

The values clarification definition of value is synonymous with the prescribed process for obtaining a value. In order for something to *be* a value, it must be: (1) chosen freely, (2) chosen from alternatives, (3) chosen after careful consideration of the consequences of each alternative, (4) prized or cherished, (5) publicly affirmed, (6) acted upon, and (7) acted upon regularly. "Unless something satisfies *all* seven of the criteria . . . we do not call it a value" (Raths, Harmin, and Simon 1966, p. 28). Similarly, one obtains a value by choosing it freely from alternatives after careful consideration and so on through the seven steps.

In values clarification preferences which do not meet all seven criteria are relegated to the category of "value indicators." This rubric includes aspirations, beliefs, attitudes, interests, feelings, worries, activities, and goals. Value indicators suggest the possibility a person may have a value and, as a result, these indicators are subjected to the clarifying response. If after clarification the indicator meets all seven criteria, then it is raised to the level of a value (pp. 30-33).

There are three difficulties with the values clarification definition of value and the concomitant process for obtaining values. First, its distinction between values and value indicators is needlessly arbitrary, since it rules out of the realm of value much human experience which we may wish to construe in value terms. Second, by insisting that regularly performed action be a criteria for value, values clarification fails to deal with the problem of determining what action(s) is entailed by a value and the problems raised by individuals who, within themselves, hold conflicting values. Third, by conflating means and ends in the definition (defining a value as the process by which it is attained), values clarification apparently argues that only through it may one reach the objective of becoming proud, enthusiastic, purposeful, and productive. These points will be developed further in the remainder of this section.

The first difficulty with the Raths, Harmin, and Simon definition can be pointed out with two illustrations. Given the values clarification definition of value, neither of the following persons could be said to have a value:

1. A priest who was reared in a family with a strong religious tradition and who claims to value his religion. (If he did not freely choose his religion from among alternatives, he does not really value his religion.)

2. A person who claims to value the stiff prison sentences given drug offenders in certain European countries. (In values clarification verbal statements do not count as actions; therefore, because this person has not acted, he does not value the stiff prison sentences.*)

These examples point out two issues not adequately treated by the values clarification definition of value: The role of habit and/or family background in determining guiding values for individuals, and the physical impossibility of acting on certain value choices.

The second difficulty with the values clarification definition of value derives from the insistence that more than verbal behavior be present before a person can be said to have a value. Although the advocates of values clarification assert this condition, they fail to address the problem of determining what actions are consistent with what values.

The problem of determining what action should follow from any stated value can be illustrated with two rather current examples. In the debate over the morality/legality of abortion, both pro- and anti-abortion forces generally express a commitment to the value of life. The dispute over which policy is more consistent with the value of life is not easily resolved, especially when the question focuses on the life of the mother over the life of the fetus or when the disagreement centers on the question of when life begins. Likewise, national debate over the propriety of bombing North Vietnam provides a similar example. Proponents and opponents of the bombing both claimed to value peace, yet obviously, they did not agree about which action best exemplified that value.

Values clarification theory provides no assistance in resolving the dilemma presented in the preceding examples. By their definition of value those who favor abortion and those who oppose it can be said to value life; similarly, those who favor bombing and those who oppose it can be said to value peace. Perhaps the advocates of values

---

*"The person who talks about something but never does anything about it is dealing with something other than a value" (Raths, Harmin, and Simon 1966, p. 29).

clarification would contend that all of these people "have values" because they act on what they claim to value. The values clarification theory of values would thus be in the position of asserting the same value can support mutually contradictory actions. Such an assertion would appear to vitiate one of the fundamental objectives of values clarification—developing values which provide a clear and consistent guide to behavior.* The previous illustrations show that, while *individuals* may feel their actions are consistent with their values, it is an open question as to what actions, if any, are entailed by commitment to particular values. Values clarification theory prefers to ignore this profound question.

Finally, the insistence that values be linked to repeated action does not speak to the case of persons holding conflicting values. Value conflicts exist not only between persons but within them as well. For example, an individual may claim to value national security and the right to privacy. This same individual may also support the wiretapping of assistants to the Secretary of State but oppose the break-in of Daniel Ellsberg's psychiatrist's office. Using the values clarification definition of value, it is not clear what might be construed about the values of this person. It might be said that he values national security because he supports the wiretapping, and in addition, he values the right to privacy because he opposed the break-in. However, the break-in was publicly justified as necessary for national security; thus if he claims to value national security, why doesn't he support the break-in? Similarly, wiretapping is generally seen as an infringement on the right to privacy; therefore, if he values the right to privacy, why doesn't he oppose wiretapping? Values clarification advocates do not provide any insight into this dilemma. They might claim that in one situation our hypothetical citizen values privacy over national security and in another situation he values national security over privacy. Such an assertion would further indicate a weakness in their definition of value. Their definition demands that a person act repeatedly on the basis of a value before it can be considered a value. Therefore, we must conclude either that intrapersonal *value* conflicts cannot exist or that our citizen values neither national security nor privacy.

------

*This objective of values clarification is variously stated throughout *Values and Teaching*, but particularly in chapters 2 and 3.

The relationship of values to action is clearly problematic.* By demanding that values yield repeatable actions, values clarification theory seriously underestimates the difficulty of determining what actions, if any, are entailed by particular values and thoroughly ignores the difficult problems presented by value conflicts.

The third difficulty with values clarification stems from its defining values synonymously with the process by which they presumably are obtained. The collapsing of the means-ends distinction in their definition of value is not *per se* inappropriate. A problem does arise, however, because the primary purpose is not to help people obtain values but rather to help them become positive, purposeful, enthusiastic, and proud. The attainment of values is not an achievement of intrinsic worth but is desired because it supposedly *leads to* the development of persons who are positive, purposeful, etc. By conflating means and ends in their definition of values and then contending that the attainment of values promotes certain desired personal qualities, the advocates of values clarification give the misleading impression that it is only through their seven-step valuing process that persons can become positive, purposeful, enthusiastic, and proud. The fallacious syllogism implied is:

Persons who go through values clarification become positive, purposeful, enthusiastic, and proud.

Johnny is positive, purposeful, enthusiastic, and proud.

Johnny has gone through values clarification.

Unless the advocates of values clarification have some special unstated definition of their four desired qualities, it seems obvious that pride, purpose, etc., can be obtained through means other than and antithetical to values clarification. Anthropologists often remark on the pride and purposiveness of members of traditional societies (Masai warriors, Samoan tribesmen, etc.). It is characteristic of traditional societies that custom guides behavior, not values or beliefs that are freely chosen after thoughtful consideration of consequences.

---

*The difficulty of conceptualizing and identifying the relationship between values and behavior is well-documented in both philosophical and social scientific research. Note, for example, Stuart Hampshire's *Thought and Action* and Gunnar Myrdal's *An American Dilemma*.

Visitors to the Chinese mainland regularly note the pride, enthusiasm, and purpose of the citizenry, and yet, Chinese education and other social institutions are typically described as indoctrinatory and propagandizing—both "nonrational" modes of values education. The advocates of values clarification do not persuasively rule out "nonrational" means of promoting pride, enthusiasm, etc. The only argument mustered against these methods is an unsubstantiated claim that ". . . those methods do not seem to have resulted in deep commitments of any sort." "They just do not seem to work very well" (Raths, Harmin, and Simon 1966, p. 40). Unless one accepts the unwarranted claim that the seven-step valuing process is more potent than other methods of attaining their desired ends, values clarification advocates are unable to defend their approach in any convincing way. To make the point with an extreme case: If we found that the distribution of a drug could efficiently and potently develop pride and enthusiasm, values clarification theory, in its present formulation, could offer no substantial objection.

Characterization of Effective Treatment

In the previous section certain difficulties stemming from the theory of values clarification were discussed. In this section the nature of the treatment process prescribed by values clarification will be considered. Advocates of values clarification contend that those who receive their treatment become positive, purposeful, enthusiastic, and proud. Assuming such results occur, we may fairly ask what is the process which brings them about?

The proponents of values clarification are not always clear, though they characterize their process as one of rational choice. They stress the rational component of valuing, particularly in the emphasis on choosing freely after thoughtful consideration of consequences. They underplay what is grossly labelled the affective domain: "Although values have some of this component, they lean more heavily toward the intellectual side" (Raths, Harmin, and Simon 1966, p. 199).

While the stress is on the rational or "intellectual" aspect of valuing, values clarification proponents prescribe a role for the teacher which derives from Carl Rogers' description of client-centered therapy. For example, the teacher who would employ value clarification is urged to be nonjudgmental, trusting, a good listener, student-centered and, at times, to express "unconditional acceptance of the student and problem" (p. 149). These are the characteristics of a client-centered therapist, and while the advocates of values clarification assert that "clarifying is not therapy" (p. 80), the striking similarity between their approach and Rogerian work demands further investigation.

To support the claim that values clarification is not therapy, Raths et al. attempt to distinguish between the symptoms of values confusion and the symptoms of emotional confusion. They state that values clarification should be employed with those who experience values confusion. Someone with emotional problems should seek help elsewhere because ". . . value-clarifying experiences are probably of little benefit and may even add to his disturbances" (p. 182).

Determining which students have unmet emotional needs and which have unmet values needs is a difficult task of assessment. The advocates of values clarification provide little guidance for making this diagnostic distinction. They define the following as "behaviors" indicative of unmet emotional needs and unmet values needs (p. 200).

Symptoms of unmet emotional needs	*Symptoms of unmet values needs*
Aggression	Overdissension
Withdrawal	Apathy
Submission	Overconformity
Regression to an earlier age	Flightiness
Psychosomatic illness	Indecisiveness
	Pretending/role-playing

This symptomology makes it difficult to determine if values clarification is treating emotional needs or value needs. For example, how do we decide if a student's behavior is overdissenting as opposed to aggressive; overconforming as opposed to submissive, etc.? The failure to make clear distinctions between emotion- and value-related manifestations increases the likelihood that values clarification may be treating problems which have traditionally been the domain of therapy—a domain values clarification claims to shun.

There is significant correspondence between values clarification and client-centered therapy regarding: (1) the conditions which produce a need for treatment; (2) the outcomes of successful treatment; (3) the key aspects of the treatment process; and (4) the role of the therapist/teacher in the prescribed treatment. Chart 1 summarizes these similarities (at the beginning of each column section is my summary followed by pertinent quotations from the authors).

The similarities between client-centered therapy and values clarification are significant enough to conclude that values clarification is, in essence, a form of client-centered therapy.* Establishing a trusting atmosphere in which a threapist or teacher is nonjudgmental and accepting may be important to the *preconditions* needed for a variety of therapeutic or educational treatments. In client-centered therapy, however, the relationship between the client and therapist and the therapist's attitude toward the client are more than preconditions, they are the *essential* features of the treatment. I contend that in values clarification also these "affective" elements are the essential features of the treatment and not preconditions which lead to some form of rational-cognitive deliberation. In summary:

1. The problems identified for treatment with values clarification are uncertainty, inconsistency, apathy, flightiness, drift, overconformity, overdissension, and role-playing.

2. Persons who overcome these problems become purposeful, positive, enthusiastic, and proud.

3. Client-centered therapy is a proven method for treating problems of uncertainty, inconsistency, etc.

4. The nonmoralizing, trusting, accepting, supportive features essential to client-centered therapy are also central features of values clarification.

------

*Testimonials from persons who have experienced values clarification further indicate the approach has an impact like that of client-centered therapy:

From a woman volunteer: "I learned that I don't allow women to influence my life as much as I do men."

From a male principal: "I learned that I'm opening up and relaxing, but I still have my inhibitions."

A fourth principal: "I relearned that I get a very nice high from sharing parts of my life with other people and hearing about theirs" (Gray 1972).

Chart 1

Similarities Between Client-Centered Therapy and Values Clarification on Certain Key Topics

Topic	Client-centered therapy*	Values clarification†
1. Conditions which produce the need for treatment	Modern society with its array of value positions makes it difficult for people to choose a satisfying way of life.	Modern society with its array of value positions makes it difficult for people to choose a satisfying way of life.
	"But in our modern culture with its conflicting subcultures, and its contradictory sets of values, goals, and perceptions, the individual tends to be exposed to a realization of discrepancies in his perceptions. Thus internal conflict is multiplied." (CCT, p. 192)	"Could it be, we wonder, that the pace and complexity of modern life has so exacerbated the problem of deciding what is good and what is right and what is worthy that large numbers of children are finding it increasingly bewildering, even overwhelming, to decide what is worth valuing, what is worth one's time and energy?" (p. 7)
	"It seems to be true that early in therapy the person is living by values he has introjected from others, from his personal cultural environment." (CCT, p. 149)	"Somehow or another the idea is held by adults that their chief function—in relationship to children—is to *tell* them things." (p. 24)
2. The outcomes of successful treatment	Persons tend to value themselves as worthwhile, become more able to function productively, develop their own self-evaluations, and become more consistent and congruent.	Persons become more productive and proud of themselves. They see their role in choosing their own values, and their verbally-stated values become more consistent and congruent with their behavior.
	"He moves toward a conception of himself as a person of worth, as a self-directing person, able to form standards and values upon the basis of his own experience. He develops much more positive attitudes toward himself." (OBAP, p. 65)	"In different words, many students have been helped to become more purposeful, more enthusiastic, more positive and more aware of what is worth striving for." (p. 12)

Topic	Client-centered therapy*	Values clarification†
	The client exhibits "...improved functioning in life tasks; improvement in reading on the part of school children; improvement in adjustment to job training and job performance on the part of adults." (CCT, pp. 184-85)	"It is especially useful for students who are difficult to motivate and are sometimes called slow learners . . . the value strategies have been found effective in moving under-achievers to normal work levels." (p. 191)
	"...the value system becomes more realistic and comfortable and more nearly in harmony with the perceived self.... Behavior continues to be consistent with the concept of self, and alters as it alters." (CCT, p. 195)	"Undergoing this, some students may find the thoughtful consistency between words and deeds that characterizes values." (p. 80)
3. Key aspects of the treatment process	An atmosphere of trust and acceptance is established in which the client examines his own feelings and experiences, and accepts responsibility for himself and his own judgments.	An atmosphere is established in which persons must be able to express their ideas and feelings without contradiction from others. The clarifying response is nonjudgmental, helping the student recognize his own confusions and his responsibility to make his own decisions.
	"The individual increasingly comes to feel that this locus of evaluation lies within himself. Less and less does he look to others for approval or disapproval; for standards to live by; for decisions and choices." (OBAP, p. 119)	"It puts the responsibility on the student to look at his behavior or his ideas and to think and decide for himself what it is he wants." (p. 53)
	"In this atmosphere of safety, protection and acceptance, the firm boundaries of self-organization relax.... It involves a reorganization of values, with the organism's own experience clearly recognized as providing the evidence for the valuations." (CCT, p. 193)	"Why can't a role be defined that would help a child take all the confusion that already exists in his mind, remove it, look at it, examine it, turn it around, and make some order out of it?" (p. 45) "The real problem is that almost no one sees the necessity for helping a child to make some order out of the confusion which has been created inside his head." (p. 24)

	Role
4. Role of the therapist/ teacher	"...interaction at this emotional level, rather than interaction at an intellectual, cognitive level, regardless of the content concerned, is the effective ingredient in therapeutic growth." (CCT, p. 160) The therapist is intimately related to establishing the process. He or she must be nonjudgmental, accepting, trusting, empathetic. The client finds "...every aspect of self which he exposes is equally accepted, equally valued." (CCT, pp. 192-93) "...he experiences a freedom from threat which is decidedly new to him." (CCT, p. 192) "In client-centered therapy, however, one description of the counselor's behavior is that he consistently keeps the locus of evaluation with the client." (CCT, p. 150) The client "...finds the therapist showing a consistent and unconditional positive regard for him and his feelings." (OBAP, p. 63) "...when the counselor perceives and accepts the client as he is, when he lays aside all evaluation and enters into the perceptual frame of reference of the client, he frees the client to explore his life and experience anew..." (CCT, p. 48)	"Values require a nondefensive, open, and thoughtful climate." (p. 106) "There is a spirit, a mood, required that we cannot satisfactorily describe or measure except to say that it seems related to a basic and honest respect for students." (p. 81) The teacher must be nonjudgmental, not "moralizing," and accepting of the students' views. He or she must provide a setting and seek to draw out the students' feelings and ideas. "...we emphasize the need for a nonjudgmental approach..." (p. 77) "...students will probably not enter the perplexing process of clarifying values...if they perceive that the teacher does not respect them. If trust is not communicated—" (p. 81) "The theory outlines a role for the teacher that is characterized by the following: 1. Unconditional acceptance of the student and the problem. 2. No advice-giving, even when that is requested, but many clarifying questions and comments. 3. Looking at the issue from the vantage point of the values of the student and not of the teacher." (pp. 149-50)

---

*All quotations from Carl Rogers, *On Becoming a Person* (Boston: Houghton Mifflin, 1961), or Carl Rogers, *Client-Centered Therapy* (Boston: Houghton Mifflin, 1965). After each quotation in the text the appropriate source is abbreviated and followed by the page reference.

†All quotations taken from Raths, Harmin, and Simon (1966). Page references included in text after each quotation.

5. Those for whom client-centered therapy is successful become purposeful, positive, enthusiastic, and proud.

6. Those for whom values clarification is successful become purposeful, positive, enthusiastic, and proud.

7. Assuming that the above points are true, there is no compelling reason to see any significant difference between the processes of client-centered therapy and values clarification in the treatment of the aforementioned problems.

8. Therefore, values clarification is successful in developing positive, purposeful, enthusiastic, and proud persons to the extent that it incorporates the essential elements of client-centered therapy.

The claim that values clarification is a form of client-centered therapy is significant in a number of ways. First, it asserts that, in spite of their protestations, practitioners of values clarification are employing a treatment which may fairly be called therapy. Advocates of values clarification should clarify their position on this point, especially since they feel that therapy is inappropriate for the problems they are treating. Second, the effective psychological processes stimulated by values clarification should not be characterized as rational-intellectual. The processes stimulated by successful client-centered therapy would best be characterized as emotional-affective. Finally, casting values education curricula in the mold of therapy, with its primary emphasis on personal dysfunctions, unnecessarily restricts the range of objectives, issues, and questions which may be encompassed by values education curricula. In the final section of this paper I will argue that values clarification represents an indefensible moral point of view which should not be promulgated by values education and which can be escaped only by first shedding the mantle of therapy.

The Moral Point of View

The advocates of values clarification consistently emphasize that there must be no "moralizing" in value education. They oppose authoritarian, indoctrinatory approaches in which the teacher or institution attempts to foist upon students a particular set of right answers to value questions. Simple rejection of indoctrination, however, does not exempt values clarification, or any program of values education, from an examination of its moral point of view.

The moral point of view of a program in value education reveals itself, to a great extent, in how the following questions are answered: What value issues form the content of the program? Are all value decisions equally valid? How are value conflicts treated? How should value decisions be made, and are some ways of making these decisions better than others?

The value issues addressed in values clarification are primarily those related to making decisions about personal preferences. The questions raised direct the student to consider how he chooses to lead his life, what career he seeks, how he uses his leisure time, what kind of person he wants to be, what kind of people he admires and what actions he would take in different situations. Values clarification does not direct students to consider value conflict dilemmas of the type cited earlier, nor do students confront what Frankena (1963, p. 47) calls ". . . the central question of normative ethics, namely, that of the basic principles, criteria, or standards by which we are to determine what we morally ought to do, what is morally right or wrong, and what our moral rights are."

Values clarification appears, at least by default, to hold the view that all values are equally valid. The accepting role of the teacher, the admonition to avoid moralizing, the avoidance of conflict, and the nurturant and trusting environment yield the distinct impression that all decisions arrived at through the prescribed process are equally defensible and acceptable. The advocates of values clarification do not seriously entertain such fundamental questions as: assuming Adolph Hitler, Charles Manson, Martin Luther King, and Albert Schweitzer held values which met the seven criteria, are their values equally valid, praiseworthy, and/or good?

As we have seen, values clarification is not oriented to interpersonal value conflict, but to some extent it considers intrapersonal conflict. This conflict is conceived as inconsistency between statements and actions. For example, if I say I wish to become a neurosurgeon but spend most of my time studying military history, through values clarification I would examine the seeming contradiction between my desires and my actions and attempt to determine what I *really* value. "Complicated judgments are involved and what is really valued is reflected in the outcome of life as it is finally lived" (Raths, Harmin, and Simon 1966, p. 27).

We have also seen that the seven-step valuing process, while apparently regarded as the best way to obtain values, is not supported by a thorough philosophical defense. Against other modes of attaining values, values clarification is presumed superior on the tenuous claim of greater potency in promoting certain personality characteristics.

The previously summarized features of values clarification support the contention that the moral point of view imbedded in values clarification is that of the ethical relativist. In its simplest definition, ethical relativism holds that one person's values are as good as another's; everyone is entitled to his own opinion; and when it comes to morality, there is no way of showing one opinion is better than another. Because values clarification appears to embrace this stance, it is worthwhile to consider some of the central arguments against relativism.

The fundamental objection to ethical relativism is that it can be used to justify virtually any activity in which an individual or a society chooses to engage. Veatch (1962, pp. 44-45) summarizes this point as follows:

Since all standards of value are utterly without foundation, since no way of life or course of action is really superior to any other, then the sensible thing for me to do is

(1) to cultivate an attitude of greater tolerance toward the various modes of life and patterns of behavior that men have chosen for themselves . . ., or

(2) to create my own set of values and attempt to enforce them with all the energy of which I am capable . . ., or

(3) to throw off all moral standards and norms of conduct and simply follow the lead of my impulses and inclinations . . ., or

(4) to go along with the crowd and merely abide by the standards of the community of which I am a member, this being the line of least resistance and the one least likely to get me into trouble and difficulty . . . .

Veatch's examples illustrate the variety of positions which can be justified by relativism, some of which, e.g., tolerance (1) and fascism (2), stand in striking opposition to one another. Persons accustomed to living in a democratic society may tacitly assume that tolerance and respect for diversity are logically entailed by relativism.* Clearly, however, if they are to remain relativists, they must

---

*Raths, Harmin, and Simon (p. 227) *may* hold such a view. In speculating about the value outcomes of values clarification, they say, "Our guess, based upon the evidence thus far available, would be that they would be those associated with the use of intelligence, the involvement of individuals in group decisions, the openness of communication, and others associated with democracy."

grant that tolerance is simply a view they happen to adopt, one which has no more to commend it than intolerance. Consequently, relativism does not provide a consistent basis from which we can determine our obligations or guide our lives—a basis which values clarification wishes to supply.

A second inadequacy of relativism is its inability to generate a satisfactory method for resolving interpersonal conflicts of value. A relativist might argue that there is no point trying to resolve such conflicts because each person's values are right for him. Nevertheless, we cannot deny that there are times when such conflicts occur and some resolution must be made. Debates over the Southeast Asian war, busing for racial balance, abortion laws, sex education, and so on attest to the existence of value conflicts which demand resolution. Relativism provides no basis for choosing among the variety of ways in which conflicts might be resolved. Blackmail, majority rule, bribery, judicial review, physical force, and rational debate are a number of ways value conflicts might be resolved. A relativist could support any of these means of conflict resolution, but he could not, in any compelling or nonarbitrary way, argue that one method is superior to another. For some reason values clarification theory, quite likely because of its inherent relativism, has chosen either to ignore or to avoid this fundamental issue.

If correct, my contention that values clarification embodies ethical relativism as its moral point of view is noteworthy for at least two reasons: First, a program of value education which devotes its attention to questions of personal preference and desire presents a truncated and myopic view of morality. A program which avoids the controversies associated with value conflict, conflict resolution, and moral justification trivializes the complexity of value issues in human affairs. Second, a values education program which, perhaps unwittingly, is grounded in ethical relativism must accept the possibility that its students will embrace ethical relativism as their moral point of view—clearly an achievement of dubious merit.

Conclusion

As a postscript to this essay I would like to speculate on why values clarification, or any program of values education, can come to represent ethical relativism.

The creators of values clarification strongly oppose authoritarian, indoctrinatory approaches to value education. Such approaches are subject to charges of being indefensibly arbitrary and violative of certain human rights. In avoiding the pitfalls of authoritarianism, however, it is not necessary to embrace ethical relativism. There does exist a number of viable approaches to value education which reject *both* relativism and authoritarianism.*

Another explanation for the relativism in values clarification may stem from what I have claimed is its notion of therapeutic value education. In developing a therapy, we are presumably concerned with helping persons recover from some malaise. Thus we would devote our energy and attention to defining, diagnosing, and treating the infirmity. The primary criterion for success would, quite reasonably, be whether our treatment worked, not whether we have exposed our clients to the full range and complexity of value issues in

---

*The following are three prominent examples which reject both relativism and indoctrination in value education. My summaries are necessarily highly over-simplified:

1. The work of philosopher John Wilson and his associates. This approach takes the view that there are identifiable capacities necessary for the practice of any morality, e.g., empathy and awareness of consequences. These capacities or "second-order" principles form the basis for curriculum in moral education. J. Wilson, N. Williams, and B. Sugarman (1967).

2. The work of Lawrence Kohlberg and his associates. As a developmental psychologist, Kohlberg has identified six "stages" of moral development which emerge in an invariant sequence. Each stage represents a philosophical point of view on various ethical issues. On philosophical grounds Kohlberg argues that the final stage of development, characterized by a full understanding of justice as equality, is superior to the earlier stages. Using psychological principles derived from research on stage development, Kohlberg presents a curriculum for moral education which facilitates and stimulates development through the stages. L. Kohlberg (1970); L. Kohlberg and E. Turiel (1971); and L. Kohlberg and R. Mayer (1972).

3. The public issues social studies curriculum developed by Donald Oliver and his associates. The curriculum is derived from value concepts assumed in the idea of a democratic society, the most abstract being respect for human dignity. The curriculum is designed to help students recognize and resolve value conflicts which arise in public policy debates. Central to the approach is instruction and practice in the use of "rational consent" in decision-making. D. Oliver and J. Shaver (1966); and F. Newmann and D. Oliver (1970). Specific curriculum materials created under the direction of Oliver and Newmann are published as *The Public Issues Series* (Columbus, Ohio: American Educational Publications).

human affairs. Our efforts in helping persons recover from their ailments may well be justifiable, even laudable, but it would be misleading to characterize our work as values education. In their efforts to help students overcome their apathy and uncertainty, the advocates of values clarification appear to be more concerned with their treatment's therapeutic effectiveness than with an examination and justification of its moral point of view.

In this essay I have subjected the theory and practice of values clarification to a rigorous and, I believe, responsible critical examination. I have identified three aspects of the approach that need further explication by its proponents: its definition of value and the role of action in that definition; its characterization of the process leading to successful treatment; and the moral point of view embodied in the approach. It was not my intention to denigrate or destroy values clarification or other efforts at developing defensible and workable programs of value education. On the contrary, I hope that this criticism has contributed to the arduous but necessary task of developing a responsible position on the role of values in education.

References

Baier, K., and Rescher, N. (eds.). *Values and the Future.* New York: Free Press, 1969.

Frankena, W. K. *Ethics.* Englewood Cliffs, N.J.: Prentice-Hall, 1963.

Gray, F. "Doing Something About Values." *Learning: The Magazine for Creative Teaching* (December 1972): 17.

Kohlberg, L. "Education for Justice: A Modern Statement of the Platonic View." *Moral Education,* edited by Nancy F. and Theodore Sizer. Cambridge, Mass.: Harvard University Press, 1970.

Kohlberg, L., and Turiel, E. "Moral Development and Moral Education." *Psychology and Educational Practice,* edited by Gerald S. Lesser. Chicago: Scott, Foresman, 1971.

Kohlberg, L., and Mayer, R. "Development as the Aim of Education." *Harvard Educational Review* 42, no. 4 (November 1972): 449-96.

Newmann, F., and Oliver, D. *Clarifying Public Controversy.* Boston: Little, Brown, 1970.

Oliver, D. *Teaching Public Issues in the High School.* Boston: Houghton Mifflin, 1966.

Raths, L.; Harmin, M.; and Simon, S. *Values and Teaching.* Columbus, Ohio: Charles E. Merrill, 1966.

Rogers, Carl. *On Becoming a Person.* Boston: Houghton Mifflin, 1961.

Rogers, Carl. *Client-Centered Therapy.* Boston: Houghton Mifflin, 1965.

Veatch, H. B. *Rational Man.* Bloomington, Ind.: Indiana University Press, 1962.
Wilson, J.; Williams, N.; and Sugarman, B. *Introduction to Moral Education.*
    Baltimore: Penguin, 1967.

PART III

The Cognitive-Developmental Approach

Introduction

Men have always been attracted by the idea that there exists in us some ideal form of the good. Certainly, we have seen the idea of man possessing a spark of the divinity reassert itself many times in intellectual thought. Plato, Rousseau, and Emerson all saw man possessing some reflection of ideal perfection. To these thinkers, the job of life was to bring the spark of the divine to the surface, to strip away the earthly trappings and the corrupting influences of society. They believed that there is something moving in man, some dynamic that is pushing toward a higher level of existence. The cognitive-developmental approach to moral education is in this intellectual tradition.

The major exponent of the cognitive-developmental approach is Professor Lawrence Kohlberg of Harvard University. Kohlberg built upon the basic insights of Jean Piaget, the Swiss psychologist, and on the educational views of John Dewey. Piaget, through close observation of children, found stages of moral thought. At various stages of development, the thought of children possesses specific characteristics. Also, Piaget discovered that during the course of their childhood, children sequentially move through clear and distinct stages of thought process. Piaget's basic insights were developed and expanded upon by Lawrence Kohlberg. Kohlberg started asking people questions about how they would respond to specific moral dilemmas and he closely analyzed their responses. He paid particular attention to the form of their answers rather than how they decided on a particular moral dilemma. In what has been an immensely revealing experiment that is still going on, Kohlberg asked seventy-five young men to respond to a series of moral dilemmas. He has continued to go back to these men every three years in the intervening twenty years. These interviews, and a good deal of related work, have been the basis for one of the most startling insights into how people change in the way that they think about moral issues. In chapter 12, Kohlberg describes his theory of moral stages and how this theory relates to the school's role in the moral education of children. Chapter 13 is a very illuminating essay by Kohlberg on the hidden curriculum in our schools. Here, Kohlberg gives particular attention to the moral implications of what is below the surface, but in the very fabric of the school experience.

Kohlberg's theory is the focus of a great deal of attention by educational psychologists and curriculum developers. In many quarters there is an attempt to use the cognitive-developmental approach in school-based programs of moral education. Three selections are included that describe attempts to apply Kohlberg's theories to the classroom. Chapter 14 is by Edmund V. Sullivan and Clive Beck, both of the Ontario Institute for Studies in Education. These two researchers have applied the cognitive-developmental approach to both elementary and secondary school classrooms in Ontario. In this article they describe their work in schools and make specific suggestions for teacher training and development. Chapter 15, by Ralph L. Mosher and Paul Sullivan, reports on a program of psychological education. While Kohlberg's theory is an important central framework for this program of psychological education, his intervention strategy, using discussion of moral issues in the classroom, is only one of several approaches used by Mosher and Sullivan to bring about greater psychological development of children. Chapter 16, by James Rest, summarizes a number of classroom applications of Kohlberg's theories and in addition further clarifies and amplifies the relationship between moral and psychological education. Chapter 17, by Anne Colby, is an interesting attempt to compare and contrast Kohlberg's cognitive-developmental approach with Raths' and Simon's values clarification techniques. The author analyzes differences but ends with suggesting how the two approaches can be integrated in the classroom.

Part III concludes with some critiques of the cognitive-developmental approach, particularly as formulated by Lawrence Kohlberg. In chapter 18, R. S. Peters, the distinguished British philosopher, very succinctly raises a series of four "omissions" of the cognitive-developmental theory. In chapter 19, Jack Fraenkel, a well-known social studies educator, raises critical questions about what he calls "the Kohlberg bandwagon." Among the most telling are those dealing with the actual application of the cognitive-developmental approach to moral reasoning in the classroom.

Although there is much work to be done to translate this most interesting theory of moral development to programs of moral education in schools, there is also a great deal of interest and activity being focused on this approach. Research and curriculum development and testing is going on in many corners of North America and elsewhere. One of the major attractions of this theory is that it holds great promise for the schools.

At the very core of Kohlberg's theory is the existence of a positive force, a telos, that is moving in the direction of more sophisticated and more comprehensive moral judgments. It becomes the task of the educator, then, to facilitate this natural impulse toward growth with an environment that supports the development of moral thinking.

12

The Cognitive-Developmental Approach to Moral Education

Lawrence Kohlberg

In this article, I present an overview of the cognitive-developmental approach to moral education and its research foundations, compare it with other approaches, and report the experimental work my colleagues and I are doing to apply the approach.

Moral Stages

The cognitive-developmental approach was fully stated for the first time by John Dewey. The approach is called *cognitive* because it recognizes that moral education, like intellectual education, has its basis in stimulating the *active thinking* of the child about moral issues and decisions. It is called developmental because it sees the aims of moral education as movement through moral stages. According to Dewey (1964):

The aim of education is growth or *development*, both intellectual and moral. Ethical and psychological principles can aid the school in the *greatest of all constructions—the building of a free and powerful character*. Only knowledge of

Reprinted by permission from *Phi Delta Kappan* (June 1975): pp. 670-75.

the *order and connection of the stages in psychological development can insure this.* Education is the work of *supplying the conditions* which will enable the psychological functions to mature in the freest and fullest manner.

Dewey postulated three levels of moral development: (1) the *premoral* or *preconventional* level "of behavior motivated by biological and social impulses with results for morals," (2) the *conventional* level of behavior "in which the individual accepts with little critical reflection the standards of his group," and (3) the *autonomous* level of behavior in which "conduct is guided by the individual thinking and judging for himself whether a purpose is good, and does not accept the standard of his group without reflection."*

Dewey's thinking about moral stages was theoretical. Building upon his prior studies of cognitive stages, Jean Piaget (1948) made the first effort to define stages of moral reasoning in children through actual interviews and through observations of children (in games with rules). Using this interview material, Piaget defined the premoral, the conventional, and the autonomous levels as follows: (1) the *premoral stage*, where there was no sense of obligation to rules; (2) the *heteronomous stage*, where the right was literal obedience to rules and an equation of obligation with submission to power and punishment (roughly ages four-eight); and (3) the *autonomous stage*, where the purpose and consequences of following rules are considered and obligation is based on reciprocity and exchange (roughly ages eight-twelve).†

In 1955 I started to redefine and validate (through longitudinal and cross-cultural study) the Dewey-Piaget levels and stages. The resulting stages are presented in the appendix to chapter 13. . . . The notion that stages can be *validated* by longitudinal study implies that stages have definite empirical characteristics (Kohlberg 1975). The concept of stages (as used by Piaget and myself) implies the following characteristics:

---

*These levels correspond roughly to our three major levels: the preconventional, the conventional, and the principled. Similar levels were propounded by William McDougall, Leonard Hobhouse, and James Mark Baldwin.

†Piaget's stages correspond to our first three stages: Stage 0 (premoral), Stage 1 (heteronomous), and Stage 2 (instrumental reciprocity).

1. Stages are "structured wholes," or organized systems of thought. Individuals are *consistent* in level of moral judgment.

2. Stages form an *invariant sequence.* Under all conditions except extreme trauma, movement is always forward, never backward. Individuals never skip stages; movement is always to the next stage up.

3. Stages are "hierarchical integrations." Thinking at a higher stage includes or comprehends within it lower-stage thinking. There is a tendency to function at or prefer the highest stage available.

Each of these characteristics has been demonstrated for moral stages. Stages are defined by responses to a set of verbal moral dilemmas classified according to an elaborate scoring scheme. Validating studies include:

1. A twenty-year study of fifty Chicago-area boys, middle- and working-class. Initially interviewed at ages ten-sixteen, they have been reinterviewed at three-year intervals thereafter.

2. A small, six-year longitudinal study of Turkish village and city boys of the same age.

3. A variety of other cross-sectional studies in Canada, Britain, Israel, Taiwan, Yucatan, Honduras, and India.

With regard to the structured whole or consistency criterion, we have found that more than 50 percent of an individual's thinking is always at one stage, with the remainder at the next adjacent stage (which he is leaving or which he is moving into).

With regard to invariant sequence, our longitudinal results have been presented in the *American Journal of Orthopsychiatry* (Kohlberg and Elfenbein 1975), and indicate that on every retest individuals were either at the same stage as three years earlier or had moved up. This was true in Turkey as well as in the United States.

With regard to the hierarchical integration criterion, it has been demonstrated that adolescents exposed to written statements at each of the six stages comprehend or correctly put in their own words all statements at or below their own stage but fail to comprehend any statements more than one stage above their own (Rest, Turiel, and Kohlberg 1969). Some individuals comprehend the next stage above their own; some do not. Adolescents prefer (or rank as best) the highest stage they can comprehend.

To understand moral stages, it is important to clarify their relations to stage of logic or intelligence, on the one hand, and to moral behavior on the other. Maturity of moral judgment is not highly correlated with IQ or verbal intelligence (correlations are only in the 30s, accounting for 10 percent of the variance). Cognitive development, in the stage sense, however, is more important for moral development than such correlations suggest. Piaget has found that after the child learns to speak there are three major stages of reasoning: the intuitive, the concrete operational, and the formal operational. At around age seven, the child enters the stage of concrete logical thought: He can make logical inferences, classify, and handle quantitative relations about concrete things. In adolescence individuals usually enter the stage of formal operations. At this stage they can reason abstractly, i.e., consider all possibilities, form hypotheses, deduce implications from hypotheses, and test them against reality.*

Since moral reasoning clearly is reasoning, advanced moral reasoning depends upon advanced logical reasoning; a person's logical stage puts a certain ceiling on the moral stage he can attain. A person whose logical stage is only concrete operational is limited to the preconventional moral stages (Stages 1 and 2). A person whose logical stage is only partially formal operational is limited to the conventional moral stages (Stages 3 and 4). While logical development is necessary for moral development and sets limits to it, most individuals are higher in logical stage than they are in moral stage. As an example, over 50 percent of late adolescents and adults are capable of full formal reasoning, but only 10 percent of these adults (all formal operational) display principled (Stages 5 and 6) moral reasoning.

The moral stages are *structures of moral judgment* or *moral reasoning*. Structures of moral judgment must be distinguished from the *content* of moral judgment. As an example, we cite responses to a dilemma used in our various studies to identify moral stage. The dilemma raises the issue of stealing a drug to save a dying woman. The inventor of the drug is selling it for ten times what it costs him to make it. The woman's husband cannot raise the money, and the

---

*Many adolescents and adults only partially attain the stage of formal operations. They do consider all the actual relations of one thing to another at the same time, but they do not consider all possibilities and form abstract hypotheses. A few do not advance this far, remaining "concrete operational."

seller refuses to lower the price or wait for payment. What should the husband do?

The choice endorsed by a subject (steal, don't steal) is called the *content* of his moral judgment in the situation. His reasoning about the choice defines the structure of his moral judgment. This reasoning centers on the following ten universal moral values or issues of concern to persons in these moral dilemmas:

1. Punishment
2. Property
3. Roles and concerns of affection
4. Roles and concerns of authority
5. Law
6. Life
7. Liberty
8. Distributive justice
9. Truth
10. Sex

A moral choice involves choosing between two (or more) of these values as they *conflict* in concrete situations of choice.

The stage or structure of a person's moral judgment defines: (1) *what* he finds valuable in each of these moral issues (life, law), i.e., how he defines the value, and (2) *why* he finds it valuable, i.e., the reasons he gives for valuing it. As an example, at Stage 1 life is valued in terms of the power or possessions of the person involved; at Stage 2, for its usefulness in satisfying the needs of the individual in question or others; at Stage 3, in terms of the individual's relations with others and their valuation of him; at Stage 4, in terms of social or religious law. Only at Stages 5 and 6 is each life seen as inherently worthwhile, aside from other considerations.

Moral Judgment vs. Moral Action

Having clarified the nature of stages of moral *judgment*, we must consider the relation of moral judgment to moral *action*. If logical reasoning is a necessary but not sufficient condition for mature moral judgment, mature moral judgment is a necessary but not sufficient condition for mature moral action. One cannot follow moral principles if one does not understand (or believe in) moral principles. However, one can reason in terms of principles and not live up to these principles. As an example, Richard Krebs and I found that only 15 percent of students showing some principled thinking cheated as compared to 55 percent of conventional subjects and 70 percent of preconventional subjects. Nevertheless, 15 percent of the principled subjects did cheat, suggesting that factors additional to moral judgment are necessary for principled moral reasoning to be translated into "moral action." Partly, these factors include the situation and its pressures. Partly, what happens depends upon the individual's motives and emotions. Partly, what the individual does depends upon a general sense of will, purpose, or "ego strength." As an example of the role of will or ego strength in moral behavior, we may cite the study by Krebs: Slightly more than half of his conventional subjects cheated. These subjects were also divided by a measure of attention/ will. Only 26 percent of the "strong-willed" conventional subjects cheated; however, 74 percent of the "weak-willed" subjects cheated.

If maturity of moral reasoning is only one factor in moral behavior, why does the cognitive-developmental approach to moral education focus so heavily upon moral reasoning? For the following reasons:

1. Moral judgment, while only one factor in moral behavior, is the single most important or influential factor yet discovered in moral behavior.

2. While other factors influence moral behavior, moral judgment is the only distinctively *moral* factor in moral behavior. To illustrate, we noted that the Krebs study indicated that "strong-willed" conventional stage subjects resisted cheating more than "weak-willed" subjects. For those at a preconventional level of moral reasoning, however, "will" had an opposite effect. "Strong-willed" Stages 1 and 2 subjects cheated more, not less, than "weak-willed" subjects, i.e., they had the "courage of their (amoral) convictions" that it was worthwhile to cheat. "Will," then, is an important factor in moral behavior, but it is not distinctively moral; it becomes moral only when informed by mature moral judgment.

3. Moral judgment change is long-range or irreversible; a higher stage is never lost. Moral behavior as such as largely situational and reversible or "loseable" in new situations.

Aims of Moral and Civic Education

Moral psychology describes what moral development is, as studied empirically. Moral education must also consider moral philosophy, which strives to tell us what moral development ideally *ought to be*. Psychology finds an invariant sequence of moral stages; moral philosophy must be invoked to answer whether a later stage is a better stage. The "stage" of senescence and death follows the "stage" of adulthood, but that does not mean that senescence and death are better. Our claim that the latest or principled stages of moral reasoning are morally better stages, then, must rest on considerations of moral philosophy.

The tradition of moral philosophy to which we appeal is the liberal or rational tradition, in particular the "formalistic" or "deontological" tradition running from Immanuel Kant to John Rawls (1971). Central to this tradition is the claim that an adequate morality is *principled*, i.e., that it makes judgments in terms of *universal* principles applicable to all mankind. *Principles* are to be distinguished from *rules*. Conventional morality is grounded on rules, primarily "thou shalt nots" such as are represented by the Ten Commandments, prescriptions of kinds of actions. Principles are, rather, universal guides to making a moral decision. An example is Kant's "categorical imperative," formulated in two ways. The first is the maxim of respect for human personality, "Act always toward the other as an end, not as a means." The second is the maxim of universalization, "Choose only as you would be willing to have everyone choose in your situation." Principles like that of Kant's state the formal conditions of a moral choice or action. In the dilemma in which a woman is dying because a druggist refuses to release his drug for less than the stated price, the druggist is not acting morally, though he is not violating the ordinary moral rules (he is not actually stealing or murdering). But he is violating principles: He is treating the woman simply as a means to his ends of profit, and he is not choosing as he would wish anyone to choose (if the druggist were in the dying woman's place, he would not want a druggist to choose as he is choosing). Under most circumstances, choice in terms of conventional moral rules and choice in terms of principles coincide. Ordinarily, principles dictate not stealing (avoiding stealing is implied by acting in terms of a regard for others as ends and in terms of what one would want everyone to do). In a situation where stealing is the only means to save a life, however, principles contradict the ordinary rules and would dictate stealing. Unlike rules which are supported by social authority, principles are freely chosen by the individual because of their intrinsic moral validity.*

The conception that a moral choice is a choice made in terms of moral principles is related to the claim of liberal moral philosophy that moral principles are ultimately principles of justice. In essence, moral conflicts are conflicts between the claims of persons, and principles for resolving these claims are principles of justice, "for giving each his due." Central to justice are the demands of *liberty, equality,* and *reciprocity*. At every moral stage, there is a concern for justice. The most damning statement a school child can make about a teacher is that "he's not fair." At each higher stage, however, the conception of justice is reorganized. At Stage 1, justice is punishing the bad in terms of "an eye for an eye and a tooth for a tooth." At Stage 2, it is exchanging favors and goods in an equal manner. At Stages 3 and 4, it is treating people as they desire in terms of the conventional rules. At Stage 5, it is recognized that all rules and laws flow from justice, from a social contract between the governors and the governed designed to protect the equal rights of all. At Stage 6, personally chosen moral principles are also principles of justice, the principles any member of a society would choose for that society if he did not know what his position was to be in the society and in which he might be the least advantaged (Rawls 1971). Principles chosen from this point of view are, first, the maximum liberty compatible with the like liberty of others and, second, no inequalities of goods and respect which are not to the benefit of all, including the least advantaged.

As an example of stage progression in the orientation to justice, we may take judgments about capital punishment (Kohlberg and Elfenbein 1975). Capital punishment is only firmly rejected at the two principled stages, when the notion of justice as vengeance or retribution is abandoned. At the sixth stage, capital punishment is not condoned even if it may have some useful deterrent effect in

---

*Not all freely chosen values or rules are principles, however. Hitler chose the "rule," "exterminate the enemies of the Aryan race," but such a rule is not a universalizable principle.

promoting law and order. This is because it is not a punishment we would choose for a society if we assumed we had as much chance of being born into the position of a criminal or murderer as being born into the position of a law abider.

Why are decisions based on universal principles of justice better decisions? Because they are decisions on which all moral men could agree. When decisions are based on conventional moral rules, men will disagree, since they adhere to conflicting systems of rules dependent on culture and social position. Throughout history men have killed one another in the name of conflicting moral rules and values, most recently in Vietnam and the Middle East. Truly moral or just resolutions of conflicts require principles which are, or can be, universalizable.

Alternative Approaches

We have given a philosophic rationale for stage advance as the aim of moral education. Given this rationale, the developmental approach to moral education can avoid the problems inherent in the other two major approaches to moral education. The first alternative approach is that of indoctrinative moral education, the preaching and imposition of the rules and values of the teacher and his culture on the child. In America, when this indoctrinative approach has been developed in a systematic manner, it has usually been termed "character education."

Moral values, in the character education approach, are preached or taught in terms of what may be called the "bag of virtues." In the classic studies of character by Hugh Hartshorne and Mark May (1928-1930), the virtues chosen were honesty, service, and self-control. It is easy to get superficial consensus on such a bag of virtues —until one examines in detail the list of virtues involved and the details of their definition. Is the Hartshorne and May bag more adequate than the Boy Scout bag (a Scout should be honest, loyal, reverent, clean, brave, etc.)? When one turns to the details of defining each virtue, one finds equal uncertainty or difficulty in reaching consensus. Does honesty mean one should not steal to save a life? Does it mean that a student should not help another student with his homework?

Character education and other forms of indoctrinative moral education have aimed at teaching universal values (it is assumed that honesty or service are desirable traits for all men in all societies), but the detailed definitions used are relative; they are defined by the opinions of the teacher and the conventional culture and rest on the authority of the teacher for their justification. In this sense character education is close to the unreflective valuings by teachers which constitute the hidden curriculum of the school.* Because of the current unpopularity of indoctrinative approaches to moral education, a family of approaches called "values clarification" has become appealing to teachers. Values clarification takes the first step implied by a rational approach to moral education: the eliciting of the child's own judgment or opinion about issues or situations in which values conflict, rather than imposing the teacher's opinion on him. Values clarification, however, does not attempt to go further than eliciting awareness of values; it is assumed that becoming more self-aware about one's values is an end in itself. Fundamentally, the definition of the end of values education as self-awareness derives from a belief in ethical relativity held by many value-clarifiers. As stated by Peter Engel, "One must contrast value clarification and value inculcation. Value clarification implies the principle that in the consideration of values there is no single correct answer." Within these premises of "no correct answer," children are to discuss moral dilemmas in such a way as to reveal different values and discuss their value differences with each other. The teacher is to stress that "our values are different," not that one value is more adequate than others. If this program is systematically followed, students will themselves become relativists, believing there is no "right" moral answer. For instance, a student caught cheating might argue that he did nothing wrong, since his own hierarchy of values, which may be different from that of the teacher, made it right for him to cheat.

Like values clarification, the cognitive-developmental approach to moral education stresses open or Socratic peer discussion of value dilemmas. Such discussion, however, has an aim: stimulation of movement to the next stage of moral reasoning. Like values clarification, the developmental approach opposes indoctrination. Stimula-

---

*As an example of the "hidden curriculum," we may cite a second-grade classroom. My son came home from this classroom one day saying he did not want to be "one of the bad boys." Asked "Who are the bad boys?" he replied, "The ones who don't put their books back and get yelled at."

tion of movement to the next stage of reasoning is not indoctrinative, for the following reasons:

1. Change is in the way of reasoning rather than in the particular beliefs involved.
2. Students in a class are at different stages; the aim is to aid movement of each to the next stage, not convergence on a common pattern.
3. The teacher's own opinion is neither stressed nor invoked as authoritative. It enters in only as one of many opinions, hopefully one of those at a next higher stage.
4. The notion that some judgments are more adequate than others is communicated. Fundamentally, however, this means that the student is encouraged to articulate a position which seems most adequate to him and to judge the adequacy of the reasoning of others.

In addition to having more definite aims than values clarification, the moral development approach restricts value education to that which is moral or, more specifically, to justice. This is for two reasons. First, it is not clear that the whole realm of personal, political, and religious values is a realm which is nonrelative, i.e., in which there are universals and a direction of development. Second, it is not clear that the public school has a right or mandate to develop values in general.* In our view, value education in the public schools should be restricted to that which the school has the right and mandate to develop: an awareness of justice, or of the rights of others in our Constitutional system. While the Bill of Rights prohibits the teaching of religious beliefs, or of specific value systems, it does not prohibit the teaching of the awareness of rights and principles of justice fundamental to the Constitution itself.

---

*Restriction of deliberate value education to the moral may be clarified by our example of the second-grade teacher who made tidying up of books a matter of moral indoctrination. Tidiness is a value, but it is not a moral value. Cheating is a moral issue, intrinsically one of fairness. It involves issues of violation of trust and taking advantage. Failing to tidy the room may under certain conditions be an issue of fairness, when it puts an undue burden on others. If it is handled by the teacher as a matter of cooperation among the group in this sense, it is a legitimate focus of deliberate moral education. If it is not, it simply represents the arbitrary imposition of the teacher's values on the child.

When moral education is recognized as centered in justice and differentiated from value education or affective education, it becomes apparent that moral and civic education are much the same thing. This equation, taken for granted by the classic philosophers of education from Plato and Aristotle to Dewey, is basic to our claim that a concern for moral education is central to the educational objectives of social studies.

The term *civic education* is used to refer to social studies as more than the study of the facts and concepts of social science, history, and civics. It is education for the analytic understanding, value principles, and motivation necessary for a citizen in a democracy if democracy is to be an .effective process. It is political education. Civic or political education means the stimulation of development of more advanced patterns of reasoning about political and social decisions and their implementation in action. These patterns are patterns of moral reasoning. Our studies show that reasoning and decision making about political decisions are directly derivative of broader patterns of moral reasoning and decision making. We have interviewed high school and college students about concrete political situations involving laws to govern open housing, civil disobedience for peace in Vietnam, free press rights to publish what might disturb national order, and distribution of income through taxation. We find that reasoning on these political decisions can be classified according to moral stage and that an individual's stage on political dilemmas is at the same level as on nonpolitical moral dilemmas (euthanasia, violating authority to maintain trust in a family, stealing a drug to save one's dying wife). Turning from reasoning to action, similar findings are obtained. In 1964 a study was made of those who sat in at the University of California, Berkeley, administration building and those who did not in the Free Speech Movement crisis. Of those at Stage 6, 80 percent sat in, believing that principles of free speech were being compromised, and that all efforts to compromise and negotiate with the administration had failed. In contrast, only 15 percent of the conventional (Stage 3 or Stage 4) subjects sat in. (Stage 5 subjects were in between.)*

_____

*The differential action of the principled subjects was determined by two things. First, they were more likely to judge it right to violate authority by sitting in. But second, they were also in general more consistent in engaging in political action according to their judgment. Ninety percent of all Stage 6 subjects thought it right to sit in, and all 90 percent lived up to this belief. Among

From a psychological side, then, political development is part of moral development. The same is true from the philosophic side. In the *Republic,* Plato sees political education as part of a broader education for moral justice and finds a rationale for such education in terms of universal philosophic principles rather than the demands of a particular society. More recently, Dewey claims the same.

In historical perspective, America was the first nation whose government was publicly founded on postconventional principles of justice, rather than upon the authority central to conventional moral reasoning. At the time of our founding, postconventional or principled moral and political reasoning was the possession of the minority, as it still is. Today, as in the time of our founding, the majority of our adults are at the conventional level, particularly the "law and order" (fourth) moral stage. (Every few years the Gallup Poll circulates the Bill of Rights unidentified, and every year it is turned down.) The Founding Fathers intuitively understood this without benefit of our elaborate social science research; they constructed a document designing a government which would maintain principles of justice and the rights of man even though principled men were not the men in power. The machinery included checks and balances, the independent judiciary, and freedom of the press. Most recently, this machinery found its use at Watergate. The tragedy of Richard Nixon, as Harry Truman said long ago, was that he never understood the Constitution (a Stage 5 document), but the Constitution understood Richard Nixon.*

Watergate, then, is not some sign of moral decay of the nation, but rather of the fact that understanding and action in support of justice principles are still the possession of a minority of our society. Insofar as there is moral decay, it represents the weakening of conventional morality in the face of social and value conflict today. This can lead the less fortunate adolescent to fixation at the preconventional level, the more fortunate to movement to principles. We find a larger proportion of youths at the principled level today than was the

---

the Stage 4 subjects, 45 percent thought it right to sit in, but only 33 percent lived up to this belief by acting.

*No public or private word or deed of Nixon ever rose above Stage 4, the "law and order" stage. His last comments in the White House were of wonderment that the Republican Congress could turn on him after so many Stage 2 exchanges of favors in getting them elected.

case in their fathers' day, but also a larger proportion at the preconventional level.

Given this state, moral and civic education in the schools becomes a more urgent task. In the high school today, one often hears both preconventional adolescents and those beginning to move beyond convention sounding the same note of disaffection for the school. While our political institutions are in principle Stage 5 (i.e., vehicles for maintaining universal rights through the democratic process), our schools have traditionally been Stage 4 institutions of convention and authority. Today more than ever, democratic schools systematically engaged in civic education are required.

Our approach to moral and civic education relates the study of law and government to the actual creation of a democratic school in which moral dilemmas are discussed and resolved in a manner which will stimulate moral development.

Planned Moral Education

For many years, moral development was held by psychologists to be primarily a result of family upbringing and family conditions. In particular, conditions of affection and authority in the home were believed to be critical, some balance of warmth and firmness being optimal for moral development. This view arises if morality is conceived as an internalization of the arbitrary rules of parents and culture, since such acceptance must be based on affection and respect for parents as authorities rather than on the rational nature of the rules involved.

Studies of family correlates of moral stage development do not support this internalization view of the conditions for moral development. Instead, they suggest that the conditions for moral development in homes and schools are similar and that the conditions are consistent with cognitive-developmental theory. In the cognitive-developmental view, morality is a natural product of a universal human tendency toward empathy or role taking, toward putting oneself in the shoes of other conscious beings. It is also a product of a universal human concern for justice, for reciprocity or equality in the relation of one person to another. As an example, when my son was four, he became a morally principled vegetarian and refused to eat meat, resisting all parental persuasion to increase his protein intake. His reason was, "It's bad to kill animals." His moral commitment to vegetarianism was not taught or acquired from parental authority; it was the result of the universal tendency of the young self to project its consciousness and values into other living things, other selves. My son's vegetarianism also involved a sense of justice, revealed when I read him a book about Eskimos in which a real hunting expedition was described. His response was to say, "Daddy, there is one kind of meat I would eat—Eskimo meat. It's all right to eat Eskimos because they eat animals." This natural sense of justice or reciprocity was Stage 1—an eye for an eye, a tooth for a tooth. My son's sense of the value of life was also Stage 1 and involved no differentiation between human personality and physical life. His morality, though Stage 1, was, however, natural and internal. Moral development past Stage 1, then, is not an internalization but the reconstruction of role taking and conceptions of justice toward greater adequacy. These reconstructions occur in order to achieve a better match between the child's own moral structures and the structures of the social and moral situations he confronts. We divide these conditions of match into two kinds: those dealing with moral discussions and communication and those dealing with the total moral environment or atmosphere in which the child lives.

In terms of moral discussion, the important conditions appear to be:

1. Exposure to the next higher stage of reasoning.

2. Exposure to situations posing problems and contradictions for the child's current moral structure, leading to dissatisfaction with his current level.

3. An atmosphere of interchange and dialogue combining the first two conditions, in which conflicting moral views are compared in an open manner.

Studies of families in India and America suggest that morally advanced children have parents at higher stages. Parents expose children to the next higher stage, raising moral issues and engaging in open dialogue or interchange about such issues (Parilch 1975).

Drawing on this notion of the discussion conditions stimulating advance, Moshe Blatt conducted classroom discussions of conflict-laden hypothetical moral dilemmas with four classes of junior high and high school students for a semester. In each of these classes, students were to be found at three stages. Since the children were not all responding at the same stage, the arguments they used with each other were at different levels. In the course of these discussions among the students, the teacher first supported and clarified those arguments that were one stage above the lowest stage among the children; for example, the teacher supported Stage 3 rather than Stage 2. When it seemed that these arguments were understood by the students, the teacher then challenged that stage, using new situations, and clarified the arguments one stage above the previous one: Stage 4 rather than Stage 3. At the end of the semester, all the students were retested; they showed significant upward change when compared to the controls, and they maintained the change one year later. In the experimental classrooms, from one-fourth to one-half of the students moved up a stage, while there was essentially no change during the course of the experiment in the control group.

Given the Blatt studies showing that moral discussion could raise moral stage, we undertook the next step: to see if teachers could conduct moral discussions in the course of teaching high school social studies with the same results. This step we took in cooperation with Edwin Fenton, who introduced moral dilemmas in his ninth- and eleventh-grade social studies texts. Twenty-four teachers in the Boston and Pittsburgh areas were given some instruction in conducting moral discussions around the dilemmas in the text. About half of the teachers stimulated significant developmental change in their classrooms—upward stage movement of one-quarter to one-half a stage. In control classes using the text but no moral dilemma discussions, the same teachers failed to stimulate any moral change in the students. Moral discussion, then, can be a usable and effective part of the curriculum at any grade level. Working with filmstrip dilemmas produced in cooperation with Guidance Associates, second-grade teachers conducted moral discussions yielding a similar amount of moral stage movement.

Moral discussion and curriculum, however, constitute only one portion of the conditions stimulating moral growth. When we turn to analyzing the broader life environment, we turn to a consideration of the *moral atmosphere* of the home, the school, and the broader society. The first basic dimension of social atmosphere is the role-taking opportunities it provides, the extent to which it encourages the child to take the point of view of others. Role taking is related to the amount of social interaction and social communication in which the child engages, as well as to his sense of efficacy in influencing attitudes of others. The second dimension of social atmosphere, more strictly moral, is the level of justice of the environment or institution. The justice structure of an institution refers to the perceived rules or principles for distributing rewards, punishments, responsibilities, and privileges among institutional members. This structure may exist or be perceived at any of our moral stages. As an example, a study of a traditional prison revealed that inmates perceived it as Stage 1, regardless of their own level (Kohlberg, Scharf, and Hickey 1972). Obedience to arbitrary command by power figures and punishment for disobedience were seen as the governing justice norms of the prison. A behavior-modification prison using point rewards for conformity was perceived as a Stage 2 system of instrumental exchange. Inmates at Stage 3 or 4 perceived this institution as more fair than the traditional prison, but not as fair in their own terms.

These and other studies suggest that a higher level of institutional justice is a condition for individual development of a higher sense of justice. Working on these premises, Joseph Hickey, Peter Scharf, and I (1973) worked with guards and inmates in a women's prison to create a more just community. A social contract was set up in which guards and inmates each had a vote of one and in which rules were made and conflicts resolved through discussions of fairness and a democratic vote in a community meeting. The program has been operating four years and has stimulated moral stage advance in inmates, though it is still too early to draw conclusions as to its overall long-range effectiveness for rehabilitation.

One year ago, Fenton, Ralph Mosher, and I received a grant from the Danforth Foundation (with additional support from the Kennedy Foundation) to make moral education a living matter in two high schools in the Boston area (Cambridge and Brookline) and two in Pittsburgh. The plan had two components. The first was training counselors and social studies and English teachers in conducting moral discussions and making moral discussion an integral part of the curriculum. The second was establishing a just community school within a public high school.

We have stated the theory of the just community high school, postulating that discussing real-life moral situations and actions as issues of fairness and as matters for democratic decision would stimulate advance in both moral reasoning and moral action. A participatory democracy provides more extensive opportunities for role taking and a higher level of perceived institutional justice than does any other social arrangement. Most alternative schools strive to establish a democratic governance, but none we have observed has achieved a vital or viable participatory democracy. Our theory suggested reasons why we might succeed where others failed. First, we felt that democracy had to be a central commitment of a school, rather than a humanitarian frill. Democracy as moral education provides that commitment. Second, democracy in alternative schools often fails because it bores the students. Students prefer to let teachers make decisions about staff, courses, and schedules, rather than to attend lengthy, complicated meetings. Our theory said that the issues a democracy should focus on are issues of morality and fairness. Real issues concerning drugs, stealing, disruptions, and grading are never boring if handled as issues of fairness. Third, our theory told us that if large democratic community meetings were preceded by small-group moral discussion, higher-stage thinking by students would win out in later decisions, avoiding the disasters of mob rule.*

Currently, we can report that the school based on our theory makes democracy work or function where other schools have failed. It is too early to make any claims for its effectiveness in causing moral development, however.

Our Cambridge just community school within the public high school was started after a small summer planning session of volunteer teachers, students, and parents. At the time the school opened in the fall, only a commitment to democracy and a skeleton program of English and social studies had been decided on. The school started with six teachers from the regular school and sixty students, twenty from academic professional homes and twenty from working-class homes. The other twenty were dropouts and troublemakers or petty

---

*An example of the need for small-group discussion comes from an alternative school community meeting called because a pair of the students had stolen the school's video-recorder. The resulting majority decision was that the school should buy back the recorder from the culprits through a fence. The teachers could not accept this decision and returned to a more authoritative approach. I believe if the moral reasoning of students urging this solution had been confronted by students at a higher stage, a different decision would have emerged.

delinquents in terms of previous record. The usual mistakes and usual chaos of a beginning alternative school ensued. Within a few weeks, however, a successful democratic community process had been established. Rules were made around pressing issues: disturbances, drugs, hooking. A student discipline committee or jury was formed. The resulting rules and enforcement have been relatively effective and reasonable. We do not see reasonable rules as ends in themselves, however, but as vehicles for moral discussion and an emerging sense of community. This sense of community and a resulting morale are perhaps the most immediate signs of success. This sense of community seems to lead to behavior change of a positive sort. An example is a fifteen-year-old student who started as one of the greatest combinations of humor, aggression, light-fingeredness, and hyperactivity I have ever known. From being the principal disturber of all community meetings, he has become an excellent community meeting participant and occasional chairman. He is still more ready to enforce rules for others than to observe them himself, yet his commitment to the school has led to a steady decrease in exotic behavior. In addition, he has become more involved in classes and projects and has begun to listen and ask questions in order to pursue a line of interest.

We attribute such behavior change not only to peer pressure and moral discussion but to the sense of community which has emerged from the democratic process in which angry conflicts are resolved through fairness and community decision. This sense of community is reflected in statements of the students to us that there are no cliques—that the blacks and the whites, the professors' sons and the project students, are friends. These statements are supported by observation. Such a sense of community is needed where students in a given classroom range in reading level from fifth-grade to college.

Fenton, Mosher, the Cambridge and Brookline teachers, and I are now planning a four-year curriculum in English and social studies centering on moral discussion, on role-taking and communication, and on relating the government, laws, and justice system of the school to that of the American society and other world societies. This will integrate an intellectual curriculum for a higher level of understanding of society with the experiential components of school democracy and moral decision.

There is very little new in this—or in anything else we are doing. Dewey wanted democratic experimental schools for moral and intellectual development seventy years ago. Perhaps Dewey's time has come.

References

Blatt, Moshe, and Kohlberg, Lawrence. "Effects of Classroom Discussions upon Children's Level of Moral Judgment." *Recent Research in Moral Development*, edited by Lawrence Kohlberg. New York: Holt, Rinehart & Winston, in preparation.

Dewey, John. "What Psychology Can Do for the Teacher." *John Dewey on Education: Selected Writings*, edited by Reginald Archambault. New York: Random House, 1964.

Hartshorne, Hugh, and May, Mark. *Studies in the Nature of Character* (3 vols.). New York: Macmillan, 1928-1930.

Kohlberg, Lawrence. "Moral Stages and Moralization: The Cognitive-Developmental Approach." *Man, Morality, and Society*, edited by Thomas Lickona. New York: Holt, Rinehart & Winston, 1976.

Kohlberg, Lawrence; Scharf, Peter; and Hickey, Joseph. "The Justice Structure of the Prison: A Theory and an Intervention." *The Prison Journal* (autumn-winter 1972).

Kohlberg, Lawrence; Kauffman, Kelsey; Scharf, Peter; and Hickey, Joseph. *The Just Community Approach to Corrections: A Manual, Part I*. Cambridge, Mass.: Education Research Foundation, 1973.

Kohlberg, Lawrence, and Elfenbein, Donald. "Development of Moral Reasoning and Attitudes Toward Capital Punishment." *American Journal of Orthopsychiatry* (summer 1975).

Krebs, Richard, and Kohlberg, Lawrence. "Moral Judgment and Ego Controls as Determinants of Resistance to Cheating." *Recent Research in Moral Development*, edited by Lawrence Kohlberg. New York: Holt, Rinehart & Winston, in preparation.

Parilch, Bindu. "A Cross-Cultural Study of Parent-Child Moral Judgment." Ph.D. dissertation, Harvard University, 1975.

Piaget, Jean. *The Moral Judgment of the Child* (2nd ed.). Glencoe, Ill.: Free Press, 1948.

Rawls, John. *A Theory of Justice*. Cambridge, Mass.: Harvard University Press, 1971.

Rest, James; Turiel, Elliott; and Kohlberg, Lawrence. "Relations Between Level of Moral Judgment and Preference and Comprehension of the Moral Judgment of Others." *Journal of Personality* 37 (1969): 225-52.

13

The Moral Atmosphere of the School

Lawrence Kohlberg

I have to start by saying that Philip Jackson is responsible for my paper, by which I mean he is "to blame."

First, he is responsible because he invented the term "hidden" or "unstudied curriculum" to refer to 90 percent of what goes on in classrooms. Second, he is responsible because he induced me to speak about the unstudied curriculum when my only qualification to do so is that I have never studied it. While I have done plenty of observing of children in and out of classrooms, such observation has always been with reference to developing personality and behavior, and not in terms of the nature of classroom life and its influence on children. Third, he is to blame because he wrote a book defining the hidden curriculum on which I based this paper, and then he prepared a document defining the unstudied curriculum in a completely different way, leaving me holding the bag.

Reprinted by permission from H. Overly (ed.), *The Unstudied Curriculum* (Washington, D.C.: Association for Supervision and Curriculum Development, 1970).

The Hidden Curriculum and Moral Education

Anyhow, I am going to revenge myself on Dr. Jackson for putting me in this awkward spot by claiming that I am the only person who is really an intellectual expert on this problem of the hidden curriculum. I say this because it will be my claim that the only integrated way of thinking about the hidden curriculum is to think of it as moral education, a topic about which few other academicians besides myself are currently concerned. To make educational sense out of the insights of Jackson, Dreeben, Friedenberg, and Rosenthal, I shall claim, you must put them in the framework of the ideas and concerns in *moral* education propounded by such writers as Emile Durkheim, John Dewey, and Jean Piaget.

To make my point, I shall start with the central question most of us have about the hidden curriculum, that of whether it educates, miseducates, or does neither. I shall claim that the answer to this question depends upon a viable conception of moral development. The question itself, that of whether the hidden curriculum educates, is posed by the very phrase, "hidden curriculum." The phrase indicates that children are learning much in school that is not formal curriculum, and the phrase also asks whether such learning is truly educative.

In *Life in Classrooms* (1968), Philip Jackson summarizes three central characteristics of school life: the crowds, the praise, and the power. Learning to live in the classroom means, first, learning to live and to be treated as a member of a crowd of same-age, same-status others.

Second, learning to live in the classroom means learning to live in a world in which there is impersonal authority, in which a relative stranger gives orders and wields power. Robert Dreeben emphasizes similar characteristics, first and foremost learning to live with authority. Both Jackson and Dreeben stress the fact that the hidden curriculum provides a way station between the personal relations of the family and the impersonal achievement and authority-oriented roles of adult occupational and sociopolitical life.

The perspectives of Jackson and Dreeben derive from a long and great tradition of educational sociology founded by Emile Durkheim in France at the end of the nineteenth century. According to Durkheim:

There is a great distance between the state in which the child finds himself as he leaves the family and the one toward which he must strive. Intermediaries are necessary, the school environment the most desirable. It is more extensive than the family or the group of friends. It results neither from blood nor free choice but from a meeting among subjects of similar age and condition. In that sense, it resembles political society. On the other hand it is limited enough so that personal relations can crystallize. It is groups of young persons more or less like those of the social system of the school which have enabled the formation of societies larger than the family. Even in simple societies without schools, the elders would assemble the group at a given age and initiate them collectively into the moral and intellectual patrimony of the group. Induction into the moral patrimony of the group has never been conducted entirely within the family. (1961, p. 231)

What this sociological tradition of Durkheim and Dreeben is telling us is that you cannot get rid of authority in the classroom, because you need people who can live with it in the bigger society. Edgar Friedenberg starts out with the same Durkheim perspective before turning it on its ear. I hesitate to restate Dr. Friedenberg. I am tempted to say that he is the only person in the world who can state a message in many syllables, and make it come across with one-syllable impact. In *Coming of Age in America* (1963, p. 43) Friedenberg says,

After the family the school is the first social institution an individual must deal with, the place in which he learns to handle himself with strangers. Free societies depend upon their members to learn early and thoroughly that public authority is not like that of the family, but must rely basically on the impersonal application of general formulae.

However, Friedenberg's observations of the hidden curriculum suggest that it is less a vehicle of socialization into a free society than that caricature of socialization we call a jail. Says Friedenberg (p. 29):

Between classes at Milgrim High, no student may walk down the corridor without a form signed by a teacher, telling where he is coming from, where he is going, and the time to the minute at which the pass is valid. There is no physical freedom whatever in Milgrim, there is no time or place in which a student may simply go about his business. Privacy is strictly forbidden. Toilets are locked. There are more different washrooms than there must have been in the Confederate Navy.

Friedenberg's style of observation of the hidden curriculum is colored by his view that its function of socialization into large-scale society means socialization into a mass middle-class society of mediocrity, banality, and conformity. From this point of view, the hidden curriculum consists of "the ways in which education subverts the highest function of education, which is to help people understand the meaning of their lives and those of others."

I have indicated how the perceived nature of the hidden curriculum rests on a prior perspective which is both a social theory and a mode of valuing. The fact that this must necessarily be the case in social inquiry, I learned in an illuminating course by Edgar Friedenberg on social science method. The observation and study of a reading curriculum rest on assumptions of both what reading is and what reading as a desirable skill ought to be. The same is true of the hidden curriculum.

Educational Consequences of Moral Education

As the educational philosopher R. S. Peters (1967, p. 6) points out, "the concept 'education' has built into it the criterion that something worthwhile should be achieved. It implies something worthwhile is being transmitted in a morally acceptable manner." To discuss the educational consequences of the hidden curriculum is to discuss whether it does or can lead to the transmission of something worthwhile in a morally acceptable manner. While Friedenberg assumes this, Dreeben claims a value-neutral stance. Dreeben (1967) concludes an earlier article by saying,

The argument of this paper presents a formulation of how schooling contributes to the emergence of certain psychological outcomes, not to provide an apology or justification for these outcomes on ideological grounds. From the viewpoint of ideological justification, the process of schooling is problematic in that outcomes morally desirable from one perspective are undesirable from another.

It is hard to understand what conclusions to draw from Dreeben's analysis if it is really value-neutral. The analysis points out that authority is necessary in adult society, so it is necessary to have a hidden curriculum by which it is learned in the school.

Nature of School Discipline

If Dreeben's analysis had real educational force, however, it is contained in the implicit value-perspective of functional sociology, the perspective that the invisible hand of societal survival guides the shaping of human institutions and gives them a value or wisdom not apparent at first glance. Durkheim, the founder of functional sociology, understood that functional sociology was not a value-free position, but essentially represented a moral point of view. Durkheim articulately and explicitly argued that the sociologist's definition of the invisible hand of the social system was also the definition of rational or scientific morality. So Durkheim goes further than saying that acceptance of authority is one of the key elements of the child's moral development.

Durkheim argues that the crowds, the praise, and the power which look so wasteful from the point of view of intellectual development are the necessary conditions for the moral development of the child. According to Durkheim,

Morality is respect for rule and is altruistic attachment to the social group. . . . although family education is an excellent preparation for the moral life, its usefulness is restricted, above all with respect to the spirit of discipline. That which is essential to the spirit of discipline, respect for the rule, can scarcely develop in the familial setting, which is not subject to general impersonal immutable regulation, and should have an air of freedom. But the child must learn respect for the rule; he must learn to do his duty because it is his duty, even though the task may not seem an easy one.

Such an apprenticeship must devolve upon the school. Too often, it is true, people conceive of school discipline so as to preclude endowing it with such an important moral function. Some see in it a simple way of guaranteeing superficial peace and order in the class. Under such conditions, one can quite reasonably come to view these imperative requirements as barbarous, as a tyranny of complicated rules. In reality, however, school discipline is not a simple device for securing superficial peace in the classroom; it is the morality of the classroom as a small society. (1961, p. 148)

Durkheim's System

I shall not go into Durkheim's system of moral education in detail in this paper except to say it is, in my opinion, the most philosophically and scientifically comprehensive, clear, and workable approach to moral education extant. Its workability has been demonstrated not in France but in Soviet Russia, where it has been elaborated from the point of view of Marxist rather than Durkheimian sociology. Like Durkheim, the Russians hold that altruistic concern or sacrifice, like the sense of duty, is always basically directed toward the group rather than to another individual or to an abstract principle. Durkheim reasons that altruism is always sacrificing the self for something greater than the self, and another self can never be greater than the self except as it stands for the group or for society. Accordingly a central part of moral education is the sense of belonging to, and sacrificing for, a group. Says Durkheim,

In order to commit ourselves to collective ends, we must have above all a feeling and affection for the collectivity. We have seen that such feelings cannot arise in the family where solidarity is based on blood and intimate relationship since the bonds uniting the citizens of a country have nothing to do with such relationships. The only way to instill the inclination to collective life is to get hold of the child when he leaves his family and enters school. We will succeed the more easily because in certain respects, he is more amenable to this joining of minds in a common consciousness than is the adult. To achieve this tonic effect on the child, the class must really share in a collective life. Such phrases as "the class," "the spirit of the class," and "the honor of the class" must become something more than abstract expressions in the student's mind. A means to awaken the feeling of solidarity is the discreet and deliberate use of collective punishments and rewards. Collective sanctions play a very important part in the life of the classroom. The most powerful means to instill in children the feeling of solidarity is to feel that the value of each is a function of the worth of all. (1961, p. 239)

A Russian Example

One of the logical but to us rather horrifying innovations in the hidden curriculum Durkheim suggests on this basis is the use of collective responsibility, collective punishment and reward. Here is how a Russian moral education manual (quoted by Urie Bronfenbrenner) tells us this and other aspects of moral education are to be done in a third-grade classroom:

Class 3-B is just an ordinary class; it's not especially well disciplined.

The teacher has led this class now for three years, and she has earned affection, respect, and acceptance as an authority from her pupils. Her word is law for them.

The bell has rung, but the teacher has not yet arrived. She has delayed deliberately in order to check how the class will conduct itself.

In the class all is quiet. After the noisy class break, it isn't so easy to mobilize yourself and to quell the restlessness within you! Two monitors at the desk silently observe the class. On their faces is reflected the full importance and seriousness of the job they are performing. But there is no need for them to make any reprimands: the youngsters with pleasure and pride maintain scrupulous discipline; they are proud of the fact that their class conducts itself in a manner that merits the confidence of the teacher. And when the teacher enters and quietly says be seated, all understand that she deliberately refrains from praising them for the quiet and order, since in their class it could not be otherwise.

During the lesson, the teacher gives an exceptional amount of attention to collective competition between "links." (The links are the smallest unit of the Communist youth organization at this age level.) Throughout the entire lesson the youngsters are constantly hearing which link has best prepared its lesson, which link has done the best at numbers, which is the most disciplined, which has turned in the best work.

The best link not only gets a verbal positive evaluation but receives the right to leave the classroom first during the break and to have its notebooks checked before the others. As a result the links receive the benefit of collective education, common responsibility, and mutual aid.

"What are you fooling around for? You're holding up the whole link," whispers Kolya to his neighbor during the preparation period for the lesson. And during the break he teaches her how better to organize her books and pads in her knapsack.

"Count more carefully," says Olya to her girl friend. "See, on account of you our link got behind today. You come to me and we'll count together at home." (Bronfenbrenner 1962)

I do not need to say any more to indicate that Durkheim and the Russians know how to make the hidden curriculum explicit, and how to make it work. Furthermore, it is clear that Durkheim has simply taken to its logical conclusion a justification of the hidden curriculum which many teachers vaguely assume, the justification that the discipline of group life directly promotes moral character. We see, however, that when this line of thinking is carried to its logical conclusion, it leads to a definition of moral education as the promotion of collective national discipline which most of us feel is neither rational ethics nor the American constitutional tradition.

Valuing the Hidden Curriculum

What I am arguing is that the trouble with Durkheim's approach to the hidden curriculum is not that of starting from a conception of moral development, but of starting from a wrong conception of moral development. Before having the arrogance to present the right conception of moral development, I want to indicate briefly how analyses of the hidden curriculum which do not articulate an explicit conception of the moral fail to provide a framework an educator can really get hold of. We have pointed out that Dreeben sees the hidden curriculum as shaped by the invisible hand of the social system without being willing to say whether what serves the social system is good or bad. In contrast, Friedenberg seems to see the hidden curriculum as shaped by pretty much the same invisible hand of society or lower-middle class society, but to see this invisible hand as bad, as destroying the hearts and minds of the poor, the aristocrats, and the nonmiddle class in general. The core difficulty of Friedenberg's analysis is his willingness to call things good or bad without systematic criteria of morality behind his judgments. This is reflected in the question, "If you don't like the values which dominate education, what set of values should dominate education?"

The core badness of the hidden curriculum, in Friedenberg's view, is its injustice, its violation of the rights and dignity of adolescents who do not meet the mass image. One might, therefore, expect Friedenberg to hold that the optimal moral consequence of a good curriculum would be the cultivation of just men, of the sense of justice. Instead he comes out for a bag of aristocratic virtues which are as arbitrary as the middle-class virtues he rejects. Put in different terms, he says, "Leave kids alone. Respect their freedom!" without asking whether an education that leaves them alone will educate them to respect the freedom of others.

The School—Transmitter of Values

If lack of explicitness in moral framework creates confusion in Friedenberg's analysis, Dreeben's and Jackson's moral neutrality presents worse puzzles in interpreting their cogent observations. For instance, Dreeben points out that the school arbitrarily demands independent performance on tasks while cooperation in tasks is considered a good thing under other circumstances. In school tests and assignments, cooperation is cheating, while it is legitimate on other occasions. Jackson makes a similar point.

Another course of action engaged in by most students at least some of the time is to disguise the failure to comply, that is, to cheat. Learning to make it in school involves, in part, learning how to falsify our behavior. (1968, p. 27)

It is not quite correct to say, as Jackson does, that the hidden curriculum of the school teaches children to cheat. More accurately, the school teaches children about cheating and leads to the development of styles of approach to the issue of cheating. In functional sociology phrases, it prepares children for life in an industrial society in which they will have to decide where and when to cheat and when not to. Recent studies confirm the old findings of Hartshorne and May (1928-1930) that schooling does not lead to increased honesty. In experimental situations allowing cheating, older children in a given school are as likely to cheat as younger children. What age and passage through school appear to do is to lead to more generalized strategies about cheating. Some older children are more likely to cheat all the time than younger children, while other older children are more likely to refrain from cheating altogether than younger children. This leaves the mean amount of cheating the same.

The point I am making is that Dreeben's analysis of the hidden curriculum suggests that it has neither the hidden nor the manifest function of developing morality. While it presents moral issues such as whether to cheat, its central norms are not moral norms but norms of independent competition and achievement. Accordingly while teachers may strive to police cheating, they will not exert any real influence over children's moral values or character. Put in a different way, Dreeben is telling us that the schools are transmitting values, but they are not what educators usually think are moral values. A good functional sociologist might reply that from the social system point of view, cultivating independent competition is more important or more *moral* than cultivating honesty, since our society is built to tolerate a lot of petty cheating but is not built to tolerate a lot of people who are not interested in making it by institutional achievement standards. It is just at this point that we have to go back to a conception of the moral before the implications of Dreeben's sociological analysis can be understood.

The Hidden Curriculum as Freedom

One final example of an approach to the hidden curriculum denies considering its use and value for moral education. This example is that of Summerhill's A. S. Neill, whose solution is to chuck out both the hidden curriculum and the concept of morality from education. Dreeben and Jackson say the hidden curriculum is authority,

Neill says chuck it out and make the hidden curriculum freedom. Friedenberg's position seems not too different, if Friedenberg were to start a school as Neill has done. Says Neill,

We set out to make a school in which we should allow children freedom to be themselves. To do this we had to renounce all discipline, all direction, all moral training. We have been called brave but it did not require courage, just a complete belief in the child as a good, not an evil, being. A child is innately wise and realistic. If left to himself without adult suggestion of any kind he will develop as far as he is capable of developing. I believe that it is moral instruction that makes the child bad, not good. (1960, p. 4)

A philosopher could while away a pleasant afternoon trying to find out just what ethical framework Neill is using when he says children are good but morality is bad. It is more instructive, however, to recognize that even at Summerhill moral problems arise and to see how Neill handles them. Some years ago, Neill says,

We had two pupils arrive at the same time, a boy of seventeen and a girl of sixteen. They fell in love with each other and were always together. I met them late one night and stopped them. "I don't know what you two are doing," I said, "and morally I don't care for it isn't a moral question at all. But economically, I do care. If you, Kate, have a kid my school will be ruined. You have just come to Summerhill. To you it means freedom to do what you like. Naturally, you have no special feeling for the school. If you had been here from the age of seven, I'd never have had to mention the matter. You would have such a strong attachment to the school that you would think of the consequences to Summerhill. (pp. 57-58)

What the quotation makes clear, of course, is that the hidden moral curriculum of Summerhill is the explicit curriculum of Durkheim and the Russians. Unquestioned loyalty to the school, to the collectivity, seems to be the ultimate end of moral education at Summerhill. Surely, however, moral education has some other aims than a loyalty to the school and to other children which might possibly later transfer to loyalty to the nation and other men. To consider what such aims might be we may start with the observation that all the writers we have discussed so far have assumed that morality is fundamentally emotional and irrational. Neill, Dreeben, and Durkheim agree on this point, differing only in their evaluation of the worth of this irrational part of life. It is assumed that the means and ends of intellectual education are one thing and those of moral education another.

Growth of Moral Character

Durkheim and Dreeben assume that learning to accept rules and authority is a concrete nonrational process based on repetition, emotion, and sometimes sanctions. The assumption is that the child is controlled by primitive and selfish drives he is reluctant to give up and that the steady experience of authority and discipline is necessary to live with rules. The notions of Dewey and Piaget, that the child genuinely learns to accept authority when he learns to understand and accept the reasons and principles behind the rules, leads moral education in a different direction, tied much more closely to the intellectual curriculum of the school. This second direction is supported by many research findings. My research and that of others indicates that the development of moral character is in large part a sequential progressive growth of basic principles of moral reasoning and their application to action.

Moral Stages

In my research, I have longitudinally followed the development of moral thinking of a group of fifty boys from age ten to age twenty-five, by asking them at each three-year interval how and why they would resolve a set of eleven moral dilemmas. We have found that changes in moral thinking go step by step through six stages, with children's development stopping or becoming fixed at any one of the six stages. These stages are defined in the appendix to this chapter. We have found these same stages in the same order in children in Mexico, Turkey, England, and Taiwan, in illiterate villages, and in the urban middle and lower classes, as figures 1, 2, and 3 indicate.

Take one dilemma, such as whether a husband should steal a drug to save his dying wife if he could get it no other way. (Sample responses to the dilemma at each stage are presented in the appendix.) Stage 1 is obedience and punishment. You should not steal the drug because you will be put in jail. Stage 2 is pragmatic hedonism and exchange. Steal the drug, you need your wife and she may do the same for you someday. Stage 3 is love, happiness, kindness, and approval-oriented. Steal the drug because you want to be a good husband and good husbands love their wives. Stage 4 is the maintenance of the social order, respect for law and order, and the loyalty to the

Figure 1

Middle-class urban boys in the U.S., Taiwan, and Mexico. At age ten the stages are used according to difficulty. At age thirteen, Stage 3 is most used by all three groups. At age sixteen, U.S. boys have reversed the order of age ten stages (with the exception of 6). In Taiwan and Mexico, conventional (3-4) stages prevail at age sixteen, with Stage 5 also little used.

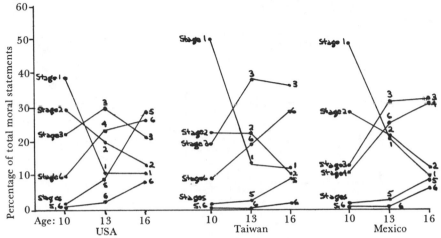

Source: L. Kohlberg and R. Kramer, "Continuities and Discontinuities in Childhood and Adult Moral Development," *Human Development* 12 (1969): pp. 93-120.

Figure 2

Two isolated villages, one in Turkey, the other in Yucatan, show similar patterns in moral thinking. There is no reversal of order, and preconventional (1-2) does not gain a clear ascendancy over conventional stages at age sixteen.

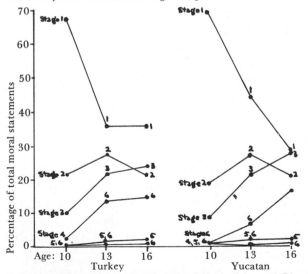

Source: L. Kohlberg and R. Kramer, "Continuities and Discontinuities in Childhood and Adult Moral Development," *Human Development* 12 (1969): pp. 93-120.

Figure 3

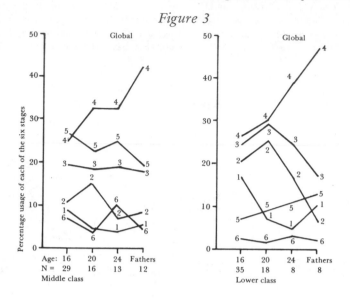

Moral judgment profiles (percentage usage of each stage by global rating method) for middle and lower class males at four ages.

Source: L. Kohlberg and R. Kramer, "Continuities and Discontinuities in Childhood and Adult Moral Development," *Human Development* 12 (1969): pp. 93-120.

the group's goals, the morality of Durkheim and the Russians. Stage 5 is social-contract constitutionalism, the definition of the good as the welfare of society where society is conceived as a set of individuals with equal rights and where rules and obligations are formed by the contractual agreements of free men. Stage 6 is the sense of principled obligation to universal human values and justice even when these are not represented in particular legal agreements and contracts in our society.

Each stage includes the core values of the prior stage but defines them in a more universal, differentiated, and integrated form. To the Stage 4 mind of George Wallace, the concept of justice is a threat to law and order, because he does not really understand the concept of a constitutional democracy in which law and order, the government, is set up to pursue and preserve justice, the equal rights of free men; and in that sense the concept of justice includes the valid elements of the law and order concept.

Let me illustrate Stage 5 and its difference from Stage 6 by a quotation from Earl Kelley's pamphlet *Return to Democracy* (1964).

A simple way to measure our efforts to educate is to judge them in the light of the tenets of democracy. . . . It is the way our forefathers decided that they wanted to live, and it is reaffirmed daily by all kinds of Americans except a very few who belong to the radical right or left. The founding fathers attempted to make the democratic ideal come to life by building our Constitution around these tenets. . . . (a) Every person has worth, has value. . . . He is entitled to be treated as a human being. He has equal rights under the law, without regard to his condition of birth or the circumstances under which he has been obliged to live. (b) The individual counts for everything. The state and school—constructed by individuals to serve individuals—are implementations of the way we want to live. . . . (c) Each individual is unique, different from any other person who has ever lived. . . . (d) Each individual has his own unique purposes, and these are the paths down which his energies can be best spent. (e) Freedom is a requirement for living in a democracy. . . . This does not mean freedom to do just as one pleases. Nobody has this right if he lives in the vicinity of any other human being, because the other human being has rights which also must be respected. . . . If we are to emphasize the learner himself, there can be no better point of reference than the democratic ideal. It has the advantage of having been agreed upon.

Professor Kelley's statement is clearly not Stage 6, although it contains a recognition of universal human rights and of justice. Fundamentally, however, Kelley is arguing that his ideal springs from a ready-made agreed-upon social-constitutional framework, one which permits social change and individual differences, but one which derives its validity from the fact that it is agreed upon, and that it has worked, rather than from the intrinsic universality and morality of its principles. If a man is confronted with a choice of stealing a drug to save a human life, however, Kelley's framework provides no clear ethical solution.

If it is recognized, however, that universal respect for fundamental human rights and for the human personality provides a moral guide defining the way in which any human should act, as well as being the established underlying values of our particular society, we are on the way to Stage 6. It is quite likely that in his personal thinking about moral dilemmas, Kelley would operate in a Stage 6 framework, but that in trying to write a public document that will gain agreement among members of a professional association, he turns to the safer ground of established actual agreement rather than that of Stage 6 principles which logically are universal though they may not be the basis of historical consensus.

For my purposes, it is not critical whether we take Stage 5 or

Stage 6 as defining a desirable level for moral education in the schools. It can safely be said that lower-stage conceptions of morality cannot define the aims of moral education, because the Constitution forbids a type of moral education which involves indoctrination and violation of the rights of individuals and their families to freedom of beliefs. This prevents us from taking the beliefs of the majority as an aim of moral education in the schools, partly because the majority has no consensus on moral issues, partly because studies show major-ity beliefs are grounded more on Stage 3 beliefs in conforming vir-tues and Stage 4 conceptions of law and order than upon Stage 5 awareness of justice and constitutional democracy.

An example of a school principal who expressed the Stage 4 beliefs of the majority has been provided by Friedenberg. The prin-cipal told his high school students they could not have a radical speaker because the speaker was against the government and the school was an agency of the government. If he had understood our constitutional system at the Stage 5 level, he would have recognized that the school as an agent of the government has a responsibility for communicating conceptions of individual rights which the govern-ment was created to maintain and serve. I am not arguing that the principal had a Stage 6 moral obligation to defy heroically an angry community of parents to see that a given radical speaker was heard. He was failing as a moral educator, however, if all he could transmit was Stage 4 moral messages to students many of whom were quite likely already at a Stage 5 level. Let us assume that all of the readers of this paper are at Stage 5 or Stage 6. What should your moral mes-sages to children be?

Moral Comprehension of Children

A series of carefully replicated experimental studies demon-strate that children seldom comprehend messages more than one stage above their own, and understand but reject messages below their own level (Turiel 1969). The studies also indicate that people can comprehend and to some extent use all stages lower than their own. As principled moral educators, you have the capacity to use lower level as well as higher level messages when you choose.

With young children, it is clear that we can make the mistake of both too high and too low a level. It is worse to make the mistake of being at too low a level because the child loses respect for the message in that case. Yet this is frequently the case. Let me quote an example of a familiar tone of Stage 3, "everything nice," from a magazine called *Wee Wisdom: A Character Building Magazine*:

"Thank you" can just be a polite little word or it can be something warm and wonderful and happy that makes your heart sing. As Boosters let us climb the steps of appreciation on a golden stairway. Let us add that magic ingredient to all our thank yous. Everyone is happier when our thanks express real appreciation.

Won't you join the boosters to climb the stairway to happiness and success. What a wonderful world it will be if we all do our part. (June 1967, p. 83)

The quotation is of course straight Stage 3, be nice and everyone will be happy. The only person who can sell that message to adolescents is Tiny Tim and he has to adopt a few unusual mannerisms to do so.

It is, of course, quite necessary to transmit moral messages at Stages 3 and 4 in the elementary school years. Even here, however, it is probably desirable to have these messages under the integrative control of higher levels. Holstein (1968) studies a group of middle-class 12-year-olds who were about equally divided between the preconventional (Stages 1 and 2) and the conventional (Stages 3 and 4) level.

Principled mothers were more likely to have conventional level children than conventional mothers. The principled mothers were capable of conventional moral messages and undoubtedly emitted them. However, their integration of them in terms of the higher level made them better moral educators even where the moral educator's task is bringing children to the conventional level.

Developing Moral Education

My research has led my colleagues and me to go on to develop experimental programs of moral education from the intellectual side. Programs center around the discussion of real and hypothetical moral conflicts. We set up arguments between students at one stage and those at the next stage up, since children are able to assimilate moral thinking only one stage above their own. The preliminary results have been encouraging, with most students advancing one stage and maintaining the advance a year later in comparison with a control group (Blatt and Kohlberg 1969). Such procedures form an explicit intellectual curriculum of moral education. Such a curriculum should not exist in abstraction; however, it should exist as a reflection upon the hidden curriculum of school life.

What is the essential nature of the hidden curriculum as a vehicle of moral growth? Our viewpoint accepts as inevitable the crowds, the praise, and the power which the school inevitably contains. How much or little crowd, praise, or discipline, or power is of little interest from our point of view. A generation of child psychology research measuring the effects of amount and type of family authority and discipline on moral character have yielded few substantial results. If these things do not define the moral-educational effects of the family, they are unlikely to define the weaker and more transient moral effects of particular schools.

The Role of the Teacher

We believe what matters in the hidden curriculum is the moral character and ideology of the teachers and principal as these are translated into a working social atmosphere which influences that atmosphere of the children. In the introduction of a recent book (Hentoff 1966, p. 8) presenting portraits of Shapiro, the principal of P.S. 119, and Boyden, the headmaster of Deerfield, Mayerson says, "Each is engaged in a diligent attempt to achieve a consistency between an articulated personal morality and the daily passage of their lives. The two schools are the sites of the working out of this ideal." Shapiro, the Harlem principal, was trained as a clinical psychologist. His ideology is one of empathy, permissiveness, and respect for his deprived children: meeting their needs, trying to keep their liveliness from dying, with no explicit concern for moral education. The ideology is one of warmth and humility and Shapiro is a warm and humble man who is against the crowds, the praise, and the power. How does his ideology, his warmth, and his humility come across to the school? I quote,

A woman announced that the assembly was being dedicated to Dr. Shapiro. He winced. Eleven girls stood and sang in unison: "Oh he is the bravest, Oh he is the greatest, we'll fight before we switch."

"Talk about brainwashing," Shapiro mumbled, slumped in a back row seat. (p. 38)

It is clear that this humble and dedicated believer in permissiveness is in firm control of the crowds, the praise, and the power.

Neill's personal characteristics are quite different from Shapiro's, yet he too has created an effective moral atmosphere. As a character, Neill is obviously dogmatic, self-assured, imposing. One could not want a stronger, more vigorous leader of a *leaderless* school. In character, he is reminiscent of Frank Boyden, the headmaster of Deerfield, who is described as being without contradiction humanitarian, ruthless, loyal, selfish, selfless, stubborn, indestructible, and infallible. Unlike Neill, Boyden believes in discipline and believes that the purpose of his school is moral character building. Like Neill, Boyden radiates a belief in the value of his school as an end in itself.

In citing Boyden, Shapiro, and Neill as masters of the hidden curriculum, I have tried to indicate that the transformation of the hidden curriculum into a moral atmosphere is not a matter of one or another educational technique or ideology or means, but a matter of the moral energy of the educator, of his communicated belief that his school or classroom has a human purpose. To get his message across, he may use permissiveness or he may use discipline, but the effective moral educator has a believable human message.

The Ends of Moral Education

We have seen, however, that this human message cannot be an ideology of education, or it will end by treating the school as the ultimate value, with the corresponding eventual morality of loyalty to the school or to an ideological doctrine of education in itself. The hidden curriculum of the school must represent something more than the goals and social order of the school itself. Our definition of moral maturity as the principled sense of justice suggests what this end must be. The teaching of justice requires just schools. The crowds, the praise, and the power are neither just nor unjust in themselves. As they are typically used in the schools, they represent the values of social order and of individual competitive achievement. The problem is not to get rid of the praise, the power, the order, and the competitive achievement, but to establish a more basic context of justice which gives them meaning. In our society authority derives from justice, and in our society learning to live with authority should derive from and aid learning to understand and to feel justice.

The need to make the hidden curriculum an atmosphere of justice, and to make this hidden curriculum explicit in intellectual and verbal discussions of justice and morality, is becoming more and more urgent. Our research studies have shown that our Stage 6 or most morally mature college students are the students most active in support of universal civil rights and in support of the universal sacredness of human life as both issues have recently come in clear conflict with authority, law and order, national loyalty, and college administrations. Research also indicates that these mature adolescents are joined by an immature group of rebellious egoistic relativists who think justice means everyone "doing his thing." It seems clear that student-administration confrontations will spread to younger and younger groups who are increasingly confused and immature in their thought about the issues of justice involved.

In the current college confrontations, it has been typical for administrators to harden into poses of what I call Stage 4 law and order thinking, or what I call Stage 5 social contract legalism. What else can they do? What else are they taught in programs of school administration? This is hard to answer because the world's great moral educators have not run schools. Moral education is something of a revolutionary activity. When Socrates engaged in genuine moral education, he was executed for corrupting the Athenian youth. I mention Socrates to indicate that it is not only America who kills its moral educators, its men like Martin Luther King, Jr., who both talked and lived as drum majors of justice.

These fatalities and many others will continue to go on as long as the dialogue about justice goes on across the barricades. The current fate of the school administrator is to find that if he keeps the dialogue out of the classroom, he will face it across the barricades with students to whom he cannot speak. The educational use of the hidden curriculum is not to prevent the dialogue by calling classroom law and order moral character, nor to cast it out on the ground that the child needs only freedom, but to use it to bring the dialogue of justice into the classroom. It is my hope that our educational research program may find worthwhile ways of doing this in the next five years. It is perhaps less a hope than a dream that the American schools will want to use it.

Appendix

Definition of Moral Stages

I. Preconventional level

At this level the child is responsive to cultural rules and labels of good and bad, right or wrong, but interprets these labels in terms of either the physical or the hedonistic consequences of action (punishment, reward, exchange of favors) or in terms of the physical power of those who enunciate the rules and labels. The level is divided into the following two stages:

Stage 1: *The punishment and obedience orientation.* The physical consequences of action determine its goodness or badness regardless of the human meaning or value of these consequences. Avoidance of punishment and unquestioning deference to power are valued in their own right, not in terms of respect for an underlying moral order supported by punishment and authority (the latter being Stage 4).

Stage 2: *The instrumental relativist orientation.* Right action consists of that which instrumentally satisfies one's own needs and occasionally the needs of others. Human relations are viewed in terms like those of the marketplace. Elements of fairness, of reciprocity, and of equal sharing are present, but they are always interpreted in a physical pragmatic way. Reciprocity is a matter of "you scratch my back and I'll scratch yours," not of loyalty, gratitude, or justice.

II. Conventional level

At this level, maintaining the expectations of the individual's family, group, or nation is perceived as valuable in its own right, regardless of immediate and obvious consequences. The attitude is not only one of *conformity* to personal expectations and social order, but of loyalty to it, of actively *maintaining,* supporting, and justifying the order and of identifying with the persons or group involved in it. At this level, there are the following two stages:

Stage 3: *The interpersonal concordance or "good boy—nice girl" orientation.* Good behavior is that which pleases or helps others and is approved by them. There is much conformity to stereotypical images of what is majority or "natural" behavior. Behavior is frequently judged by intention—"he means well" becomes important for the first time. One earns approval by being "nice."

Stage 4: *The "law and order" orientation.* There is orientation toward authority, fixed rules, and the maintenance of the social order. Right behavior consists of doing one's duty, showing respect for authority, and maintaining the given social order for its own sake.

III. *Postconventional, autonomous, or principled level*

At this level, there is a clear effort to define moral values and principles which have validity and application apart from the authority of the groups or persons holding these principles and apart from the individual's own identification with these groups. This level again has two stages:

Stage 5. *The social-contract, legalistic orientation.* Generally with utilitarian overtones. Right action tends to be defined in terms of general individual rights and in terms of standards which have been critically examined and agreed upon by the whole society. There is a clear awareness of the relativism of personal values and opinions and a corresponding emphasis upon procedural rules for reaching consensus. Aside from what is constitutionally and democratically agreed upon, the right is a matter of personal "values" and "opinion." The result is an emphasis upon the "legal point of view," but with an emphasis upon the possibility of changing law in terms of rational considerations of social utility (rather than freezing it in terms of Stage 4 "law and order"). Outside the legal realm, free agreement and contract are the binding elements of obligation. This is the "official" morality of the American government and Constitution.

Stage 6: *The universal ethical principle orientation.* Right is defined by the decision of conscience in accord with self-chosen *ethical principles* appealing to logical comprehensiveness, universality, and consistency. These principles are abstract and ethical (the Golden Rule, the categorical imperative); they are not concrete moral rules like the Ten Commandments. At heart, these are universal principles of *justice,* of the *reciprocity* and *equality* of the human *rights,* and of respect for the dignity of human beings as *individual persons.*

A Moral Dilemma and Sample Responses

In Europe, a woman was near death from a special kind of cancer. There was one drug that the doctors thought might save her. It was a form of radium that a druggist in the same town had recently discovered. The drug was expensive to make, but the druggist was charging ten times what the drug cost him to make. He paid $200 for the radium and charged $2,000 for a small dose of the drug. The sick woman's husband, Heinz, went to everyone he knew to borrow the money, but he could only get together about $1,000, which is half of what it cost. He told the druggist that his wife was dying and asked him to sell it cheaper or let him pay later. But the druggist said, "No, I discovered the drug and I'm going to make money from it." So Heinz got desperate and broke into the man's store to steal the drug for his wife.

Should the husband have done that? Why?

Musammer—age 10   *Stage 1*   *Turkish*

1. No. It's not good to steal. (Why?) If you steal some other's things one day he will steal yours, there will be a fight between the two and they will just put both in prison.

2. (Is it a husband's duty to steal the drug? Would a good husband?) No. He must go and work in order to earn the money for the drug. (If he can't?) One must give him the money. (If nobody gives?) If they don't she will die—he should not steal. (Why not?) If he steals they will put him in prison.

3. (Does the druggist have the right to charge that much for the drug if the law allows him?) No—if he charges so much from the villagemen then they won't have enough money.

4. (If it were your wife who were dying?) I will not steal. I would let her die.

5. If I stole they would tell on me and put me in prison—so would not.

6. They should put him in jail because he stole.

Hamza—age 12   *Stage 2*   *Turkish*

1. Yes, because nobody would give him the drug and he had no money, because his wife was dying it was right. (Wrong not to?) Yes, because otherwise she will die.

2. (Is it a husband's duty to steal the drug?) Yes—when his wife is dying and he cannot do anything he is obliged to steal. (Why?) If he doesn't steal his wife will die.

3. (Does the druggist have the right to charge that much for the drug?) Because he is the only store in the village it is right to sell.

4. (Should he steal the drug if he doesn't love his wife?) If he

doesn't love his wife he should not steal because he doesn't care for her, doesn't care for what she says.

5. (How about if it is a good friend?) Yes—because he loves his friend and one day when he is hungry his friend would help. (If he doesn't love friend?) No—when he doesn't love him it means his friend will not help him.

6. (Should the judge punish him?) They should put him in jail because he stole.

Iskender—age 17   *Stage 4*   *Turkish*

1. He should not have stolen—he should have asked for the drug and they would give him the drug. (They didn't.) He should go some-where else. (Nowhere else to go.) He should try to work for the drug. (He can't.) Then it would be right to steal and not let his wife die because she will die and for that moment it would be right—he had to steal because his wife would die—he had to steal for the first and last time.

2. It is all right to steal when he can't do anything else—for the first and last time and then he should go out to work. (His duty?) It's not his duty to steal, but it is his duty to feed her.

3. (Did the druggist have the right to charge so much?) It's not right—laws are set up to organize people and their living—he charges so much because he is not human—if he thinks of others he must sell things so that everybody can buy.

4. (If he doesn't love her, should he steal the drug?) Because they are married he must—loving and feeling close to her has nothing to do with it. They must be together in bad or good times. Even if it's someone else who is dying he should steal. If I was in his place I would steal if I didn't know the man who was dying. He should do it only once to save somebody's life—if it's a question of death he should steal but not for anything else.

5. (Should the judge send him to jail?) It is up to the judge to decide. If he thinks the man stole just for this once and had to steal to save his wife then he would not put him in jail, but if he thinks the man will do it again and that it will become a habit then he should put him in jail. If the judge is understanding he would find a job for this man who is not working.

James   *Stage 5*   *American college*

1. Heinz did only what he had to. Had I been Heinz, I would probably have done the same thing. In any event, however, Heinz

must be prepared to go to jail for breaking into a store. Breaking into the store was not "right," but the lesser of two wrongs.

2. (Is it his duty?) Every husband must decide which of the two wrongs—letting his wife go without the drug or stealing—is greater *to him*. I would steal.

3. (Did the druggist have the right to charge that much or keep the drug?) The druggist had the *right* to charge that much, although perhaps he should not have. I consider the druggist a despicable human being, even though he was acting within his rights.

Richard   *Stage 6*   *American adult*

1. (Should Heinz have done that?) Yes. It was right; human life and the right to it are prior to, and more precious than, property rights.

2. (Is it a husband's duty to steal the drug for his wife if he can get it no other way?) It is the husband's duty to do so. Any good husband whose ethical values were not confused would do it.

3. (Did the druggist have the right to charge that much when there was no law actually setting a limit to the price?) In a narrow legal sense, he had such a right. From a moral point of view, however, he had no such right.

4. (Heinz broke into the store and stole the drug and gave it to his wife. He was caught and brought before the judge. Should the judge send Heinz to jail for stealing, or should he let him go free? Why?) He should suspend the sentence or dismiss the charge since Heinz did no moral wrong.

References

Blatt, M., and Kohlberg, Lawrence. "The Effects of a Classroom Discussion Program upon the Moral Levels of Preadolescents." *Merrill Palmer Quarterly* (1969).

Bronfenbrenner, Urie. "Soviet Methods of Character Education, Some Implications for Research." *American Psychologist* 17 (1962): 550-65.

Dreeben, Robert. "The Contribution of Schooling to the Learning of Norms." *Harvard Educational Review* 37, no. 2 (spring 1967): 211-37.

Durkheim, Emile. *Moral Education.* New York: Free Press, 1961.

Friedenberg, Edgar Z. *Coming of Age in America: Growth and Acquiescence.* New York: Random House, 1963.

Hartshorne, Hugh, and May, Mark. *Studies in the Nature of Character* (3 vols). New York: Macmillan, 1928-1930.

Hentoff, Nat, and McPhee, John A. *Our Children Are Dying* and *The Head-*

master: Frank L. Boyden, of Deerfield. Two books in one volume with an introduction by Charlotte Mayerson. New York: Four Winds Press, 1966.

Holstein, Constance. "Parental Determinants of the Development of Moral Judgment." Ph.D. dissertation, University of California at Berkeley, 1968.

Jackson, Philip W. *Life in Classrooms.* New York: Holt, Rinehart & Winston, 1968.

Kelley, Earl. *Return to Democracy.* Washington, D.C.: National Education Association, Elementary Instructional Service, 1964.

Neill, A. S. *Summerhill: A Radical Approach to Child Rearing.* New York: Hart, 1960.

Peters, R. S. *Ethics and Education.* Chicago: Scott, Foresman, 1967.

Turiel, E. "Developmental Processes in the Child's Moral Thinking." *New Directions in Developmental Psychology*, edited by P. Mussen, J. Heavenrich, and J. Langer. New York: Holt, Rinehart & Winston, 1969.

14

Moral Education in a Canadian Setting

Edmund V. Sullivan and Clive Beck

Perhaps at the outset, before discussing moral education in the schools, a distinction between the Canadian and United States legal systems is relevant. A crucial legal distinction is that in Canada no sharp separation between church and state functions is written into law. In particular, the issue of moral and religious education in the public schools of Ontario, where we work, although a sensitive topic, is not an openly contentious one, as it is in the U.S. The climate for exploratory moral education programs in our province has been quite favorable for several reasons. When we started our initial work at the Ontario Institute for Studies in Education (OISE), a Commission on Moral and Religious Education was working to provide guidelines for moral and religious education in the schools (Ontario Department of Education 1969). This commission's deliberations drew heavily from a conference on moral education held at OISE and particularly from a paper prepared for the conference by Lawrence Kohlberg (see Beck, Crittenden, and Sullivan 1971). One of the recommendations of the commission was to encourage exploratory programs and

Reprinted by permission from *Phi Delta Kappan* (June 1975): pp. 697-700.

research in moral education. Specifically, the OISE staff was encouraged to work along these lines. At this time we formally started our research project in moral education and have had the encouragement and blessing of the Ministry of Education from that time to the present. The general atmosphere for exploring issues and questions related to moral education in Ontario schools is very cordial at this time.

Pilot Programs

Our discussions in this section are derived from personal involvement as teachers in pilot courses in value education in both the elementary and secondary schools.

A major motive in our efforts at the elementary level was our desire to understand children's thinking on value issues during the middle years of childhood. Initially, the work of Jean Piaget and Kohlberg was most informative. Our work was restricted mostly to students in the later elementary school years. Our general rationale for selection of teaching approaches was as follows:

1. Selection of topics relevant to the student's life situation. We have used a contextual rather than an individualistic approach. We sought to deal with issues that can be termed "the individual and society." Our work cannot be termed "guidance" or sensitivity training and should therefore be considered different from the "values clarification" approach of Sidney Simon and his associates.

2. Selection of topics readily adaptable to different approaches based on background, interest, and concerns of different groups of students.

3. Selection of methods that stimulate attention to cognitive aspects of moral development. Initial testing and evidence of other investigators showed that fifth-grade students are at a preconventional level of moral reasoning in Kohlberg's stage scheme. We did not confine ourselves to a single moral dilemma approach. Instead, we experimented with a variety of methods—all designed to stimulate analysis, discussion, and response to value issues.

4. Selection of methods that would draw on student resources and on their power to help each other work through problems and issues.

These broad criteria reveal a basic concern of the OISE project. Our aim has been for flexibility and adaptability in learning situations. We decided originally not to package curriculum materials, but we are now having some second thoughts on this strategy. Our concern about packaged material stems from the conviction that we can best assist teachers in suggesting uses of materials without adding to the quantity of material.

A key notion in all of our work with students and teachers is that of "structure." The complexity of value questions and the unease with which both teachers and students begin critical examination of value issues require, it seems to us, some ground rules and boundaries. We have observed free-wheeling, nondirective classes where students become dissatisfied and disenchanted with vagueness and looseness. Our own approach is to attempt to give students an initial sense of structure and order through what we call the "principled discussion" method (Beck 1971). We outlined topics for fifth- and sixth-graders under the broad heading of "human relations." For each of the topics, we offer guiding questions for the discussion. At first glance this structure seems rigid, but in fact it allows ideas to be examined within a broad framework. We have labeled this framework a minicourse in human relations, with the following content topics, each of which might occupy about two forty-minute periods: (1) rules people give us; (2) the place of rules in society; (3) exceptions to society's rules; (4) the individual's need for other people; (5) helping other people; (6) the self and others; (7) the place of law, judges, and police; (8) the place of governments and other authorities; (9) law breaking and the place of punishment, etc. In all, there are twenty topics suggested under this one unit.

Children were given study notes on each of these topics to provide a structure—a sense of direction for the learning session or sessions.

Evaluation of our work in the elementary schools was both formal and informal. Of specific interest here is our formal evaluation procedure. Since we were interested in how children deliberate on moral issues, we found Kohlberg's moral reasoning directly relevant. In the fall of 1970, we interviewed forty-two students who deliberated on Kohlberg's moral dilemmas. These students were divided into two groups: (1) those who would participate in our minicourse in ethics (the experimental group) and (2) those who, as a group, were matched on age, IQ, and social class status but who did not participate in the minicourse (control group). We assessed these students, using Kohlberg's moral dilemmas, over a two-year period at three intervals. A pretest was given to all the students before the experimental group started to work with value issues. The first posttest was given at the end of the semester. The second or follow-up was given to both groups one year after completion of the course. The interviews were scored in order to determine the stage of the child's moral reasoning. Briefly, Kohlberg's (1971) framework encompasses three levels subdivided into six stages of moral reasoning:

Level I—Preconventional
    Stage 1. Punishment and obedience orientation
    Stage 2. Naive instrumental hedonism
Level II—Conventional
    Stage 3. Interpersonal concordance (good boy—nice girl)
    Stage 4. Law and order orientation
Level III—Postconventional, Autonomous, or Principled
    Stage 5. Social contract legalistic orientation
    Stage 6. Universal ethical principles

On the pretests, all the students were assessed as being at the preconventional level, and the two groups were similar on this account. Both groups at the first posttest showed an advancement toward conventional stages, but there was some indication that the experimental group was somewhat more accelerated in this development. Finally, in a posttest follow-up done a year after the minicourse was completed, the experimental group showed significantly more and higher levels of conventional reasoning, i.e., Stage 4 thinking. Looking at the results more descriptively—that is, from the difference between the control group which showed some development in moral reasoning without formal help and the experimental group which participated in the twice-weekly discussions—we would say that both groups show a general developmental trend from predominantly Stage 1 thinking on the pretest to predominantly Stage 3 on the posttest. The differences between the two classes are seen in: (1) the emergence of Stage 4 reasoning in both the posttest and follow-up for the experimental class while no Stage 4 thinking was apparent in the control-group children; (2) after the first year, the experimental children no longer responded at Stage 1 (external authority . . . avoid punishment), but began thinking more at Stages 2 and 3; on the other hand, the control-group children did not drop Stage 1 thinking as drastically. As with the control group, the experimental group begins with the same reliance on external authority structures (preconventional), but by the end of the first year these students had definitely swung to an orientation in which they began to think more independently, using ideas of fairness, reciprocity, and equal sharing. At the same time, a few students began thinking in the larger context of society.

Note that our elementary school work is tentative and exploratory, not definitive. It helps us in the effort to bring theory and practice into harmony.

Secondary Schools

Our work with adolescents preceded our elementary school efforts, and the major part was carried out in two different secondary schools over a period of about four years. In the first school, Mr. Beck took over a third-year class in the humanities two days per week to discuss moral issues. Students at this age level are normally in what Kohlberg calls the conventional morality stage. For the most part, the issues raised in class were designed to produce reflection on moral conventions and to consider alternative, sometimes novel, solutions. Thus we encouraged what Kohlberg calls postconventional morality. During the initial meetings with the students, we had a direct discussion of moral theories and principles. The teacher structured the class much more at the beginning, then increasingly relinquished control of topics as the class progressed. The discussions were always informal, however, in a relaxed atmosphere. This class lasted for only one semester, and we were not sure what we could accomplish in so short a period.

The class consisted of seventeen students who volunteered to participate in an "experimental" ethics course. A matched comparison group (control) was assessed on moral reasoning at various times but had not attended the "experimental" ethics course.

Members of the experimental ethics class were encouraged by the teacher to discuss a number of topics. Although the following sequence was not rigidly adhered to, and side topics were introduced occasionally, the topics were in general as follows: (1) some distinctive features of moral goodness; (2) myself and other people; (3) an individual's need for other people; (4) acting out of moral reasons; (5) the place of mixed motivations; (6) the importance of spontaneity and single-mindedness; (7) the place of moral principles and rules; (8) the value of the act versus the value of the rule; (9) conscience; (10) justice, equality, and fairness; (11) developing mutually beneficial solutions; (12) moral diversity; (13) the pursuit of happiness; and (14) an analysis of various virtues and vices.

The course of study was as much an experiment for us as for the students and the school. We reasoned that discussion and disagreement among a group of peers would produce some conflict in their moral thinking and dissatisfaction with their present perception of moral relationships, which was generally at conventional and preconventional levels. Our purpose as educators would be to draw out those ideas that embodied a more critical attitude toward moral issues through asking questions and helping the students to sustain this kind of thinking in discussion. Since most of our students were reasoning at the conventional level (Stages 3 and 4), we attempted for the most part to delve into the reasoning behind conventional norms, an understanding which we would typify as postconventional reasoning. At least from the point of view of moral reasoning, the results of our efforts can be seen in figure 1.

When the ethics class ended, there seemed to be no detectable difference between the experimental and control groups. At first we attributed this to the fact that the class was too short in duration. More informal interviews with students, however, made us think that we had accomplished more than was indicated by the Kohlberg moral judgment questionnaire. The students in the ethics course seemed more reflective; their informal statements and evaluations of the course indicated a considerable amount of conflict, which we felt to be possibly growth producing. The following summary helps give an impression of student attitudes near the end of the sessions.

After T's summary, it struck some of the students that we had been going around in circles in this course and had learned very little that we didn't already know. There followed a half-hour discussion of the value of the course, and how such a course might be conducted. Some felt we should be more concrete, discussing and solving particular moral problems. Others (especially IJ) felt that we were quite specific enough, and it would be rather boring discussing each other's

Figure 1
Mean Percentage of Stage 5 Usage for Each Group at Each Test Time

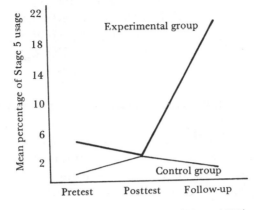

Source: Beck, Sullivan, and Taylor, *Interchange* (Winter 1972), pp. 28-37.

personal problems. OP felt that if we became too personal there would be a strong pressure to conform and we would all end up the same. She said that she had noticed already how one or two members of the class sometimes made scornful comments about particular individuals' points of view. Several students commented that the course had enabled them to think more carefully about moral problems. T said that it is difficult just to sit down and recall what one has learned in a course, especially when one has no textbook to provide markers. He wondered whether it might help to look at some historical theories in moral philosophy, and a number of students thought that that might be a good idea. He asked whether the students would like more blackboard notes to take down (more than the usual two or three points), but the consensus was that two or three points were plenty. In general, there was a feeling of (1) not having "learned" very much from the course, (2) having quite enjoyed the discussions, and (3) having profited in a rather vague way from the course.

Experience of conflict and struggling with seemingly unresolvable (since not resolvable at the conventional level of moral thinking) social problems might, not surprisingly, lead to a sense of frustration and retreat from new and interesting forms of moral reasoning. In this light, the follow-up results are particularly intriguing. It would seem that the passage of time had tempered the feeling of conflict, and natural life experiences had produced opportunities for exercising some of the postconventional notions and skills gleaned from the classes. At any rate, the fact that the change that occurred was a Stage 5 change is reassuring, since it was in the direction of this kind of thinking that we had hoped to encourage our students.

To summarize, it would seem that the significant increase in moral reasoning detected for the experimental group in the follow-up was the result of an increase in Stage 5 thinking.

Findings of this nature, at both the elementary and secondary levels, encourage us to pursue our assessment in a more long-term developmental perspective, where this is possible. In this we distinguish ourselves from other sentiments about educational evaluation, e.g., educational behaviorism and educational technology. We are aware of the problems related to a "developmental" perspective:

A major appeal of educational behaviorism is its objective statement of criterion measures. It is much more difficult to specify criterion measures for developmental growth than for the immediate acquisition of specific, correct responses. Not only is it difficult to specify criteria for developmental change, but teachers rarely work with a student long enough to observe a significant change in development. . . . Developmental change is difficult to detect, especially in age-graded classes. With the exception of some nongraded schools, few schools are organized to highlight developmental change. . . . One does not measure a child's developmental stage every day, but one uses this way of thinking as a background feature for viewing the child's day-to-day behavior. (Hunt and Sullivan 1974, p. 59)

The developmental perspective we are espousing does not always bring with it the joys we hope for in our work. After this initial effort in the secondary schools, we launched a full-scale effort for two semesters in another school. By this time we had devised an elementary ethics textbook for high school students and had identified other materials to bring to the classroom for discussion purposes. In our enthusiasm, both of us attended and conducted these classes, and also had some graduate students assisting us from time to time. At least from the point of view of Kohlberg's moral assessment, our efforts appeared to produce negligible results. The discrepancy between the results at this school and the one where we previously had been successful made us reflect on ways in which the two courses may have differed. First, the teaching format changed when we worked in the latter (unsuccessful) school, which we shall call School B. We used a structured textbook in School B that was not available when we worked at School A. Although the content was postconventional in orientation, it nevertheless reflected the initial interests of the teachers and not the students. This may have put the students in a conventional set to accept our ideas as a source of expert authority. Second, School B differed from School A in the number of instructors who taught the class. In School A only one instructor taught the class for a semester. At B the classes were led by five different instructors. The first-semester classes were conducted with the two major directors of the project (Beck and Sullivan), who worked jointly with the students, and the second-semester classes were conducted by three other OISE colleagues who conducted the class individually. The presence of so many different instructors may have caused the course to become disorganized because of so many different points of view. Probably the most beneficial arrangement was at School A, where there was a sustained postconventional orientation given by one teacher. Third, we felt that a difference in the school atmospheres also could have been a factor in the discrepancy in results. Even from the study at School A, we would have to conclude that our course by itself did not produce the significant increase in Stage 5 reasoning, since there was no significant difference between the experimental and control group at the end of the course, i.e., in the posttest. The change occurred one year later (i.e., follow-up) with an interim in which no course in ethics was offered. Our own feeling was that our course interacted with other significant factors in the school atmosphere to produce the increase in Stage 5 reasoning. In other words, our ethics course was a catalyst for change when combined with other factors. Our own subjective evaluation of the two secondary schools in which we have worked is that they were different in atmosphere. We felt that School A was more open and democratic in structure than School B.

The Teacher and School Atmosphere

Our experience in two high schools made us aware of the "hidden curriculum" discussed by critics of the school. We became much more sensitive to how the structure of the school can implicitly encourage a certain kind of morality—to be more specific, an authoritarian, conventional one. Many of the efforts of individual teachers to help students toward a postconventional (Stages 5 or 6) level of moral development are frustrated by a school atmosphere and organization which constantly emphasize lower-stage values and principles. Or, to put the point more positively, a school atmosphere and organization which exhibit postconventional features can greatly facilitate the development of students toward higher moral stages. Unfortunately, most school systems are run on broadly authoritarian lines; a relationship of mutual trust, respect, and cooperation between student and teacher is extremely difficult to cultivate in such an environment.

Teachers can do much to create the appropriate environment in the classroom. To begin with, they can learn intellectual humility and a willingness to admit ignorance, acknowledge a mistake, or modify views in the face of sound counter-arguments by students. The teacher should not pose as an intellectual genius nor as an infallible source of knowledge. There are considerable pressures upon him from parents, the public, and even the students to maintain such a posture, but he must resist these forces. In particular, teachers must learn to give full acknowledgement of, and make constant use of, the expertise of students. Only in this way can a spirit of cooperative search for knowledge and wisdom be developed in the classroom.

The teacher should show respect for the student as a person. This is easily said and repeated, but we often overlook the enormous backlog of authoritarianism toward younger people which exists in society. Permissiveness is not what is needed; that is not respect. We are only "permissive" to inferiors. The teacher must treat students as other *people*, who have a diversity of abilities and desires (just as he/she has), and with whom he/she happens to be engaged in certain semi-personal, cooperative activities. It is true that the teacher has been given a degree of authority over students, but this authority should be exercised only insofar as a sizable majority are convinced that it is necessary for the cooperative activities in which they are engaged. The teacher is a resource person, chairperson, leader; but these roles should be exercised only insofar as is deemed useful by the group. If most of the students in a class feel at a particular point that such a role is not needed, or that someone else could fill it better, that settles the matter. All of those people are unlikely to be wrong, although it is possible that they could be.

But while these arrangements and relationships are being established in the classroom, the school as a whole may be militating against the objectives of the particular teacher. A great deal of research remains to be carried out in the area of nonauthoritarian school organization and its effects upon moral development. Some experiments have been performed, and there are various books and articles on free schools, open schools, and nonauthoritarian schools in general. It is difficult to draw conclusions from these experiments. Many free schools have been either too small or too short-lived or too unusual in some other way for us to make predictions about what might happen in a large school in a total system. Open-plan schools have been tried fairly extensively over a long period in some areas, but where they have succeeded it is difficult to tell why this is so—and there have been many failures. Furthermore, it is questionable whether open-plan schools, working within a basically authoritarian system, can really be nonauthoritarian. Sometimes, perhaps, they become even more authoritarian than usual, because of the difficulties of maintaining conventional "order" in an open-plan situation. This fact highlights the basic problem of bringing about institutional changes favorable to moral development in the schools: It is difficult to change the classroom without a change in the structural arrangements and authority channels of the school itself.

We are also struck by the possibility of the teacher's moral level influencing the classroom discussion. Our own conviction is that teachers at a postconventional level of morality are needed to stimulate higher levels of moral reasoning in students. This does not necessarily make the teacher a moral rebel or a danger to school order. In most instances, postconventional moral arguments recognize the need for conventions, but they base the merits of the conventions on sound reasoning rather than on some unquestioned authority. Certain discussions on contemporary social issues may take students and the teacher into areas where there are no clear authoritative sources. The teacher must indicate to the student his own fallibility on such matters, if and when they arise in a classroom discussion. It would seem difficult for Stage 4 conventional "law and order" teachers to put themselves in this kind of role because there will be a latent fear that, if the teacher does not have all the answers, his classroom authority will be eroded. Since the structure of the class usually leaves the teacher in a controlling position, he is typically the initial modulator of the level of the classroom discussion. If the teacher's emphasis is on the maintenance of "law and order" and "authority," the discussion is not likely to venture into levels where authority is questioned on rational grounds.

There is usually a selective process in education, and, ordinarily, teachers who are successful in professional educational circles have conventional moral values. This is not necessarily an indictment of the teaching profession, since there are many good reasons which give support to conventional morality. The school is an agent of socialization; part of its mandate is to help parents and society in the inculcation of conventional moral norms. No one would argue that contemporary schooling is failing in its attempt at this mandate. The only problem is that much of conventional morality does not match up with the problems presented to the student in contemporary society. In school he is learning conventional morals that appear archaic. We do not wish to argue that everything new under the "moral sun" has an aura of sanctity about it, but it is imperative with our rapidly changing value systems to examine both old and new values alike. The problem with most teacher training institutions is that they are the fortress of most conventional norms. The teacher who finishes training is well aware of the "tried and true" conventions that have kept the school going for years. These conventions are known as the collective wisdom which all new teachers need in order to get by and succeed in their task. The final outcome of this whole process, which is subsequently supported by the very structure of the school, is a predominance of teachers who remain for the most part in the conventional stages (Stages 3 and 4) of morality. The emphasis on "law and order" in the school is important, but it inhibits some aspects of the educational process.

One might ask, therefore, Is there a necessity for teacher training in areas related to moral education? The answer, from looking at our project, is an unqualified yes. All the teachers and observers who have done practicums with us stressed the importance of serious reflection in the teacher training colleges in all areas of the curriculum which are value laden. From our work we conclude that the range of the previous statement covers most subjects in the curriculum. Our practicum participants stressed the importance of moral dimensions in such varied topics as history, social studies, and comparative religion. No doubt this stress can be seen in other subjects, e.g., humanities, literature, etc.

To break the kind of set in the teacher training institutions which is described above will be no easy task. Looking back on our practicums, we can see that teachers quite unconsciously fell into teacher-centered class formats, even when they thought they were avoiding them. It will be very important in the future to help generate environments other than the teacher-centered format to alleviate some of the challenges of moral indoctrination.

It will also be important for psychologists and other social scientists to be sensitive to how their theories and findings are used in teacher preparatory colleges. One example will suffice, using Kohlberg's stage theory. It may occur, as it did in our work with teachers, that these people are interested in the moral development stages à la Kohlberg. The question that educational psychologists must ask is whether the psychological characteristic as it is described will have effects on a teacher's attitude which may be detrimental. For example, by telling a teacher that one child is at an "instrumental hedonist" stage, while another is at the "good boy—nice girl" stage, does he run the risk of having the teacher negatively evaluate one stage over another in a stereotype, rather than take a developmental perspective? It seems that this is not a rare occurrence, and we are increasingly becoming aware of the moral issues that it creates for social scientists when they give out personality labels to the public (see Ryan 1971). In one of the schools in which we worked, we inquired of the whereabouts of a student in one of our biweekly classes; we were told that the teacher asked him to leave the class "because he was a wise guy and a Stage 2." It is important to be constantly sensitive to the fact that the assessment instruments that we devise and the labels we use can easily be made tools of victimization by ourselves and the teachers with whom we work.

References

Beck, Clive M. "Moral Education in the Schools: Some Practical Suggestions." *Profiles in Practical Education*, no. 3. Toronto: Ontario Institute for Studies in Education, 1971.

Beck, Clive M.; Crittenden, Brian S.; and Sullivan, Edmund V. (eds.) *Moral Education: Interdisciplinary Approaches.* New York: Newman Press, 1971.

Hunt, David E., and Sullivan, Edmund V. *Between Psychology and Education.* Hinsdale, Ill.: Dryden Press, 1974.

Kohlberg, Lawrence. "Stages of Moral Development as a Basis for Moral Education." *Moral Education: Interdisciplinary Approaches*, edited by Clive

M. Beck, Brian S. Crittenden, and Edmund V. Sullivan. New York: Newman Press, 1971.

Ontario Department of Education. *Report of the Committee on Religious Education in the Public Schools of the Province of Ontario.* Toronto: The Department, 1969.

Ryan, William. *Blaming the Victim.* New York: Vintage, 1971.

15

A Curriculum in Moral Education
for Adolescents

Ralph L. Mosher and Paul Sullivan

Introduction

Guidance has had a long search for its identity. Historically, counselors began by matching man and job. Assessment, in the form of the testing of intelligence, academic achievement, job aptitude, vocational interest, and personality followed. Most recently, the field has been preoccupied with providing psychotherapy or psychological counseling to troubled children, adolescents, and adults. Guidance has had important influence, both real and symbolic, on education. It has consistently argued the importance of emotional, social, and vocational development in an educational system giving priority to intellect; it has valued the individual against the institution and believed in his potential. Guidance has promised much and delivered too little, yet it remains an important ideology in public education.

But as the little red schoolhouse recently has come under increasing criticism so, too, has the little white clinic. Less than half the counselors in the United States have had training in psychological

An earlier version of this chapter appeared in *Focus on Guidance* (January 1974).

counseling. "Longitudinal studies indicate that these fields (counseling, guidance and school psychology) failed to successfully prognose, much less cure, mental illness partly because they confused mental illness with deviance from the middle-class norms of the schools" (Kohlberg 1971).

Guidance has been a stepchild. It has derived its theory from other sources: industrial psychology, educational psychology, clinical psychology, and psychiatry. We believe that counseling must transcend its derivative status and overcome a passivity and inefficacy in the face of great human pain, confusion, and need. The time is opportune both for a rigorous accounting and for a reformulation of counseling's objectives. New initiatives are essential. They should come from an honest appraisal of what guidance has and has not done, a comprehensive view of the many factors which affect growth and learning in this culture, and an acknowledgment that the problems we face are larger than the survival of counselors per se.

A New Rationale for Guidance

A basic need in counseling is for theory which will enable the field to move beyond a primary concern with the treatment or rehabilitation of atypical individuals or subpopulations (e.g., school underachievers, the emotionally disturbed, drug-dependent adolescents). John Dewey argued that the stimulation of human development is the basic objective of education. And Lawrence Cremin has said that guidance is the most characteristic child of the progressive movement in American education. We believe that the education of the person must be whole: i.e., it must stimulate cognitive or intellectual growth, moral sensibilities and reasoning, emotional growth, social skills, vocational competencies, aesthetic development, and physical maturation. Within a concern for overall ego or personal development, then, we believe that guidance should provide educational experiences which help every individual grow as a person—specifically in terms of moral, emotional, social, and vocational development. Obviously, these are major and crucial aspects of human development. They are the dimensions which have historically concerned and at least implicitly unified the fields of counseling, guidance, and school psychology. Thus, we both reassert and reformulate generic objectives in arguing that the stimulation of personal, emotional, ethical, social, and vocational development for all is the basic justification for the professional specialty of guidance.

We believe further that counseling should provide leadership in educational and psychological programs to stimulate human development on these dimensions. Counselors, as we see it, will work where crucial educational effects on ego, emotional, and moral development occur: in schools, with teachers and students; in the community, with parents and the numerous educational resources which exist there. Functionally, this means the counselor must have the ability to analyze, prescribe, and act for psychological growth on individual, organizational, and community levels. He will cooperate with others in stimulating development in individuals and in the organizations or social systems which affect their growth.

It is essential to be specific about the means by which the counselor is to accomplish these very ambitious objectives. Obviously, it is presumptuous to suggest that counselors can realize these aims by themselves. But we envisage a guidance counselor who knows more, does more, and has different priorities than at present. The requisite theoretical and educational programs already exist to make it possible for counselors to be moral educators. We have at least three reasons for focusing counselors' attention on moral education. The first reason has already been set out: the basic purpose of education, and of guidance, is the stimulation of individual development. The course in moral education we will describe is an example of an educational program designed to stimulate overall ego development in adolescence (Mosher and Sprinthall 1971). Secondly, we believe that counselors should be knowledgeable of the substantial theoretical and educational experimentation now going on in moral education. Third, we believe that counselors are uniquely confronted by the moral dilemmas with which children and adolescents struggle, and that they have skills and contributions essential to effective programs of moral education. For these reasons we suggest that counselors act as moral educators. Rather than claiming to be "value neutral" (a claim debunked a decade ago by Shoben's argument that counselors are, in fact, "smugglers" of school and adult values) we believe that counselors should join teachers, administrators, and parents in the development of systematic programs of moral education in the school.

Moral Development

Our curriculum work in moral education draws heavily on Kohlberg's empirical and theoretical study of moral development. Because of Kohlberg's (1973) contributions we have a relatively clear blueprint for this aspect of adolescent development. We know the characteristics of adolescent moral thinking, its progression, and some of the experiences critical to its stimulation. While the major educational and curricular applications of Kohlberg's theory remain to be done, we believe that the theoretical understanding of moral development now available allows that practical work to go forward with dispatch and promise.

We will first review, briefly, Kohlberg's moral development theory, as it provides the basis for our curriculum. In addition, a reasonably sophisticated understanding of the theory permits the teacher better to comprehend the flow of adolescent argument about moral dilemmas, to categorize it (i.e., to differentiate stages and subtleties in moral discussion), and to make appropriate responses (e.g., clarifying questions, probes, counter-arguments at a higher stage). Finally, the theory suggests educational experiences beyond the analysis or discussion of moral issues (e.g., the importance of role-taking) which may have important developmental consequences.

In Kohlberg's conceptualization "moral" refers basically to thought processes, i.e., to judgment, reasoning, or decision making in situations where the person has conflicting responsibilities. Moral principles are principles of choice for resolving conflicts of obligation. This reflects the strong cognitive and philosophic elements in the theory. "Moral" is not simply a tag to be attached to actions of which we approve. Morality is an overall mental structure, a means for deciding what one should or should not do in situations involving competing moral values. Each stage of moral development has a characteristic way of resolving such conflicts. These stages of moral development are empirically derived. Kohlberg has found that these characteristic ways of thinking about moral choice exist across class and culture; they are universal and developmental.

The principles one uses in making decisions develop from the egocentric, limited, and externally derived canons usually characteristic of younger children to the autonomous, universal, and inclusive principles which characterize the highest levels of moral reasoning. Moral thinking becomes increasingly differentiated and integrated in the course of development. Each successive stage produces more complex, more cognitively and philosophically satisfactory principles. At the highest level, principles such as justice provide a universal mode of choosing, one which we would want all people to adopt in all situations.

Moral Education for Adolescents

The course we will describe is intended primarily for juniors and seniors in high school. A modified version will be tested shortly with sophomores. The course presently is taken for credit as a social studies elective. It could, as logically, be offered in a guidance, human development, psychology, or philosophy curriculum. The course can be taught both within a regular four period per week schedule or as an after school course for three hours once per week. It is designed to be taught for one semester or during a full year.

The course is introduced to the students in a relatively simple and straightforward way. They are told that they will be taking a course in ethical or moral reasoning; that the fundamental purpose of the experience is to have them think deeply and at length about a variety of complex social and personal moral dilemmas or issues. We suggest certain general synonyms for the term "moral"—questions of "right" and "wrong," value issues, questions of individual rights, obligations to others, etc. We emphasize that our purpose is not to teach a set of right and wrong answers. The point is to allay for the adolescent or his parent any concern that the course will involve indoctrination or preaching.

We will use the term "phase" to describe distinctive and sequential stages in the course. However, the educational experiences characteristic of these several phases do not need to be offered in the order we use. They are best seen as units or components in an overall course which involves high school students in systematic intellectual analysis of moral dilemmas and in a variety of role-taking experiences (e.g., "ethical" counseling with other adolescents or acting as moral educators with peers or younger children). The basic learning paradigm is to involve the adolescents' ways of thinking about moral questions and issues with the perspectives and thought of other adolescents and the teacher. The student is then put in "real" situations or experiences where he must apply moral thought to the ethical problems or dilemmas of other people.

Personal Introductions

Phase 1 of the course involves personal introductions. The student is asked to introduce himself and, if he chooses, to talk about some recent experience of special significance. Some students make extended introductions in which they talk about experiences with drugs, learning experiences, disciplinary problems, or problems with boyfriends or girlfriends. Other students (those less verbal, less secure in a new group) introduce themselves briefly and with some embarrassment. The teacher supports the student and often in a subtle way focuses on the personal moral issues mentioned.

Dilemma Discussions

Phase 2 of the course involves discussion and analysis of moral dilemmas through the case study method. We use two kinds of case study materials. The first is films, either full length or edited segments of feature films with depict ethical dilemmas. The use of films as a stimulus for classroom discussion is hardly a new educational technique. Nonetheless, using films specifically to stimulate moral discussion was suggested originally by seeing "The Godfather." Among other things, it is a modern American morality play. We subsequently used the films "Deliverance," "Serpico," "Judgment at Nuremberg," "On the Waterfront," and the TV dramatization of the Andersonville Trial. A number of films from the Learning Corporation of America series, "Searching for Values," also were used. The latter series is made up of edited versions of fourteen feature length films, focusing on salient moral dilemmas. We have tested these films sufficiently to feel that at least two-thirds of them are useful in generating moral discussions with adolescents.

Our experience is that appropriately selected films are very powerful stimuli to moral discussion and reasoning. There are several reasons for this. Film is the medium of this generation, and in very subtle and potent ways can personalize moral issues. Michael Corleone, the young Don in "The Godfather," is a very compelling figure for adolescents—one with whom they can and do identify. Further, one does not have to be a good reader to be able to understand issues in a film. Our use of film has simply *worked*. We did find it important to ensure that everyone in the class had recently seen the film to be discussed, to avoid arguments about facts. The problem that a particular feature film may not be available when the teacher wants a class to see it will be solved as film series (such as those by Guidance Associates, Learning Corporation of America, and Encyclopedia Britannica) become more extensively available. We also encourage teachers to experiment with moral discussion of new feature films and not to rely exclusively on canned series.

We also use written case materials. *Moral Reasoning—The Value of Life* by Alan Lockwood (1972) is an excellent example. We used this inexpensive paperback unit book as a text for the course. It contains a series of brief, well-written, and arresting case studies on the issue of life and its value. Certain of the case titles suggest the nature of the situations dealt with: "Should the Baby Live?" (a mother's responsibility to a seriously retarded baby), "Too Old To Keep Alive," "Hitler Must Be Killed," "The 'Wasting' of a Village" (Lieutenant Calley and the massacre at My Lai). Discussion questions are suggested for the students, and there is a treatment of the psychology of moral development. Coupled with a film such as "The Right To Live: Who Decides?" (in the Learning Corporation of America series) and with the television film "The Andersonville Trial," an in-depth discussion of the value of a human life can be developed. Our experience, however, is that a class can reach a point of saturation in the discussion of any moral issue, no matter how basic. When that occurs we move on to other case materials or issues and, perhaps, return at a later point.

Teaching Counseling Skills

Phase 3 of the course involves teaching counseling skills to the students. Why do we do this in a course designed to stimulate moral development? In part, because of a serendipity. Some years ago we used the Kohlberg moral development scale as one developmental measure to assess the effect of teaching counseling to high school students (Mosher and Sprinthall 1971). We selected the instrument because it was designed to measure growth-developmental change and not because of any postulated relationship between learning to counsel and moral development. What we found, to our surprise, was that students studying counseling for a semester developed, on the average, about a third to a half stage in terms of measured moral reasoning. This was a change roughly equivalent to that achieved by Blatt in courses designed specifically and directly to analyze and discuss moral dilemmas and, thereby, to effect moral development.

On reflection, it became apparent to us that adolescents, in learning to counsel, at first responded to personal dilemmas in the lives of people they were attempting to help by judging behavior as appropriate or inappropriate or by writing the person a prescription —telling him what to do. The cumulative effect of the experience of counseling under supervision was that the adolescent came to see that human problems are very complex and different and that judging another person's behavior or suggesting what to do is not really very helpful. In short, we were training adolescents to understand a person's ideas, feelings, and dilemmas in more complex, comprehensive, and subtle ways.

There are, we now see, further theoretical reasons to assume that training in counseling may contribute to moral reasoning. Kohlberg suggests that at least two central things are happening in the process of moral development. One is that the individual's capacity for empathy develops; the other has to do with the emergence of a more comprehensive understanding of the principle of justice in human relationships and human social units. Clearly, in teaching adolescents to counsel, we are offering them systematic theoretical and, especially, *applied* training in empathy. By that we mean, very simply, to accurately identify and sensitively respond to the feelings and ideas of another person. Whatever the approach to empathy training, the essential point is that this training coincides almost exactly with a major component in the development of greater moral sensitivity. The effect of counseling is also due to the role-taking which occurs in responding empathically. Role-taking and empathy have much in common. In a larger sense, we are talking about a generic strand in ego development. In short, there is a solid basis in Kohlberg's theory to support what we stumbled upon—but found to work—in an earlier phase of curriculum development.

Theoretically, counselors are in the best position to teach counseling, and we argue for their inclusion in moral education programs. But counselors, too, are somewhat insecure in teaching high school students. The way we teach counseling has been described at length elsewhere and will not be extensively recapitulated here. (See Mosher and Sprinthall 1971; Dowell 1971; Griffen 1972; Sprinthall 1973;

Mackie 1974.) Nonetheless, a brief overview of the procedures we employ may be useful. A unit on counseling probably should not take less than six weeks of the course time (i.e., eighteen to twenty hours) and could be expanded to occupy to large part of one semester. It will be recalled that during the students' personal introductions the teachers often "model" some counseling responses. They listen and respond to the central feelings, personal concerns, or ethical issues raised by the students in a supportive and, at that point, nonconfronting way. The counseling phase of the course moves through a general sequence of experiences for the students. We first involve them in exercises adapted from Carkhuff in which they are asked as helpers to respond to brief "role plays" of "client" personal problems done by other students. They are taught to rate their responses for degree of empathy, specificity, and related counseling behavior, argued by Rogers, Carkhuff and others as essential to effectiveness. We then ask them to prepare a longer case-problem or ethical issue to be discussed with a counselor, divide the students into pairs, and have them alternate in the roles of helper or counselor and client. These discussions are taped. One or more of them will be analyzed and discussed before the group as a whole. The supervision is quite specific and intensive. The tapes are then individually analyzed with the two students present, and the feedback of the student who has been the "client" is used as the final criterion of the perceptiveness and sensitivity of the "counselor." Students make a number of these tapes in both roles, work with different students, and are supervised in so doing.

The issues which the students introduce are almost always personal issues, although there is no formal pressure that their role-play cases be so. For example, one girl talked in her first tape about a problem in her own family. An older brother, already convicted of one charge of selling drugs, had left a cache of dope in the home where she found it. It was evident to her that he was again selling drugs, a fact he admitted when confronted. The ethical issue was whether she should tell her father about her brother's pushing or keep silent: *to honor her father and "rat" on her brother.* The dilemma was further complicated by the fact that her father was not well and that the older brother had been for some years a source of disappointment and very real worry for both parents. In addition, she had been throughout (or saw herself as) a dutiful daughter—essentially straight, not a drug user. Yet the older brother got a disproportionate amount of the parents' attention, concern, and time; she felt herself somewhat taken for granted as a steady and reliable daughter. Not surprisingly, she had real feelings of anger toward the brother for the way he treated both his parents and her. She saw her dilemma as an opportunity to get back at the brother, but had concomitant feelings of guilt about doing so. It is worth mentioning that this complex ethical issue was introduced by the girl in the first session. In a sense, it is a classic Stage 3 dilemma in Kohlberg's terms: A good girl and daughter who really wants to do the right thing for others in her family. If she tells her father, as she feels she must, she tells on (and prejudices) her brother—which he has asked her not to do.

Another girl talked about the problem of a friend—the oldest child in a family of six in which the parents were divorced. Late in the evening she picked up an extension phone to hear her mother planning an assignation with the husband of one of the mother's best friends. The obvious question is what does she do with that kind of information. These cases are dramatic illustrations of the kinds of personal ethical issues raised in counseling, and they lead to another question relative to a course in moral reasoning: Should the teacher deal with the issue in abstract terms or in direct terms? Our position is that the teacher should attempt to do both things. That is, he should help the student analyze the dilemma, *and* help the student decide on some resolution. It is a delicate matter for the teacher to avoid either being wishy-washy or trying directly (or subtly) to persuade an adolescent of the "rightness" of a particular course of action. But a thorough examination of the problem, the possible courses of action and their consequences, plus support for the individual's reasoned decision seems to be the responsible path for the teacher.

Teaching Teaching Skills

Phase 4 of the course involves training high school students to be moral educators with younger children. This gives them systematic experience in role-taking. We put them in a real role—as a teacher —where they can apply or use, under supervision, what they have learned about moral development and moral reasoning. Our experience in related courses, where high school students have taught in elementary schools or counseled on community "hot lines" or in peer counseling programs at the high school level, suggests to us that these kinds of role-taking experiences are growth producing. By being involved in teaching moral reasoning to younger children or peers, the adolescent's own moral development will be stimulated. One learns by doing. (The writers' own understanding of moral development theory and ethical analysis has become much more comprehensive under the stimulus of creating this curriculum and teaching it to adolescents. We expect this will be true for most teachers.) The opportunity to see how younger children reason about moral dilemmas, and to teach moral reasoning, offers to adolescents a broader understanding of aspects of human growth. It also gives them an enhanced sense of personal competency. But the basic reason is to deepen and make more comprehensive their own understanding of moral issues.

This phase of the course consists of a weekly seminar and a practicum lasting most of a semester. The practicum opportunities include teaching in religious schools (where adolescents typically act as student aides) and in regular elementary classrooms. Guidance Associates now has available filmstrip case material for use in the elementary classroom especially adapted to the concerns and attention span of younger children.

An important aspect of this phase is the ongoing seminar and supervision of the adolescents. We help the students prepare for the moral discussions and then allow them to analyze what occurred. On-the-spot supervision of the actual teaching is provided as often as possible; classroom discussions are tape recorded for future review. Our plan has the adolescent co-teach with at least one other teenager. This affords mutual support; it is also invaluable to have more than one person leading a discussion, since each sees the discussion in somewhat different terms or perspectives and can respond to things the other does not see—both during the discussion and when analyzing it afterward.

The weekly seminar serves several functions. Cases, materials, and teaching strategies are prepared, including learning more about Kohlberg and related theories, framing specific stage arguments, asking questions that elicit an individual's reasoning about moral issues, etc. Also, the seminar is a place to examine how well particular discussions went, which arguments or tactics were effective, what ways of reasoning were used, etc. Finally, members of the group can provide support for one another as well as share their experiences.

Evaluation

Employing a series of measures of psychological growth as estimates of the dependent variable, the results indicated quite clearly that the combination of dilemma discussions, counseling skills, and actual cross-age teaching induced significant and positive psychological development. Using the Kohlberg Test of Moral Maturity and the Loevinger Test of Ego Development as estimates of stage growth, the results were compared on a pre-post basis for the experimental class and across two "control" groups, e.g., two regular high school classes. The pupils in all three classes were in the last two years of secondary school with an average age of sixteen years. There were no subgroup differences between males and females on the pretest scores so each class was treated statistically as a single unit. The Kohlberg Test results are presented in tables 1 and 2.

Table 1
Summary of Pretest and Posttest Means and Standard Deviations for the Kohlberg Moral Judgment Interview

Group	N	Test	Score	Test	Score
Experimental class	14	Pre	M 301.07 SD 47.01	Post	M 344.93 SD 46.71
Control class 1	14	Pre	M 263.57 SD 24.35	Post	M 272.36 SD 36.54
Control class 2	14	Pre	M 234.64 SD 31.26	Post	M 239.14 SD 36.34
All	42	Pre	M 266.43 SD 44.23	Post	M 285.48 SD 59.44

Table 2
Analysis of Covariance for Kohlberg Moral Judgment Interview

Source	df	SS′	MS′
Between	2	10258.40	5129.20
Within	38	20213.92	531.94
Total	40	30472.32	

$F = 9.6411$
$P < .001$

The Scheffe test was used to make multiple comparisons of the adjusted group means. These data are summarized in table 3. There was a highly significant difference between the experimental class and control class 1 and between the experimental class and control class 2 but no differences between the control classes. Figure 1 is a graph representing the movement of pretest to posttest means for each of the groups.

Table 3
Scheffe Multiple Comparisons Test

		Group A	Group B	Group C
	Means	312.64	275.02	268.76
Control class 1	275.02	37.62*		
Control class 2	268.76	43.88*	6.25	

df = 2,39
*indicates p < .001

Figure 1
Graph of Group Pretest and Posttest Means for
Kohlberg Moral Judgment Interview

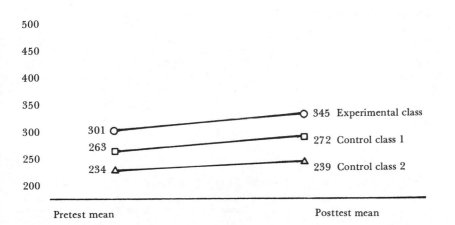

The Loevinger Test results are presented in table 4. The pretests and posttests on the Loevinger Sentence Completion Test were subjected to an analysis of covariance with the pretest scores being

Table 4

*Summary of Pretest and Posttest Means and Standard Deviations
for the Loevinger Sentence Completion Test*

Group	N	Test	Score	Test	Score
Experimental class	14	Pre	M 5.43 SD 1.09	Post	M 7.21 SD 1.18
Experimental class	14	Pre	M 5.78 SD 1.25	Post	M 5.57 SD 1.40
Experimental class	14	Pre	M 5.07 SD 1.14	Post	M 4.57 SD 1.09
All	42	Pre	M 5.43 SD 1.17	Post	M 5.79 SD 1.63

the covariate. Table 4 is a summary of pretest and posttest means
and standard deviations for this measure.

Table 5 summarizes the data from the analysis of covariance.
There was a highly significant difference between the groups as indicated by the F score. Table 6 presents the data from the Scheffe test
of the adjusted group means. There was a highly significant difference between the experimental class and the control classes and,

Table 5

Analysis of Covariance for Loevinger Sentence Completion Test

Source	df	SS'	MS'
Between	2	43.73	21.86
Within	38	17.56	.46
Total	40	61.29	

F = 47.30
p < .001

Table 6

Scheffe Multiple Comparisons Test of Adjusted Group Means

		Group A	Group B	Group C
	Means	7.21	5.25	4.89
Control class 1	5.25	1.96*		
Control class 2	4.89	2.33*	0.37	

df = 2,39
*indicates p < .001

once again, no difference between the two control classes. Figure 2 is a graph of the movement from pretest to posttest for each of the groups.

Figure 2
Graph of Group Pretest and Posttest Means for
Loevinger Sentence Completion Test

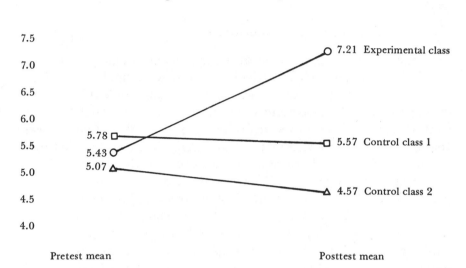

The overall results, then, indicate that the high school pupils who discuss and analyze moral dilemmas and then teach or lead dilemma discussions with other pupils exhibited significant developmental shifts. The combined experience of learning about dilemmas and teaching others formed an active curriculum for the teenagers. An earlier attempt at Minnesota yielded negative results in one class. In that class, high school pupils discussed and analyzed moral dilemmas but did not actively participate in teaching other pupils. The results indicated that there was no change on pre- to posttests with the Kohlberg and the Loevinger tests. In other words, when high school pupils discussed dilemmas for an entire term yet did not apply their learning to a real situation there was no significant shift in their own cognitive structures. The way they thought about issues of social justice and the level of complexity of their definitions of developmental ego stage remained essentially unchanged (Schaeffer 1974). However, when the moral dilemma format was combined with actual teaching then cognitive-developmental shifts occurred. In this manner the results are parallel to a series of other high school classes developed at Harvard and at the University of Minnesota (Dowell 1971; Erickson 1974, 1975; Rustad and Rogers 1975; Hurt and Sprinthall 1975). Significant cognitive-developmental changes appear to be associated with curriculum materials which involve active social role-taking by teenagers.

Conclusion

Space limits a description of other programs in moral education currently being tested. Of particular interest to counselors is Grimes' (1974) classroom program in which sixth-grade students and their mothers jointly discussed and wrote moral dilemmas. Highly significant effects on the moral reasoning scores of the children were found. Of equal importance, the training of the mothers aided them in their traditional role of moral educators with their own children.

Similarly, Haynes (1975) worked with adolescents and their parents to study and change the "justice structure" of the family as a new form for family education and counseling. DiStefano (1975) taught moral reasoning about sexual and interpersonal dilemmas to adolescents. Paolitto (1975) investigated role-taking experiences for junior high school children and their effects on the preadolescent's moral development. A project to train counselors and social studies teachers to teach moral education as part of high school psychology and American history is under way in Brookline, Massachusetts. Experiments in creating just high school units are beginning in Cambridge, Massachusetts and Newport, California.

The essential point is that the creation of ways for counselors and psychologists to educate for moral development in children and adolescents (and to empower parents as moral educators) is proceeding. Whether counselors and psychologists will join these programs of developmental education is unsure. Sometimes it seems that members of the profession would rather make schedule changes than experiment with an innovative program. But the very creation of such programs is a sign of professional health.

References

DiStefano, Ann. "Teaching Moral Reasoning About Sexual and Interpersonal Dilemmas." Ph.D. dissertation, Boston University School of Education, 1975.

Dowell, R. Chris. "Adolescents as Peer Counselors: A Program for Psychological Growth." Ph.D. dissertation, Harvard University, 1971.

Erickson, V. L. "Psychological Growth for Women." *Counseling and Values* 18, no. 2 (1974): 102-16.

Erickson, V. L. "Deliberate Psychological Education for Women: From Iphigenia to Antigone." *Counselor Education and Supervision* 14, no. 4 (1975): 297-309.

Griffen, Andrew. "Teaching Counselor Education to Black Teen-Agers." Ph.D. dissertation, Harvard University, 1972.

Grimes, Patricia. "Teaching Moral Reasoning to Eleven Year Olds and Their Mothers: A Means of Promoting Moral Development." Ph.D. dissertation, Boston University School of Education, 1974.

Haynes, Sheila. "The Justice Structure of the Family: A Focus for Education and Counseling." Ph.D. dissertation, Boston University School of Education, 1975.

Hurt, B. L., and Sprinthall, N. A. "Psychological and Moral Development for Teacher Education." *Journal of Moral Education* (1975).

Kohlberg, Lawrence. *Collected Papers on Moral Development and Moral Education.* Cambridge, Mass.: Laboratory of Human Development, Harvard University, 1973.

Lockwood, A. *Moral Reasoning—The Value of Life.* Middletown, Conn.: American Educational Publications, 1972.

Mackie, Peter. "Teaching Counseling Skills to Low Achieving High School Students." Ph.D. dissertation, Boston University School of Education, 1974.

Mosher, R., and Sprinthall, N. A. "Psychological Education: A Means to Promote Personal Development During Adolescence." *The Counseling Psychologist* 2, no. 4 (1971).

Paolitto, D. "Role-Taking Opportunities for Early Adolescents: A Program in Moral Education." Ph.D. dissertation, Boston University School of Education, 1975.

Rustad, K., and Rogers, C. "Promoting Psychological Growth in a High School Class." *Counselor Education and Supervision* 14, no. 4 (1975): 277-85.

Schaeffer, P. "Moral Judgment: A Cognitive Developmental Project." Ph.D. dissertation, University of Minnesota, 1974.

Sprinthall, N. A. "A Curriculum for Secondary Schools: Counselors as Teachers for Psychological Growth." *School Counselor* 5, no. 3 (1973): 361-69.

16

Developmental Psychology as a Guide to Value Education: A Review of "Kohlbergian" Programs

James Rest

The enthusiasm that Kohlberg and his associates have recently generated in value education programs lies not so much in new curriculum materials and new teaching techniques, nor in the demonstration of spectacular results in their pilot programs, but rather in the way they discuss their general directions and purposes in terms of philosophical and psychological theory and research. Kohlberg has characterized his efforts as "warmed-over Dewey," and refers to John Dewey as "the only modern thinker about education worth taking seriously" (Kohlberg 1971). Dewey laid out an educational program in broad philosophical terms. It was not, however, until Piaget's work that a psychology was begun which "developed the general premises of Dewey . . . into a science of great richness and logical and empirical rigor." Following Piaget, Kohlberg has worked "to make Dewey's ideas concrete," and Kohlberg's associates, in turn, have worked on "an application of Kohlberg to a high school curriculum" (Sprinthall 1971b). Educational programs with such a venerable lineage (Dewey-Piaget-Kohlberg, and so forth), have

Reprinted by permission from *Review of Educational Research* 44, no. 2 (1974), pp. 241-59.

created interest because of the intellectual heft behind them and the promise of initiating something more than a superficial, piecemeal, short-lived fad.

A review of these current educational programs entails a consideration of the way in which the foundational ideas have been extended in educational practice and a consideration of their distinctive features. I shall not review the psychological research on which the programs are based but rather the way in which the conclusions from research are used to guide program construction. The gist of this review is that "Kohlbergian" value education programs are based on ideas that separately have widespread acceptance and that have been around for some time; the programs integrate and "concretize" these basic ideas in new ways, although many further developments are necessary before one can claim to have successfully developed a distinctively new kind of educational program. Some next steps in program development will be suggested.

The Fundamental Ideas

Structural Organization

The rationale of the programs can be discussed in terms of three fundamental ideas: "structural organization," "developmental sequence," and "interactionism." The aspect of behavior of most interest to a cognitive developmentalist is a person's basic problem-solving strategies and structural organization: what stimuli are attended to; how these inputs are organized in terms of categories, concepts or images; what integrating principles or synthesizing operations are used to formulate plans, to make decisions, and so forth. Jerome Bruner presented this idea in *The Process of Education* (1960), eloquently stating that education should primarily emphasize problem-solving strategies, fundamental concepts, and the basic structure of the academic disciplines, because these are the basic tools of thought for making sense out of experience, organizing plans of action and decision making. If one acquires a basic tool of thought, he has enhanced his competence in dealing with that domain of human functioning and he has also gained something usable outside the classroom in a changing world. Similarly, Kohlberg has contended that moral education should not be aimed at teaching some specific set of morals but should be concerned with developing the organizational structures by which one analyzes, interprets and makes decisions about social problems.

In making the person's cognitive structure the focus of value education, the developmentalist conceptualizes educational aims differently from other approaches to value education. Cognitive-developmental value education differs from the "socialization" or indoctrination approaches, for the cognitive-development approach aims not at producing mere conformity with the state's, the teacher's, or the school's values, but at developing capabilities in decision making and problem solving (Carr and Wellenberg 1966; Durkheim 1925; Jones 1936; Kohlberg and Turiel 1971). A cognitive-developmental approach also conceptualizes educational aims differently from advocates of behavioral objectives, for cognitive structures are not specific public performances (although, of course, their assessment is inferred from empirical data) but general, internalized conceptual frameworks and problem-solving strategies. The developmentalist also parts company with humanist psychologists who emphasize transitory affective feeling states (openness, spontaneity, joy), for the focus is upon the acquisition of structured competencies that transfer to later life and have a *cumulative* effect in enhancing and enriching life. The developmentalist sees cognitive structure as the framework by which affective experiences are interpreted, and by which the strong, emotional experiences of today are translated into the commitments of tomorrow. Structure is emphasized; not the transitory awareness or feeling state. The cognitive-developmental approach, like the value clarification approach (e.g., Raths, Harmin, and Simon 1966), advocates the desirability of clear thinking and explicit knowledge of one's values, but the cognitive developmentalist contends that certain problem-solving strategies are more adequate than others and that certain concepts are better tools of thought than others. The cognitive-developmental approach does not make complete ethical relativity and value neutrality the cornerstones of value education which the value clarification approach does.

Developmental Sequence

Cognitive developmentalists are struck by the obvious fact that newly born babies lack the competencies of adults. These competencies must be acquired, and the developmentalist attempts to analyze fully-developed competence in terms of discriminations, thought-operations, and rule systems that underlie the competence—in short, the cognitive structure. Developmentalists further attempt to depict the course of the way in which these structures are built up, which components come first and are prerequisites for the later elaborations. The developmentalist describes the successive elaboration of more complicated and differentiated structures out of simpler ones in terms of stages. The developmentally earlier "lower" stages are prerequisites of the "higher" stages; the more complicated higher stages deal more effectively with problems of wider scope and greater intricacy than do the lower stages. Hence stages are sequenced in a certain order because the earlier stages are less difficult and are attainable before the later stages. Higher stages are said to be "better" than lower stages in the sense that the higher structural organizations can do a better job in analyzing problems, tracing out implications, and integrating diverse considerations.

The developmentalist is not indifferent to which cognitive structure a person ultimately ends up with since analysis indicates that some cognitive tools are better than others. The goal of education, then, is to stimulate development step by step through the stages. In the case of moral education, Kohlberg contends that, because very few people now reach the highest stage, this is not a trivial matter of trying to speed up development a little towards an end where all are going anyway. There are three corollaries to this general goal: (1) the educator should be interested in facilitating development as far as possible, even in people who may never reach the highest stages; (2) even if at a certain time the educator cannot move a particular person to a new stage, he should try to prevent fixation at the lower stage and try to keep things "fluid" enough that progress may come about at a later time; and (3) the educator should strive to facilitate "horizontal" development as well as "vertical," that is, not only to push for new structures but to extend the full use of an acquired structure to new domains of activity and problem areas.

If the developmental psychologist really reaches his goal of charting the course of development of a competence, then educators indeed have some very useful information. The characterization of the highest stage of development gives a psychological analysis of some competence—e.g., Piaget's stage of formal operations gives us an analysis of what it means to be logical; Kohlberg's Stage 6 provides a description of what mature moral judgment consists; the psycholinguist's characterization of the highest stage of grammar development gives an analysis of what it takes to construct completely grammatical sentences. Note that there is much more specificity here in a characterization of cognitive structure than the honorific labels often used to define educational objectives (such as "creative," "self-actualized," "good citizen," "well-adjusted," and so forth).

Furthermore, if the educator has a step by step description of the development of some competence, then he has a means of ordering progress (knowing which changes are progressive), of locating people along this course of development, and therefore of anticipating which experiences the student will most likely respond to and from which he will profit. The adage that the teacher should meet the student at the student's level can be given precise and operational meaning if the course of development is defined and the student's level can be assessed. Knowing the course of development enables one to optimize the match between children and curricula and also serves as a guide for sequencing curriculum. Accordingly, at the propitious time, problems that are manageable yet challenging can be introduced to create an interesting learning experience in itself, and, at the same time, to serve to set up the prerequisite components for problems at the next level.

Kohlberg (1971) has criticized many moral education programs for either underestimating the sophistication of children by trying to teach a simplistic virtue-always-pays morality, or in overshooting the comprehension of children with abstract and abstruse doctrines. In short, these programs ignored the notion of developmental sequence and did not match curriculum with the developmental level of the students. Kohlberg and Lockwood (1970) have more generally questioned whether the new social studies and the structure-of-the-discipline approaches (those inspired by Jerome Bruner) to curriculum revision are to be faulted on the same point, namely that the level of reasoning presupposed by these curricula is inappropriately high for most students for whom it is intended. According to Kohlberg, such new curricula often presuppose Piaget's stage of formal operations or Kohlberg's Stages 5 and 6, and high school students typically are not there yet, thus students miss the fascination and relevance that their teachers see in the new curricula.

Interactionism

The third fundamental idea, "interactionism," concerns the way in which cumulative, developmental change takes place and the process by which cognitive structures are progressively elaborated. If we use the computer as an analogy to the human mind, we might say that a person's cognitive structure is the program by which he processes inputs (experience) and generates outputs (behavior). The computer analogy is used by many theorists to depict human thinking, but the distinctive point of the interactionist view has to do with how these "programs" get into the head. Interactionists deny that these cognitive structures are "wired-in" biologically or genetically; they also deny that these cognitive structures are simply reflections of environmental contingencies, as if a person just swallows whole the organizational patterns around him. Instead, the interactionist view is that the human computer (using analogy again) is a *self-programming* computer such that new programs are developed to more adequately organize experiences and give clearer directions for action. As the child notices certain regularities in the environment and establishes behavioral patterns that interact effectively with the environment, we say that the child has built up certain cognitive structures. As the child encounters new and different experiences which cannot be understood adequately or reacted to in terms of established structures, the child seeks to revamp his way of thinking. The new experience interacts with previously established cognitive structures to prompt the search for more adequate structures. Once a new "program" is found which can successfully "compute" the new situation, the program becomes part of the person's repertoire. Therefore, the essential condition for the cumulative elaboration of cognitive structure is the presentation of experiences which "stretch" one's existing thinking and set into motion this search-and-discovery process for more adequate ways to organize experience and action.

Note that the type of changes which are of interest here are those which are fundamental, long-term, and cumulative—not changes which reflect situational fluctuations, or temporary conditions which fluctuate, reverse, or cancel out the effects of each other.

The educational implications of interactionism have long been recognized by educators in terms of "discovery learning," "the Socratic method," and so forth. Discovery learning no doubt provided a basic justification for the expense of physics and chemistry labs used in high school teaching. Perhaps value education and social studies education have been among the last areas to work on this idea (Fenton 1967), although programs such as Hunt and Metcalf's (1968), or Oliver and Shaver's (1966), are premised on the discovery method. A result of this approach in social studies has been the introduction of discussion of genuinely controversial issues into public schools. Since the teacher is no longer primarily an answer-giver but a process-facilitator, controversial topics in school need not entail indoctrination but can furnish a source of meaningful and spirited inquiry for students. Similarly, Kohlbergian moral education programs have not only included the discussion of controversial issues in their programs, but have made it the staple item. The chief activity of these value education programs then is the student's search rather than the teacher's answers. There are two reasons why the student's search should be the chief activity: (1) didactic teaching of values seemed to be largely ineffective when it was tried in the 1930s (Kohlberg 1971); (2) didactic teaching of values in public schools is unconstitutional and philosophically unjustifiable (Kohlberg 1971; Wilson, Williams, and Sugarman 1967).

The teacher's function is to stimulate this "stretching and searching" process. Kohlberg recommends in addition that a teacher facilitate upward movement by providing models of thinking which are one stage above the student's current level. Kohlberg does not speak directly to the point of whether +1 modeling is essential to change or is just catalytic to change, but there are two reasons to suppose that +1 modeling is not essential: first, cognitive developmentalists, including Piaget, usually describe the acquisition of new structures in terms of the single individual trying to reorganize his thoughts, not learning from a model; and second, new cognitive structures can be evolved in the absence of higher stage models (who was +1 for Socrates?).

There is another difficulty with Kohlberg's recommendation to provide +1 modeling. Kohlberg (1971) states that, "If moral communications are to be effective, the developmental level of the teacher's verbalizations must be one step above the level of the child" (p. 42). Yet Kohlberg criticizes the new social studies curricula because they require a higher stage of reasoning (Piaget's stage of formal operations or Kohlberg's Stages 5 and 6) than evidenced by the students (Piaget's stage of concrete operations, Kohlberg's Stages 3 and 4). What appears to be a contradiction might be resolved by making a distinction between the level or stage of the teacher's selective modeling activities and the level of thinking presupposed by a curriculum —but Kohlberg does not explicate this apparent contradiction.

Implementation

The three fundamental ideas of structural organization, developmental sequence, and interactionism compose the rationale of cognitive-developmental programs in value education. The bulk of the writing about Kohlbergian programs has been devoted to arguing its rationale rather than detailing programs or discussing results. Nevertheless, it is important to consider how these basic ideas have been carried out in concrete application. Implementation will be discussed in terms of four practical questions:

1. In what arrangements do teachers and students interact? (For example, one-to-one; homogeneous or heterogeneous grouping; small or regular size classes; lectures, discussion groups, practicums, seminars, projects, field experiences.)
2. What is the curriculum? (What materials or experiences are provided or structured by the teacher?)
3. What is the teacher's role? (How are students' tasks defined and supported by the teacher? What interventions does the teacher make? What skills are important for the teacher to have?)
4. How does one assess progress? (How are overall effects measured? How are specific materials and day-do-day teacher behaviors and student behaviors evaluated? How is individual progress evaluated?)

Kohlberg's Own Programs

Blatt Studies. Kohlberg has been directly involved in the design and conduct of a number of education programs (Blatt 1969; Blatt and Kohlberg 1974; Boyd 1973; Hickey 1974; Selman and Kohlberg 1972). Descriptions of these programs are hard to come by and the main sources of published information about them are contained in general discussions of the approach (Kohlberg 1971; Kohlberg and Turiel 1971). The Blatt studies were the initial pilot projects. In these, students met with a teacher in small classes (nine-thirteen people) several times a week for about a quarter of a year. "Moral dilemmas" were read aloud by the teacher, followed by class discussion. Interestingly, a stage mix of students (i.e., having students whose predominant stage was different) was considered advantageous because the heterogeneity increased divergence of viewpoints and thereby added more conflicts, challenges, and interest to the discussions. Stage mix also was considered advantageous in furnishing modes of thinking at many levels so that on a probabilistic basis there would be a +1 mode of thinking modeled for almost everyone in the group sometime in the discussion (that is, thinking modeled at one stage above a subject's current stage). Presumably the teacher provided the +1 modeling for the most mature student in the group. Therefore, most of the +1 modeling would come from within the group itself, cast in the terminology and vernacular of the group.

Blatt's "curriculum" consisted of a number of dilemmas and probing questions to initiate the discussion. The rest of the resources would be generated from within the group itself. The dilemmas used by Blatt were much like the dilemmas used by Kohlberg in assessing moral judgment. In effect, Blatt's curriculum was an extension of Kohlberg's assessment procedure using hypothetical dilemmas. The teacher's role was to introduce the dilemma; to encourage class members to take a stand on what ought to be done and to explain why; to encourage confrontation and mutual probing by the class members of each other's reasoning without personal assaults (encouraging the clash of ideas, not personalities); to encourage listening and paying attention to each discussant's points and evaluation of the adequacy of the arguments; to furnish occasional high stage responses as the +1 modeling of the highest students; to interject a probe question here and there; to reflect and summarize group deliberations; and to facilitate good group-discussion process. Upon deciding that profitable discussion had been exhausted on a dilemma, the teacher would then move on to the next one. Blatt assessed the pre-post gains of his students by Kohlberg's instrument and reported that, in general, students gained more by the experience than did the controls. In addition, he reported that the gains were patterned by the student's initial pretest stage—that is, Stage 2 subjects tended to move to Stage 3; Stage 3 to Stage 4; Stage 4 to Stage 5, and so on. With this differential pattern of movement upward, Blatt argues that the treatment effect cannot be construed as merely learning slogans or repeating the utterances of the teacher because all subjects did not change in the same way but changed in relation to their pretest stage.

Blatt's work was the first step toward building a moral education program based on the cognitive-developmental perspective. It was a bold venture considering the poor results of intervention studies in other areas of cognitive-developmental research (e.g., the Piagetian conservation training studies). There are, however, some programmatic questions worth raising about this form of value education. While the program does emphasize student searching and the engagement of truly controversial issues, and while it does emphasize the basic structure of reasoning, it nevertheless only half-heartedly implements the notion of optimal curriculum match and the sequencing of curriculum to build cumulative results. The dilemmas used were not classified for their raising particular stage-specific considerations, nor would there have been an advantage in doing so when used with a stage-heterogeneous group. This kind of program does not seem to utilize one of the few opportunities that the teacher (using nondidactic method) has to arrange conditions to optimize curriculum-student match. The curriculum seems to consist of an assortment of dilemmas with no strategy embodied in their sequencing (ideally, shouldn't the insights gained through discussion of one dilemma lay the foundation or prerequisites for the next problems?). Whatever the cumulative effect, it does not seem to be designed by the program. From the point of view of a curriculum writer, paragraphs which verbally depict some moral dilemma are a rather impoverished set of materials. Films, simulation games, stories, historical documents, role playing, and so forth, can also depict moral dilemmas, and do so more vividly and dramatically. A regimen of dilemma after dilemma is a rather dull academic diet. One also wonders how students are going to find out about the world outside themselves if all they do is listen to each other discuss and opine (or is that supposed to be the job of other courses?).

We can raise some questions about the role of the teacher in Blatt's programs. A large part of the teacher's role is facilitating group process, and knowledge of developmental psychology does not particularly prepare one for this role. The skills for a group discussion leader are not prescribed by Kohlberg's moral stages nor does developmental psychology in general furnish guidelines for this crucial component of "Kohlbergian" education programs. Since Blatt's own background was in clinical psychology, we cannot tell to what extent his training in this aspect of psychology accounts for his program's success as opposed to his utilization of the principles of developmental psychology. Nevertheless, there are two possible ways that knowledge of stage characteristics could contribute to the teacher's effectiveness. By being familiar with stage characteristics and therefore familiar with recurrent types of thinking, the teacher is better prepared to understand the intent and meaning of the utterances of students. First, by being better "cued in" beforehand, the teacher can better reflect, summarize, and amplify students' remarks. Second, Kohlberg and others urge the teacher to respond to children with a verbalization one step above the level of the child. Surely knowledge of developmental psychology is necessary here (at least, knowledge of Kohlberg's scoring system). But is it really possible for a teacher to code a child's statement, to decide what stage is above it, and to compute a response all in the time frame of conversational exchanges? Judging from the amount of time it takes to stage score a regular interview and the amount of time it takes to compose unambiguous stage-prototypic statements, it is unrealistic to expect a teacher to be computing +1 retorts to students in a group discussion. Perhaps with special training, such responses to recurrent statements would be possible—but in any case, Kohlberg's advice to teachers is enormously difficult to carry out.

The Prison Studies. The discussion-of-moral-dilemmas program which Blatt initiated in Sunday school and high school settings was taken by Hickey (1974) into a prison setting. Hickey found that modifications were necessary—since, not surprisingly, the group dynamics among prisoners are more complicated than in Sunday school. Descriptions of Hickey's work constantly allude to these problems but do not give much detail—one expects that Hickey's own previous experience in prison work was crucial here. Moreover, instead of using prepared hypothetical dilemmas as the basis for discussion, the group came to use their own dilemmas and issues relating to prison life. Hence the "curriculum" shifted towards real concerns of the prisoners in their common setting. The role of the "teacher," however, was still that of discussion leader.

In addition, Hickey and a group from Harvard sought to extend their sphere of influence beyond the discussion group into the prison setting itself. One aspect of this was to study the prison as a social system operating according to a certain kind of "morality." Scharf (1974) developed an interview and classification system to indicate the way in which prisoners view "the moral atmosphere" of the prison (i.e., their view of the ways in which the rules functioned, the ways in which guards relate to prisoners, and the ways in which prisoners interact with each other). His major findings were that prisoners tend to view the practicing morality in a prison at a low stage (perceiving the justice practices of the institution as governed by power and obedience morality or an instrumental exchange morality) and that prisoners conceptualize prison life at a lower stage than their moral judgments of hypothetical dilemmas. Hence prison life gives the inmate little impetus for developing a higher stage understanding of the moral basis for law, society, and cooperation.

With the rules of the prison viewed as coercive and illegitimate, and with the inmate peer culture viewed as exploitative, the discussion groups could be only partially effective. Therefore, changes in the actual social environment of the prison were sought. Hickey and the Harvard group obtained permission to change the social system of a small ward (about twenty inmates). Their tactic was to train prison staff in novel roles, such as moral discussion leaders, and to organize the "model cottage" as a democratic organization (within certain constraints of the larger institution). Prisoners and staff met not only in moral discussion groups, but also to formulate governing rules, to solve problems, and to make group plans. The strategy was that such a social organization would complement the discussion group and would furnish experiences in social roles that promote moral development. Moreover, an aftercare program was developed in which the released inmate continued to participate in discussion groups with staff and other released prisoners, thus providing an opportunity for continuing discussion of problems and decision making.

Presentation of the results of the prison program are mostly anecdotal and preliminary as yet. While the discussion-of-dilemmas is still the heart of the program, it is obvious that many new components have been added about which Kohlberg's six stages of morality and even developmental psychology have little to say (e.g., group discussion skills, dynamics of changing social organizations, individual counseling, parole management, and so forth). Furthermore, some criticisms of the Blatt studies still apply to the prison program: half-hearted application of the principle of optimum curriculum match and programmatic sequencing of curriculum; restriction of curriculum resources to those inside the participants' heads; and the unrealistic expectation that the discussion leader can compose +1 verbalizations on the spot.

The prison studies will provide information on the relation of moral judgment to the influences of social environments and whether increases in moral judgment make a difference in behavior patterns once the inmates are released from prison. Positive results would of course be spectacular; negative results, however, with this extremely problematic population would not preclude the possibility of more favorable results with a less problematic population.

Other Projects. Kohlberg and his students have made a number of additional innovations which have extended the original program ideas and materials: (1) A moral education course for college undergraduates included not only the discussion-of-dilemmas format but also readings and discussions of classic moral philosophers (Boyd 1973), thus extending the resources available in the curriculum. (2) Selman and Kohlberg consulted with Guidance Associates (1972) in making a set of filmstrip-records that depict moral dilemmas for discussion by young elementary school subjects. The color pictures and accompanying sound track artfully dramatize moral dilemmas to interest and provoke discussion among youngsters. (3) Lockwood (1972) has prepared a booklet, *Moral Reasoning—the Value of Life,* as part of a social studies series developed by Oliver and Newmann (Oliver and Shaver 1966). The booklet is especially interesting for integrating Kohlberg materials with the format developed by Oliver and Newmann. Instead of paragraph-long dilemmas (characteristic of the Blatt studies), a more extended presentation of actual documented cases is used to set up discussion (for instance a discussion of Bonhoeffer's complicity in the plot to kill Hitler, Calley and My Lai, etc.). Historical, legal, and sociological background is provided to enrich and deepen the discussion. And the discussion guides help to analyze the formal aspects of discussion along the lines suggested by Oliver and Shaver (1966). (4) The Moral Education Project of the Ontario Institute for Studies in Education is an ongoing research and development project for curriculum materials, teaching methods, teacher training, and theory elaboration. This ambitious, broad-gauge enterprise has set up moral education programs in elementary and high schools in Canada and has published books containing many practical suggestions and possible topics and materials for moral education (Beck 1971, 1972; Beck, Crittenden, and Sullivan 1971).

Sprinthall and Mosher. Recently Sprinthall (1971a) has described a "deliberate psychological education" program as "an application of Kohlberg to a high school curriculum." Mosher and Sprinthall (1970) however did not initially set out to "prove" a theory—as did Kohlberg and his immediate associates—but rather to work pragmatically on a general problem. The problem which Sprinthall and Mosher started out with was this: today's youth have great difficulty in attaining self-identity, in making important choices, and in resisting alienation from the major institutions of society; schools are not doing much to help youth in finding self-definition, in resolving value conflicts, or in determining self-direction; even psychological guidance services are generally ineffective because they function on the sideline of school activities and are overloaded with purely administrative functions. In short, the problem is: how can psychological growth be made a major and deliberate part of our educational system, and how can the resources of psychologically trained personnel be better employed?

Sprinthall, Mosher, and a number of resourceful graduate students went into high schools and tried a variety of programs. One approach was to teach a course in child and adolescent development with lectures, films, and discussion groups. On the other side of the spectrum was a T-group approach which deemphasized content and focused on group process. They felt that neither of these approaches was effective. The approach that seemed to be most effective was one that combined a practicum experience with a seminar which examined the practicum experience. In other words, what worked best was to involve the high school students in some practical psychological work (e.g., counseling other teenagers, serving as teacher aides in elementary school, working in a nursery school, and so forth) and to meet in a seminar to discuss both the principles of academic psychology relating to their work and the personal meaning of their experiences and their responsibilities in these new roles. Sprinthall and Mosher contend that this combination of "doing psychology" and "learning psychology" produces not only the most learning of psychological content but also the most personal psychological growth.

The sense in which the deliberate psychological education

program is based on developmental psychology (or is "Kohlbergian") is a complicated issue. Just as the Blatt programs and the prison programs draw on expertise other than that which just comes from knowing developmental psychology and six stages of morality, so also Sprinthall and Mosher's program draws on other bases, only much more so. Sprinthall, Mosher, and their associates seem to draw very heavily on Rogers, as well as Erikson (1968), Elkind (1967), Carkhuff (1969), in addition to Kohlberg. Furthermore, the scope of Sprinthall and Mosher's aims is much wider than *moral* education, although moral education is one component of "personal psychological growth." And whereas some subject matter of deliberate psychological education is distinctively *morality*, there are many other nonmoral components such as communication and counseling skills, cross-age teaching and tutoring, improvisational dance and drama, identifying and labeling emotions, and so forth.

The relation of the deliberate psychological education program to Kohlbergian developmental psychology is most evident in abstract discussions of the general aims of the program, of its stage appropriateness, and of the rationale for the practicum-seminar format. As in Kohlberg's discussion of the general aims of moral education, Sprinthall argues (1972a) that the aims of deliberate psychological education must be tied into a general philosophy of education and a philosophy of values. Merely to set forth "authenticity," "peak experience," "real self," and so forth as goals without also placing these honorific labels within a larger framework is rejected. They also reject making the goal of their program simply achievement in academic psychology or prevocational training for future psychologists (high school "prepsych" training like "premed" training). In the Deweyan-Piagetian-Kohlbergian tradition the aim of the program is to foster cumulative structural development, that is, to acquire ways of organizing and understanding experience, ways of planning and organizing one's activity which are enhancing cumulatively and in a long-term way (Kohlberg, 1971). For Kohlberg, this, in effect, means fostering development in moral judgment towards Stage 6, and Stage 6 is defined operationally in terms set forth in the scoring guides of the stages. Mosher and Sprinthall admit that they cannot specify in detail what they mean by "personal development" because the theory and research of developmental psychology is lacking on this matter. They state,

A major problem confronting psychological education is the lack of an adequate theory of personal or emotional development. . . . We do not set out a precise theoretical definition of what we mean by personal development in adolescence. Yet some of the central processes of personal growth in adolescence are evident. They include the development of a more complex and more integrated understanding of oneself; the formation of personal identity; greater personal autonomy; a greater ability to relate to and communicate with other people (e.g., peers and the opposite sex); the growth of more complex ethical reasoning; and the development of more complex skills and competencies—in part by trying pre-vocational and "adult" roles. (1971, pp. 10-11)

In discussing program aims, then, Sprinthall and Mosher accept Kohlberg's general argument that aims should be defined in terms of development. However, Sprinthall and Mosher cannot go very far in this because the kind of developmental psychology that they need does not exist. Consequently, they are limited to relating developmental psychology to their program in a piecemeal fashion and by extrapolation from subareas (like Kohlberg's moral judgment area).

In Sprinthall and Mosher's discussion of adolescence as a stage, they go along with Kohlberg in advocating the general argument that program should be matched to developmental level. They cite several strands of developmental psychology to support the stage appropriateness of their program. They cite Piaget in contending that not before adolescence would their program be appropriate, for with the emergence of formal operational thought comes the capacity to conceive of oneself in the future as being a variety of possible selves, each with certain probabilities of actualization based on evidence. This, they argue, sets a lower limit for the initiation of their program and points out that certain cognitive prerequisites are usually established with adolescence which make their program meaningful. Kohlberg's research on moral stages is cited as supporting the age-appropriateness of their program since the period of adolescence usually involves consolidating an understanding of conventional social institutions and is timely for beginning the shift from "conventional" morality to "principled," autonomous morality. Erikson's (1968) view that the chief developmental crisis of adolescence is identity formation also supports the timeliness of their program. Elkind's (1967) discussions of the special egocentrism of adolescence is also cited as necessitating an explicit program in personal identity to move youngsters out of a state of exaggerated self-reference and privatism into a more integrated and encompassing concept of self.

While these various strands of developmental psychology can be used as a *general* justification for having a program in "personal development" for adolescents, Sprinthall and Mosher do not derive specific day-by-day guidance for program construction from these theorists. For instance, if one were to make specific use of Kohlberg's moral judgment stages, one would determine the developmental level of a specific group of individuals and then use the stage characteristics in day-by-day planning of problems, points-of-view, distinctions, cognitive operations, activities, and so forth, that would be most crucial for those individuals to work on. Ideally and ultimately, one expects a program that claims to be based on developmental psychology to be able to justify in detail the specific kinds of tasks and experiences that are set up for students, the order in which they are undertaken, and the way in which particular kinds of activity are matched with the student's developmental level. Otherwise, *any* program which makes self-identity its focal content can claim to be just as grounded in developmental psychology as Sprinthall and Mosher's. This is not to say that the program was haphazard or had no logical progression; the problem is that it is not articulated with any research-based developmental psychology.

One last comment on curriculum: not having a theory of personal development makes it difficult to know what activities are and are not suitable for personal development. It is difficult to see the unity in a program that has options including peer counseling, moral discussions, teaching elementary school children, and improvisational dance. In what way are these alternative paths to the same goal? What activity in the arts, music, humanities, social sciences, or sports, would not be equally suitable?

The practicum-seminar format of the deliberate psychological education program is related to the cognitive-developmental notion of interactionism. Certainly the experience of being a tutor, a nursery school helper, or a peer counselor must have been a new, challenging, and stretching experience for the high school students. The seminar would seem to have prompted the process of trying to make sense out of the practicum experience, in setting up the formulation of new frameworks for understanding and interacting with others. The combination of activity and responsibility with reflection and "academic" psychology would seem to be an ingenious format for implementing the "interactionist" point of view and less artificial than the original Blatt format which used short verbally presented hypothetical situations as the stimulus material. According to the cognitive-developmental theory, this format should facilitate basic structural change in students' personality organization.

But again, making the case in the abstract still leaves the details to be specified. Mosher and Sprinthall's (1970, 1971) published accounts do not give enough details on how specific issues arising in the practicum are dealt with in the seminar. Indeed, coordination of practicum with seminar would be a major problem with this format. How, for example, are discussions, films, readings of academic psychology related to practicum experiences? Does the teacher wait until some student raises a point before suggesting a relevant reading? Does the whole group read the same source or just those who raised the issue? If individuals in the group are reading different things, and experiencing different problems, what commonality is there in discussion? Are topics in the seminar programmed in some logical, cumulative order or is the seminar without structure? If structured, how is this synchronized with the practicum experience?

One feature that the Sprinthall-Mosher program does not stress is for the teacher to furnish +1 modeling. In this regard it differs from the Kohlberg programs, but this feature has already been criticized. On the other hand, a feature in the Sprinthall-Mosher program which is important in cognitive-development theory but has not been emphasized in Kohlberg programs is the provision for new social role-taking experiences. Sprinthall (1972b) points out that teenagers typically have little experience in the social roles of teacher, counselor, or caretaker and that assuming these responsibilities greatly expands the "experience-table" of most adolescents. He reports that many students felt that having this kind of real responsibility for others was the key growth element.

Assessment of the Mosher and Sprinthall (1970) program is still in the preliminary phases; reported results are generally positive but not spectacular. There are several kinds of assessment that could be relevant: (1) *Overall personal development.* Sprinthall and Mosher admit that global measures of this are problematic, however they used the Loevinger and Wessler (1970) ego development scale. (2) *Major subcomponents of personal development.* Sprinthall and

Mosher assessed moral judgment, using Kohlberg's scale. They could have, but did not assess other major aspects of personal development, for example, Erikson's ego identity statuses as assessed by Marcia (1966) and communication skills and person perception (Flavell, Botkin, Fry, Wright, and Jarvis 1968). Is progress in one subarea related to progress in other subareas? (3) *Psychological skills.* They assessed counseling skills on rating scales devised by Carkhuff (1969). Other skills such as teaching effectiveness in elementary school or nursery school, drama, and dance improvisation were not assessed. (4) *Knowledge of psychology.* No data were reported on formal testing, on child development theory and research, learning theory and research, or counseling theory, but it would be interesting to know how knowledge about psychology is related to psychological skills and personal development. (5) *Student evaluation.* Sprinthall and Mosher do not report the basis for evaluating individual student's performance in ways that were fed back to the students. (6) *Student interest and involvement.* Some unobtrusive measures of student interest came from attendance counts but no data are reported. Unsolicited comments were another source of information about interest, and more formally, questionnaires filled out by students at the end of the course were used, but results are not published. (7) *Prerequisites for the program.* Measures of cognitive capacities (Piaget's formal operations, as discussed by Mosher and Sprinthall 1971) and perhaps certain personality variables might be assessed so as to determine readiness for the program and likelihood of positive change. Different students may be entering at different levels of development and according to theory, this should be relevant to the type of program that the students have. (8) *Process evaluation.* In addition to knowing how effective overall the program was, we would want to know which parts facilitated which changes, what teacher interventions or program experiences were more valuable than others, what student behaviors indicate movement forward, etc. Sprinthall and Mosher have begun this type of evaluation in analyzing tape recordings of peer-counseling sessions, and in presenting anecdotally segments of seminars in which significant events were taking place, but much work remains to be done in developing a framework for systematically analyzing practicum and seminar experiences.

Future Prospects

Developmental psychology guides the educational programs we have discussed in global, programmatic ways, but not in day-by-day planning or analysis. So far these programs have articulated their general aims in terms of developmental psychology and have described their general strategy for creating a "stimulating environment" using the concepts of developmental psychology. Attention is paid to specific stage characteristics in pretest and posttest assessment. However, the specific characteristics of stages of development are not used to define more proximate objectives which a teacher could use in deciding what to emphasize or provide for specific individuals at a specific time. The question therefore remains as to whether educational programs can be related in detailed ways to specific stage characteristics and whether there is any advantage in doing so.

Future work can be envisaged as proceeding on several fronts. First, we would hope that developmental psychologists will furnish precise statements of developmental sequences. Sprinthall and Mosher lament not having a developmental theory of "personal development" to work with. Kohlberg is still making major changes in his scoring system of stages of moral judgment; the empirical verification of stage details is far from complete. Flavell (1970) in reviewing the present state of work in social cognition in general contends that work in this direction has only just begun. Potentially, however, the contribution that developmental research can make to program development would include the following: (1) psychological analysis of competence in a given domain; (2) step-by-step description of the development of the competencies; (3) assessment instruments for locating individuals on the courses of development; (4) characterization of the conditions for progressive structural change; and (5) models and instruments for analyzing the flow of events and interactions in an educational program.

Second, the contributions of curriculum developers are needed. Developmental psychology does not uniquely prescribe the curriculum which Blatt used as the only one possible. Developmental psychology at best might be able to prescribe what specific concept, problem, or discrimination is most propitious for a given subject to deal with at a given time, but this does not determine the materials, the activity, or the experiences which are to be used. Developmental psychology may be useful in specifying objectives and useful for sequencing activities, but it does not furnish a complete pedagogy or curriculum materials. One hopes educators who want to use developmental psychology as a guide to value education will not have to devise curriculum materials "from scratch" but will be able to select and adapt much of the existing material (the case studies, films, simulation games, role-playing episodes, novels, exercises and problems in social studies, and so forth). One might envision the developmental psychologist providing a list and schedule of basic concepts and problems, for example, and the curriculum developer preparing materials and defining activities appropriate to each developmental component. It will take much research to determine what works best with what students under what conditions.

Third, the clinical or teaching skills necessary to facilitate these developmental processes need to be specified. This review has called attention to the crucial role played by group discussion skills, and other pedagogical skills in the programs now under way. This component should not be underplayed just because it is not the special province of developmental psychology. If the hope is to develop prototype programs that can be replicated, details must be available on goals and assessments, curriculum and activities, and pedagogy.

One might ask whether attempting to pilot such programs now is not premature. Would not educators be advised to wait until developmental psychology is further along? Judging from the reports of the participants in the programs, they generally seem to feel that the pilot programs were at least as beneficial as their usual programs, and many participants were more positive than that. Furthermore, the charge of being premature only applies if one assumes that the only way that program development and psychological theory progress is from lab to field application. Among others, Kohlberg, Sprinthall, and Mosher have contended that advances in developmental psychology and in education are most likely to come from collaboration on educational research enterprises whereby the researcher and practitioner share each other's problems, perspectives, and ideas.

References

Beck, C. M. *Moral Education in the Schools: Some Practical Suggestions.* Toronto: Ontario Institute for Studies in Education, 1971.

Beck, C. M. *Ethics.* New York: McGraw-Hill, 1972.

Beck, C. M.; Crittenden, B. S.; and Sullivan, E. V. *Moral Education: Interdisciplinary Approaches.* Toronto: University of Toronto Press, 1971.

Blatt, M. "Studies of the Effects of Classroom Discussion upon Children's Moral Development." Ph.D. dissertation, University of Chicago, 1969.

Blatt, M., and Kohlberg, L. "The Effects of Classroom Moral Discussion upon Children's Level of Moral Judgment." *Moralization: The Cognitive Developmental Approach,* edited by L. Kohlberg and E. Turiel. New York: Holt, Rinehart & Winston, 1974.

Boyd, D. "From Conventional to Principled Morality." Unpublished manuscript, Harvard University, 1973.

Bruner, J. *The Process of Education.* Cambridge, Mass.: Harvard University Press, 1960.

Carkhuff, R. R. *Helping and Human Relations.* New York: Holt, Rinehart & Winston, 1969.

Carr, D. B., and Wellenberg, E. P. *Teaching Children Values.* Freeport, Ill.: Honor Your Partner Records, 1966.

Durkheim, E. *Moral Education.* New York: Free Press, 1961.

Elkind, D. "Egocentrism in Adolescents." *Child Development* 38 (1967): 1025-34.

Erikson, E. H. *Identity: Youth in Crisis.* New York: W. W. Norton, 1968.

Fenton, E. *The New Social Studies.* New York: Holt, Rinehart & Winston, 1967.

Flavell, J. H. "Concept Development." *Carmichael's Manual of Child Psychology* (3rd ed., vol. 1), edited by P. Mussen. New York: John Wiley & Sons, 1970.

Flavell, J. H.; Botkin, P. T.; Fry, C. L.; Wright, J. W.; and Jarvis, P. E. *The Development of Role-Taking and Communication Skills in Children.* New York: John Wiley & Sons, 1968.

Hickey, J. "Designing and Implementing a Correctional Program Based on Moral Development Theory." *Moralization: The Cognitive Developmental Approach,* edited by L. Kohlberg and E. Turiel. New York: Holt, Rinehart & Winston, 1974.

Hunt, M. P., and Metcalf, L. E. *Teaching High School Social Studies* (2nd ed.). New York: Harper & Row, 1968.

Jones, V. *Character and Citizenship Training in the Public Schools.* Chicago: University of Chicago Press, 1936.

Kohlberg, L. "The Concepts of Developmental Psychology as the Central Guide to Education." *Psychology and the Process of Schooling in the Next Decade,* edited by M. Reynolds. Minneapolis: University of Minnesota Audio-Visual Extension, 1971.

Kohlberg, L., and Lockwood, A. "Cognitive Developmental Psychology and Political Education." Boulder, Col.: Speech for Social Science Consortium Convention, 1970.

Kohlberg, L., and Turiel, E. "Moral Development and Moral Education." *Psychology and Educational Practice,* edited by G. Lesser. Chicago: Scott Foresman, 1971.

Lockwood, A. *Moral Reasoning—The Value of Life*. Middletown, Conn.: American Educational Publications, 1972.

Loevinger, J., and Wessler, R. *Measuring Ego Development* (vols. 1 and 2). San Francisco: Jossey-Bass, 1970.

Marcia, J. E. "Development and Validation of Ego Identity States." *Journal of Personality and Social Psychology* 3 (1966): 551-58.

Mosher, R. L., and Sprinthall, N. A. "Psychological Education in Secondary Schools: A Program to Promote Individual and Human Development." *American Psychologist* 25 (1970): 911-24.

Mosher, R. L., and Sprinthall, N. A. "Psychological Education: A Means to Promote Personal Development During Adolescence." *The Counseling Psychologist* 2 (1971): 3-83.

Oliver, D., and Shaver, J. P. *Teaching Public Issues in the High School*. Boston: Houghton Mifflin, 1966.

Raths, L.; Harmin, M.; and Simon, S. *Values and Teaching*. Columbus, Ohio: Charles E. Merrill, 1966.

Scharf, P. "The Effects of the Justice Structures of Penal Institutions upon the Moral Judgments of Inmates." *Moralization: The Cognitive Developmental Approach*, edited by L. Kohlberg and E. Turiel. New York: Holt, Rinehart & Winston, 1974.

Selman, R., and Kohlberg, L. *First Things: A Strategy for Teaching Values*. New York: Guidance Associates, 1972.

Sprinthall, N. A. "A Program for Psychological Education: Some Preliminary Issues." *Journal of School Psychology* 9 (1971a): 373-82.

Sprinthall, N. A. "The Adolescent as a Psychologist: An Application of Kohlberg to a High School Curriculum." *School Psychology Digest* (1971b): 166-75.

Sprinthall, N. A. "Humanism: A New Bag of Virtues for Guidance." *Personnel and Guidance Journal* 50 (1972a): 5-11.

Sprinthall, N. A. "A Curriculum for Psychological Development: Learning Psychology by Doing Psychology." Paper presented at the 49th meeting of the American Orthopsychiatric Association (April 8, 1972b).

Wilson, J.; Williams, N.; and Sugarman, B. *Introduction to Moral Education*. London: Penguin, 1967.

17

Two Approaches to Moral Education

Anne Colby

In recent years teachers have been exposed to two major approaches to moral education: the values clarification methods advanced by Simon and his colleagues and Lawrence Kohlberg's theory of moral development as he applies it to education. I intend to compare values clarification with the cognitive-developmental (Kohlbergian) perspective by responding to these questions: Are Kohlberg and Simon addressing themselves to the same issues? Can one adopt both approaches without being inconsistent on a theoretical level? Do their psychological assumptions agree or conflict? Do their philosophical assumptions agree or conflict? Are their classroom methods or strategies interchangeable? I will argue that although the values clarification and moral development approaches seem incompatible in some areas, integration of the two is both possible and desirable.

Raths, Harmin, and Simon, in *Values and Teaching* (1966), provide a comprehensive statement of values clarification theory and methods. This approach is less concerned with the particular content of values than with the "valuing process." A value must meet seven

Reprinted by permission from *Harvard Educational Review* 45, no. 1 (February 1975), pp. 134-43.

process criteria. It should be chosen freely from alternatives after thoughtful consideration of the consequences. It should be prized, cherished, affirmed, and acted upon. Guidelines are derived from these criteria to help children learn the valuing process:

1. Encourage children to make choices and to make them freely.
2. Help them discover and examine available alternatives when faced with choices.
3. Help children weigh alternatives thoughtfully, reflecting on the consequences of each.
4. Encourage children to consider what they prize and cherish.
5. Give them opportunities to make public affirmations of their choices.
6. Encourage them to act, behave, and live in accordance with their choices.
7. Help them to examine repeated behaviors or patterns in their lives. (pp. 38-39)

The second part of *Values and Teaching* describes classroom methods for putting the general guidelines into practice. For example, sample questions or "clarifying responses" that teachers might use are: "Is this something that you prize?" "Did you consider any alternatives?" "Was that something that you yourself selected or chose?" The "value sheet," a different means to the same end, consists of a provocative statement and a series of questions each student answers in writing. One value sheet uses several quotations to encourage children to think about courage:

Courage is generosity of the highest order, for the brave are prodigal of the most precious things.
                                                              —*C. C. Colton*

True courage is to do without witness everything that one is capable of doing before all the world.
                                                      —*La Rochefoucauld*

Courage is like love: It must have hope to nourish it.   —*Napoleon Bonaparte*

Courage leads starward, fear toward death.   —*Seneca*

Brave men are brave from the first.   —*Corneille*

The courage of the tiger is one, and the horse another.   —*Ralph Waldo Emerson*

Ultimate bravery is courage of the mind.   —*H. G. Wells*

Grace under pressure.   —*Ernest Hemingway*

1. What does the word "courage" mean to you?
2. Do you think courage manifests itself? How?
3. Do you think everyone possesses courage? How? If not, why?
4. Are you proud of your level of courage? Discuss. (p. 99)

In addition to teaching methods, *Values and Teaching* includes guidelines for starting a values clarification program, for dealing with school administrators, and for evaluating a program once it is under-way. The authors also attempt to answer the questions that teachers usually ask. This emphasis on practicality is typical of the values clarification approach and is probably one reason for its popularity.

Values Clarification (1972), by Simon, Howe, and Kirschen-baum, is a handbook of seventy-nine practical strategies for clarifying values. Each strategy includes a statement of purpose, detailed proce-dures, helpful notes to the teacher, and suggestions for adapting or extending the strategy. Most of the strategies can be used at widely varying age levels with fairly minor changes in content, and in several cases suggestions are made for adding new content.

As in *Values and Teaching*, the strategies relate to the valuing process, and some involve the seven valuing criteria directly. In the "values grid," students list their positions on a number of issues such as water pollution or abortion and decide which of the seven criteria each opinion meets. The students' intended focus is not on defending the content of their convictions but rather on becoming aware of how they were arrived at. Often class discussions are suggested to give students the chance to explain their choices.

Values and Teaching ends with a literature review which points out the methodological weaknesses of efforts to evaluate the values clarification program. There is some evidence that increased clarity of values results in increased purposiveness (Klevan 1957), school achievement (Raths 1960; Lang 1962) and involvement and interest (Brown 1966). However, only Lang's study controlled for the possi-bility that changes were due to the quantity rather than the kind of attention given. Even if the behavioral effects were clearly docu-mented, one could not assume that changes in "values related behav-ior symptoms" were due to the mediation of clarified values unless one identified the behavioral symptoms themselves with unclear values.

The values clarification approach concentrates on the careful choice of values but has no underlying theoretical structure. Kohlberg's approach to values, on the other hand, is based on a cognitive theory which specifies how moral development occurs.

In many ways, Kohlberg's theory of moral development (1969, 1973) parallels Piaget's theory of general cognitive development. According to Kohlberg, as a child develops he actively constructs a moral world view and uses the same structure of reasoning to analyze different moral situations. A child's reasoning becomes more mature and adequate as he grows older because, in interacting with people and trying to solve moral problems, he will be bothered by inconsistencies and will reorganize his thinking to deal with them. This cognitive growth seems to occur in the same sequence of stages for all people.

As a child advances through moral stages, she becomes more and more able to see other people's points of view on a situation, to understand that they may differ from her own and to take them into account in coming to a conclusion about what she ought to do.

Attempts to verify important aspects of Kohlberg's theory have yielded promising results. The universality of the stage sequence has been documented cross-culturally (Kohlberg 1969) and the results of a longitudinal study of American boys supports the irreversibility of the developmental sequence (Kramer 1968). The reality of moral stages as structured wholes is documented by high degrees of consistency across various verbal situations or contents (Kohlberg 1969).

Attempts have been made to stimulate the development of more mature moral judgment in schools, colleges, and prisons. The most widely used method has been the moral discussion. The participants discuss a hypothetical dilemma, delineate the moral issues involved, justify their moral positions and interact with group members at stages other than their own. The moral discussion can be used from early childhood through adulthood by varying the content of hypothetical dilemmas and the level of abstraction at which issues are discussed. Here is a dilemma intended for elementary school children:

Holly is an eight-year-old girl who likes to climb trees. She is the best tree-climber in the neighborhood. One day while climbing down from a tall tree she falls off the bottom branch but does not hurt herself. Her father sees her fall. He is upset and asks her to promise not to climb trees any more. Holly promises.

Later that day, Holly and her friends meet Shawn. Shawn's kitten is caught up in a tree and can't get down. Something has to be done right away or the kitten may fall. Holly is the only one who climbs trees well enough to reach the kitten and get it down but she remembers her promise to her father. (Selman and Kohlberg 1972)

Unless groups are at an advanced level of cognitive sophistication, the issue of justification (how one supports or justifies a moral statement) is raised in a simplified way by asking them to think and talk about these kinds of questions: "What do you think X should do and why?" "What are the best reasons you can think of to support that?" "Is that a good reason?" An understanding of the is/ought distinction (the relation between what one would do versus what one should do in a situation) can also be pursued on many levels. Even fairly young children can discuss each questions as these: "What *should* X do?" "What do you think X *would* do if she or he were really in this situation?" "What would you do if you were in the situation?" "Do you always do what you should do?" "Why or why not?" "What is something you didn't do even though you thought you should have done it?" For more sophisticated groups, the dilemmas can be made more complex, the participants can be challenged to justify their positions more thoroughly, and discussion may include metaethical as well as normative ethical issues.

Recently some prison and school moral development programs have been expanded into self-governing "just communities" in which day-to-day conflicts rather than hypothetical dilemmas are resolved in group meetings. These emphasize consistency between judgments and actions which is less prominent when only hypothetical moral dilemmas are discussed.

The moral development and values clarification perspectives share several psychological assumptions. Both approaches are cognitive rather than behavioristic or psychoanalytic: they focus on the child's thinking about or conception of values and moral issues rather than on external environmental or internal unconscious pressures to respond in a particular way. Both approaches aim for increased clarity of thinking as the student develops, and both are primarily concerned with increasing the adequacy of cognitive *processes* rather than imparting particular beliefs or values as did traditional approaches to character or religious education. The two, however, have different criteria for cognitive adequacy. Simon and other values clarification advocates emphasize independence of decision making, careful consideration of alternatives and consequences, and willingness to stand up for and live in accordance with one's beliefs. While Kohlberg would probably agree that these qualities are good and important, his theory concentrates on qualitative changes in reasoning as it matures. The stages themselves are descriptions of these changes.

Although Simon believes that his strategies will help stimulate growth through Kohlbergian stages (Simon and Kirschenbaum 1973), Simon's domain and emphasis differ radically from Kohlberg's. Simon is interested in clarifying a broad range of values of which moral values are only a small part. Self-knowledge and self-esteem are essential goals in his programs. While it is hard to argue with Simon's premise that people should learn to make all kinds of decisions in a careful and reasonable way, Simon's failure to distinguish between moral and nonmoral values can be confusing. For example, in a typical values clarification exercise, "values voting," group members are asked such questions as "How many [of you] have ever dyed your hair a different color?" "How many would like to take up glider soaring?" and "How many think we should legalize mercy-killing?" (*Values Clarification,* pp. 41-48). Though all these questions are related to self-knowledge and thus to values clarification, only the third asks a moral question. The failure of values clarification to treat moral and nonmoral questions as fundamentally different obscures such philosophical issues as ethical relativity (the view that validity of a moral judgment is relative to the values or needs of the individual or culture) and adequacy of justification.

A second difference between the values clarification and moral development approaches is that the former is concerned with the descriptive "is," the latter with the prescriptive "ought." In the "value sheet" strategy developed by Raths, Harmin, and Simon, the instructions to the student are: "Read each of the eight situations below and try to identify *what you would do* in each case" (p. 86). An analogous Kohlbergian moral discussion would require that participants consider the prescriptive question, "What should you do . . ." in addition to the predictive/descriptive question, "What would you do . . ." (Colby, Speicher, and Blatt 1973).

The absence of prescriptive (should/ought) considerations from values clarification processes is related to their failure to make the moral-nonmoral distinction. One can hardly say that people *should* be interested in glider soaring. At least the "should" in this nonmoral question may mean something quite different from the "should" in

"One should steal a drug to save someone's life." One *should* fly a glider if one has certain desired goals like having fun; however, one is not obligated to have fun in this particular way. But if stealing a drug to save someone's life is morally right, one should do it; one is *obligated* to do it whether one wants to or not. Simon is interested in having people clarify the values they hold, but once the values are clear, it is an open question whether these values are good. His great care to avoid value imposition excludes prescriptive considerations and confuses the philosophical issues.

In *Readings in Values Clarification*, Simon and Kirschenbaum (1973) wonder "why Kohlberg thinks that I convey such overwhelming relativism" (p. 63). Two reasons for such an impression have been discussed, the lack of any moral-nonmoral distinction and the avoidance of prescriptive considerations. The following statements further support this impression: "The two (clarifying values) approaches described below are not based upon the assumption that absolute goods exist and can be known. They view values as relative, personal and situational" (Simon and Kirschenbaum 1973, p. 11). It is not clear, however, that Simon is relativistic in the metaethical sense, i.e., that he holds that there can be no objectively valid rational way of justifying one moral value judgment against another, or that two contradictory moral judgments may both be valid or true. Rather, in reacting against the simple-minded, absolutist, and traditional moralities foisted upon children, Simon may wish simply to emphasize the degree to which general moral principles must be tailored to the details of each interpersonal situation. I suspect that Simon is insufficiently clear about the distinction between tolerance for differences of opinion and the relativist notion that all opinions are equally justifiable. If this is a misinterpretation, the lack of a coherent statement of philosophical assumptions in values clarification literature is at least partially at fault.

Without facing the philosophical issues more squarely, Simon, Howe, and Kirschenbaum cannot offer a moral justification for clarifying people's values. Teachers help students publicly affirm and act on their beliefs by using such strategies as "self-contracts." The teacher says:

In this activity, you are going to make a contract with yourself about some change you would like to make in your life. It can involve starting something new, stopping something old, or changing some present aspect of your life. For example, perhaps you might want to do something about ecology. You might want to make a self-contract which says, "For the next week, I will turn out the lights each and every time I leave my room, thus saving electricity, thus cutting down on the pollution from the electric company. (*Values Clarification*, pp. 319-20)

It is not clear, however, what the teacher "ought" to do when a student decides that he has been suppressing his desire to cheat on tests and will make a self-contract to act on his feelings by cheating any time he can. Raths recognizes this possibility as a problem for values clarification and offers a solution:

If the teacher thinks his students are not yet ready to judge the issue of honesty, to use an example, he should not pretend that he permits them to do so. He should up and tell them, "Students, we cannot let you decide this for yourselves right now. This decision is one that is too complicated (or dangerous) to give you." (*Values and Teaching*, p. 113)

At one point this limitation is backed by a moral justification: "You may choose what you believe best, but some behavior can't be permitted because it interferes too much with the freedom or rights of others" (*Values and Teaching*, p. 113). Further scrutiny of the justification shows that the desire to avoid evaluating the moral adequacy of differing values positions interferes with a coherent resolution of the cheating problem.

Ginger: Does that mean that we can decide for ourselves whether we should be honest on tests here?
Teacher: No, that means that you can decide on the value. I personally value honesty; and although you may choose to be dishonest, I shall insist that we be honest on our tests here. In other areas of your life, you may have more freedom to be dishonest, but one can't do *anything any time*, and in this class I shall expect honesty on tests.
Ginger: But then how can we decide for ourselves? Aren't you telling us what to value?
Sam: Sure, you're telling us what we should do and believe in.
Teacher: Not exactly. I don't mean to tell you what you should value. That's up to you. But I do mean that in this class, not elsewhere necessarily, you have to be honest on tests or suffer certain consequences. I merely mean that I cannot give tests without the rule of honesty. All of you who choose dishonesty as a value may not practice it here, that's all I'm saying. Further questions anyone? (*Values and Teaching*, pp. 114-15)

This teacher avoids a moral justification for her position, as this would imply that the opposite position is inadequate or wrong. This is an unsatisfying solution to the problem. If no moral justification is required for the limitations she places on her students' choices, they tend toward the arbitrary imposition against which the values clarification approach is reacting. Raths, Harmin, and Simon give prudential arguments against imposing values on the students in too many areas, but in the end leave the teacher free to impose his own values without ample justification where the consequences of free choice would be "distasteful or dangerous." The teacher is encouraged to have students act on all values except those she selects out in what must seem to them an arbitrary fashion. A teacher's equal approval of all acts based on values is not a neutral stand either, for the teacher seems to be sanctioning all the values expressed. The student may come to believe that any action is morally justified if it is sincere or "authentic."

An advantage of the Kohlbergian approach is that the teacher has grounds for giving and requiring respect for an individual's opinions and values without sanctioning those opinions or values as morally adequate. He can recognize the student's right to hold and express views without having to maintain that those views are right or justifiable and so should be acted upon. Ideally, a moral development program is run democratically so that decisions about rules and discipline are made by the group as a whole. Even in classrooms where this is not done the teacher's authority is not arbitrary, as it is in values clarification, since any decision must be justified by the teacher and open to challenge by the students.

In spite of the differences between values clarification and moral development, their goals are not radically disparate. Both aim to sensitize people to values or moral issues, to give them experiences in thinking critically about such issues, to encourage judgment-action consistency and to build a sense of self-confidence and interpersonal trust. It might be useful to think of the relationship between values clarification and moral development strategies as a division of labor. Values clarification helps people to know and accept themselves, to be able to make choices freely and carefully. Moral development strategies help them to subject those values and choices to critical evaluation from a moral perspective and, it is hoped, to act morally as well as sincerely.

Where the values clarification approach tends to confuse rather than clarify thinking about *moral* issues, ideas from Kohlberg's approach could be added: discussion questions focusing on considerations of fairness, the is/ought distinction, sensitivity to moral issues in general, and the distinction between moral and nonmoral questions.

While the moral development approach, optimally used, aims to build self-confidence, trust, and responsibility as well as to increase sophistication of moral thinking, the programs incorporated into traditional schools lack the specific methods for attaining these goals that values clarification has to offer. Curricula using hypothetical moral dilemmas alone tend to neglect the important fact that self-knowledge, self-concept, ego ideal, and lifestyle choices are inextricably bound up with moral choices. Here values clarification materials have useful contributions.

For borrowing across approaches to be viable, some revision is needed on both sides. Two changes can be made in the values clarification strategies to integrate them with moral development objectives. First, specifically moral considerations could be integrated into the strategies. Simon, Howe, and Kirschenbaum describe a simulation activity in which students pretend to be trapped in a cave. Each student is asked to give reasons for why he or she should be at the head of the dig-out line and thus have the best chance of survival. Students are asked to describe both what they want to live for and what they have to contribute to others in the world (pp. 287-89). As it is now, the strategy does not demand that the students consider the situation from the point of view of fairness, nor does it encourage them to examine the justice of basing life and death decisions on one's personal expectations or potential societal contributions. A moral development approach would require that these issues be considered.

Second, when considering moral and nonmoral aspects of a situation, students could be encouraged to differentiate between the two, for clear thinking about moral issues involves the ability to determine which facts are morally relevant. Likewise, the distinction between "is" and "ought" must be clarified. In a dilemma where students are asked to imagine being trapped in a cave-in with no way of digging out, the decision is whether cannibalism is justified if it will increase the chances that some survivors will be rescued. While it is interesting and important for the students to discuss their feelings about the situation, certain considerations have little moral relevance, like the question "How does human flesh taste?" One might well be less inclined to cannibalism if human flesh tastes terrible, but this is hardly a moral argument against it. To clarify such distinctions the teacher must ask students to think about the differences between moral and nonmoral issues in each dilemma and in general.

In addition to these specific changes, a general shift in emphasis would bring the values clarification strategies even more in line with what Kohlberg has found fruitful. Since the particular content of a choice is less important than the reason behind the choice, the major emphasis should be on the discussions which occur after the pencil and paper exercises (votes, rankings, and forced choices) are completed. The students need to pull together a general conceptual scheme from the large numbers of specific choices they have made, to see some consistency and to draw a few generalities from the many specifics. This may be implied by Simon, Howe, and Kirschenbaum, but might be misinterpreted by teachers because the major part of many strategies consists of lists of questions or rankings. Students must think and talk about why they voted, ranked, or chose as they did; they must also consider whether theirs were good choices and, most importantly, why.

Insights from the use of values clarification material in the classroom also provide useful suggestions for moral development methods. In *Values and Teaching*, Raths, Harmin, and Simon caution teachers against using large group discussions for four reasons. First, participants in the heat of a value discussion often become defensive of positions they might not even hold. Second, the participants often are motivated by factors irrelevant to the issue being discussed, such as desires to please other students and/or the teacher, and thus the thoughtful, deliberative aspects of valuing often become diluted with emotional considerations. Third, teachers must be sensitive to motivating participation by the less aggressive students in the group. Fourth, discussion can generate undue pressure on individuals to accept the group consensus. These suggestions apply to Kohlbergian groups as well, but the teacher must remember that moral development is not a completely individual process and requires social interaction, taking others' perspectives, and resolving inconsistencies in one's thinking.

The values clarification approach could also help teachers deal with a problem they often have when working with Kohlberg's approach. This is the tendency of children to avoid making a moral decision by finding a nonmoral solution to a dilemma. In response to

Holly's cat-in-the-tree dilemma, children will suggest that the children ask a parent to retrieve the cat, look for a ladder, or coax the cat down with some fish. Usually these solutions are ruled out by the teacher in an attempt to focus the children's attention on the conflict between truth and concern for the cat or between child-parent duties and friendship. It might be fruitful to encourage this tendency to search for feasible alternatives as a first step in discussing the dilemma. Later the teacher could lead the discussion into the moral conflict. In this way one dilemma could be used to achieve both values clarification and moral development objectives.

Raths, Harmin, and Simon also caution teachers against using "why" questions. The reasons behind each choice are crucial to Kohlberg's approach, and "why" questions cannot simply be eliminated. Raths argues that asking a student to justify her position can be detrimental to self-confidence or self-esteem because it questions her assertions and puts her in a defensive position. Students might also espouse reasons which are not their own to satisfy the teacher. There is some validity to these objections, and instructions to teachers using Kohlberg's approach should take them into account. "Why" questions need to be asked sensitively and with sincere interest in the student's thinking rather than as challenges provoking a defensive reaction. The opportunity to admit that one is not sure why she feels the way she does must always be open to the student as well.

Although in many ways the moral development and values clarification approaches do conflict, it is possible to use them in a complementary way without being inconsistent. I have sketched the outline of a possible theoretical integration of the two approaches and given some advice for coordinating classroom activities. The rest of the integration must be done by curriculum writers and teachers as they develop programs using both approaches. Though using the two together without careful thought could increase confusion and contradictions, a thoughtful combination could probably accomplish more than either approach alone.

References

Brown, G. "An Investigation of a Methodology for Value Clarification: Its Development, Demonstration, and Application for Teachers of the Elementary School." Ph.D. dissertation, New York University, 1966.

Colby, A.; Speicher, B.; and Blatt, M. "Hypothetical Dilemmas for Use in Moral Discussions." Cambridge, Mass.: Center for Moral Education, Harvard University, 1973.

Klevan, A. "An Investigation of a Methodology for Value Clarification: Its Relationship to Consistency in Thinking, Purposefulness, and Human Relations." Ph.D. dissertation, New York University, 1957.

Kohlberg, L. "State and Sequence: The Cognitive-Developmental Approach to Socialization." *Handbook of Socialization Theory and Research*, edited by D. Goslin. New York: Rand McNally, 1969.

Kohlberg, L. "Continuities in Childhood and Adult Moral Development Revisited." *Life-Span Developmental Psychology*, edited by P. Baltes and K. W. Schaie. New York: Academic Press, 1973.

Kramer, R. "Moral Development in Young Adulthood." Ph.D. dissertation, University of Chicago, 1968.

Lang, M. "An Investigation of the Relationship of Value Clarification to Underachievement." Ph.D. dissertation, New York University, 1962.

Raths, J. "An Application of Clarifying Techniques to Academic Underachievers in High School." Ph.D. dissertation, New York University, 1960.

Raths, L.; Harmin, M.; and Simon, S. *Values and Teaching*. Columbus, Ohio: Charles E. Merrill, 1966.

Selman, R., and Kohlberg, L. *First Things: A Strategy for Teaching Values*. New York: Guidance Associates, 1972.

Simon, S.; Howe, L.; and Kirschenbaum, H. *Values Clarification: A Handbook of Practical Strategies for Teachers and Students*. New York: Hart, 1972.

Simon, S., and Kirschenbaum, H. *Readings in Values Clarification*. Minneapolis: Winston Press, 1973.

18

Why Doesn't Lawrence Kohlberg Do His Homework?

Richard S. Peters

Someone said of Bernard Shaw that he was like the Venus de Milo. What there was of him was excellent. The same, I think, needs to be said of Kohlberg. The trouble is, however, that Kohlberg remains quite impervious to criticisms of the limitations of his view of moral education. He has never answered, for instance, a series of very constructive criticisms leveled against him by myself and Bill Alston in the Binghampton conference of 1969 (see Mischel 1971). It is not that the stuff he continues to ladle out is not very good. It is, and I have made much use of it myself (see Peters 1974). It is simply that he remains oblivious of the many other important aspects of moral education, and there is a danger that the unwary will think that he has told the whole story. In a commentary of this length, I can only list the main omissions:

1. He suffers from the rather touching belief that a Kantian type of morality, represented in modern times most notably by Hare and Rawls, is the only one (see Peters 1973 and Murdoch 1970). He

---

Reprinted by permission from *Phi Delta Kappan* (June 1975), p. 678.

fails to grasp that utilitarianism, in which the principle of justice is problematic, is an alternative type of morality and that people such as Winch have put forward a morality of integrity in which the principle of universalizability is problematic (see Winch 1972 and Kierkegaard 1961). I think this can be carried forward, actually. A morality of courage as exemplified by train robbers, the old "virtue" of Machiavelli's *Prince*, is a defensible morality. So also is a more romantic type of morality such as that of D. H. Lawrence, in which trust must be placed in "the dark God within." It is either sheer legislation to say that Kohlberg's morality is the true one, or it is the worst form of the naturalistic fallacy which argues from how "morality" is ordinarily used to what morality is.

2. He does not take "good-boy" morality seriously enough either from a practical or from a theoretical point of view. Practically speaking, since few are likely to emerge beyond Kohlberg's Stages 3 and 4, it is important that our fellow citizens should be well bedded down at one or the other of these stages. The policeman cannot always be present, and if I am lying in the gutter after being robbed it is somewhat otiose to speculate at what stage the mugger is. My regret must surely be that he had not at least got a conventional morality well instilled in him. Theoretically, too, the good-boy stage is crucial; for at this stage the child learns from the inside, as it were, what it is to follow a rule. Unless he has learned this well (whatever it means!), the notion of following his *own* rules at the autonomous stage is unintelligible. Kohlberg does not appreciate, either, that moral rules have to be learned in the face of counter-inclinations. Otherwise there would, in general, be no point to them. Hence the necessity at these stages for the type of reinforcement advocated by Skinner and others and for the modeling processes so stressed by Bronfenbrenner in his *Two Worlds of Childhood* (1971). In particular, he ignores the masterly chapter on "The Unmaking of the American Child." He seems sublimely unaware, too, of the mass of evidence about other aspects of moral education collected by Hoffman in Mussen's *Carmichael's Manual of Child Psychology* (1970).

3. As Bill Alston stresses in his article (see Mischel 1971) and I stress elsewhere, Kohlberg, like Piaget, is particularly weak on the development of the affective side of morality, of moral emotions such as "guilt," "concern for others," "remorse," and so on.

4. Finally, Kohlberg, in his references to ego strength, sees the

importance of will in morality, but offers no account of the type of habit training which encourages or discourages its growth.

I and others have written a great deal about these other aspects of morality and moral learning and development; it is a pity that Lawrence Kohlberg does not start doing some homework!

References

Bronfenbrenner, Urie. *Two Worlds of Childhood*. London: Allen & Unwin, 1971.

Kierkegaard, Sören. *Purity of Heart*. London: Fontana Books, 1961.

Mischel, Theodore. *Cognitive Development and Epistemology*. New York: Academic Press, 1971.

Murdoch, Iris. *The Sovereignty of Good*. London: Routledge & Kegan Paul, 1970.

Mussen, Paul H. (ed.) *Carmichael's Manual of Child Psychology*. New York: John Wiley & Sons, 1970.

Peters, Richard S. *Reason and Compassion*. London: Routledge & Kegan Paul, 1973.

Peters, Richard S. *Psychology and Ethical Development*. London: Allen & Unwin, 1974.

Winch, Peter. *Ethics and Action*. London: Routledge & Kegan Paul, 1972.

19

The Kohlberg Bandwagon: Some Reservations

Jack R. Fraenkel

The enthusiasm which Lawrence Kohlberg and his theory of moral stages has generated recently for a "moral reasoning" approach to values education has been quite impressive. Conferences, workshops, articles, even books dealing with the approach have proliferated. Lots of people are jumping on the bandwagon. Nevertheless, many others are wary of having teachers and curriculum developers jump too quickly on the moral stages bandwagon for a number of reasons. In this article, I wish to discuss briefly what some of these concerns are. I shall not review in detail the psychological research upon which Kohlberg's theory is based (See Kurtines and Greif 1974; Simpson 1974, for criticisms of this research), but rather offer some comments about the nature of the theory itself, and the way in which some of the basic ideas in the theory have been extended into educational proposals and teaching models. Particular attention will be paid to some of the conclusions and suggestions offered by Edwin Fenton (1976) and Barry Beyer (1976). The adequacy of the theory as a rationale for values education will then be considered.

Reprinted by permission from *Social Education* (April 1976), pp. 216-22. Copyright National Council for the Social Studies.

The Basic Ideas of Kohlberg's Theory

Much of Kohlberg's thinking is rooted in the earlier thinking of John Dewey (1916, 1932) and the stage theorizing of Jean Piaget (1932). Rest (see chapter 16) has identified three fundamental ideas as lying at the heart of Kohlberg's theory. These he labeled "structural organization," "developmental sequence," and "interactionism." *Structural organization* refers to the fact that developmental psychologists like Kohlberg consider the development of a person's cognitive structure—the way in which a person analyzes and interprets data, and makes decisions about personal and social problems—to be of crucial importance in that person's overall growth and development. *Developmental sequence* refers to the fact that Kohlberg and others who hold similar beliefs view the development of a person's cognitive structure in terms of stages, with the developmentally earlier and less complex "lower" stages being viewed as prerequisites to the "higher" stages. A major purpose of education for a developmentalist is to foster individual movement through these stages.

Kohlberg interviewed children and adults in a variety of cultures (nine at last report: see chapter 12), and identified three levels of moral development—the preconventional, the conventional, and the postconventional. Each of these levels contains two stages within it, for a total of six stages of moral reasoning. These stages can be briefly described as follows:

Stage 1: a morality of punishment and obedience (physical consequences determine what is right);

Stage 2: a morality of instrumental hedonism (satisfying one's own needs is what is right);

Stage 3: a "good boy—nice girl" morality (maintaining good relations with others and obtaining their approval is what is right);

Stage 4: a morality of maintaining "law and order" (obeying authority and "doing one's duty" is what is right);

Stage 5: a morality of contract, of individual rights, and of democratically accepted law (standards critically examined and agreed on by the society as a whole determine what is right);

Stage 6: a morality of individual principles of conscience (the decision of one's conscience, in accord with self-chosen principles, appealing to logical comprehensiveness, universality, and consistency, determines what is right).

The stage of moral reasoning that a particular individual has achieved is determined by having judges evaluate the person's responses to a hypothetical "moral dilemma"—a story in which an individual is faced with a moral choice. The stories are philosophical in nature, and involve questions of responsibility, motive, or intention. An individual's stage is not determined by the nature of the choice that he or she makes with regard to a moral dilemma, but rather on the basis of the reasons the individual gives for the choice.

Like Piaget, Kohlberg not only argues that progression through these stages is sequential and invariant, but also that not very many people reach the highest stages. He has stated that only ten percent of adult Americans reason at the postconventional level (see chapter 12). Furthermore, the six stages are viewed as universal, holding true in all cultures, with each stage representing a higher level of reasoning than the one immediately preceding it. Though individuals do not skip stages, they may move through them either quickly or slowly, and an individual may be found half in and half out of a particular stage at a given time. As individuals progress through the stages, they become increasingly able to take in and synthesize more and different information than they could at earlier stages, and to organize this information into an integrated and systematized framework. Kohlberg has also argued that higher-stage reasoning is morally better than lower-stage reasoning (see chapter 12).

Interactionism refers to the process by which a person's cognitive structure is developed. As a child develops and notices certain regularities in his environment, he develops a pattern of behavior (a cognitive structure) to deal with these regularities—a way of thinking about the world. As the child grows and matures, however, he undergoes experiences for which his previously developed cognitive structure is inadequate; he thus seeks to revamp his way of thinking in order to make sense out of the new experience. When he finds a new way of thinking which enables him to understand the experience, his cognitive structure—his way of thinking about the world—is accordingly changed. An essential ingredient for intellectual growth—for the cognitive development of the child—therefore, is the opportunity to engage in a number of new and different experiences which will cause him or her to try to reorder his or her existing way of thinking and to seek out more adequate ways to organize and interpret data.

Some Reservations About the Theory

A first reservation lies in the argument for the universality of the stages. Even though Kohlberg states that the six stages he has identified hold for all nine of the cultures that he has examined, this is a rather small sample from which to infer the sweeping conclusion that the description of moral development for all people in all cultures has been found, or even to infer that the concept of justice, fundamental to the reasoning inherent in the higher stages (5 and 6), is endorsed by all cultures. Turnbull, for example, in *The Mountain People* (1972), describes some of the behaviors of the Ik people of northeastern Uganda. The Ik at one time had been a peaceful society who cooperated to hunt for food, and who honored their dead with burial ceremonies. More recently, the Ugandan government decided to make the Ik's tribal grounds into a national park, and accordingly moved them to a new and very crowded living area on a steep mountainside. As a result of this move the Ik appear to have developed values which are the very antithesis of justice. For example, Turnbull observed a group of them laughing when a young child grabbed a hot coal from a fire and screamed in pain. Young Ik laughed with pleasure as they beat an elderly Ik with sticks and threw stones at him until he cried. An entire village came to the edge of a cliff that a blind woman had fallen over and laughed as she suffered in agony. As a two-year drought destroyed the Ik's crops and starvation set in, hoarding food and keeping it from one's family and from the elders of the tribe became honorable and was viewed as a mark of distinction. Old people were abandoned to die, and burial ceremonies to honor the dead were no longer held. After living with the Ik for eighteen months, Turnbull summed up his experiences in the following words:

The Ik teach us that our much vaunted human values are not inherent in humanity at all, but are associated only with a particular form of survival called society, and that all, even society itself, are luxuries that can be dispensed with. (1972)

As Peters (see chapter 18) has suggested, Kohlberg and his advocates appear to suffer from the belief that a morality based on the concept of justice is the only type of morality that is defensible. This puts him and his supporters in a somewhat difficult position, for they are forced to defend the proposition that justice is a universally held and admired concept. Unfortunately, there is just too much evidence to the contrary around for this to wash.

A second reservation lies in the assertion that higher-stage reasoning is not only different, but morally *better* than lower-stage reasoning. Such a notion (that higher means better) seems to be an impossible one to prove. If higher-stage reasoning is better it should contain or possess something which lower-stage reasoning does not. And if this is true, it is difficult to see how those reasoning at the lower stages would be able to understand the arguments of the individuals at the higher stages. And if they cannot understand the arguments, it is difficult to see why they would be inclined to accept such reasoning as being better than their own as a justification for various actions. If higher is not better, then there doesn't seem to be any justification for trying to "improve" the reasoning of children by helping them to move through the stages. Scriven (see chapter 20) argues in a similar vein:

The put-up or shut-up question [is] whether someone at an "intermediate" stage of moral development is more wrong (or less right) on moral issues than someone at a "higher" stage. If the "lower" stage subjects are not demonstrably wrong, then there's no justification for trying to change them, i.e., for moral education. If they *are* demonstrably wrong, then there must be a proof that they are wrong, i.e., a proof of the increasingly objective nature of the moral standards (or processes) of higher stages; but no satisfactory proof of this has ever been produced. . . .

Thirdly, since Kohlberg himself estimates that a majority of people do not get beyond Stage 4, it would seem important to devise ways to get everyone up to and firmly entrenched at this stage. Peters (see chapter 18) writes "[Since] few [individuals] are likely to emerge beyond Kohlberg's Stages 3 and 4, it is important that our fellow citizens should be well bedded down at one or the other of these stages. The policeman cannot always be present, and if I am lying in the gutter after being robbed it is somewhat otiose to speculate at what stage the mugger is. My regret must surely be that he had not at least got a conventional morality well instilled in him."

The conventional level (Stages 3-4) of reasoning is important for another reason. "At this stage the child learns from the inside, as it were, what it is to follow a rule. Unless he has learned this well (whatever it means!), the notion of following his own rules at the autonomous stage is unintelligible." Children must understand and appreciate the importance of rules in general for both personal and societal survival (can you imagine a society existing without at least some rules?), as well as what can happen when rules are disregarded and/or taken lightly by large numbers of people, before the idea of developing and following one's own rules begins to make any sense. It is certainly important to realize that rules may be unjust, but the question of *when* and *whether* to disobey an unjust (or any) rule is an important one to explore *explicitly* with children, using a variety of incidents and analogies. We surely do not want to develop in the young a tendency to take rules too lightly (nor, of course, to view them as inviolate and absolute), and this can only be avoided by helping them to realize the value of, as well as to practice, following rules which at times go against their inclinations. Indeed, a key element of morality, it seems to me, lies in the understanding that "resistance to temptation" can be rewarding in its own right. Neither Kohlberg, nor any of his associates, has emphasized the importance of getting as many students as possible to the level of conventional morality. (Fenton's (1976) statement that "we should aim to raise the level of moral thinking of all children" to Stage 4, however, is a hopeful sign in this regard.) As yet, however, few specific strategies for developing in children a sense of the importance of rules (and, more importantly, a realization of the fact that giving in to one's inclinations frequently brings neither happiness nor satisfaction) have appeared.

Fourthly, the theory places rather unrealistic demands on classroom teachers once they *do* engage students in moral discussions. Kohlberg (1971a) has stated, "If moral communications are to be effective, the developmental level of the teacher's verbalizations must be one step above the level of the child" (p. 42). If what Kohlberg says is true, this requirement presents at least two problems. Since Kohlberg has stated that only ten percent of the population reaches Stages 5 or 6, the laws of probability suggest that there are many teachers who themselves reason at the lower stages, and who accordingly are likely to come in contact with students reasoning at stages higher than their own. Will such teachers be able even to understand, let alone help, such students? How can a teacher who reasons at Stage 3, for example, be expected to present a Stage 5 argument to a

Stage 4 student (so as to foster stage growth) if he or she cannot understand what such an argument is?

Furthermore, even if enough Stage 5 teachers could be found, they would still face a considerable amount of practical difficulty as they interact with students, no matter what the stages of the students may be. Since intellectual development and chronological age are not always the same, most teachers are likely to find that they have children at a variety of stages within their classrooms. It would probably be most unusual, in fact, to find a classroom in which all of the students were at the same stage. Theoretically, at least, this is all to the good, for the divergence of viewpoints would promote more conflict and variety of opinion in class discussions. But remember that Kohlberg argues that children must be exposed to a stage of reasoning one stage higher than their current stage if stage development is to be fostered.* To do this, a teacher must listen to several responses of each student, figure out what stage of reasoning these responses suggest, and then either frame an appropriate "one stage higher" response during ongoing class discussions, or mix the students with others who are reasoning one stage higher so that they may hear their arguments. This seems to be asking an awful lot from busy classroom teachers.

---

*Not all of Kohlberg's supporters appear to agree with this requirement, however. Beyer (1976) writes: "Teachers need not be able to identify the stages of reasoning their students use in order to be able to lead moral discussions. . . . Teachers who learn to encourage students to respond to each other can usually engage them in arguments at contiguous stages." This statement is rather puzzling. How can a teacher engage students in arguments "at contiguous stages" if he or she can't recognize the stages in the first place? If we take this statement at face value, Beyer appears to be saying, "Don't worry. Just engage the students in discussion, and growth in moral reasoning will occur." But he then goes on to say that teachers "with experience and with re-reading reports of Kohlberg's research . . . can become more skilled at identifying the stages at which their students reason." Evidently he is not sure himself about how important it is for teachers to be able to locate students at a particular stage. He can't have it both ways—either teachers need to know what the stages are and be able to recognize them when they hear them (so that individuals reasoning one stage apart can be placed together in order to promote development through the stages), or they don't. If they don't, they can forget about stage theory and just do what conscientious teachers have done all along—try to engage students in discussions about important issues without specifically trying to get individuals exposed to the views of individuals one stage higher. The question remains: Is being able to identify a moral stage important or isn't it?

Some Reservations About Fenton's Generalizations
Concerning Kohlberg's Research

Professor Fenton (1976) offers eleven conclusions which he feels Kohlberg's research supports. A careful examination of these claims, however, leads one to believe that Fenton has not been critical enough in his examination and analysis of this research. Not only are Kohlberg's arguments for the universality of his stages and the notion that "higher is better" open to question, but many of the other conclusions that Fenton draws are not supported convincingly by Kohlberg's research. First of all, the fact that there really are *six* stages has by no means been established. Only three individuals have been identified as being at Stage 6—Kohlberg himself, one of his graduate students, and Martin Luther King (Kohlberg 1971b).

Secondly, it is not even agreed that all of the stages are qualitatively different. Norman Williams (Williams and Williams 1970), for example, has suggested on the basis of data that he has collected, that Stages 3 and 4 appear to be alternative or parallel rather than sequential steps in a person's development.

Thirdly, even the notion of stages is challenged. Social learning psychologists like Mischel, for instance, argue that regular changes over time in the moral judgments of children may be due simply to the fact that as children grow older, they are reacted to differently by most of the adults with whom they come in contact. Since parents and other adults talk differently to young children and adolescents, it should not be surprising that verbal responses of first and second graders are different from those of teenagers (Mischel 1974).

Fourthly, Fenton's claim that "the most reliable way to determine a stage of moral thought is through a moral interview" depends on what he means by the word "interview." Rest (1975), for example, has developed an objective test (the Defining Issues Test) which asks students to rank prototypic statements of the "crucial issue" involved in a dilemma, from which he then draws inferences about their level of moral reasoning. Rest presents data which show that his test compares favorably with Kohlberg's test with regard to power of results, replications, and sample sizes in the studies conducted. Rest has concluded that "there are almost limitless formats for collecting moral judgment data" (1975, p. 112). Furthermore, Fenton's statement that "trained scorers show ninety percent agreement in identifying stage" is not supported by Kohlberg's own research. In his most recent scoring system, Kohlberg (1974) reports: "Interjudge agreement on this data was only 66 percent for major stage agreement." That's a long way from ninety!

Fifthly, Fenton's claim that all people move through these stages in an "invariant sequence" is contradicted by Simpson (1974) who points out that the research to which Kohlberg appeals has only demonstrated this among Stages 2, 3, and 4. And the claim that a person "reasons predominately at one stage of thought" seems more a preferred way of looking at the responses of people to moral dilemmas than a proven fact. Bull (1969), Williams and Williams (1970), and Wright (1971) have suggested alternative models, each of which is supported by a considerable amount of data.

Lastly, Fenton's assertion that "deliberate attempts to facilitate stage change in schools through educational programs have been successful" needs to be qualified somewhat. In some of the studies that have been cited by Kohlberg and others, many students showed no stage movement at all. In Kohlberg's 1969 study, for example, which is frequently cited as the basis for longitudinal trends in stage movement, just about one-third (32.6 percent) of the students involved showed an overall upward stage change, while only eight out of the total sample of forty-three showed one-step upward change (Kohlberg and Kramer 1969, p. 105). In the study which she conducted in 1973, Holstein found that only seven students out of a total sample of fifty-two moved up one stage over a three-year period, with some thirty-three (63.5 percent) showing some general upward movement (Holstein 1973). And in the studies in Boston and Pittsburgh which Kohlberg describes in chapter 12, he states that only "about half" of the teachers involved (twenty-four) were able to stimulate upward stage movement. And even that was only from one quarter to one-half a stage.

The point of all this is not to discourage teachers from thinking about stage theory and research. There is much in Kohlberg's work that is extremely interesting and useful. I have used much of it myself. But I am wary at this point of being too sure about what we know—of offering a neat bundle of eleven (or however many) generalizations about moral development research without at the same time pointing out those aspects of these research findings which are open to question or alternative interpretation.

I think it particularly important for those who review research findings and discuss their implications for social studies education to indicate what we don't know—that is, what questions such research leaves unanswered. This would help the profession in general to view conclusions based on research findings for what they almost always are—hypotheses demanding continual investigation and refinement rather than statements of established fact.

Reservations About Some of the Educational Suggestions Based on the Theory

There is no question, I think, that the influence of Kohlberg's theory has been considerable. As Rest has mentioned, "Educational programs with such a venerable lineage (Dewey-Piaget, Kohlberg, and so forth) have created interest because of the intellectual heft behind them and the promise of initiating something more than a superficial, piecemeal, short-lived fad" (see chapter 16). Nevertheless, the manner in which the basic ideas inherent in the theory have been extended into proposals for teaching raises a number of issues and questions which, at least so far, have remained unattended to by moral reasoning advocates. Let us consider a few of them here.

First is the issue of what Rest calls "optimal curriculum match" (see chapter 16). As mentioned earlier, a major goal of education so far as Kohlberg and other developmentalists are concerned is to *stimulate* development through the stages of moral reasoning. If this can be done, educators would have some very useful information. Rest writes:

The characterization of the highest stage of development gives a psychological analysis of some competence—e.g., Piaget's stage of formal operations gives us an analysis of what it means to be logical; Kohlberg's Stage 6 provides a description of what mature moral judgment consists. . . . Note that there is much more specificity here in a characterization of cognitive structure than the honorific labels often used to define educational objectives (such as "creative," "self-actualized," "good-citizen," "well-adjusted," and so forth).

Furthermore, if the educator has a step-by-step description of the development of some competence, then he has a means of ordering progress (knowing which changes are progressive), of locating people along this course of development, and therefore of anticipating which experiences the student will most likely respond to and from which he will profit. . . .

The chief strategy advocated by educators specifically interested in furthering moral development in social studies classrooms, however, is the discussion of moral dilemmas (Galbraith and Jones 1975; Beyer 1976). While these dilemmas do provoke controversy and the sorts of questions included in the strategy do encourage students to analyze alternatives (though the *explicit* and *sustained* consideration of *consequences* appears minimal), these writers do not pay much attention to the notions of optimal curriculum match and curriculum sequencing mentioned by Rest. They do not consider the fact that different kinds of dilemma issues may be more profitable (in the sense of promoting interest and discussion) at different grade levels; that dilemmas which deal with stage-specific kinds of concerns may be called for in order to appeal to students who are reasoning at different stages; or that one dilemma might be used to build on another so as to further cognitive growth. (The idea of using alternative dilemmas—with the original situation changed to some degree —as a follow-up to the original discussion, however, is a step in this direction. See Galbraith and Jones 1975, p. 19.) The notion of sequencing dilemmas is not discussed.

One gets the uneasy feeling at times that the advocates of moral discussions have gotten carried away by their own enthusiasm. For example, Beyer (1976) makes a number of statements which are either unsupported testimonials (e.g., "the most productive discussion involves small group discussions followed by a discussion involving the entire class"); value judgments (e.g., "a significant number of students should favor one course of action, while others should favor another"); or unrealistic in what they propose (e.g., "After students hear or see the dilemma, the teacher should ask questions in order to help students to clarify the circumstances involved in the dilemma, define terms, identify the characteristics of the central character, and state the exact nature of the dilemma and the action choice open to the central character. Little more than five minutes need be devoted to this part of the strategy").

Indeed, Beyer's (1976) assertion that a program of moral discussions will improve learning skills, improve self-esteem, and improve attitudes toward school seems to be a bit strong for even the converted to swallow whole. No evidence is provided to support this sweeping claim. Why should participating in a moral discussion (or

any discussion, for that matter) *ipso facto* help students develop
listening skills or improve their self-esteem? Discussions can be conducted poorly or well; the mere assertion of their value does not improve a person's skills or change his or her attitudes. It would seem
more likely that the manner in which a discussion is conducted
would be the crucial factor involved.

A word, too, is in order about the nature of the dilemmas themselves. Some of the ones that I have seen which Kohlberg, Fenton,
Beyer, Galbraith, et al., cite are rather narrow in scope (e.g., "Should
Jill give Sharon's name to the Security Officer?") and affect only one
or a few individuals (e.g., "Should a Christian girl in Nazi Germany
break the law and jeopardize her family by hiding her Jewish friend
from the Gestapo?"). This is apparently intentional; Beyer (1976)
states that a moral dilemma "should be as simple as possible. The
dilemma should involve only a few characters in a relatively uncom-
plicated situation which students can grasp readily. Complicated
dilemmas confuse students who are then forced to spend time clarifying facts and circumstances rather than discussing reasons for suggested actions."

This sort of rationale can be objected to on a number of counts.
First, dilemmas in real life are rarely simple. Secondly, students need
to be exposed to a wide variety of different kinds of issues and
dilemmas as they move through the grades, particularly ones which
can affect the lives of many people, so that they will become aware
of the sorts of problems which exist in the world (e.g., "Should the
President of the United States 'send in the marines' against the oil-
producing nations if they will not supply us with oil?"). Thirdly, one
wonders how students are to learn to sort out and analyze the facts
involved in complicated issues they will face in real life (e.g., abortion, taxation, local control of schools, euthanasia, jury duty, busing,
drug usage, environmental contamination, the right of public employees to strike, etc.) if they get little practice in doing so in
schools? And fourthly, students *need* practice (and lots of it) in
"clarifying facts and circumstances" if they are to find out about the
nature of the world in which they live.

The notion of sequencing dilemmas in some fashion seems in
order here, with one possibility being that of making them increasingly more complex, abstract, and difficult as students progress
through the grades. Such a scheme might entail students in the

elementary grades being presented with fairly simple interpersonal and intrapersonal conflicts revolving around such concepts as fairness, reward, punishment, responsibility, authority, and conscience. As students move on into junior and senior high school, they can at each grade level be presented with dilemmas involving larger and larger groups of people, including governments and international agencies. Such dilemmas, not only interpersonal, but also intergovernmental and global (involving more than two governments), could focus on such additional concepts as honor, duty, contract, property, civil liberties, and obligation. This might be one way of providing more breadth in the types of dilemmas to which students are exposed, and also of promoting the more fundamental, long-term, and cumulative change with which developmentalists are concerned.

It also should be pointed out that the strategy for guiding moral discussions suggested by Beyer (1976) and Galbraith and Jones (1975) is only one of many possibilities that might be used. The steps which these authors present do offer teachers some concrete ideas for getting a moral discussion started in the classroom, but care must be taken not to infer that this is the "one and only" way to go about the matter. Not only do other models exist (Hunt and Metcalf 1968, p. 134; Fraenkel 1973, p. 266) for teachers to consider, but also they can be encouraged to create their own strategies and models when and where appropriate.

Furthermore, we are not even sure that it is the discussion of the dilemmas themselves which brings about stage movement. It is certainly conceivable that a sensitive and concerned teacher, one who continually engages students in conversation and asks them questions, and lets them know by his or her comments and actions that he or she is interested in what they have to say, may be the independent variable in this regard. The discussion of moral dilemmas may be irrelevant. Perhaps the discussion of nonmoral controversial issues would do just as well. At this point, we just don't know.

More than anything else, the discussion of moral dilemmas seems to be a very limiting sort of strategy to recommend. In the first place, discussion does not work very well or for very long with children below the age of ten or so. You simply can't have much of an intellectual discussion with third and fourth graders. Other ways of presenting information about moral relationships and dilemmas, such as the use of models and concrete examples, must be used. Secondly, the use of case studies, which is what moral dilemmas are, focuses on specific instances rather than general principles. This often presents a problem in that only a few children in the class see the particular issue involved in the case as interesting or having applicability to them. An emphasis instead on more general principles (e.g., that one often has to make exceptions to rules), however, allows reference to a large number of examples by both teacher and students, thereby increasing interest and involvement on the part of the whole class (Beck 1972, p. 45). And finally, the likelihood of several *different* types of alternative suggestions being proposed by a class of students reasoning at Stages 2 or 3 (which Beyer and Fenton say is where most high school students are likely to be) does not seem to be very great. A more appropriate strategy, it seems to me, would be to encourage teachers (and curriculum developers and publishers) to not only present dilemmas to students in interesting and exciting ways and in a variety of formats (printed, oral, visual), but also to present them with a range of alternative solutions (at various stage levels) for resolving the dilemmas. As a part of the discussion of the dilemma, the teacher could then include a systematic consideration of the various alternatives. This would not in any way preclude, of course, having students suggest their own alternatives in addition to those presented. I am struck by Clive Beck's notion that perhaps one reason that a lot of people do not develop morally is because better alternatives have not occurred to them. They continue to react in conventional ways frequently because they perceive no other way of reacting. The above suggestion would, in Beck's words, "extend their imagination" (Beck 1972, p. 44).

Kohlberg's Theory and Values Education

Is the rationale behind the moral reasoning approach a sufficient one for values education? The answer to this question, I think, must be no. Certainly the development of a child's ability to think rationally about moral issues is important. Indeed, it is very important. And there is no denying that insufficient attention has been paid to the development of reasoning in general, let alone moral reasoning in particular in our classrooms in the past. But children need to develop not only intellectually but also emotionally if they are to become fully functioning and psychologically whole human beings. In fact, it is becoming clear to a lot of us that intellectual and emotional development are interdependent—that oftentimes the failure of someone to grasp the meaning of something is due to a lack of emotional sensitivity on his or her part. As Beck points out: ". . . what is needed is an *interactive* approach. Often we try to help a child understand a particular aspect of ethical theory: for example, we try to help him understand the need for reciprocal relationships (as in promise-keeping and formation of contracts); and we find that we fail, because there is a lack of sensitivity, a lack of concern, a lack of emotional development—a lack of *noncognitive* development—which prevents him from having this cognitive insight. On the other hand, there are cases where we try to help a person become more sensitive to other people and their needs and more disposed to help them, and the [problem] is his lack of *understanding* of the place of concern for others in a person's life" (1972 pp. 41-42).

The development of such an interactive approach, it seems to me, is a matter of the highest priority. What sorts of content and strategies that such an approach should contain, of course, is at this point an open question. Also open are the questions of how the content should be sequenced and when and where the strategies should be used. To be able to answer these questions in any kind of intelligent fashion, we are going to have to get clear in our own minds and in the profession about what the term "values education" means. What does it mean to say that someone is educated in values? What sorts of skills, attitudes, knowledge, etc., does such a person possess that others not so educated do not? How do we determine the degree to which a person is becoming educated in values—in short, how do we assess growth in this regard? And what specifically can teachers do to help students become "values educated"?

The ideas of Kohlberg and his supporters provide us with valuable food for thought in this regard. So, too, does the work of those who have proposed approaches which differ from Kohlberg's (Raths, Harmin, and Simon 1966; Oliver and Shaver 1966; Newmann and Oliver 1970; Hunt and Metcalf 1968; Fraenkel 1973; Scriven 1966, 1971, and chapter 20 of this volume; Shaver 1976). But none of these approaches is the last word on the subject. We need to have lots of models and strategies proposed, and then lots of research which tests and compares the effectiveness of these models and strategies in promoting both short- and long-range emotional and intellectual development. What is lacking at present is any sort of educational theory which *integrates* psychological notions about *both* intellectual and emotional development, together with a philosophical consideration of what values education should be about. This would appear to be a goal toward which all who are interested in seeing a comprehensive program of values education implemented in social studies classrooms might direct their efforts.

References

Beck, Clive. "The Development of Moral Judgment." *Developing Value Constructs in Schooling: Inquiry into Process and Product,* edited by James A. Phillips, Jr. Worthington, Ohio: Ohio Association for Supervision and Curriculum Development, 1972.

Beyer, Barry K. "Conducting Moral Discussions in the Classroom." *Social Education* (April 1976): 194-202.

Bull, Norman J. *Moral Judgment from Childhood to Adolescence.* London: Routledge & Kegan Paul, 1969.

Dewey, John. *Democracy and Education: An Introduction to the Philosophy of Education.* New York: Macmillan, 1916.

Dewey, John, and Tufts, James H. *Ethics* (rev. ed.). New York: Henry Holt, 1932.

Fenton, Edwin. "Moral Education: The Research Findings." *Social Education* (April 1976): 188-93.

Fraenkel, Jack R. *Helping Students Think and Value: Strategies for Teaching the Social Studies.* Englewood Cliffs, N.J.: Prentice-Hall, 1973.

Galbraith, Ronald E., and Jones, Thomas M. "Teaching Strategies for Moral Dilemmas. An Application of Kohlberg's Theory to the Social Studies Classroom." *Social Education* (January 1975): 16-22.

Holstein, C. "Moral Judgment Change in Early Adolescence and Middle Age: A Longitudinal Study." Unpublished manuscript, 1973.

Hunt, Maurice P., and Metcalf, Lawrence E. *Teaching High School Social Studies.* New York: Harper & Row, 1968.

Kohlberg, Lawrence. "The Concepts of Developmental Psychology as the Central Guide to Education: Examples from Cognitive, Moral, and Psychological Education." *Psychology and the Process of Schooling in the Next Decade: Alternative Conceptions.* Minneapolis: University of Minnesota Audio-Visual Extension, 1971a.

Kohlberg, Lawrence. "From Is to Ought: How to Commit the Naturalistic Fallacy and Get Away with It in the Study of Moral Development." *Cognitive Development and Epistemology,* edited by Theodore Mischel. New York: Academic Press, 1971b.

Kohlberg, Lawrence. "Comments on 'The Development of Moral Thought' by Kurtines and Greif." Unpublished manuscript, 1974.

Kohlberg, Lawrence, and Kramer, R. "Continuities and Discontinuities in Childhood and Adult Moral Development." *Human Development* (1969): 93-120.

Kurtines, William, and Greif, Esther B. "The Development of Moral Thought: Review and Evaluation of Kohlberg's Approach." *Psychological Bulletin* (August 1974): 453-70.

Mischel, W. "A Cognitive Social Learning Approach to Morality and Self-Regulation." *Morality: Theory, Research, and Social Issues*, edited by Thomas Likona. New York: Holt, Rinehart & Winston, 1974.

Newmann, Fred M., and Oliver, Donald W. *Clarifying Public Controversy, An Approach to Teaching Social Studies*. Boston: Little, Brown, 1970.

Oliver, Donald W., and Shaver, James P. *Teaching Public Issues in the High School*. Boston: Houghton Mifflin, 1966.

Piaget, Jean. *The Moral Judgment of the Child*. London: Routledge & Kegan Paul, 1932.

Raths, Louis; Harmin, Merrill; and Simon, Sidney B. *Values and Teaching*. Columbus, Ohio: Charles E. Merrill, 1966.

Rest, James. "The Validity of Tests of Moral Judgment." *Values Education Theory/Practice/Problems/Prospects*, edited by John R. Meyer, et al. Waterloo, Ontario: Wilfrid Laurier University Press, 1975.

Scriven, Michael. *Value Claims in the Social Sciences*. Boulder, Col.: Social Science Education Consortium, 1966.

Scriven, Michael. *Student Values as Educational Objectives*. Boulder, Col.: Social Science Education Consortium, 1966.

Scriven, Michael. "Values and the Valuing Process." Unpublished manuscript, 1971.

Shaver, James P. *Facing Value Decisions: Rationale Building for Teachers*. Belmont, Calif.: Wadsworth, 1976.

Simpson, Elizabeth L. "Moral Development Research: A Case Study of Scientific Cultural Bias." *Human Development* 17 (1974): 81-106.

Turnbull, Colin. *The Mountain People*. New York: Simon & Schuster, 1972.

Williams, N., and Williams, S. *The Moral Development of Children*. London: Macmillian, 1970.

Wright, Derek. *The Psychology of Moral Behavior*. Baltimore: Penguin, 1971.

PART IV

The Cognitive Approach

Introduction

Part IV contains a collection of viewpoints that will take us in a somewhat different direction. The cognitive or moral reasoning approach has a long tradition in schools. From the time of Socrates, to the medieval universities, to the academies and colleges of early America, a major aim of education was to aid men to think rigorously and carefully about ethical issues. Behind this tradition is a bedrock assumption that moral reasoning can be successfully taught and, indeed, that the development of moral reasoning is perhaps the most legitimate aim of education.

In chapter 20, Michael Scriven, the philosopher of science, raises some serious questions about the developmentalist views of Kohlberg and the "affectivist" views of Raths and Simon. He attempts to build a case for a strictly cognitive approach to moral education through a rigorous program of formal instruction. In chapter 21, Gary Wehlage and Alan L. Lockwood examine the values education aspects of several current curricula in the social studies. The authors give special attention to the relationship of moral relativism to these curricula. Chapter 22, by Donald Oliver and Mary Jo Bane, raises questions about the limitations of approaching moral education through curriculum and instruction strategies. Finally, in chapter 23, Irving Kristol argues that schools must stop short-changing the young by not placing demands on them. Schools should stand for and enforce certain values by reasserting academic and behavioral standards of excellence, standards that have been put aside in recent years.

20
Cognitive Moral Education

Michael Scriven

Recent interest in "humanistic" and "affective" education, as well as in developmental psychology, has combined with the great reawakening of interest in moral education to deemphasize the cognitive approach. This paper will point in the other direction. It is written as a cognitivist or rationalist polemic, for the sake of brevity and to encourage discussion. Personal caveats are appended rather than interspersed.

The Cast of Characters

The history of moral education in the U.S. is, by and large, a history of failure.* Documentation, if needed, runs from Hugh Hartshorne and Mark A. May's 1928 study to the National Assessment of Educational Progress data and Watergate. There are three leading contenders with their own favorite explanations of this failure. These may be labeled *affectivism, developmentalism,* and *cognitivism.*

---

*It is clear from Urie Bronfenbrenner's book *Two Worlds of Childhood* (1971) that generalizing to the USSR is risky; other sources suggest that Scandinavia and China may also be exceptions.

Reprinted by permission from *Phi Delta Kappan* (June 1975), pp. 689-94.

According to the affectivists, the failure resulted from treating moral precepts taught in school as if they were something to be memorized like the rules of grammar or historical facts, whereas— they would say—they have no connection with action except via affect, which was almost totally ignored. In short, children learned the rules but had no interest in applying them; they passed the written (cognitive) tests but failed the behavioral ones (which require both cognitive and affective gains). In practice, says the affectivist, moral education must be treated as essentially a matter of feeling, affect, attitude. Appropriate modes of teaching follow from this approach, e.g., role playing, model presentation, the use of inspirational material, etc.

According to the developmentalist, the failure resulted from using a single treatment of a moral issue with a developmentally heterogeneous group (typically age-mates) scattered across many stages of moral development, resulting in negligible net impact. One might as well try to teach theology to a random sample of European waifs by reading Aquinas to them in Latin; to only a few would it even make sense, let alone teach theology. The proper approach, says the developmentalist, is to match the "treatment" to the "diagnosis."

According to the cognitivist, the failure was due to a colossal underestimation of the difficulty of moral problems and analysis— indeed, of morality. One might as well suppose he could teach nine-year-olds the calculus by having them memorize the dozen formulae from the end-page synopsis of a calculus text. The children could not have passed a serious written test, only superficial ones. And, having no real understanding of what morality is all about, they had no reason to take it very seriously when it conflicted with their own interests.

It might seem that a fourth point of view should also be mentioned, namely, that of the religionist. Religionists often blame moral laxity on lack of adequate religious education. But which religious education? The many answers can be treated as varying mixes of the three previous ingredients. For example, a traditional Jesuitical approach is high on cognitivism, low on affectivism, with just a dash of developmentalism. The low-church Episcopalian often reverses the order of the first two components. (Almost all Jesuits, however, think the affective component crucial though small; in a way, it corresponds to what they call grace.) The simple problem with the religionists, however, is that it is their efforts at moral education which were studied and were shown to have failed. Not that they failed with every pupil, of course; but their batting average as moral teachers appears to be no higher than that of TV or Marxist atheism.

The affectivists and developmentalists think that essentially all forms of religious education have failed either through slighting affect or development, or through incompetent treatment of these elements. The cognitivist thinks they failed because they were built on recognizable falsehoods or improbabilities illogically and superficially applied.

Many other well-known approaches to education are hybrids of the three "ideal types" described. Lawrence Kohlberg certainly, Piaget probably, is a developmentalist-cognitivist; the values clarification people and the (British) Lifeline Project people are affectivist-cognitivists. The usual public school approach (i.e., excluding the subject from the official curriculum) must be classified along with any indoctrinational approach as de facto affective, since in fact it commits itself to moral education by nonreasoning means, by example, habit, social pressure, and punishment.

The Cognitivist Perspective

From the cognitivist's perspective, the hard-core affectivists are a bunch of do-gooders whose highest aim is to develop a "positive attitude" in some direction which is either undefined or undefended, and is very likely to be different in itself or in its specific implications for every authority on affective education. That's about as much of a contribution to morality as getting everyone into a panic is to fire fighting. Affect as an end in itself only replaces moral apathy with moral anarchy. Affect must—says the cognitivist—be entirely subservient to the cognitive approach. It has a place, but only as the last supplement in the pedagogy of ethics. First must come the legitimation of ethics itself, then the legitimation of moral education, then the cognitive structuring of moral education, then the teaching of the basic cognitive elements in ethics—and only then the affect, the icing on the cake. Three of these five steps, one might suppose, represent "tooling up" for moral education rather than doing it. But in the case of moral education, one cannot justify doing it unless one has done this kind of preparation, for one can hardly teach what one cannot show to be true: Having done it, it becomes part of what one teaches. One finds little serious treatment of these essential presuppositions in the work or the curriculum of the affectivists. The omission is not just serious; it is sinful.

From the cognitivist perspective, the developmentalists are a bunch of crypto-authoritarians who are exposed in their true colors by their answer to (or their failure to answer) the put-up or shut-up question of whether someone at an "intermediate" stage of moral development is more wrong (or less right) on moral issues than someone at a "higher" stage. If the "lower" stage subjects are not demonstrably wrong, then there's no justification for trying to change them, i.e., for moral education. If they *are* demonstrably wrong, then there must be a proof that they are wrong, i.e., a proof of the increasingly objective nature of the moral standards (or processes) of higher stages; but no satisfactory proof of this has ever been produced (or endorsed) by the developmentalists.* Nor is this accidental. If there *were* such a proof, who could understand it and find it persuasive? Either the lower stages *can*, in which case it isn't a higher stage proof and hence is morally inferior and should be ignored by truly moral people—and hence provides no basis for action in the field of moral education; or the lower stages *can't* understand it, in which case *they* have no good reason to move "upward," in which case *we* have no justification for moving them against their will—and, in fact, no justification for thinking they should be moved, since the proof is pragmatically circular; i.e., it only proves the highest stages are highest to highest stagers. So the activity of moral "uplift" is, in any case, unjustified on the basis of the developmentalists' own assumptions. (So the cognitivist argues.) The problem with stage theory, to sum it up, is that a proof that higher means better would either refute stage theory (if every intelligent person could appreciate it) or would be circular—that is, self-refuting or self-serving. That doesn't look like a very healthy ideology for moral education, in the cognitivist's view.

It might seem that one could avoid some of this criticism by distinguishing between the *process* of moral reasoning at various

---

*Kohlberg, the great figure among the developmentalists, has, very much to his credit, made a serious effort to supply part of such a proof.

stages and the *product,* i.e., the particular moral views expressed. On this point the cognitivist simply says that the process may be a legitimate concern of the pedagogue, but the product is what gets the passing grade, or purgatory. If the product isn't morally defensible, we need a new process. The developmentalist has to come through with a hierarchy that will show "higher" stages hold morally superior positions. Or else they aren't higher.

Finally, the cognitivist refers to a fifth group: the behavior modists, the Skinnerians. Although they see themselves as being at the opposite pole from the affective humanists, the cognitivist sees the behavior modification psychologists as being in the same situation, i.e., as having an engine, but no rudder—or at least no compass. A careful study of the actual goals adopted in "behavior mod" work with children, prisoners, or draftees reveals an uncritical acceptance of Establishment/authoritarian values, disinterest in what are normally taken to be higher values, and no interest at all in determining which of the two should be supported (see Scriven 1973, pp. 422-45). In short, the behavior modists can't—indeed, don't even try to—provide the very structure of the subject they are teaching, implicitly or explicitly.

Speaking of implicit and explicit, the cognitivist reserves the last dregs of scorn for the inactivists, who see that the ship is sinking but feel that it may make things worse if people try to find the lifeboats. Being conservative is one thing; insisting on group suicide is another. The inactivist may well be right to be nervous about the affective or developmental or religious "way of salvation"; but he is a traitor to shy away from cognitivist moral education, almost literally a traitor, for surely a cognitive approach is required if understanding and support for the Constitution and Bill of Rights—as opposed to recitation of them—is to be achieved. The implicit value system of a school or a parent that resists the minimum necessary requirements for teaching real understanding of those documents is contradictory to the explicit value system of those documents, i.e., of this country. Now, the "minimum necessary requirements" are at least those we would impose if those documents were purely cognitive—for no one denies they are at least that; they do have a literal meaning. If we take good teaching procedures from the nearest thing we have to purely cognitive areas, areas such as science or math or grammar, we can easily show that these procedures are *not* followed with regard to teaching the Constitution—which, for the cognitivist, is perhaps the most important part of the defensible secular morality of this society. And they are not followed, because of the opposition of inactivists. (More details on this below.)

It will be clear from the preceding that the cognitivist thinks the foundations of ethics, as well as everyday moral reasoning (done within the framework of ethics), are matters for reasoning to investigate and establish—and that reason in fact shows ethics to have solid bases, just as it shows the Constitution and Bill of Rights to be well based. For the cognitivist, it seems obvious that law and morality should be thought of as sensible, reasonable institutions—in principle, at least. What is puzzling is that a society founded on a strict and strong commitment to the "objectivity," that is, the rationality of a Bill of (political) Rights should act as if moral rights were somehow so totally different that treating them as part of the cognitive curriculum is almost unheard of. The cognitivist's suspicion is that some very odd politics or philosophy must have got in the way of the obvious here. That suspicion is confirmed when we discover that the California Bar Association staff, dispensing their excellent materials, never runs into political opposition, although the content of those materials is largely moral education. When called by that name, treatment of the same topics in a similar way by other projects is greeted with the usual hysteria.

Now, what explains this relativism about ethics by that name, by comparison with absolutism about political ethics? And relativism is the key issue, for it is out of relativism that the noncognitive approaches spring. If relativism were not justified, we would treat ethics just like any other social studies subject such as civics or government.

The Roots of Relativism

There are three main ideological supports for ethical relativism. The first is a misconception or exploitation of pluralism. The second is the social sciences' ostracism of ethics, in the name of the doctrine of "value-free social science." The third is the common philosophers' claim that the concept of ethics as a set of social principles based on experience and judged by the extent to which they further the welfare of mankind—roughly, the utilitarian concept—involves some philosophical fallacy.

We'll return to the first of these arguments later. The second and third are perhaps too technical for this context; a discussion of them will be found elsewhere (see Scriven 1974). Suffice it to say that contemporary professional opinion has swung strongly back toward what has to be the commonsense view—that the sciences are not free of value judgments, and that a utilitarian view of ethics, as of the law, involves no terrible fallacy (Quinton 1973).

As the cognitivist sees it, this unhealthy alliance between bad methodology in the social sciences and bad theory in the area of ethics explains both the dearth of work on moral education for thirty years (the term and its cognates do not appear in the leading anthologies of educational research published only a few years ago) and the erroneous direction which that work has (largely) taken now that it has begun again. Full understanding of the complex arguments about these errors is not something easily achieved; but it must now be regarded as a minimum prerequisite for competent work in educational research or innovation. Without it, the staff and students of schools of education, and of departments of psychology and sociology—and hence eventually the children in our schools—will continue to be fed erroneous concepts of ethics, or deprived of all that science and education can do for them in that area. But let us return to the practical realm, to the question of how morality should be taught, assuming for the moment that the enterprise is legitimate.

The Noncognitivists' Last Stand

Surely, it will be said, there is at least this much truth in the positions of the affectivist and the developmentalist: There can be no viable approach to moral education that does not allot equal time (more or less) to the affective dimension and that does not individualize its offerings to the developmental status of the individual student.

The cognitive comeback is not conciliatory. To the affectivist, the reply is threefold. First, the affective dimension of moral education is in general immoral. Second, it is in general ineffective. Third, it is probably unnecessary. (We shall return to these charges in the next section.) To the developmentalist, the cognitivist merely replies that the question of primary concern is not what level of moral argument will "reach" (i.e., affect) the student, but what level(s) is/are correct; it (or they) may well not be the "highest" in the developmental sense. Once it is determined which moral reasons are good reasons, then we can face the pedagogical problem in the same way that we do when teaching mathematics: We have to discover appropriate points of entry into the student's mind and sequences therefrom that lead to an understanding of correct moral reasoning. It is then to be expected that pedagogical routes exist and can be found that follow a different sequence from the "natural sequence" of moral stages, since that is merely the untutored response to social interactions during the maturing years. We do not expect that the optimal curricular sequence in medical school would match the sequence of learnings that would be acquired by someone developing medical skills by trial and error while responding to the medical needs of an isolated tribe. The study of "developmental stages" in the medical knowledge of witch doctors would be of some sociological or anthropological interest, but of only incidental interest to the designer of a medical curriculum. For much of the witch doctor's "knowledge" would be false and much would be lacking. Cognitive moral education—as the Jesuits, who took it seriously, long since discovered—takes many years, even when highly systematized. The developmentalists, like the "readiness" researchers, may well be able to provide helpful hints as to the limits of feasibility; but since they are not studying the efforts of students to master a systematic curriculum with the help of expert teacher-leaders, their findings will be no more than hints. Moreover, like readiness research, developmental research is extremely difficult, and one must rate its results as relatively unreliable on general inductive grounds, at least until far more replication by independent groups occurs.

The inescapable major point is that, at the moment, the developmental approach has not validated most of what it does teach, or the way in which it teaches, and hence is not a justified approach. This is not to say that what it does is wrong; it is to say that we don't know whether it's wrong without considerably more explicit attention to the problem of justification than it's receiving. Study of the values implicit in the Kohlberg work in prisons and schools is encouraging—but procedures for moral education which treat their own values in less than a totally explicit way are bound to be used by others, less sensitive, in a less defensible way. In disciples, of Kohlberg as of Skinner, the justification tends to get lost and only the procedures remain.

Immoral Affective Education

The cognitivist thinks affective education, with limited exceptions, tends to be immoral, ineffective, and unnecessary.

The basic moral problem with affective "education" (in the moral domain) is that it consists of the attempted modification of affect/attitudes/values in other ways than through the use of reason. This is pretty close to a definition of manipulation rather than education. Obviously, there is little agreement about how to define affective education, so one could easily argue that there's something *someone* has called affective education which isn't open to the above objection. However, a recent (unpublished) survey suggests that most of the paradigms people refer to by that title and that have any moral component involve *some* of the objectionable activity. (On the other hand, Norm Newberg's affective education operation in the Philadelphia school district clearly goes far beyond this, has very little moral component, and might equally well be called Excitement Education.)

While it's true that some education appears to achieve some (sometimes most) of its effect through nonrational influences, this by no means shows it to be affective by the above definition, since such effects are achieved either unintentionally or subsequently to the use of reason. It is the *deliberate* attempt at *directly* affecting the value system *without* either preliminary or collateral legitimation to the recipient that we identify as improper, the classic examples being subliminal advertising, some variants of brainwashing, religion for toddlers, and lobotomies. The "integrity of the person" must be respected by the educator, and should be respected by the parent, as early as is possible; it is that respect which requires that there be explanation, justification, and permission before tampering with values. It is the sense that this integrity is being violated that leads us to reject with distaste the Jesuit claim that if they can get hold of children before age six, they have them for life. In the cognitivist view, moral education for prerational children must be absolutely minimal, preferably reversible, and its content must be culturally, not parentally, legitimated.

The impropriety of affective education in the moral domain is all the more serious because of the intimate connection between morality, action, self-concept, and the well-being of others. Hence, the cognitivist argues, the only legitimate basis for moral education is the cognitive one, the only one open to public and personal scrutiny. This is not to say that affective techniques are *necessarily* illegitimate. The older student, convinced by cognitive considerations of his or her need for affective change, may voluntarily enlist in an affective workshop, much as he (or she) might sign away the right to control his (or her) own body when convinced by rational means that surgical intrusion is necessary. Since we have not raised affective treatment to (even) the level of efficiency of surgery, this is not exactly a pressing possibility.

Indeed (here we turn to the second point in the cognitivist reply to the affectivist), affective techniques are still novelties, still experimental, still badly in need of research and evaluation. This is no time to act as though they provide a workable, let alone legitimate, alternative approach to moral education.

Another dimension of the impropriety of the affectivist approach is shared with the behavior modist and the developmentalist: the lack of legitimation or indeed consistency in content, in the values that are taught. A noncognitive or nonrationalistic approach to moral education involves the same kind of absurdity exhibited by those who talk of "Judeo-Christian morality" as if that term had a single referent or indeed a distinctive core. There are plenty of moral doctrines that have been alleged to be a part of the necessary core of moral education in the Judeo-Christian tradition with just as much enthusiasm as they have been alleged to have no place in it. The bans on suicide and abortion are obvious examples. Most less specific doctrines are usually to be found in every other moral tradition, not excluding the atheist moral tradition; hence there appears to be nothing distinctive to which the Judeo-Christian label applies. Moral educators with Ph.D.s in psychology (or in education) aren't going to do any better if they don't have a legitimated set of doctrines and implications to work from. And if they *can* develop these, they might as well try teaching the skills they used in developing them— cognitive skills—since that at least is defensible and may be all that's needed.

Which brings in the final question of necessity. On all grounds, there seems no need, at this primitive stage in moral education, to make any moves towards the affective approach. We have an excellent alternative, which seems just as likely to produce the desired affective changes as an affective orientation. To that we now turn.

The Cognitive Curriculum

The cognitivist never loses sight of the fact that correct moral action is going to require affect as well as cognition. But the cognitivist thinks that the best way to achieve affective change may be through use of a cognitive curriculum. And, for the reasons set out in the previous section, it may be the only defensible approach. There is nothing paradoxical about this position, any more than there is about the claim that the best measure of essay-writing ability is a multiple-choice test. It is just that one's unreflective intuition is inclined to favor a match in style between tests and treatments, or between teaching style and criterion style.

So, even granted that there are two necessary components in the *objectives* of moral education, the cognitive and the affective (i.e., the skills of moral analysis and the motivation to act in accordance with the results of sound moral analysis), it by no means follows that the *process* of moral education should include a substantial slice of affective education. What should it include? The moral curriculum can be covered very well under three headings. The first component is knowledge about and understanding of the facts, including arguments and positions, involved in moral issues; this covers a big sweep of knowledge and the more that is covered the better.

It is a common mistake to underestimate the enormous body of knowledge that is required in order to cope competently with currently and prospectively important moral issues. (But reading a book like Glanville Williams's *The Sanctity of Life and The Criminal Law* rapidly converts skeptics.) Some of this knowledge will be picked up while covering other subjects in the regular curriculum, but much of it is best learned in connection with discussion of the moral issues which hinge on it, for reasons of efficiency as well as interest. The knowledge involved covers knowledge of arguments and positions as well as knowledge of what we usually call "the relevant facts"; and it covers understanding as well as rote knowledge. Understanding is tested by requesting the student to extrapolate the viewpoint that is said to be understood, to handle a novel situation. Role playing, a common practice in affective education, may be involved here; but its purpose is simply to generate cognitive understanding. It is not unlikely, the cognitivist believes, that *real* (cognitive) understanding will in fact lead to sympathy, etc., that is, to an alteration of affect. Indeed, it is partly for this reason that the cognitivist sees no necessity for (as well as an impropriety in) a direct effort in the affective dimension.

The second subdivision of the moral curriculum involves the cognitive skills of moral reasoning, developed to the level of confidence where they can be exercised in social argumentation (which involves both the distractions of irrelevant emotions—not that *all* emotions are irrelevant—and the necessity for very rapid response). Moral reasoning is of course related to scientific and legal reasoning, but since only the most constricted and formalistic approaches to these are normally provided for students, if any at all, it will be characteristic of moral education for some time to come that this component will require a great deal of time. Listening to the original Watergate hearings (Ervin Committee) provided an impressive demonstration of the simple lack of capacity for moral reasoning that characterized trained lawyers like John Ehrlichman. (Note, as an example, his justification of the break-in aimed at getting Daniel Ellsberg's psychiatric dossier. He drew an analogy with breaking into a bank vault containing a map with the location of a hydrogen bomb timed to blow up Washington the next day.) We often talk as if this weakness were a matter of moral "sensitivity." And so it is, but *not* in the sense that it can't be trained by cognitive means; an exactly analogous "sensitivity" to the overall rightness or wrongness of an *estimate* or a *proof* is one of the goals of math education, as good a paradigm of the cognitive as we need.

Looking at the National Assessment of Educational Progress results in the area of civics and social studies, one realizes that American youth are almost totally illiterate in this area. For example, they may enthusiastically accept an abstract moral truth, e.g., freedom of speech or equality of rights. But they may have absolutely no capacity to relate it to specific decisions and situations in which it is involved.

The third area to be covered in the moral education curriculum is the nature, origin, and foundation of ethics—sometimes called metaethics—and involving such questions as, What is it that distinguishes morality from convention, orders, self-interest, etc.? Nothing is more clearly distinctive of morality today than the way in which this area is treated in school, press, and home. The great unanswered and often unspoken question for most children is, Why should I be moral? It is unanswered either because parents and teachers do not know how to answer it or because they produce some false answer, e.g., about avoiding hell-fire, which is of course as feeble as the evidence for hell, and the feebleness of *that* evidence becomes known to almost every child who can read or who has agnostic playmates. This question is often unspoken, by children who sense what is often pathetically clear, that their parents or teachers not only have no answer, but feel embarrassed that they have none. When most schools and homes can give no sensible reason for being moral, and when being moral is often rather a drag, why should we look any further for an explanation of the lack of personal or public morality in the White House or outside it?

The effect is not only on ethics but on patriotism. It is absurd to suppose that children who at age six are totally conscious of the fact that their parents frequently lie while often proclaiming that lying is inexcusable are not by that age well aware that the rhetoric of their politicians bears little relation to reality. The deep cynicism instilled by repeated experiences of this kind has almost destroyed the basis for a commitment to morality or loyalty to the country, to democracy itself. There is no short way back from where we are now. No economic controls, no new legislation can fix us up. The only hope lies in a new start, a new look at ourselves, a willingness to work up from the alphabet to a defensible culture without acting as if "everyone knows" that *this* or *that* is the right thing to do, or approve of, or enjoy. And that is why the moral curriculum has to be committed to eternal willingness to investigate every claim it considers, to support every inclination it favors, to examine what it is doing as well as what others are doing. This critical orientation is an inevitable consequence of the study of historical and cross-cultural ethics, part of the third component. The three make up a large cognitive curriculum. If we try it, we will find out whether it does produce an affective shift. Unless we try it, we are not doing the obvious minimum to meet an emergency, and we have no license for any other approach.

Implementation

A major political problem for the schools will have to be overcome if this kind of moral curriculum is to be introduced, just as one had to be overcome with sex education and evolutionary education, and with "modern" literature and dress styles every time they change. A good deal of what has to be said, in the third area particularly, is going to run contrary to the views of many families. To take one point that can be put kindly, rather than crudely, but which cannot be avoided: One will have to point out that (and show why) the only sense in which religion or conscience provides a basis for ethics is a psychological one. This is another of the great unspoken truths recognized by most people in our society who have thought about it, but which is not yet acceptable as public utterance. The simple truth is that it's damned hard sledding today to find a literate *theologian* who believes the contrary, let alone a significant number of experts on metaethics. As long as we allow the bigots to control our schools on this, that long is our society doomed to the aimless relativism that has brought it to its knees today. There is nothing demeaning in the role of conscience and religion as sources of inspiration, of support, but not of justification; it was a view good enough for Buddha, Mahomet, Confucius, and the prophets, and in the view of many, good enough for Jesus. More is less—to claim more than that is to achieve less. People know better. Most of the values education material available for schools today simply chickens out on this kind of issue; it tippy-toes around, doing "values clarification," which usually begins by teaching the untenable distinction between value judgments and statements of fact that instantly establishes relativism as the norm (since objectivity is thus denied to value judgments, including moral value judgments). We won't get far with that approach.

And we won't get far with the "avoid controversy at all costs" approach which has been the worst side effect of local control of schools, now reinforced by West Virginia's Kanawha County troubles. Moral education is education for citizenship, for mature life, and is exactly like vocational education in that it will be useful exactly to the degree that it faces real-life problems—and that *means* controversy.

The confusion of *pluralism*, of the proper tolerance for diversity of ideas, with *relativism*—the doctrine that there are no right and wrong answers in ethics or religion—is perhaps the most serious ideological barrier to the implementation of moral education today. The dilemma seems simple: Either we teach a specific set of moral tenets —in which case we reject the views of others and hence (apparently) pluralism—or we teach "empty ethics" ("be good and avoid evil"), which we well know to be a waste of time. There is of course a third path: teaching how to do moral analysis from any given basis, teaching various views of ethics and within ethics, and then letting the chips fall where they may. Values educators, like science educators, have rightly stressed this possibility. They have been less careful in avoiding the attractions of relativism when going the process route. It is morally and pedagogically correct to teach *about* ethics, and the *skills* of moral analysis rather than doctrine, and to set out the arguments for and against tolerance and pluralism. All of this is undone if you also imply that all the various incompatible views about abortion of pornography or war are equally right, or likely to be right, or deserving of respect. Pluralism requires respecting the right to *hold* divergent beliefs; it implies *neither* tolerance of *actions* based on those beliefs *nor* respecting the *content* of the beliefs. Some actions are morally indefensible, even if done "in conscience"—that is, because dictated by our beliefs (e.g., sacrificing one's children to one's gods); and some beliefs are false, even if we respect the right of people to hold them (e.g., the belief that there is a supreme being who requires the sacrificial killing of his followers' children). There is an objectivity of fact—not a perfect objectivity of knowledge—on which ethics must be built, or rot away. It does not justify intolerance, but neither does it justify relativism or a moral education that teaches relativism or implies it.

Justification

Whence comes the objectivity that the cognitivist claims for that view of ethics? From the same place as all claims to objectivity, be they in science, math, law, or, for that matter, chess criticism: from the possibility of providing a supportive argument that places the matter beyond reasonable doubt. It is now beyond reasonable doubt that Richard Nixon lied about his lack of knowledge of the Watergate coverup; and it's also beyond reasonable doubt that he or his henchmen did a great many things, including lying, breaking the law, abusing authority, accepting bribes, offering bribes, etc., that were morally wrong. Are these value judgments or statements of fact? They are *both*, itself a fact which effectively destroys the fact/ value distinction as normally presented. There's no puzzle about the objectivity of moral value judgments: Some of them are definitionally true ("murder is wrong"); some of them empirically true ("Ehrlichman lied under oath," "firing Cox was indefensible," "de facto suicide is sometimes an obligation and sometimes a sin"); they are in this respect no different from statements about atoms or card games. You don't have to begin moral proofs with *arbitrary* moral axioms. You begin them, if challenged, with the definitions of the moral terms they employ and no other assumptions, just as in an argument about atoms or opening leads in bridge. There's nothing mysterious or arbitrary about showing why the constitutional freedoms (for example) are morally desirable, or why equality of rights is a better maxim than the alternative to it. The great smokescreen of relativism has somehow been generated out of the warm little fires of the freedoms of religion and speech, out of pluralism, a feat which testifies only to our total incompetence in moral reasoning—our gullibility, not our generosity. The objectivity of ethics depends not on anyone's stage of moral development, though its *appeal*—its motivating power—of course depends on that. Ethics is as objective and as debatable and as emotional a matter as that of identifying the best soccer team in the World Cup before the final.

Conclusion

How much time should be devoted to the moral curriculum? What is a realistic answer, given what we know about the limits on educational effectiveness? To improve the country significantly, 10 percent of the total curriculum K-12; to save the country, perhaps 33 percent? Since many of the most important skills of reasoning and investigation, and many of the most interesting facts of the social and biological sciences, and (as Donald Oliver and James Shaver showed) a great deal of history can be learned using moral education as the vehicle, the net intrusiveness is not as great as these figures would suggest. To suggest less would be naive; to suggest this much is optimistic as a prediction, but reasonable as a basis for experimentation.

There are many other questions that have to be answered in order to set out in full the cognitivist alternative. It is to be hoped that enough has been said to make it a real alternative. The failure of conventional moral education in the past—that is, its failure to affect the moral behavior of its victims though somewhat affecting some of their thinking—is just seen by the cognitivist as showing the lack of any effort to provide an understanding of the *connection between* the two dimensions, and the lack of really *serious* training in the cognitive component.

Is the cognitivist right? I said that I would append some personal qualifications to this presentation. Its principal function has been to set out an approach which in our present state of ignorance has a strong claim to be considered as the best prima facie candidate. Only experimentation will show whether the cognitivist is right. But the position, as expressed here, is awfully hard on the supporter of alternative approaches; on the motley assortment of affectivists, developmentalists, religionists, and behavior modists that he puts on the "enemies list." Perhaps I can sum up my demurrers by saying that some of my best friends are among those enemies.

References

Bronfenbrenner, Urie. *Two Worlds of Childhood.* London: Allen & Unwin, 1971.

Hartshorne, Hugh, and May, Mark A. *Studies in Deceit.* New York: Macmillan, 1928.

Quinton, Anthony. *Utilitarian Ethics.* London: Macmillan, 1973.

Scriven, Michael. "The Philosophy of Behavioral Modification." *The Seventy-Second Yearbook of the NSSE, Part I.* Chicago: University of Chicago Press, 1973.

Scriven, Michael. "The Exact Role of Value Judgments in Science." *Program Development in Education,* edited by J. Blaney et al. Vancouver, B.C.: University of British Columbia Press, 1974.

21
Moral Relativism and Values Education

Gary Wehlage and Alan L. Lockwood

One of the recent trends in curriculum is the development of values education materials and teaching strategies. There is no definitional consensus among educators regarding what may be called a values education curriculum. The label does not stick to any one thing. For purposes of this paper we will consider values education curricula to be those which totally or in part express a point of view about how values should be treated in the classroom.

The explicit purpose of most values education curricula is usually given in terms of aiding students in understanding value choices and eventually arriving at more informed or better value decisions. In this paper we are interested in values education to the extent it deals with *moral* values. More specifically, we wish to separate moral from nonmoral values and examine curricula to see if there is reason to believe that students will be aided in making more defensible moral decisions. Our purpose is to criticize several existing values education curricula and to offer a tentative framework for an acceptable moral point of view that would allow students to arrive at defensible moral judgments and decisions.

A first step in this process is to distinguish between moral and nonmoral value judgments. In general terms, this distinction is between those values which involve human rights, welfare, and justice and those which do not. Nonmoral values include esthetics, personal taste, and those objects and procedures which are instrumental to valued goals.

To be more specific, we can safely assert that a preference for Bach over the Beatles is a nonmoral choice. Similarly, a preference for the parliamentary form of government as opposed to the system in the United States which separates legislative from executive branches is also a nonmoral value. The particular organizational form of government preferred in a political democracy is an instrumental value problem. As such it is a nonmoral consideration, while a choice of political democracy over oppressive dictatorship almost certainly would involve a consideration of moral issues.

In general, then, a distinction can be made between those values which involve morality (human rights, welfare, justice) and those which do not. We are aware that an important gray area exists between these two categories. Nevertheless, this distinction is important because, as we will show later on, moral and nonmoral values should not be treated in the same way when trying to make judgments and decisions. In examining values education curricula we will search to see if this distinction is made for students and teachers. To the extent this distinction is not made it is likely that students will be encouraged to treat moral choices in a relativistic manner. Moral relativism is, in our judgment, an indefensible philosophical position and, therefore, is indefensible as part of a values education curriculum.

Moral Relativism: An Unacceptable Point of View

Moral relativism is more than the simple *descriptive* claim that persons or cultures frequently hold different values. It is more than the fact that honest men can arrive at different value judgments. Moral relativism is the *prescriptive* view that all values, including moral values, should be considered equally valid. This position prescribes that in matters of morality no opinions can be shown to be better than others. Richard Brandt (1959, p. 272), finding its roots in the thought of Protagoras, summarizes relativism as the contention: *"There are conflicting ethical opinions that are equally valid."*

In our day-to-day discussions we frequently hear the following claim: "Well, you have your opinion and I have mine and there is nothing more we can do about it. At least we know where we stand, but our values are different and we all know that a person's values can't be proved right or wrong." This claim confuses matters because it does not distinguish between moral and nonmoral values. We would agree that nonmoral values are legitimately relative. (One's preference for Bach is relative to other possible choices.) However, we cannot accept the contention that all moral choices are equally valid.

Our fundamental objection to moral relativism is its "permissiveness" regarding the central question of ethics. If we ask the question, "What criteria or standards should we use in making moral value decisions?," the relativist would reply: "It doesn't make any difference, all criteria are equally valid." Thus the relativist stance cannot possibly help us resolve any conflict in which moral values are in dispute. The relativist can only offer the following advice: "If you need some way to resolve your moral value conflict, choose any way you wish. All are equally appropriate and morally defensible."

Relativism can "justify" any moral choice or way of life because any considerations, reasons, or standards are acceptable as guides or directions for decision making. There is an important sense, then, in which relativism provides us with *no* guidance for dealing with moral problems. If all ways are equally valid we don't know which way to go. Henry Veatch (1962, pp. 44-45) summarizes a variety of moral viewpoints, some mutually contradictory, which could logically be held by persons espousing moral relativism:

Since all standards of value are utterly without foundation, since no way of life or course of action is really superior to any other, then the sensible thing for me to do is:
(1) to cultivate an attitude of greater tolerance toward the various modes of life and patterns of behavior that men have chosen for themselves . . . , or
(2) to create my own set of values and attempt to enforce them with all the energy of which I am capable . . . , or
(3) to throw off all moral standards and norms of conduct and simply follow the lead of my impulses and inclinations . . . , or
(4) to go along with the crowd and merely abide by the standards of the community of which I am a member, this being the line of least resistance and the one least likely to get me into trouble and difficulty . . .

As relativists faced with moral value choices, we could logically choose to do whatever we wish and allow others to do whatever they wish; do whatever we wish and force others to do what we wish; or do whatever others wish us to do. In our view such a position demeans the significance of moral issues. By saying, in effect, "anything goes," the central question of ethics is rendered meaningless.

Moral Relativism and Social Studies Curricula

In examining a social studies curriculum to determine if it espouses moral relativism we consider two aspects. First, if it is determined that no distinction is made between nonmoral and moral values in either the rationale or materials, there is reason to believe that ethical relativism will be promoted. This conclusion is not logically necessary but there is good reason to believe that when teachers and students are not required to treat the two classes of values differently they will not do so of their own accord. In other words, the position that all value decisions can be made in the same way promotes moral relativism because value relativism is acceptable in the nonmoral domain.

A second and related consideration involves the use of standards or criteria for making moral value judgments. Even if the distinction between the two classes of values is drawn, the claim may still be made that moral value decisions are essentially matters of personal preference and that, consequently, such decisions are not subject to any general standards of judgment. The notion that moral value judgments are personal is usually derived from the view that no principles or criteria can be generally and publicly applied. The evidential clues for this position are usually found in phrases indicating the need for each person to make a unique decision which is "right" for him. For example, in discussing the actions of the Nazis in Germany: "Killing the Jews was wrong from my point of view, but for the Nazi it was the right thing to do because of what they believed in." Therefore, if a curriculum claims that moral value decisions are essentially personal because no general criteria, principles, or standards can be applied in such a situation, then ethical relativism is being reflected. In summary, then, any values education curriculum can be judged for its stance on ethical relativism by determining: (1) if there is a distinction made between nonmoral and moral values; and (2) if there is some notion of general standards which take decisions out of the personally subjective realm.

Values Clarification

The first curriculum to be examined is the values clarification approach as outlined by Raths, Harmin, and Simon (1966). They offer no distinction between moral and nonmoral values. This is particularly important in view of the fact that they deliberately take a relativistic stance about values in general. They claim that "because life is different throughout time and space, we cannot be certain what values, what lifestyle, would be most suitable for any person" (p. 28).

Presumably one must choose values from experience. The implication is that what might be wrong today will be right tomorrow depending on the experiences a person has. The authors go on to say that "whatever values one obtains should work as effectively as possible to relate one to his world in a satisfying and intelligent way." This is the criterion the authors present for determining what values a person ought to hold. The last phrase may seem to save them from relativism but, in fact, their use of "satisfying" and "intelligent" permits people to hold and act on *any* value.

The process by which one determines if a value is satisfying and intelligent is summarized as:

Choosing: freely from alternatives after thoughtful consideration of the consequences of each alternative;

Prizing: cherishing, being happy with the choice, willing to affirm the choice publicly;

Acting: doing something with the choice repeatedly, in some pattern of life. (p. 30)

It should be obvious that *any* value or value system can meet these criteria. Adolph Hitler and Martin Luther King could equally satisfy the requirements; each went through the steps and arrived at values which were satisfying and intelligent to them.

The essence of values clarification is found in the individual examining his own values in a highly personal way. An important strategy in this approach is to avoid having students challenged by conflicting points of view. Argument, conflict, and a testing of values is minimized because there is no public test of adequacy for moral judgments. For the teacher all notions of criticism or evaluation of a student's choices are to be avoided. "It puts the responsibility on the student to look at his behavior or his ideas and to think and decide for himself what it is he wants" (p. 53). The nearly exclusive emphasis on personal judgment eliminates any notion that general standards can be applied to a judgment. "By definition and by social right, then, values are personal things" (p. 37). In short, your value is right if it is right for you, based on the life you want to lead.

Their position is defensible only to the extent one is concerned with nonmoral values. A nonmoral decision is appropriately made after one considers his unique experiences and preferences. Whether one chooses to spend a weekend canoeing or visiting his mother-in-law is a nonmoral personal value decision. However, for decisions involving moral values such as life, liberty, property, and civil rights, mere personal preferences cannot be the grounds for decision making. Some general, public criteria must be applied.

The failure of Raths, Harmin, and Simon to differentiate between moral and nonmoral values while at the same time insisting that value decisions are essentially personal preferences is a serious limitation in their rationale and methods. By treating all values alike and by claiming values are highly personal, we find that values clarification promotes a relativistic position. One can "justify" any moral decision with their approach and that is ethically irresponsible. For further criticism of the values clarification approach, see chapters 10 and 11.

In arguing that values clarification promotes an unacceptable moral point of view, we do not claim that the teaching strategies are without pedagogical usefulness. We recognize that many of the techniques developed in values clarification are quite effective in achieving certain purposes, such as getting students to articulate what they value. In the final analysis, however, teaching techniques must be judged on their unintended as well as intended effects.

Taba Strategies

The second example is the Taba curriculum as developed and interpreted by Jack Fraenkel. Two of the Taba teaching strategies are explored here in terms of ethical relativism. Fraenkel (1973) offers a description of the Taba strategies designed to help students consider values, but makes no distinction between moral and nonmoral considerations. For example, the following situational dilemma for role playing is offered to suggest how a teacher might stimulate discussion of value problems:

A group of your friends want to "rough up" and "work over" another student they feel is a "stool pigeon" and "teacher's pet." They want you to join them, and suggest you're a "chicken" if you do not. What do you do? (p. 249).

Ordinarily one would view this kind of situation as raising a moral value issue. In asking the student "what do you do?," the teacher is calling for a judgment about actions that involve the right to physical well-being of another person. Any time one is considering a choice involving physical violence against a person, moral considerations are involved.

It is clear that the Taba approach is willing to ask children about *moral* dilemmas and decisions. Similarly the approach also advocates that teachers ask students to consider nonmoral values involving parental approval of their friends, or what to do about making a new student in class feel at ease. In short, the approach lumps moral and nonmoral values together when using a particular strategy. There is no reason to believe teachers or students would distinguish between the two classes in using the various strategies.

An examination of the teaching strategies reveals that the Taba approach also fails to meet our second consideration with respect to relativism. There is no concept of general criteria for judging the morality of a decision. Fraenkel's explication of the Taba approach is very explicit in directing teachers to be accepting of *whatever* a student says in discussing a value problem. In one strategy, labeled "exploring value conflicts," the teacher is told to create an atmosphere in which one uncritically accepts both the value judgment and the reasons given for a particular action (p. 251). When a student is encouraged to judge his own past actions, the teacher is "to prevent others from entering the discussion . . ." in an effort to avoid challenges to the student's statements (p. 244).

In the final step the teacher is to quiz the student as to possible inconsistencies within his own statements, i.e., "How does that agree with the reasons you gave earlier?" (p. 244). This possible challenge regarding consistency is, of course, internal to the student's arguments. There is a clear directive not to allow other students to inject different standards of judgment into the discussion. Never should the teacher imply that other standards might prevail; each student creates his own standards of judgment.

Fraenkel states that "teachers must be careful *not* to approve or disapprove of various student responses, but to accept all replies as legitimate expression of student feelings" (p. 250). While there is much to be said for teachers building student trust by being "accepting" in attitude, such a style becomes ethically irresponsible when it is carried to the point of moral relativism. In summary, the Taba strategies for values education fail to distinguish between moral and nonmoral, and they do not encourage the development of general criteria to test moral decisions.

Science Research Associates

The third curriculum to be analyzed is the SRA Social Science Laboratory approach (Lippitt, Fox, and Schaible 1969). The authors present three approaches to discussing values, and several examples of values under discussion in the classroom. In developing a rationale, there is no explicit statement regarding the distinction between moral and nonmoral values. There is a distinction drawn between personal values held by individuals and general societal values, values of social classes, and values of ethnic groups. An exploration of values is justified as an effort to get students to understand how behavior is influenced by values, that consequences result from acting on values, and that people disagree over what values to hold. While the SRA rationale sees the handling of value controversy as an important dimension of social education, there is no explicit distinction between moral and nonmoral.

In terms of our second criterion, the development of general standards beyond mere personal preferences, the SRA materials are also deficient. As was the case with the Taba approach, there seems to be a confusion between being accepting, open, and nonthreatening toward students, on the one hand, and being ethically relativistic on the other. For example, the following dialogue is offered as an exemplary teaching style when discussing values with children (p. 31):

Mrs. Morgan: You see, we get our values in different ways. (Teacher summarizes the discussion and reinforces the atmosphere of openness at the same time.) We live in a country where people can have many different ideas about what is good or bad. Some of our parents believe one thing and some believe another. The same thing goes for our friends. Learning about many different values helps us to think about our own values and why we believe them and whether we should think about changing them. Tommy?

Tommy: I wouldn't change my idea unless it was wrong. Isn't there always one right value, Mrs. Morgan? (Student appeals to teacher's authority. Note how teacher handles this trap.)

Mrs. Morgan: Well, Tommy, some values are certainly wiser than others.

This may be because people have thought about them more carefully, or because many people have tested and decided on some value at many different times. In our classroom, we want to listen to everyone's values, whether or not they agree with ours. (Teacher again reinforces open atmosphere.)

Mrs. Morgan says that some values are "certainly wiser than others," but at the same time she does not give very strong reasons why some are wiser than others. This seems inconsistent in view of · the explicit demand by the curriculum that teachers continually ask students to give reasons why *they* hold a particular value. We suspect that the defense of a value position requires much more than evidence that people have thought about it carefully or decided on it many times in the past. There are, of course, numerous examples of people developing careful statements justifying murder, slavery, abridgement of political rights, and religious persecution. Also, the fact that many people hold a value is not sound justification.

The statement in the above dialogue that some values are wiser than others indicates that the authors might be against ethical relativism, but they default in the absence of any systematic treatment of why such relativism is inappropriate. The message that would seem most likely for teachers and students is that "anything goes," if you can give some reasons why you hold a particular position.

Mrs. Morgan seems to accept and approve the notion that people have different positions on what is "good or bad." ("Some of our parents believe one thing and some believe another.") But she then suggests that people should think about their values to see if they should be changed. But why would anyone want to change a value? Tommy indicates one changes a value if it is "wrong." What criteria can be applied to decide that a value is "wrong"? Mrs. Morgan suggests that Tommy's question is misguided because there may be several "right" values. However, the authors do not give any criteria for determining a value as being "right." Mrs. Morgan can only fall back on the notion that having thought about a value carefully makes it right. While we agree that careful thought is certainly to be encouraged, this in itself does not deal with the Hitlers who claim their values are to be preferred as the result of their careful thought.

The ambiguity regarding moral values found in the SRA curriculum seems inconsistent with the stated objective of the curriculum that scientific method and systematic procedures be taught to children. The lack of a clear position on ethical relativism is a flaw in the effort to have children use the tools of social science. If students think they are learning to engage in careful thinking about moral decision making, they are probably misled.

Reflective Thinking

One approach to social studies which is not a specific curriculum but nevertheless has had significant impact on the field is the reflective thinking approach of Hunt and Metcalf (1968). They clearly advocate an approach to values education and devote an entire chapter to value analysis and clarification. Their focus on controversy stemming from competing and inconsistent beliefs about individual and social choices reflects a concern with moral education.

Their rationale deals extensively with moral values but at no point do they distinguish between moral and nonmoral values. Moreover, they offer the following statement suggesting a relativistic point of view about all value judgments:

Value judgments are relativistic, as are all scientifically made judgments of fact. A judgment of fact is true *relative* to the chosen definition of truth; a judgment of value is right *relative* to what a person is or wants to be. Judgments of both fact and value can be made reflectively, if we recognize the values of relativism as opposed to the values of absolutism. (p. 141)

This assertion leads to confusion regarding their approach because they also contend that some values are more important than others for the operation of a democratic society. Furthermore, they see the central ethical commitments of a democratic society as a basis for judging the worth of other values. For example:

Some people when faced with interpersonal conflicts involving an ideal and a specific behavior, resolve the conflict by rejecting the ideal. One who favors equality and segregation and who comes to see them as inconsistent may reject equality. We assume that democratic-reflective study of such issues is more likely than unreflective procedure to resolve them in the direction of fuller commitment to democratic ideals. Our position advocates reflective reconstruction of beliefs as a means of clarifying and preserving the central ideal of democracy. (p. 58)

In other words, they are willing to say that the central ideals of democracy are preferable over alternatives. There is no equivocation here.

The authors discuss the problem of using the reflective approach as a method to test decisions within the democratic value structure. The role of the teacher is to support and maintain the value principles of democracy but at the same time allow for the diversity of more specific values within this framework. Within the reflective method a wide range of value judgments are possible. Ultimately, however, Hunt and Metcalf believe that every student has to decide whether his basic character is to be democratic-reflective in its central values. Such a decision is highly personal but teachers of social studies can help students to make it reflectively:

We want students to be consistent in their values—but we also want them to justify values by recourse to criteria derived from a philosophy to which they subscribe. Whether they choose to subscribe to a democratic philosophy is their decision to make—probably the most important decision in their lives. (pp. 141-42)

While Hunt and Metcalf obfuscate their position by seeming to advocate moral relativism, in fact their position separates democratic values from those personalistic values which are generally nonmoral. Also, they clearly believe democratic values to be better than the alternatives. While Hunt and Metcalf recognize that one cannot force students to accept the moral values of democracy, teachers do have an obligation to help them work through a tested philosophy. Students presumably arrive at a commitment to democratic values because they are morally more defensible.

In terms of general criteria for moral value decisions, Hunt and Metcalf take a strong position. Their concept of reflective thinking requires the testing of claims for evidence, consistency, and the consequences of action. In addition to the methodological criteria of reflective thinking, value claims must be tested in terms of how they promote the central ethical commitments of a democratic society.

Public Issues Curriculum

Finally, we come to the "public issues" approach (Oliver and Shaver 1966; Newmann and Oliver 1970). This curriculum relies on a rationale similar in certain respects to the Hunt and Metcalf approach. In *Clarifying Public Controversy,* Newmann and Oliver take a position which clearly confronts the question of ethical relativism, and reject it as indefensible.

We see three facets to the general problem of evaluation. The first involves ethical relativism. Some claim that we should not make judgments as to whether some views are better, more rational, or valid than others. Relativists maintain that groups and individuals harbor different standards of goodness, justice, morality, and that there are no universal absolutes by which one man or group could legitimately judge another. This position is reflected in familiar preaching for tolerating different cultures, "Live and let live," "The natives are not inferior to us, only different—they have their values, we have ours," "You should judge a group by *its* own values, not yours, the outside observer," "Findings in psychology that demonstrate ways in which individual perceptions and attitudes are influenced by cultural surroundings; findings in anthropology demonstrating various value systems throughout the world; and the democratic value of toleration all have been used to support a relativistic view that, in an extreme form, suggests that no person or group should judge the positions or behaviors of another," "Though we Americans believe in free enterprise, the Russians do not. Their system might be right for them, but wrong for us," "According to Jimmy's values, it's alright to dodge the draft, but according to mine it's wrong. He had his life—I have mine. Nobody can say whose is better." (p. 279)

Recognition of the general issue of ethical relativism is clear in these statements. Newmann and Oliver go on to say that the reasoning offered by relativists is "an escape from problems we believe must be confronted, which is why we cannot accept a relativistic position." This sets the public issues rationale apart from most curricula. Newmann's unequivocal stand against relativism is flawed only by a failure to help students distinguish the moral from the nonmoral. He does, however, offer guidelines for recognizing the general moral values of our society.

Regarding the problem of general criteria for moral decision making, the public issues approach establishes a set of substantive criteria for avoiding relativism. The public issues approach asserts that several values are more fundamental than others:

Construing public controversy in America as manifestations of conflict among several values in a large and diverse American creed, we postulate individual human dignity as the most fundamental value of all. We assume considerable disagreement and ambiguity in the definition of human dignity, but suggest two phenomena as requisite to its fulfillment: freedom of choice among diverse alternatives, and rational consent as a process by which to deal with conflicts arising out of the pluralism we advocate. The conception of citizenship education advanced in this book attempts to define and implement, for the most part, one value: rational consent. Exercising rational consent requires persons to clarify and justify their views on public issues in conversations with peers. (p. 33)

This position implies that human dignity, freedom of choice, and rational consent are the moral foundations of a democratic society. These moral values are supreme and are used to judge the worth of policies which purport to facilitate a democratic society.

In judging the public issues approach in terms of our two criteria, we find that no distinction is made between moral and non-moral. However, Newmann explicitly confronts relativism as inadequate and suggests there are general standards which can be applied to test the ethical quality of a policy. These standards involve the ideal of human dignity through freedom of choice and procedures of rational consent. In summary, any policy which violates the value of rational consent or denies freedom of choice from among alternatives is morally wrong because it ultimately violates our concept of human dignity.

Formulating an Acceptable Curriculum

We have argued in this paper that any values education curriculum should avoid propagating moral relativism. In order to do this a distinction should be drawn between moral and nonmoral values, and some notion of general standards of judgment should be explored. Any values education curriculum must be able to show teachers and students that they are embracing an acceptable moral point of view, and that their moral judgments are defensible. While this might seem to be an excessively demanding criterion, it is nothing more than educators have demanded in the nonvalue realm of curriculum. Most of the "new social studies" curricula devote considerable time and space to showing how a process, procedure, or set of scientific assumptions and methods produce warranted conclusions and knowledge. For example, the recent materials from Mehlinger and Patrick, *American Political Behavior* (1972, pp. 9-15), is a systematic attempt to provide a more adequate point of view on knowledge of political behavior. The entire text attempts to help students understand the behaviorists' point of view and why this perspective is the best way to learn about and understand political phenomena.

In the next few pages we will suggest several characteristics exhibited by a defensible moral point of view which avoids relativism. These characteristics are general in nature and do not specify conclusions on particular moral problems. Different moral judgments can exist within their framework. At the same time, some kinds of moral reasoning are rejected. We believe these characteristics provide a general set of criteria to be used in developing defensible moral judgments.

While it is not easy to make the distinction between moral and nonmoral value questions, it is essential in values education that this distinction be made. If one starts with the assumption that nonmoral values are legitimately relativistic, then this class of values needs to be separated. For example, questions about abortion, public nudity, the use of drugs, cigarette smoking, the eating of nonunion lettuce and grapes, etc., must first be analyzed in terms of the morality or nonmorality of the value issues at stake. If, for example, it is determined that cigarette smoking is essentially a nonmoral value issue, then it is rightly a personal matter to be determined by the relative values of each individual.

Values issues cannot generally be defined a priori as moral or nonmoral. By asking people to separate the moral from the nonmoral they are compelled to clarify what issue is at stake. In a particular controversy, for example, it may be that one faction asserts that morality is involved while another argues that a nonmoral choice is involved. This kind of situation arises, for example, in much of the controversy over ecological or environmental problems. Some people construe air and water pollution as a nonmoral value choice. The problem is conceived as a cost-benefit choice between those who desire clean water and those who want the cheap production of certain goods. Others, however, contend that there is a moral choice of right and wrong involved in the destruction of ecological systems which affects the rights and welfare of people. Thus, some are willing to talk about a "land ethic" which requires the preservation of ecologically viable systems for generations unborn, while others speak in terms of "trade-offs." Part of the environmental controversy, then, revolves around disagreement over the nature of the value choices.

Generally, it is appropriate to start with the position that whenever the rights of a person (life, liberty, property) are involved, moral values are under consideration. If, at times, it becomes distressingly difficult to show why something is or is not a moral issue, then at least people can become aware of the complexity of this matter called morality. The distinction does not always have to be clear and easily applied to make the effort worthwhile. Once it has been established that a particular value problem is moral in nature, there are several caveats that should be kept in mind. An acceptable moral point of view recognizes potential conflict. According to an old story, a father sending his son off to the big city gave this advice: "Son, remember, if in doubt, always do right." The point, of course, is that moral problems are rarely presented to us as a simple choice of right versus wrong. Frequently we are confronted with complex questions involving choices between competing notions of goodness or rightness. If moral dilemmas were simply a matter of choosing right over wrong, there would be no problem. Part of the job of moral education is to help students identify the moral dimensions of value conflicts. Such general values as honesty, security, life, freedom, law and order, privacy, and equality may conflict in certain situations. An acceptable moral curriculum helps students to become aware of conflicts and to consider the implications of moral judgments and moral actions.

A second caveat is that moral education cannot unequivocally instruct us as to what actions are right or wrong. Commitments to particular moral values do not automatically tell us what actions are consistent with those values. For example, two persons may agree on the sanctity of human life but disagree over the moral propriety of abortion. In short, if everyone were to accept the same set of general moral values, there would still be important arguments over what actions would be consistent with those values.

In general, an acceptable moral point of view not only helps people distinguish between moral and nonmoral values, it also keeps them alert to the potential for conflict among general moral values. In addition, people are reminded that even when there is agreement or commitment to a general value, determining appropriate action is still problematic. An acceptable moral point of view anticipates problems inherent in the serious consideration of moral issues. However, stimulating an awareness of these problems should not give students the impression that an absence of consensus on moral judgments and actions means that moral relativism is acceptable.

The second characteristic of an acceptable moral point of view is the assumption that there are general criteria for establishing and defending moral judgments. A curriculum with an acceptable moral point of view must take a position on the criteria that can be used to determine which reasons are more or less defensible. Moral education takes one beyond the notion that self-interest or personal tastes and desires are adequate grounds for making moral decisions. Therefore, there is the need to establish general criteria for making moral judgments. These criteria need to be publicly recognized and applicable to the reasons people give to support particular moral opinions and actions.

We can begin establishing our criteria by eliminating some factors as satisfactory defenses for moral reasoning. First, one cannot rely solely on conformity to law, customs, or the dictates of religion to provide criteria for a defensible moral judgment. Certain laws, customs, or religious beliefs can be judged immoral. For example, at certain points in history slavery and genocide have been supported by law and religion. One can always reasonably ask: "Is that law, custom, or religious belief morally right?"

Another factor in making moral judgments is behavior. While behavior is important, it cannot serve as the sole consideration. For example, we would judge differently a person who donates money to a worthy cause so that he can obtain a tax break and a person who donates because of a commitment to the worthiness of the cause. While the observable behavior of both persons is the same, their intentions are different. Similarly, if a person is coerced into committing an act which is generally considered wrong (e.g., robbing a bank), a different judgment occurs when that same action is done willfully. There are other factors, such as insanity, which absolve a person of moral responsibility for certain behavior. In general, conformity to certain behavioral standards is not a sufficient criterion for defending a moral judgment.

One general criteria that should be included in an acceptable moral point of view is the notion of the "informed reasoner." This concept is not easily defined, but, as we use it, it requires that one have knowledge of the empirical state of affairs surrounding a moral problem and some ability to predict the consequences of various courses of action. A person might, for example, find evidence that the generation of electric power is a serious health hazard in that pollution from the burning of fossil fuels and radiation from nuclear energy have been directly or indirectly responsible for illness and death. A person believing in the sanctity of life might conclude that there should be an immediate cessation of these means of generating electricity. The consequences of such a policy would most certainly bring about much suffering and most likely lead to starvation and death. Clearly, a broad understanding of the consequences of particular choices is essential in making acceptable moral decisions.

The accurate prediction of the most important consequences of an action is often extremely difficult. It is obvious that the unintended results of some actions plague us with social problems that seem unavoidable. Even with the most thoughtful consideration of consequences it is sometimes not possible to predict with certainty the effects of actions on the rights and interests of others (e.g., the current debate over the dangers of nuclear power). Nevertheless, there are better and worse ways of gathering data and predicting consequences and we all have a moral obligation to do the best job possible of taking into account the effects our proposed action might have on others.

As indicated earlier, an acceptable moral point of view transcends the authority of law, custom, and religion and recognizes that there is more to morality than performing certain behaviors. The quality of one's reasoning on moral matters is paramount. Moral reasoning must employ defensible principles. Principles can be defined as general statements which apply to a range of situations. For example, the "golden rule" is a principle which may guide one's thinking in a variety of human relationships. Principled reasoning results in judgments which are not based on narrow self-interest or slavish obedience to law, custom, or religion. Philosophers do not agree on the specific definitions of such principles but there is general agreement that defensible moral principles must provide both consistency and generality for our moral judgments.

Consistency is a necessary characteristic if one desires to avoid capricious and arbitrary judgments. If one concludes that contradictory behaviors are equally moral, or that a judgment is moral today but immoral tomorrow, we become hopelessly confused. We cannot obtain guidance from inconsistent reasoning. The characteristic of generality is also a significant quality of principled moral thought. Generality requires us to defend our judgments as adequate not simply in one particular case but in all similar cases. What is right in situation X must also be right in all similar situations. The generality criteria helps insure fair treatment to all parties in a moral situation.

Engaging in principled moral reasoning does not provide unequivocal solutions to all moral problems. However, principles which meet the criteria of consistency and generalizability provide anchors for our moral reasoning. If one does not insist on principles then self-interest and bias may reign. For example, a person would be free to formulate ethics which provide exceptional treatment for himself. As Brandt (1959, p. 263) points out, "This, of course, would be fatal to the hope that ethical thinking can provide a reasonable adjudication of conflicts of interest—'reasonable' adjudication in the sense of being made by appeal to principles suited to command respect from all parties to a dispute."

Conclusion

In this paper we have argued that moral relativism is an unacceptable point of view and indicated that some curricula embody this view. An acceptable moral point of view for values education should help students consider the difference between moral and nonmoral issues. It should also help them see that some moral value judgments are more defensible than others. In developing the general criteria which lead to defensible judgments, a number of considerations should be kept in mind. First, one is obligated to be informed on relevant empirical matters and do the best job possible in anticipating the consequences of particular judgments and actions. Second, one should consider whether moral decisions pass the tests of consistency and generality. The discussion of moral issues within this framework can avoid the pitfalls of relativism on the one hand and moral indoctrination and absolutism on the other.

References

Brandt, Richard. *Ethical Theory*. Englewood Cliffs, N.J.: Prentice-Hall, 1959.

Fraenkel, Jack R. *Helping Students Think and Value*. Englewood Cliffs, N.J.: Prentice-Hall, 1973.

Hunt, Maurice P., and Metcalf, Lawrence E. *Teaching High School Social Studies*. New York: Harper & Row, 1968.

Lippitt, Ronald; Fox, Robert; and Schaible, Lucille. *The Teacher's Role in Social Science Investigation*. Chicago: Science Research Associates, 1969.

Mehlinger, Howard, and Patrick, John J. *Teacher's Guide to American Political Behavior*. Lexington, Mass.: Ginn & Company, 1972.

Newmann, Fred M., and Oliver, Donald. *Clarifying Public Controversy*. Boston: Little, Brown, 1970.

Oliver, Donald, and Shaver, James. *Teaching Public Issues in the High Schools.*
    Boston: Houghton Mifflin, 1966.
Raths, Louis; Harmin, Merrill; and Simon, Sidney B. *Values and Teaching.*
    Columbus, Ohio: Charles E. Merrill, 1966.
Veatch, H. B. *Rational Man.* Bloomington, Ind.: Indiana University Press, 1962.

22

Moral Education: Is Reasoning Enough?

Donald W. Oliver and Mary Jo Bane

Many people assume that some form of secular moral education should take place in the schools. But what kind of moral education? And how should the schools provide it?

In this paper, we first describe a social studies curriculum which we believe meets the criteria for moral education defined as training in moral reasoning. We then describe some of the difficulties we have encountered in teaching the approach, and our intuitions about its limitations. Primarily we are troubled by the fact that we have not dealt with nonrational moral sensitivities. In the last part of the paper, we discuss the problems of carrying on moral education in a broad sense within the existing school system, and suggest some modifications that we believe are necessary.

Values and Public Issues

For the past several years we have been developing a social studies curriculum directed at the clarification of public issues

Reprinted by permission from Clive Beck, Brian S. Crittenden, and Edmund V. Sullivan (eds.), *Moral Education: Interdisciplinary Approaches* (New York: Newman Press, 1971).

through the use of rational strategies within a framework of courteous and disciplined discussion. This curriculum is based on a number of premises regarding what talk about public issues should be and what kind of people do the talking. It assumes that the people doing the talking are committed to the process of reasoned discussion as a means of resolving value disputes, and that, to some degree, they are concerned about the welfare of the broader community as well as their own self-interest.

A number of more specific assumptions are made regarding the purpose and function of value concepts. We assume that when faced with a public dispute in which it is difficult to determine who is right or wrong, or when it is difficult to say whether the community or individual parties in the dispute should make this decision, one should search for general principles of ethical or moral conduct; and that the use of general moral principles allows us to develop stable and predictable ways of resolving conflicts.

We postulate, moreover, that, although the use of general values applied to social and political conduct allows us to judge public policies more reliably and consistently, these values often clash. It is our position that looking for value conflict or value tension is a more realistic approach to social controversy than searching for some overriding principle that will tell us the correct solution to any particular problem. For, although such broad principles as respect for human dignity or justice may be essential bases of judgment in a controversial situation, it is often difficult to communicate the strength of one's position on the basis of general but ambiguous principles. We believe that throughout history men have developed more specific value categories which may be thought of as both elements of and bridges to the more basic values of human dignity and justice, such values as:

The right to think, to believe, to speak, to worship as one's conscience or personal experience dictates.

The right to be secure from physical attack or injury.

The right to make agreements with other men and have these agreements respected.

The right to have one's personal property protected from seizure and destruction.

It is clear, however, that defining some ultimate good, such as human dignity, in more specific value terms does not resolve controversy. It simply provides a public rhetoric by which the controversy might be more easily clarified. In this sense our curriculum efforts have been directed mainly at identifying the intellectual and procedural strategies that are used in talking about public controversy. It is assumed that such clarification will at least facilitate compromise, temporary accommodation of basic differences, or agreement within the community of advocates.

The basic value premise of the curriculum may be called "rational consent," the implicit agreement that controversy is to be accommodated or resolved by reflection and conversation rather than force or coercion. Specific procedures which allow the business of the community to be carried on, and the mechanics of governmental decision making, are looked upon simply as the formal ritual which legitimizes the product of prior reflection.

An element obviously missing from this model is the whole political-process component, factional in-fighting, and the use of various kinds of semi-coercive methods and power plays within the world of real politics. While we understand the critical importance of this missing component, we have chosen to help the school do what we feel it might do best. We have little doubt that young people can best learn the principles of power politics in the real world, not in artificial simulation situations in the classroom (see Newmann 1968).

Clarification Through Discussion

The approach used in the Harvard Social Studies Project can be divided into three basic elements: (1) the analysis of public controversy in terms of prescriptive, descriptive, and analytic issues; (2) the use of distinct strategies for justification and clarification of one's views on such issues; and (3) systematic attention to the discussion process as one deals with a controversial issue.

Identifying Issues

Any given situation or case can stimulate controversy in a number of directions, depending upon the type of question that concerns the participants or observers. By way of illustration, we might look at the Stamp Act controversy, a series of events which led up to the American Revolution:

In 1765 the English Parliament passed a Stamp Act which required that stamps be bought and placed on all public documents used by the American Colonists. The major purpose of the Act was to raise revenue for the continuing administration and defense of the Colonists, especially against unfriendly Indians on the western frontier. However, the Act set off a wave of protest and violence, which was completely unforeseen by the English. In Boston, mobs marched through the streets, set fire to the governor's mansion, and threatened the lives of anyone who might attempt to administer the Act. An almost complete boycott went into effect; either the law was violated and public papers were given out within the stamp, or legal transactions requiring stamps were suspended. All along the eastern seaboard, any English official who sought to land, store, or sell stamps was intimidated and threatened with physical injury. Stores of stamps were burned on the New York waterfront. Largely because the boycott began to threaten the prosperity of English merchants who sold goods to the Colonists, the Act was repealed.

Prescriptive Issues

This historical case provokes disagreement on several levels. One level involves judgments about what should or ought to have been done, given the information available. Judgments concerned with the legitimacy or the rightness of actions and policy are prescriptive issues: Was it right for the English to impose the Stamp Act in the first place? Should governmental acts be imposed only when the people affected are adequately represented? What kinds of protests would one consider reasonable? At what point is one justified in using violence and abandoning legal methods of protest? We could further classify prescriptive issues in such categories as:

Personal conviction and conscience. What should you do as an individual in the Stamp Act situation?

Public policy. Should parliament have passed such an act without the consent of the American colonists?

Ethics. Which value is more important: the right of the colonists to representation or the maintenance of a peaceful, orderly society?

Law. Were the Americans adequately represented under the English constitutional system of the day?

These types of prescriptive issues are related. The purpose of differentiating them is simply to show ways in which we might clarify our thinking by carefully defining the issues we choose to discuss.

Descriptive Issues

After identifying a number of prescriptive issues, a discussion of the Stamp Act might turn to a different set of questions. Was violence actually necessary to bring about the repeal of the Stamp Act? Did the Stamp Act seriously affect the commercial interests of the colonists? Was there a long tradition of acceptance of virtual representation by the colonists as a means of legitimizing parliamentary action? Were the motives of the troublemakers in the colonies based mainly on constitutional principle or mercenary greed? Questions like these focus on problems of fact—describing people's behavior, interpreting what the world is actually like, or explaining why certain circumstances presumably occur.

Analytic Issues

Finally, we identify analytic issues. These questions focus not on what *should* be done, or what is the actual state of affairs, but on what is the most useful meaning or interpretation of a word, phrase, or problem. In the Stamp Act situation there is clearly a definitional problem in the word "representation." A broader and perhaps more important type of analytic dispute arises over the way we interpret the issue under discussion. For example, one person may see the issue of "adequate representation" as a strictly legal or constitutional issue. He seeks to answer the question by studying English constitutional arrangements of the eighteenth century. A second person may see "adequate representation" in moral terms: to what extent should the person affected by a law have some say in the creation of the law? In order for these two people to discuss the term "adequate representation" productively, they would first have to reach some agreement on which of these issues is more important or which should be discussed first.

Although we have distinguished prescriptive, descriptive, and analytic issues as different types of problems, they usually cannot be kept separate during a discussion of an issue. The purpose of dealing with them separately here is to suggest that there are various aspects of inquiry which can be separated when a discussion becomes murky or unproductive.

Strategies of Justification and Clarification

The Analogy. One powerful technique, which we feel is central to the clarification of prescriptive issues, involves dealing with an issue within the context of a number of related cases. Thus we might begin with a specific case such as the Stamp Act situation, identify a relevant issue arising out of the case (should violence be used as a method of gaining increased representation in government), identify another case (or analogy) that is similar in that it raises similar value conflicts (for example, student violence on the Columbia University campus), and see how we feel about a policy as it applies to the second case.

The power of the analogy is that it provokes discussants to make distinctions and qualifications that strengthen and clarify value positions. The person who supports violence in the Stamp Act situation but who denounces violence at Columbia must find some critical distinction between the two situations. (One might assert, for example, that students were voluntarily members of the Columbia community, and could withdraw if they so chose, whereas the colonists were not voluntary members of the British Empire.) Thus, one might start with a position that violence can be justified under extreme circumstances to gain representation in a group or community and move to the qualified position that violence is justified as a method of gaining representation only when the community in which you seek representation provides no opportunity for voluntary withdrawal.

Evaluating Evidence. In dealing with descriptive issues, the major problems lie in accumulating and evaluating evidence, and in understanding logical relationships among different types of evidential statements. Students can be taught various canons of reliability and distinctions such as that between associative and causal claims.

Defining Terms and Making Distinctions. There are a number of strategies for dealing with definitional problems: using an authoritative source; searching for synonyms on the basis of common experience; searching for general criteria as they are induced from specific examples.

Discussion Process

There is a subtle and important link between the analytic process by which issues are defined and positions justified, and the quality of the interpersonal setting within which discussion takes place. We have loosely called this link the discussion process. It includes being sensitive to what others are saying in a discussion, the ability to summarize where the discussion is, especially points of agreement and disagreement, the ability to challenge the direction or relevance of another individual's argument. While these may sound somewhat elementary to sophisticated adults, we have found that high school students are lacking in such skills. Discussion is usually construed by students as catharsis or combat. As catharsis, the purpose of talking is to get something off your chest; as combat, the object is to "win" the argument. The notion that discussion might serve to clarify one's own values requires radical reorientation of classroom discussion. As we shall point out later in the paper, the heart of this issue is creating a group climate in which the student takes other discussants seriously enough to break the set of "performing for the teacher."

As should be clear from the above discussion, we assume that rational strategies used in the discussion of societal conflict provide the basis of a type of moral education. In essence the educational process involves a subtle relationship between individual valuations and the use of moral disciplined strategies as a means of clarifying or justifying such valuations. The educational outcome is not the acquisition of substantive values, such as equality, justice, or property rights. It is assumed that students already have these values. The outcome is presumably the student's ability to work through increasingly more complex principles of conduct as he attempts to justify his own point of view in the presence of contrary views expressed by his fellow students and teachers. The source of these complex principles is induction through rational discussion. It is also assumed that the student develops a tendency to re-examine his principles in the light of societal change, for the values themselves require constant redefinition as they are applied to new situations.

Relationship to Modern Ethical and Psychological Thought

We see the public issues approach as moral education, although this may conflict somewhat with the older use of that term in the social studies. The older view advocates the teaching of democratic virtues: the importance of voting, respect for "community helpers," love of country, the fostering of charitable feelings towards those less fortunate, etc.

Our own view of moral education clearly focuses on moral reasoning, and is more in line with the conclusions expressed by Benn and Peters:

Our view about morality, therefore, which we have expounded by considering the contributions of the main schools of moral theory can be summed up as follows:

i. A moral rule differs from a customary one in that it implies the autonomy of the individual. A rule becomes moral by being critically accepted by the individual in the light of certain criteria.

ii. The criteria can be summarized by saying that the rule should be considered in the light of the needs and interests of people likely to be affected by it with no partiality towards the claims of any of those whose needs and interests are at stake.

iii. The acceptance of such criteria is implied, albeit in a minimal degree, by the notion of rationality in the sense of reasonableness.

Our contention is therefore, that there is a sense in which moral philosophy or ethics, which is the attempt to make explicit the criteria in terms of which rules are morally justified. itself exemplifies, in a minimum degree, the acceptance of the criteria which it attempts to make explicit. (1959, p. 63)

If this is morality, then one might clearly describe our efforts in social studies education as moral education.

The basic definition of morality developed by such moral philosophers as Benn and Peters is also the basis of Kohlberg's approach to moral education. Kohlberg's studies of the moral reasoning of children show that as the child develops the reasons he gives for advocating a particular response to a moral dilemma become increasingly more complex. The young child is oriented towards punishment and naive hedonism; as he grows older, he passes through a stage of conventional morality and gradually develops a more thoughtful, principled approach. Throughout this process, the concept of justice held by the child becomes more differentiated and more attuned to the rights of others, based on equality and reciprocity. Kohlberg sees moral education as the stimulation of this natural developmental process which leads to mature moral reasoning:

A definition of the aim of moral education as the stimulation of natural development appears, then, to be clear-cut in the area of moral judgment, which has considerable regularity of sequence and direction in development in various cultures. Because of this regularity, it is possible to define the maturity of a child's moral judgment without considering its content (the particular action judged) and without considering whether or not it agrees with our own particular moral judgments or values or those of the American middle-class culture as a whole. In fact, the sign of the child's moral maturity is his ability to make moral judgments and formulate moral principles of his own, rather than his ability to conform to moral judgments of the adults around him. (1967, p. 179)

Our experience in teaching the public issues approach seems to confirm many of Kohlberg's observations concerning moral education. Our goal, like Kohlberg's, is to develop the moral reasoning abilities of our students. It seems, however, that most of our students— relatively mature high school students of average ability—operate from Kohlberg's Stages 2, 3, and 4. Their orientation towards a controversial problem is that the major actors avoid trouble and maximize their own individual interests, unless some naturally endowed traditional authority intervenes. They hold vague notions that some things are "morally right," but tend to justify laws by traditional criteria of authority rather than by abstract legal or moral principles. They have tremendous difficulty in operating easily with our value conflict model, which we can now label a Stage 5 or 6 conception of morality.

The results of these three streams of intellectual activity—Benn and Peters' concept of moral reflection in a democratic state, Kohlberg's notion of natural development stages leading towards increasingly mature moral reflection, and our own educational efforts to implement a curriculum and teaching dialogue centering on more complex modes of moral justification—are all based on common assumption about the nature of human discourse. All assume that man is or can be a rational animal, that he seeks greater complexity in the manipulation of verbal arguments, and that he can become engaged in abstract social and political issues in a somewhat impersonal way without such a deep investment of his own psyche that it will warp his perceptions.

Problems with the Approach

In teaching our program, we have assumed that students can learn to carry on productive discussions about public issues under the leadership of a trained and sensitive adult. We have used various forms of discussion, from teacher-dominated to entirely student controlled, and have supplemented these discussions with didactic instruction in the analysis of argument. For "content," we have relied on various types of cases—stories, journalistic narratives, historical accounts.

We have, however, encountered various problems in using the approach in the classroom. Although students sometimes become very excited about the issues raised by the cases, they seldom seem to take the issues seriously in a personal sense. They enjoy the combat of discussion and the opportunity to express their opinions, but they are not generally sensitive to the arguments of other people. When the issue is one in which they seem personally involved, the discussion becomes a repetition of opinions rather than an attempt at clarification. When the issue does not seem particularly important, discussion becomes a game in which the object is either to second-guess the teacher and arrive at the right answer or to overwhelm the other participants psychologically. These attitudes make it difficult to carry on productive conversations in the classroom. We suspect, also, that there is very little transfer of learning to situations outside the classroom, since discussion is viewed as "another schoolroom game."

There are, of course, some techniques which might be tried within the framework of our program to deal with some of these problems. We might extend our range of concern to personal as well as public decisions. Presumably such situations would be more relevant to the students, but would, at the same time, provide an opportunity to teach strategies for making rational moral decisions.

Questions, for example, could be phrased in personal rather than general terms: "Should *you* participate in civil disobedience in protest against the Vietnam war?" rather than "Should peace groups use illegal means in pursuit of their aims?" Or homey examples might be used, such as the trumpet player's situation analyzed by Hare (1963, pp. 114, 194). Should I, and by implication everyone, be allowed to play my trumpet in any place and at any time that I desire to do so? This question provides Hare, and could provide classroom teachers, with an opportunity to examine the relationship between individual freedom and social good and to attempt to develop general procedures for dealing with such conflicts. Or the class might consider important issues in their own lives, for example premarital sex and love, in individual and social terms (see Fletcher 1967, pp. 125-40).

Efforts might also be carried out to deal more systematically with students' different levels of cognitive and moral development. This is suggested by Kohlberg's finding that people at one stage of development can understand moral arguments at one level above their own and can be trained to move to this level, but that they cannot understand or move two or more levels up.

For example, students discussing the Stamp Act case might use arguments that reflect a Stage 3 level of moral development: they might argue that what the Sons of Liberty did was right because "that was what good patriots did" or because the British were being "bad rulers," without being able to specify what their labels mean or imply. These students might be presented with Stage 4 arguments, those emphasizing preservation of authority, rather than with social contract or natural rights arguments. It might be argued, for example, that the Sons of Liberty were wrong because they were breaking laws and disrupting the legitimate government of the empire. It might be possible in this way to lead the students through the stages of moral argument without losing them along the way.

We believe, however, that although these techniques would improve the effectiveness of training students in the processes of moral judgment, they do not resolve a more general problem of moral education. The more fundamental question is whether or not most people engage in the kind of moral reasoning advocated by our curriculum, and even if they do, whether this kind of reasoning is but an insignificant part of something we might call the moral personality. One could argue, for example, that we should be more concerned with moral sensitivity than with moral reasoning. Or perhaps a sensitivity to paradox and tragedy in human nature (rather than consistency and universality in moral rules) is a far more powerful force in the expression of man's inherent humanity than the use of reasoning strategies in the development of flexible moral principles.

The Limits of Reason

The bonds that tie together a moral community of men cannot rest simply on a common sense of intellectual justice. Perhaps more important than such attributes as consistency, universality, and impartiality is an intuitive notion of man's physical, moral, and intellectual limitations. And it is quite conceivable that the essentially tragic nature of man's being can be communicated only through ritualistic celebration and metaphor. Perhaps educators, philosophers, and psychologists should join with theologians and sensitive youth in a search for the kind of powerful metaphor with which our Christian heritage once provided us. We somehow need to create myths and celebrations by which we can project the common joys, sorrows, and compassion that we share simply by the fact that we are human.

We can see the limitation of rational analysis by looking more deeply into some of the great issues of life—love, work, violence. The issue of violence, for example, requires a broad conception of appropriate educational experiences. Our discussion of the Stamp Act defined the issue of violence in utilitarian terms, asking when the benefits of violence were greater than its costs. In this sense, violence is a technique that can be used for achieving important human goals after a rational decision that no other means are available. The need for violence is eliminated when justice and personal fulfillment are available to all people, and when institutions for resolving conflicts operate as they should.

It seems equally reasonable, however, to consider violence on several other levels. Man lives in a naturally violent universe. Matter is created and transformed in gigantic stellar explosions. On earth, living things kill and are killed in a dynamic food cycle. Man's violence, even though it seems to be of his own making, may merely be a reflection of his position in nature. From another perspective, institutionalized violence is sometimes identified as a symptom of a society gone mad, while individual violence may represent an appropriate response to an insane social order. On a third, more personal level, men's physical and emotional violence towards each other may reflect a psychological fact. The dark and tragic side of man exists, whether its roots are assumed to lie in original sin or in the Oedipus complex. Violence may fulfill basic needs.

The story of Christ is one of struggle and tragedy, temptation and death, agony and joy. Contemporary literature, which has few real heroes, most often reflects the paradox and the irony of human existence. The world of absurd novels and drama—of John Barth, Thomas Pynchon, Edward Albee—is not a world in which reasoned discourse leads men to justice and equality. The closest we come to popular heroes are John and Robert Kennedy. They were men of tragedy, who celebrated life with joy and zest, killed in absurd drama.

Within this context, the possibility and specific nature of "utopia" becomes critical. W. H. Auden (1958, pp. 168-69) suggests that there are two kinds of "dream pictures of the Happy Place where suffering and evil are unknown," the Edens and the New Jerusalems:

Glancing at a lampshade in a store window, I observe it too hideous for anyone in their senses to buy: He observes it is too expensive for a peasant to buy.

Passing a slum child with rickets, I look the other way, He looks the other way if he passes a chubby one . . .

You can see, then, why, between my Eden and his New Jerusalem, no treaty is negotiable.

In my Eden we have a few beam-engines, saddle-tank locomotives, overshot waterwheels and other beautiful pieces of obsolete machinery to play with: In his New Jerusalem even chefs will be cucumber-cool machine minders.

In my Eden our only source of political news is gossip: In his New Jerusalem there will be a special daily in simplified spelling for non-verbal types.

In my Eden each observes his compulsive rituals and superstitious tabus but we have no morals: In his Jerusalem the temples will be empty but all will practice the rational virtues.

Applying Auden's metaphor to our own assumptions about society, it would seem that the Happy Place which our "natural discourse" curriculum encourages students to envisage and work towards is a New Jerusalem. This is a world of the social scientist rather than the theologian, of the intellect rather than the emotions. Encouraging students to dream of Edens, to confront the tragedy and irrationality in human life, and to think metaphorically as well as analytically should also be part of the educational process, if we are to leave the questions truly open.

There is also a question of whether it is psychologically possible to separate ethical decisions and political ideology from total life style. Smith, Bruner, and White (1964) showed us how complex is the relationship between opinion and total personality; Lane (1962) found the roots of political ideology in individual styles of dealing with the world as a whole. White and Lippitt (1960, p. 244) speak of a "psychological core of democracy" including "open-mindedness to influence from others; self-acceptance or self-confidence and friendliness and good will in attitudes and actions toward others."

Kenniston's (1968) study of young radicals is an especially interesting illustration of the problem. His interviews with a number of the leaders of the New Left Vietnam Summer Movement revealed that these "young radicals" were from affluent, warm, permissive homes; they were unusually intelligent, open, and honest; they were deeply committed to working towards justice and equality within the system, through nonviolent means. Kenniston also found, however, a deep-rooted concern with violence.

Many of their earliest memories involve conflict, outer anger, and inner fear. They were, throughout their childhoods, especially sensitive to the issues of struggle within their families and communities. Although in behavior most of these young radicals were rather less violent than their contemporaries, this was not because they were indifferent to the issue, but because their early experience and family values had taught them how to control, modulate, oppose and avoid violence. Verbal aggression took the place of physical attack. They learned to argue, to compromise, and to make peace when confronted with conflict. . . .

I have mentioned the many tensions—psychological, interpersonal, and organizational—that are related to this issue in their work. The avoidance and control of violence, whether in international warfare, political organizations, small groups, or face-to-face personal relations, is a central goal and a key psychological orientation in the New Left. Many of the problems of the Movement are related to the zealous effort to avoid actions and relations in which inner aggression or outer conflict may be evoked. . . .

The position of the psychologically non-violent revolutionary in opposition to a violent world is paradoxical . . . for all his efforts to control violence, cataclysm, and sadism, the young radical continually runs the danger of identifying himself with what he seeks to control, and through a militant struggle against violence, creating more violence than he overcomes. The issue of violence is not resolved for these young men and women. (pp. 254-56)

This analysis suggests that violence has profound psychological implications, which should be treated in any serious discussion. It might be more appropriate to talk about the morality of violence by considering the underlying personality dynamics than by debating the usefulness of violent strategies in the American Revolution.

We believe, therefore, that great issues of the human spirit, such as feelings and expressions of violence, must be dealt with on a level deeper than that suggested by such phrases as "justification strategies" or "moral reasoning." We believe that education should encourage people to examine the relationships of men to their societies or to the universe not only through the rational analysis of "case studies," but also through the genuine attempt to create and wonder about a profound, perhaps religious, experience.

Moral Education and Schools

One way to approach this in the schools is through the development of new programs in the humanities. The present trend in teaching both social studies and English is to organize them as academic disciplines patterned after those in the university and to emphasize methods of scholarly thought. Traditionally, the humanities deal with art, music, and literature largely in historical or "critical" terms, as works to be experienced for the purpose of critical analysis. We believe there is a need for more profound educational "happenings" through which one might focus on a variety of conceptions of the human condition. Certainly art, music, literature would play a part in the creation of such happenings, but so might television, movies, and drama—media which are now considered to be mainly entertainment.

We would argue that the relatively modern distinctions between work and education, religion and entertainment, prevent "humanities" teachers from dealing with some of the most powerful happenings available for education. One might ask, for example, whether "2001," "The Graduate," "Alice's Restaurant," "Easy Rider," and "Midnight Cowboy" are educational films, religious films, or entertaining films to be seen at the neighborhood theatre? Is the time, effort, and money required to create such films spent in the interest of education, religion, or entertainment? From our point of view, such films are both educational and religious.

These distinctions were undoubtedly useful in the development of an affluent technological society: education is preparation for work and occurs between the ages of five and seventeen; work is what happens Monday through Friday; recreation and entertainment happen on weekends and in evenings; religion happens on Sunday. We see a profound questioning of these distinctions today, especially among young people.

There is a crisis of meaning, created essentially by affluence and the accompanying cynicism of youth regarding the necessity of work as the core of man's existence. The crisis has been compounded by the inability of three major institutions, school, work, and church, to deal with the redirection of energy previously channelled into economic development.

The conventional school is still tied to the goals of "getting ahead" in vocational and materialistic terms, although the availability of so much material wealth suggests that this is no longer a pressing need. Even those schools that are making a sincere effort to provide a free and human learning environment and to develop curricula based on important questions in the humanities find it difficult to make significant changes in the perceptiveness and willingness of students to raise important social and personal questions honestly. We interpret this failure as an indication of a conflict between the goals and structure of the existing school and the goals of the humanities. Fundamental questions are most appropriately discussed in small groups of equals; the school is organized in large groups of students led by an authority figure. The humanities question the authority and structure of institutions; the school demands acceptance of authority and standard behavior patterns in order to carry out its work. The school is therefore faced with an inescapable dilemma when it attempts to carry on serious inquiry in the humanities in the same environment where it teaches conventional knowledge.

The work institutions in general have not considered it part of their function to evaluate the society or the individual's place in it. It is unlikely that the Ford Motor Company, for example, would encourage its workers to question whether Fords should be made at all, or whether the resources of the company should be allocated to a different goal of the society. Nor are Ford employees apt to raise questions of their own position in the society—whether personal satisfaction comes from spending forty hours a week on an assembly line, or whether a flexible schedule might be a more civilized way to organize one's life.

At the same time, the world view of religious institutions whose traditional task has been the consideration of ultimate meaning is often carried forth with obsolete forms and rituals. At best, they raise social and ethical issues and promote community service, but they are outside the significant processes of life for most people.

Beyond Schools

The problem requires a view of the educational process as a continuing experience in thoughtful self-exploration. To create conditions for this type of experience will require fundamental changes in our existing educational institutions.

We feel that the exploration of one's self, one's values, and one's personal relationships can be promoted by membership in a group of people who hold different views of reality but who are constantly engaged in a search for a truer and more personally relevant view. A group's interaction forces each of its members to respond in some way to the views of the others, whether by rejection, assimilation, or accommodation. For the group to be influential, it must be important enough to the individual that he takes seriously the thoughts and feelings of the others. The situation must be comfortable enough that each person can reveal himself to some degree to the others. The relationships must be truly open and egalitarian. No member's thoughts should be rejected out of hand, nor should any member's be accepted uncritically.

We feel that this type of group situation is vital to the examination of those deep-rooted values and attitudes formed within the intense emotional setting of the family or early childhood group. Under ordinary circumstances, personality patterns are remarkably persistent. Only in powerful, emotionally laden environments has research uncovered significant reorientations of values (see, for example, Jacob 1957, Newcomb 1943). Although value-change in itself is not our goal, we do feel that the examination of values—which, if done seriously, implies the possibility of change—should be the primary emphasis of moral education. And we feel that this can take place only in the type of group situation described above.

This is quite different from the learning groups that commonly exist in schools. We would hope that, within our groups, adults and young people would deal with each other as people engaged in a common search for life's meaning, not as occupants of roles. Young people typically deal with adults almost exclusively in the fulfillment of obligations. They rarely have close contact with adults who represent a variety of professions, social classes, or philosophies, or with adults who have neither a parental or teaching role. The school setting is uniform and stylized. The teacher is trained to maintain a certain "distance" from the students; he can never become too personal. Conversation is usually carried on in the form of "public pronouncements" rather than tentative explorations of private feelings. Even students' views of themselves tend to be stereotyped; often, young people do not see each other in any role other than that of students.

In order to operate well, we feel that our "moral learning groups" need other freedoms not commonly part of the school, besides freedom from status distinctions. The school tends to limit somewhat arbitrarily both the topics studied by the students and the way in which they are studied. Much of the current culture—movies, TV, advertising, rock music—is ignored by the school. The student is expected to define himself and his society in terms of ideals and conventions of presentation that are at least partly outmoded. He deals primarily with written "classics" but is not encouraged to think seriously about what Simon and Garfunkel or television advertising are saying about the present human condition. Moreover, students are required to read, think, and express themselves verbally. Visual and musical expression, so much a part of the "outside" culture, are a very minor part of the school curriculum. Finally, the style of knowing in the school, as in the society generally, is heavily biased towards rational analytic knowledge. The "hippie" and existential preference for personal, intuitive knowing is seldom even acknowledged.

We feel that the schools operate within a very limited range of human experience. We would like to see them dealing with the whole gamut of modern culture, the whole range of personal feelings and perceptions, and all the forms of expression imaginable.

This philosophy raises serious problems of implementation. How can we do all this? Who is to decide on an agenda with an infinite number of possibilities? We feel that another type of freedom is demanded here. Each group, as a group, should be free to choose its own topics, its own schedules and settings, and its own procedures. Groups should have a large bloc of time, free from other obligations, and access to all types of resources. They should also have skilled leaders to help the group get through its procedural problems without abdicating responsibility to a small group or riding roughshod over minority factions.

We feel, then, that procedural freedom and freedom from traditional status distinctions are necessary to create mutually trusting groups in which real moral education—the examination of deeply rooted and important values—can take place.

It is not easy to imagine institutional settings in which these groups could exist. We have had some experience with an intensive summer experience that met many of our criteria: a range of ages among the members, close egalitarian relationships, and procedural freedom. This seemed quite successful, and leads us to consider the possibility of summer camps or vacation schools, when group members are free from other responsibilities, as workable settings.

Another possibility is to release students from conventional studies for a large bloc of time, perhaps six or eight weeks, sometime during their high school career. This would have the same benefit of affording complete freedom in scheduling.

We are also exploring the possibility of groups that take only part of an individual's time. We are finding that a group that meets once a week, in addition to a full school or work schedule, does not generate the necessary commitment. Perhaps releasing students from that half of their school time normally given to English, social studies, and "frills" would be adequate. We are currently trying such an arrangement.

Conclusion

Teaching students to handle personal, social, and political issues with more sophisticated modes of moral reasoning seems to us a legitimate goal of the public school. Our own curriculum efforts have been directed at making explicit the strategies by which value positions can be justified, largely in the context of oral discussion. We have developed case materials to provide the teacher and student with an easily accessible base from which to explore these issues. It is clear from both the work of Kohlberg and our own clinical intuitions that students operate with relatively primitive modes of justification and see conversation more as a forum for combat, catharsis, or persuasion, than as a context for the clarification of personal value premises upon which public policy issues are grounded.

Although our own efforts are presently looked upon as somewhat "radical" in the field of social studies, mainly because they are an assault on the traditional disciplines of history and the social sciences, we feel that our society's values are being questioned by too many people for teachers to continue to ignore the importance of moral analysis in the classroom. Our concern is that once a conception of "moral education" gets into the classroom, people will somehow assume that it has a significant impact on the student. Our own research indicates that this is not the case. Students may do better on pencil-and-paper tests measuring complexity of the reasoning process, but their spontaneous dialogues are little affected. Even if one assumes that we will learn how to affect the latter, it is still doubtful that much will carry over into day-to-day decision making.

The reasons for our skepticism are numerous. The language we use to describe moral reasoning directed at personal conflict or social controversy is highly analytical and abstract; the conflicts and controversies are far more complex and visceral than the structures we can apply to them. Controversy is, in fact more powerfully described through the metaphors of the dramatist, which transcend public language. Young people's growing distrust of the formal analysis of moral issues and their faith in existential or situational solutions to moral dilemmas suggests that systems for analyzing these issues not only must be based on solid philosophical ground, but also must be psychologically meaningful and relevant. And finally, we are skeptical of formal schooling as a situation in which the analysis of personal and moral issues might take place. The press of time and large numbers of students leads teachers to structure and rigidify modes of thinking, which should be open and spontaneous. Moreover, our experience indicates that the great percentage of students value reflection, not as an end in itself, but only as a means of clarifying decision and action in the real world. The schools have shown little inclination to facilitate (or even allow) students the opportunity to test the consequences of moral decision making in the community at large.

The revolt of young people in so many spheres of human activity—politics, education, art, personal lifestyle—is an effort to reinterpret and change traditional arrangements in society. As we see it, the great need for young people (and perhaps adults alike) is not simply the opportunity to discuss and justify personal or social decisions about events in the world. They need the opportunity to project themselves in rich hypothetical worlds created by their own imaginations or those of dramatic artists. More important, they need the opportunity to test out new forms of social order—and only then to reason about their moral implications. It is quite clear that school is not a likely place for this kind of activity to occur, and that the traditional social science disciplines provide but meager forms of knowledge to help us imagine, act on, and interpret that world. We need new institutions which legitimize the right of adolescents and adults to spend time reflecting and planning social action. We need a broader base of knowledge from which the reflection will spring than that traditionally stressed in schools and universities. And we need to consider the fields of ethical analysis and socialization, as philosophers and psychologists talk about these fields, as but one mode of clarification, and perhaps a relatively minor one at that.

References

Auden, W. H. "Vespers" from "Horae Canonicae." *Selected Poetry of W. H. Auden.* New York: Modern Library, 1958.

Benn, S. I., and Peters, R. S. *The Principles of Political Thought.* New York: Free Press, 1959.

Fletcher, J. *Moral Responsibility: Situation Ethics at Work.* Philadelphia: Westminster Press, 1967.

Hare, R. M. *Freedom and Reason.* Oxford: Clarendon Press, 1963.

Jacob, P. E. *Changing Values in College.* New York: Harper & Row, 1957.

Kenniston, K. *Young Radicals.* New York: Harcourt, Brace & World, 1968.

Kohlberg, L. "Moral Education, Religious Education, and the Public Schools: A Developmental View." *Religion and Public Education,* edited by Theodore Sizer. Boston: Houghton Mifflin, 1967.

Lane, R. E. *Political Ideology.* New York: Free Press, 1962.

Newcomb, T. M. *Personality and Social Change.* New York: Holt, Rinehart & Winston, 1943.

Newmann, F. M. Contribution to "Political Socialization in the Schools." *Harvard Educational Review* 38, no. 3 (summer 1968).

Smith, M. B.; Bruner, J.; and White, R. W. *Opinions and Personality.* New York: John Wiley & Sons, 1964.

White, R. K., and Lippitt, R. O. *Autocracy and Democracy.* New York: Harper & Row, 1960.

23

Moral and Ethical Development in a Democratic Society

Irving Kristol

I have been asked to speak about "moral and ethical develop-ment in a democratic society," and I should like to begin by taking as my text a long report that appeared in the September 2, 1974 issue of *The New York Times.* Under the heading "A Coed Camp That's Run Like a Mountain Resort," the reporter gives us a glowing account of Camp Keowa, New York—a camp for 200 teen-age boys and girls run by the high school division of the Boy Scouts of Amer-ica. It is a quite radical departure from the Boy Scout camps of yesteryear. There are no uniforms, and no bugles are blown for reveille—because, the reporter explains, "Teen-agers are too sophis-ticated for that kind of stuff these days." The campers go to bed when they please, rise when they please, and pass the day as they please. The only rules are no drugs, no liquor, and no coed showers. According to the *Times,* the kids absolutely loved this new kind of camp, and the final paragraph of the story consists of the following enthusiastic endorsement by one of the campers:

Reprinted by permission from *Moral Development, Proceedings of the 1974 ETS Invitational Conference* (Princeton, N.J.: Educational Testing Service, 1975).

"The best part of all was that we didn't have to clean up our cabins," said Edward Meyer, 16, of Brooklyn, who spent much of his time at camp playing poker and wound up winning $50. "Our floor was covered with garbage. And nobody made us pick it up."

Mind you, this is a Boy Scout camp, and—as we all know—the Boy Scouts have always had it as their overriding aim to promote the moral development of young people. Presumably, Camp Keowa is engaged in this task and, according to the *Times* reporter, the young people interviewed, and the camp officials quoted, it is having an extraordinary success. True, the floors of the cabins seem to be covered with garbage. But is that any real cause for concern? What has garbage to do with moral development?

I think that's a very interesting question, and not at all a merely rhetorical one. Most of us who were middle-aged were, after all, raised to think that there was indeed some kind of connection between the people's garbage and the people's morals. Were we wrong? Were we, as the *Times* suggests, a generation that suffered from a deficiency of sophistication? It seems to me that the question is worth exploring, and I can think of no better way to begin than by lingering over that word in the title of the subject which has been given me—the word "development."

Letting Morality Happen

"Development" is such a curious word, so tantalizingly neutral and therefore so ambiguous in defining our relation to morality. After all, the title could easily have been "moral and ethical education in a democratic society." Why wasn't it? Well, I assume the reason is that the sponsors of this conference were not all certain that it is a proper function of education to shape young people according to any specific set of moral standards; and the phrase "moral education" does imply an activity of that sort. The term "development," on the other hand, suggests that morality is something that exists embryonically within every child—rather like an intelligence quotient—and that education can be satisfied by encouraging it to unfold toward its fullest potentiality. "Morality," in this view, is something that *happens* to one. And education then becomes a process of "liberating" human possibilities for this eventual happening rather than of defining human possibilities in an approved way.

This is certainly a very convenient notion for a teacher, or for anyone in a position of authority, because it means that he (or she) need not himself have any firm moral beliefs, to say nothing of providing a moral model of any kind. The process of "development" can then be regarded as a purely technical problem—a problem of means, not of ends—and the "solution" is to get people (young people, especially) to have feelings about morality and to think about morality: to be morally sensitive and "morally aware," as we say. Once this has been successfully accomplished, the task of education is finished. What kinds of people emerge from this process is something we can leave to the people themselves freely to decide; the final disposition of their moral sentiments and ideas is their business, not anyone else's.

It's all very odd and most interesting. It's rather as if an expert in gardening were to compose a manual on "botanical development in a suburban landscape." He would then give you all sorts of important information on how things grow—weeds as well as flowers, poison ivy as well as rose gardens—without ever presuming to tell you whether you should favor one over the other, or *how* to favor one over the other. In fact, there are no such gardening manuals—precisely because any gardener will indeed have some definite ideas as to what a garden might look like. Different gardeners will have different ideas, of course; but there will be a limit to this variety. The idea of a garden does not, for instance, include an expanse of weeds or of poison ivy. And no gardener would ever confuse a garden with a garbage dump.

In contrast, we seem unable or unwilling to establish defining limits to the idea of a moral person. We are, as it were, gardeners with all the latest implements and technology, but without an idea of a garden, and unable even to distinguish between a garden and a garbage dump. Is this a function of mere ignorance? Or mere timidity? I think not. Rather, we have a kind of faith in the nature of people that we do not have in the botanical processes of nature itself—and I use the word "faith" in its full religious force. We really do believe that all human beings have a natural *telos* toward becoming flowers, not weeds or poison ivy, and that aggregates of human beings have a natural predisposition to arrange themselves into gardens, not jungles or garbage heaps. This sublime and noble faith we may call the religion of liberal humanism. It is the dominant spiritual and intellectual orthodoxy in America today. Indeed, despite all our chatter about the separation of church and state, one can even say it is the official religion of American society today, against which all other religions can be criticized as divisive and parochial.

I happen not to be a believer in this religion of liberal humanism, but this is not the time or place for theological controversy and I am not, in any case, the best qualified person for such a controversy. What I want to point to, and what I wish to discuss, is the *political and social crisis* which this religion of liberal humanism is evidently provoking. I shall not try to controvert the liberal-humanist thesis that there is no superior knowledge available as to how people should be morally shaped, nor shall I try to disprove the thesis that the people will, if left alone, shape themselves better than anyone or anything can shape them. I shall simply remark what I take to be a fact: Though the majority of the American people may well subscribe to some version of this religion—and I think they do—they end up holding in contempt all the institutions in which the ethos of this religion is incarnated. Indeed, and incredibly enough, they become increasingly "alienated" from these institutions, and end up feeling that these institutions are in some way "unresponsive" and "irrelevant" to their basic needs. And not only "unresponsive" and "irrelevant," but actually "repressive" as well. It is a historical fact of some significance, I would say, that though schools were never particularly popular institutions among young people, it is only in recent years, as our schools have ceased trying to "form" young people and have tried instead to "develop" them, that the school has come to be widely regarded as a kind of prison.

The Legitimacy of Institutions

What we are talking about is the *legitimacy* of institutions, and what I am suggesting is that the moral neutrality of our institutions, especially our educational institutions, ends up robbing them of their popular legitimacy. Nor does it matter if this moral neutrality is, at the moment, popularly approved of and sanctioned by public opinion. It *still* ends up depriving these institutions of their legitimacy. One does not, after all, have to be a particularly keen student of history or psychology to know that people will accept or tolerate or even praise institutions which, suddenly, will be experienced as intolerable and unworthy. Institutions, like worm-eaten trees, can look healthy and imposing, until they crumble overnight into the dust. If you look at the *cahiers* submitted to the French Assembly on the eve of the great revolution, you will find not a breath of dissatisfaction with the monarchy—not a hint of republican aspirations. Similarly, early in 1964, an opinion poll among students at the University of California at Berkeley found that the overwhelming majority thought very well of the school and believed they were getting an excellent education there. Nevertheless, both Louis XVI and Clark Kerr soon found themselves riding the whirlwind. Such abrupt eruptions of profound discontent, catching us all by surprise—whether we are talking about the rebelliousness of racial minorities, or young people, or women, or whomever—are characteristic of American society today. They are also characteristic of a society whose institutions—whether they be political institutions, or schools, or the family—are being drained of their legitimacy—that is to say, of their moral acceptance.

We try to cope with this problem by incessantly "restructuring" our institutions so as to make them more "responsive" to popular agitation. But that obviously does not work very well. The more we fiddle around with our schools, for instance, the more energetically we restructure and then re-restructure them according to the passing fancy of intellectual fashion, the more steadily do they lose their good repute. In desperation, many of our reformers are falling back on the proposition that such symptoms of discontent are really signs of good health and vigor—that it is *natural* for people to become more dissatisfied as things get better, and as they learn to appreciate the possibilities of even further improvement. Of all the absurdities of contemporary political sociology, this must rank as the most bizarre. It amounts to saying that, as the people's condition improves, they are bound to feel worse rather than better—more unhappy rather than more content. But surely the purpose of improvement is to make men and women feel satisfied, not more dissatisfied —otherwise, in what sense can we talk of "improvement" at all?

It is a peculiarly perverse and morose view of human nature which claims that men's inevitable response to good actions is to feel bad. It is a view of human nature which, though desperately proposed by liberal humanism to explain the peculiar behavior of its believers, makes nonsense of the creed of liberal humanism itself, which cannot possibly subsist on the premise that the perfect human condition is one in which men are better off than ever before but feel miserable as never before. The unthinking way in which we nevertheless echo the thought that lively dissatisfaction is a form of "creativity," and that the generation of such "creativity" is a token of reformist success rather than a sign of reformist failure—this is a declaration of intellectual bankruptcy, and nothing else. It is nothing more than a way in which reformers secure an ideological credit card, good in perpetuity, which they can then indefinitely bank on regardless of their cash condition.

The irony of our present situation, as I see it, is that, as our institutions try to become ever more "responsive" to their constituencies, the people seem to put less and less faith in them generally. One can only conclude that either there is something wrong with the idea of "responsiveness" as we currently understand it, or that there is some fault in our idea of "the people" as we currently understand it. I should like to suggest that there is something wrong with both of these ideas, as we currently understand them—and that, ultimately, we are talking about a single error rather than a dual one: an error in the way we conceive the relations between a people and their institutions in a democratic society.

Strategies of Responsiveness

There is an old Groucho Marx chestnut about how he resigned from a club immediately upon being elected to membership—his resignation being prompted by the thought that any club which would elect him a member couldn't possibly be worth joining. I think that, in this old chestnut, there is a lesson for all of us about "responsiveness." More and more of our institutions have been "reaching out" for "greater participation" and "greater involvement" —and an ever-larger number of those new recruits to full membership in the club have been quietly resigning, in fact if not in formality. To which our clubs seem to answer: "That's alright. Resigning is a way of belonging, and maybe the best club is one consisting of members who have resigned." This is the conclusion, at any rate, the Boy Scouts seem to have reached.

It is not easy to say to what degree our various strategies of "responsiveness" are motivated by sly cunning or plain self-deception. Thus, in the heyday of campus protest over the Vietnam war, and amidst an upsurge of political radicalism in general among college students, Congress decided to lower the voting age to 18. Now, to the best of my knowledge, there was not a single protest meeting on any American campus on the issue of a lower voting age. Similarly, to the best of my knowledge, Congress did not receive a single mass petition from young people on this matter. Nevertheless, Congress decided that, in the face of all this unrest, it couldn't simply remain mute and impassive. So it decided to be "responsive" in its way. It didn't end the Vietnam war, and it didn't abolish capitalism, but instead passed a constitutional amendment lowering the voting age to 18. That amendment was promptly ratified by the requisite number of state legislatures, and shortly thereafter Richard Nixon was elected President by an overwhelming majority of the popular vote, and unrest on the campus was replaced by apathy. One cannot say Congress intended things to work out this way—most of the liberals who were the ardent proponents of a lower voting age certainly did not. But, in retrospect, there is reason to concede some substance to the lament of student radicals that a sort of con game had been practiced upon them.

So, one of the ways in which we are characteristically "responsive" is to give dissatisfied people what they have not asked for and what there was never any sound reason for believing they really wanted. Thus, when nonwhites in the ghettos of New York City began to express dissatisfaction with the fact that their children were being graduated from high school without even being able to read or reckon at an elementary school level, they were promptly given "community control" over their local school boards and "open admissions" to the senior city colleges. But if you look back at the course of events, you will discover that there never was any real popular demand for either "community control" or "open admissions." Neither of them had any bearing on the problems at hand. As a matter of fact, any authentic conception of "community control" stands in rank contradiction to the practice of busing students for purposes of integration, which is also under way in New York's schools. What is the point of giving citizens "control" over their local schools when their children are being bused away to be taught in other schools? And, as concerns "open admissions," what is the point of admitting into college high school graduates whose problem is that they cannot read at an eighth-grade level? How does that solve the problem?

But we are also "responsive" in another, seemingly more candid but actually even more cunning, way. This is to give people what they are actually demanding—or at least what some are vociferously demanding—in the tranquil knowledge that these demands are misconceived anyway, and that their satisfaction is a meaningless gesture. That is what has happened with regard to parietal rules, course gradings, class attendance, curriculum requirements, nominal student representation on various committees, and so forth, on so many of our college campuses, and even in our lower schools as well. The strategy here may be defined as follows: When confronted with protest, dissatisfaction, and tumult, unburden yourself of your responsibilities but keep all your privileges, and then announce that your institutions have enlarged the scope of "participation" and "freedom" for all constituents. Since "participation" and "freedom" are known to be good democratic things, you have the appearance of rectitude and the reality of survival.

This complicated game of "responsiveness" has been skillfully played these past years and has enabled a great many institutions to maintain and secure their imperiled positions. In that sense, it has been unquestionably successful. In a deeper sense, however, it has gained nothing but time—a precious enough gain, but only if one realizes that it is simply time that has been gained, and that this time must be used productively if the gain is to be substantial rather than illusory. It is not my impression that any such realization exists, or even that people in authority are reflecting seriously on the events of the past decade. The question of the diminished legitimacy of our institutions is not being confronted—in the hope, no doubt, that it has gone away of its own accord. But I do believe it a serious error to think it has gone away, despite the sullen calm which now pervades our society. It seems to me, rather, than more and more people are showing more and more contempt for that club—the club which consists of the collectivity of our institutions—to which they have been elected. They may have ceased to abuse the facilities so excessively, but they are certainly not using them productively, nor do they show the slightest inclination to pay their dues. As a matter of fact, their attachment is so obviously fragile that no one has asked them to pay any dues.

But who wants to belong to a club where you don't have to pay dues of any kind? What kind of a club is that?

The Importance of Obligations

It has been argued, by political philosophers and educators through the ages, that it is unwise to give people rights without at the same time imposing on them obligations—that rights without obligations make for irresponsibility, just as obligations without rights make for servility. Edmund Burke pushed this thesis a little further when he declared that it was part of the people's rights to *have* obligations—that an absence of obligation means a diminution of humanity, because it signifies a condition of permanent immaturity. But I would say we can extend this line of thought even further, and declare with some confidence, based on our own more recent experience, that obligation is not only a right but a *need*—people upon whom no obligations are imposed will experience an acute sense of deprivation. It is our striking failure to recognize this phenomenon of *moral deprivation* for what it is which explains our fumbling and even cynical response to the dissatisfaction that Americans are expressing toward their institutions.

I would claim that the main point which emerges from the American experience of late is that people do not have confidence in themselves—that people do not have respect for institutions which, instead of making demands upon the people, are completely subservient to their whims. One can even make the point more generally: Just as people will have no sense of prideful belonging to a society that has so low an opinion of them that it thinks it absurd to insist that people become better than they are, so they will feel equally alienated from a society that proclaims so high an opinion of them that it finds it absurd to insist that they need to become better than they are.

Institutions that pander to citizens—and I use that word "pander" advisedly—in an effort to achieve popularity may get a good press for a while. Our mass media, for which pandering is an economic necessity, are naturally keen to see other institutions remake themselves in the media's own image—to become "responsive" the way a television station or network is responsive. "Responsiveness," here, means to satisfy popular appetite or desire or whim or fancy— or, rather, to satisfy what is thought at any moment to be popular appetite or desire or whim or fancy. Such "responsiveness," being timely and circumstantial, is thought also to be "relevant." But amidst the noise of mutual self-congratulation, what is lost sight of is the fact that these institutions, floating on clouds of approval and self-approval, have uprooted themselves from that solid ground of moral legitimacy from which all institutions receive their long-term nourishment.

Do I exaggerate? Well, let me be specific about the problems of ghetto education—problems which I know you are all seriously concerned with, if not directly involved with. We have had, during the past decade, dozens of bold innovations in the schooling of slum kids, each of them claiming to be more "responsive" and more "relevant" than the previous ones. Some of these innovations have even rediscovered forms of classroom organization and techniques of pedagogy that were popular a hundred years ago—and you can't be more innovative than that! Each innovation, at some moment, is held up to us as a "breakthrough," is the subject of enthusiastic magazine articles and television reports—on the order of the *Times* report on Camp Keowa—is quickly imitated by enterprising school administrators elsewhere, and is generally judged to be a success before any results are in. Then it quietly vanishes, and nothing more is heard about it as attention focuses on some still newer innovation, by some other bold educational reformer who has "broken through" encrusted tradition and has come up with an even more "responsive" and "relevant" program. In general, the criteria of "relevance" and "responsiveness" mean the degree to which the new educational scheme panders to the appetites, the fancies, the whims of the students, and avoids anything that looks like an exercise of authority.

Meanwhile, back in the ghetto, there continues to exist a whole set of successful schools which no one pays any attention to. These schools are successful in the most elementary yet crucial terms: There is a long list of parents trying desperately to register their children in these schools, the truancy rate and transfer rate are low, there is less juvenile delinquency, a lower rate of drug addiction among all students, and academic achievement levels tend to be

slightly higher than average. I am referring, of course, to the parochial schools in the ghetto, which no one writes about, which the
media ignore, but which—in the opinion of parents and students alike
—are the most desirable of all ghetto schools. Many of these parochial schools are in old buildings with minimal facilities—a pitiful
library perhaps, a squalid gymnasium perhaps, a spartan lunchroom
perhaps. Anyone who had ever taken the trouble to open his or her
eyes to the existence of these schools would not have been aston-
ished and taken aback—as so many were—by the findings of the Cole-
man report that the condition or even nonexistence of such physical
facilities had little connection with educational achievement.

Why are the parochial schools in the ghetto so well regarded?
The answer is obvious: They are *self-respecting* institutions, demanding institutions, with standards that students are expected to meet.
Many of them even have and enforce dress codes, as a symbolic gesture of self-affirmation. By making such demands upon their students, they cause their students to make demands upon themselves—
and, most important, cause their students to realize that the only
true moral and intellectual "development" occurs when you do make
demands upon yourself. And this—the habit of making demands
upon ourselves—is something that we learn from being taught it, by
precept and example.

The Case for Authority

I suppose what I am saying can be and will be interpreted as just
another critique of what we call "permissiveness." I should be unhappy if this happens because I so intensely dislike both that term
and its associations. People who indiscriminately attack "permissiveness" are themselves victims of a confusion between authority and
authoritarianism—a confusion they share with the very tendencies
they criticize. "Permissiveness" and "authoritarianism" are indeed
two possible poles of moral discourse—they are, both of them, the
poles that come into existence when the center no longer holds. That
center is *authority*, by which one means the exercise of power
toward some morally affirmed end and in such a reasonable way as
to secure popular acceptance and sanction. Legitimate authority is
not always reasonable, since this authority is exercised by people
who are not, in the nature of things, always reasonable. No one is

always reasonable, and legitimate authority is therefore always open to criticism and correction. But if authority may be flawed in its means of operation, both "permissiveness" and "authoritarianism" are flawed in their goals, which are morally void and substanceless. This second flaw, clearly, is infinitely more important than the first, since it induces a kind of technocratic mania, with exponents of "permissiveness" figuring out ever new ways of "liberating" the citizen, but having no idea as to what he is being liberated for, while exponents of "authoritarianism" are busy figuring out how to control people for the sole purpose of securing the power of existing institutions, with no serious conception as to the ultimate purpose of this power.

The "permissive" person is all for change, especially "social change"; the "authoritarian" person is all for "stability," especially "social stability." But there is something inherently ridiculous in being *for* change without having a clear and vivid perception of the kind of person and the kind of political community you want such change to bring about. Besides, if there is one thing certain in this world, it is change, which is but a descriptive term for the natural processes of birth, growth, decline, and death. The political problem is neither producing change nor suppressing it, but coping with it—adapting to it in the least costly and most beneficial way.

Similarly, the "authoritarian" person is all for stability. But stability is, in its own way, as inevitable as change. When we say stability, we mean a condition in which the arrangements of our lives, individual and collective, acquire a meaning and a value—it represents a victory over the continual flux of things, a temporary mastery over chance and destiny. The human race needs such meanings, both individual and collective, if it is to claim entitlement to the term "human." A meaningless life and a meaningless polity are insupportable and intolerable. So there is little point in singing the praise of stability *per se*. Just as one wants to know the answer to the question "change for what?," so one wants to know the answer to the question "stability for what?"

And the answers to these questions are provided by authority, properly understood. I am not talking about *power*, which is the capacity to coerce. I am talking about *authority*, in which power is not experienced as coercive because it is infused, however dimly, with a moral intention which corresponds to the moral sentiments and moral ideals of those who are subject to this power. Education, in its only significant sense, is such an exercise in legitimate authority. And when educators say that they don't *know* what their moral intention is, that they don't *know* what kinds of human beings they are trying to create, they have surrendered all claim to legitimate authority.

At that point, it really doesn't much matter whether they resort to an "authoritarian" mode of governance, with a blind and wilful reliance on tradition, or on a "permissive" mode of governance, which encourages blind and aimless "development." I must say, for my own part, that had I to choose between these two modes, I would opt for the "authoritarian" in the hope that a mechanical repetition of the forms just might reawaken and neutralize the dead substance that used to give these forms meaning and legitimacy. But this would be an extreme and desperate condition, and just as extreme cases make for bad law, extreme conditions make for bad educational philosophy, and it is the better part of wisdom not to linger too long over them. What so many of us fail to see, however, is that the prevailing "permissiveness" is also an exercise in desperation, which is bound to be self-defeating. "Moral development," as now conceived, creates moral deprivation—a hunger of the soul for moral meanings—which is far more devastating and dangerous than any physical hunger. And this hunger of the soul will, in the end, satisfy itself by gratefully submitting to any passing pseudoauthority, which will be coercive in the extreme—and will be accepted *because* it is so coercive, because it does offer an escape from a dreadful, meaningless freedom. Those kids at Camp Keowa, dressed like slobs and sitting amidst their garbage and playing poker—they will, in all likelihood, end up by enthusiastically joining some movement which puts them in uniform, gives them songs to chant in unison, and sets them to work cleaning up every speck of dirt, under threat of the severest penalties. Having liberated them from the traditional authority of the Boy Scouts, we shall certainly end up delivering them to some newer, some rigid, and more brutal authoritarianism.

I can already hear the plaintive rejoinder: But where on earth, in this bewildered age, are our educators going to discover this moral authority without which authentic education is impossible? Who is going to give us the answers to questions about the meaning of our individual and collective lives? I recognize both the cogency and poignancy of this lament: Ours is indeed a bewildered age. But I would, at the risk of offending many of you, say this: If you have no sense of moral authority, if you have no sovereign ideas about moral purpose, you ought not to be educators. There are many technocratic professions, in which for all practical purposes the knowledge of means suffices—but education is not one of them. An educator who cannot give at least a tentative and minimally coherent reply to the question "Education for what?" is comparable to a clergyman who cannot explain the purpose of religion. We have many such clergymen. They, too, talk about "moral and ethical development." They, too, wonder why so many young people seem bored with the institutions their parents enlist them in. And they, too, in desperation drop anything old in favor of anything new. Having lost sight of their goals, they become the captives of intellectual and ideological fashion.

Is it so different with our educators? I fear not, though I should like to think otherwise. And I'll begin to think otherwise when, at a conference such as this, I see listed on the agenda a session on "educational chic." That is an event I most sincerely look forward to.

Postscript

24

What Can Be Done?

David Purpel and Kevin Ryan

It is not our intention to present the reader with a cookbook of precise steps to take in order to develop a program of moral education. Quite the contrary, we have tried to present the complex, layered nature of moral education. Our aim has been to introduce the multiplicity rather than prescribe the particular. And, while not taking a particular stance and a specific approach to moral education, we nevertheless strongly believe that this area of human life is a major part of the schoolman's territory. We believe, still further, that there should be some quiet urgency in attending to it. We can, therefore, suggest some plan of attack on this vast and tricky terrain. This chapter, then, is an attempt to outline for the schoolman what can be done.

First Steps: Examination of What Is

Moral education is not a matter of choice. It is in the very fabric of schooling. While it can be ignored, it cannot be eradicated. Education is a value-laden human activity. Values are built into the curriculum of the school, the way children are grouped, the choice and training of teachers, the composition of the school board and the administrative staff, and the school's budget allocations. Morality is intertwined in the many human interactions. The use of authority, including how rewards and punishments are meted out, also carries with it a moral message.

The first step of the practitioner is to find out what is going on in the school that has relevance to this issue. In chapter 5, we suggested that moral education is inevitable and invited the reader to look at various manifestations of moral education in both the visible and invisible curriculum. We suggest making a "moral inventory" of one's own school; we have already indicated a number of places to look for morally loaded practices which we summarize below.

The Visible Curriculum

1. Moral aspects of the traditional curriculum can be examined through visiting classes, inspecting curriculum guides and texts, and examining broad programs such as career education and sex education.

2. A more subtle form of moral education is built into the many stories, myths, and folktales that are told and retold in the schools.

3. Moral dicta have often been codified into statements such as "love thy neighbor" or "make love not war." These sayings and other proverbs, mottoes, and epigrams carry with them moral imperatives. They are seen and heard by schoolchildren, and need to be surveyed and analyzed for their instructional impact.

The Hidden Curriculum

1. *The Classroom Culture.* What is the quality of the moral life of the classroom? How are controversial issues resolved? How is misbehavior defined and then dealt with? How do teachers and students interact with one another? What sorts of things does the teacher reward and punish?

2. *Other Formal School Activities.* What values are conveyed in school assemblies and pep rallies? What is being given attention and what is not being given attention? When emotions are stirred, to what end are they stirred?

3. *Peer Culture.* What are the dominant cliques in the school and what are the values that they represent? What groups or individuals are least honored? What values do they represent? How do the "strong" students relate to "weak" students?

4. *School Culture.* What does the school as an institution stand for and communicate to the young? What regulations are most honored? Which ones are most easily violated?

The intention of such a survey is not to identify all the places that the school has fallen down but, rather, to get a balanced and comprehensive view of what is actually going on.

Community Views

Schoolpeople need to be in touch with the social climate surrounding moral education. The proof of the importance of moral education is that so many people feel so passionately about it. There are few parents who do not want their children to grow up with a firm understanding of right and wrong. However, once one starts probing what is meant by "good" and "bad," or by "moral behavior," divisions develop and passions are often aroused.

We believe that schools do not belong to educators but to all the people. Parents have a particular interest in the school and their views need particular attention. Teachers are professionals, not automatons. They have attitudes and perspectives that need to be listened to. Children, too, have thoughts and feelings about their education. Moral education has always been a mission of the school, but its form takes different shapes and different intensities at different times. It is important to know what the present climate of support or reservation is. To do that we suggest the following steps for school leaders:

1. Bring together some teachers and citizens (possibly some members of the school board) to plan and conduct a survey of the school and the community. The purpose of the survey is to ascertain what people mean by moral education (teaching a set of values? religious education? sex education? citizenship?).

2. Communicate to the public what is currently going on in the school and what are some of the alternative approaches to moral education.

3. Indicate what the school leadership believes to be the appropriate role of the school in moral education and the nature of the programs they would like to see implemented.

There are other questions that need to be examined in this

process: Is there an information gap? Around what issues? For which groups? Are there ambiguous or confusing areas? Are there individuals or groups who need to be given a special hearing and with whom there should be special dialogue?

Finally, this information needs to be put in a form that can be useful to policy making. It can also serve as the basis for further investigation and study of specific school policies to be implemented.

Long Run Goals

We have discussed some ways to begin the process of dealing with moral education. We feel that these are vital first steps in developing policy, but the basic substantive questions for practice remain. We want this book to provide schoolpeople with specific and concrete help in developing policies and practices for moral education. We have tried to present a representative sample of the most cogent and relevant writings in the field. However, we are well aware that the field provides serious problems for practitioners. In reviewing the contents, we realize that we may have inadvertently increased the problems by emphasizing their complexity as well as the limitations of the various approaches. Therefore, we feel it would be irresponsible to leave the reader at this point with pious platitudes on the need to strive ever onward and upward. We wish to address ourselves openly and frankly to the questions of "what can and should we actually do" now that we have come to understand or rediscover the *importance, complexity,* and *inevitability* of moral education. Our basic themes have been (1) that the moral aspects of education are the most vital and fundamental ones, but (2) their translation into sound educational practices is beset by extraordinarily tangled, controversial, and potentially explosive difficulties even though (3) a great deal of moral education does go on in public schools.

There is really no rational way of escaping the responsibility of moral education short of a determined effort to pretend that the issues are either not there or will soon go away. Such an orientation (or strategies that amount to the same thing) is simply not appropriate for the responsible professional. The educational practitioner is not a bemused and innocent commentator. Practitioners, if they are to be professional, cannot engage in the luxury of avoiding difficult decisions or making them the basis of personal comfort. We cannot be responsible educators without making conscious and deliberate decisions on moral education. At the same time, we must realize that our decisions will have to be made within a context of insufficient understanding, inadequate data, and incomplete research. It is also probable that they will be received with skepticism, criticism, and controversy. Hardly an attractive prospect! However, educators are often, if not usually, required to practice with insufficient theory, guided by ambiguous if not conflicting social policies. Our recommendations to practitioners can be grouped into three categories—confrontation, inquiry, and commitment.

Confrontation

We have shown that there are a number of significant moral education approaches now available for classroom application. However, none of these approaches is without its deficiencies and difficulties, and none merit unqualified approval. If a school adopts an existing program, it should be with the understanding that the program is unlikely to satisfy completely the requirements of valid moral education.

Our conviction is that practitioners must confront this problem squarely and directly. We simply have to face the harsh realities of the field—the ambiguities, the controversies, and the perplexities. Whatever we do in this field (and no doubt in others) we are bound to offend some group, principle, research, orientation, convention, or tradition. It is up to the practitioner to make an operational synthesis out of this chaos.

Confronting these realities can serve as a liberating rather than a paralyzing force. Acknowledging the limits of research and the lack of social consensus can allow us to work without the expectation of finding complete answers. We are all forced to proceed with humility in this area. We need to help each other, and we need to resist the guilt often induced by those without humility. Our strength as educators does not (and perhaps should not) lie in finally resolving classic dilemmas or settling ultimate questions. Rather, it resides in two abilities: (1) being able to pose appropriate questions and (2) acting in sensible, pragmatic ways that sometimes approximate wisdom. It has become increasingly unpopular to invoke "common sense" as a guideline for educational practice, and with some justification; we have certainly seen the limitations of a great deal of conventional wisdom.

However, we must not ignore the resources of personal and individual insight, understanding, and judgment. Given the limitations we have mentioned, we really have no alternative but to supplement the public and professional dialogue with our own judgments and decisions. Not to act is to act irresponsibly.

Inquiry

Even though we have stressed the limitations of the theoretical research and development efforts, and have encouraged practitioners to apply their own skills and judgments, we want to reaffirm the critical necessity for educators to become well informed on the issues and seriously involved in the quest for valid policies. For practitioners, this inquiry must be accompanied by at least tentative operational conclusions, always subject to continuous and critical review.

We need to have special insights into and understandings of the complex dimensions of moral education. We need to know about the conflicting approaches, the inherent political and social considerations, the philosophical and psychological frameworks, and the problems of classroom applications. We need to decide which issues to present to students. Original sin? The moral dimensions of the Vietnam war? The petty thievery in Miss Grundy's third-grade classroom? We also need to reflect on how students should deal with moral issues. Logically? Empirically? Intuitively? Emotionally? Most important, we have to develop a set or sets of moral guidelines. Should they be situational? Developmental? Marxist? Judeo-Christian? Pragmatic? Relativist? Fortunately, we do not have to deal with these issues in isolation, since there is a vast, brilliant, and continuing tradition of scholarship on both basic and applied aspects of moral education.

Further inquiry should help us see in stark outline the quality and direction of the moral education that exists in our schools. It should also help us bring to the surface what we actually believe. While there is value in encountering the expert what we ourselves believe is of particular importance. Once in touch with our own informed views, we can not only test these views with associates and through further readings, but also in the world of educational practice. Again, it remains for the practitioner to confront the difficulties involved, to make the most honest and thorough inquiry possible, to supplement these findings with his own experiences and intuitions, and to make the wisest possible decision.

Commitment

Finally, and perhaps of greatest importance, there must be a significant degree of moral commitment by educators. We must ourselves pursue moral goals and seek to employ moral responses in our profession, and we must wrestle with the complexities and difficulties of behaving morally in our own lives. As teachers, this quest should be manifested for our students in our behavior, in the questions we pose, and in the decisions we make. It is a human imperative to search for goodness and a professional imperative to put moral considerations into practice. Modeling is a powerful technique for moral education, and young people often take their cues from what adults do more than from what they say. We must therefore be aware of our own moral commitments and attempt to act from a meaningful, articulated, and informed moral viewpoint.

We view our task as involving colleagues, students, and parents in a mutual quest for moral insight. We need to pursue this mutual quest rigorously and honestly, with the courage to admit that our knowledge is insufficient. As professionals, we should have particular expertise in guiding this quest, but it makes sense to openly admit that we all need to continue to learn, inquire, and struggle when it comes to finding moral meaning. Certainly, the fears of indoctrination and manipulation would be sharply decreased if teachers were to consider themselves as students in this field. Why do we not say to colleagues, students, and parents: "Look, we're all agreed that we want to behave in accordance with the highest moral principles. As we all know, there's not much agreement on what those principles are, and even when we agree on them we don't seem to know how to apply them in specific situations. Since there are no clear answers, we will have to study hard in this area. We don't have answers but we can provide and guide opportunities for study. We know some books to read, questions to raise, exercises to develop, and experiences to provide which we think can help us to reduce the confusion. We also need help, so won't you join us in this most difficult and important search? No doubt from time to time we'll make mistakes, get angry with each other, get confused, and become frustrated—not because we want to or because we are stupid, evil, or insensitive—but because the issues themselves are so thorny and so basic. These discomforts are part of the price we will have to pay for this opportunity. We need to help each other and proceed on the basis that we are all acting if not in wisdom, at least in good faith."

Conclusion

We have presented a framework for practitioners, involving confrontation, inquiry, and commitment. Within this framework, of course, educators may arrive at a variety of conclusions. Many of these have been discussed in this book, e.g., formal curriculum programs and school governance. As we have already stressed, school leaders must become aware of ongoing school practices and must engage the entire community in a dialogue on moral education. It may be that these discussions, reflections, musings, and deliberations will result in a decision not to alter anything in the school. Or it may be decided that the proper area of emphasis is teacher education or inservice training. Or administrative policies, or curriculum, or the hidden curriculum, or various combinations of policies.

The bottom line, then, is not a recommendation for any particular form of moral education but rather our urgent and unshakeable conviction that educators must make informed decisions on moral education in the schools. We cannot dismiss the validity of any decision, even "doing nothing," but we find it unacceptable to deal with the issues mindlessly or carelessly. The way educators respond to the issues of moral education will have profound effects upon our entire way of life.

Education is simply not value-free. One cannot involve a child in schooling from the time he is six until he is seventeen or twenty-one and not affect the way he thinks about moral issues and the way he behaves. Nor can one legitimately evade the responsibilities we are urging by dismissing moral education as a fad. Certainly, education has been burdened with a continual procession of bandwagons that march by loudly, stridently, and then fade out until the next one comes along. It is true that the current activity in moral education has many of the characteristics of faddism. It is also true that the underlying issues are eternally relevant. What changes is not the value and importance of moral education but the interest in it. Ironically enough, because of the bandwagon effect, we have to work harder at sustaining interest and work in moral education, and resolve to go on even after the inevitable fade of the music.

Resources

Resources

Selected Bibliography

Beck, Clive. *Moral Education in the Schools: Some Practical Suggestions.* Toronto: Ontario Institute for Studies in Education, 1971.

Beck, Clive. *Ethics.* New York: McGraw-Hill, 1972.

Beck, Clive; Crittenden, Brian S.; and Sullivan, Edmund V. (eds.) *Moral Education: Interdisciplinary Approaches.* New York: Newman Press, 1971.

Bettelheim, Bruno. "Reflections: The Uses of Enchantment." *The New Yorker* (December 10, 1975): 50-114.

Dewey, John. *Moral Principles in Education.* New York: Philosophical Library, 1959.

Durkheim, Emile. *Moral Education.* New York: Free Press, 1961.

Educational Testing Service. *Moral Development, Proceedings of the 1974 ETS Invitational Conference.* Princeton, N.J.: Educational Testing Service, 1975.

Graham, Douglas. *Moral Learning and Development.* New York: John Wiley & Sons, 1972.

Harmin, Merrill; Kirschenbaum, Howard; and Simon, Sidney B. *Clarifying Values Through Subject Matter.* Minneapolis: Winston Press, 1973.

Hartshorne, Hugh, and May, Mark. *Studies in the Nature of Character.* Vol. I: *Studies in Deceit.* Vol. II: *Studies in Service and Self-Control.* Vol. III: *Studies in Organization of Character.* New York: Macmillan, 1928-30.

Hoffman, Martin L. "Moral Development." *Carmichael's Manual of Child Psychology,* edited by Paul H. Mussen. New York: John Wiley & Sons, 1970.

Jones, Vernon. *Character and Citizenship Training in the Public Schools.* Chicago: University of Chicago Press, 1936.

Kohlberg, Lawrence. *Collected Papers on Moral Development and Moral Education.* Cambridge, Mass.: Laboratory of Human Development, Harvard University, 1973.

Kohlberg, Lawrence, and Selman, Robert L. *Preparing School Personnel Relative to Values: A Look at Moral Education in the Schools.* ERIC Clearinghouse in Teacher Education, 1972.

Kuhmerker, Lisa. *A Bibliography on Moral Development and the Learning of Values in Schools and Other Social Settings.* New York: Center for Children's Ethical Education.

Makarenko, A. S. *Problems of Soviet School Education.* New York: Progress Publishers, 1965.

Overly, N. V. (ed.) *The Unstudied Curriculum.* Washington, D.C.: National Education Association, 1970.

Piaget, Jean. *The Moral Judgment of the Child.* New York: Free Press, 1965.

Raths, Louis; Harmin, Merrill; and Simon, Sidney B. *Values and Teaching.* Columbus, Ohio: Charles E. Merrill, 1966.

Simon, Sidney B., and Kirschenbaum, Howard. *Readings in Values Clarification.* Minneapolis: Winston Press, 1973.

Simon, Sidney B.; Howe, Leland; and Kirschenbaum, Howard. *Values Clarification: A Handbook of Practical Strategies for Teachers and Students.* New York: Hart, 1972.

Sizer, Theodore and Nancy F. (eds.) *Moral Education.* Cambridge, Mass.: Harvard University Press, 1970.

Sugarman, Barry. *The School and Moral Development.* New York: Barnes & Noble, 1973.

Sullivan, Edmund V. *Moral Learning: Findings, Issues, and Questions.* New York: Paulist Press, 1975.

Wilson, John; Williams, Norman; and Sugarman, Barry. *Introduction to Moral Education.* Baltimore: Penguin, 1967.

Sources of Materials and Information

American Institute for Character Education, P. O. Box 12617, San Antonio, Tex. 78212.

Center for Children's Ethical Education, 2 West 64th Street, New York, N.Y. 10023.

Center for Moral Education, Larsen Hall, Harvard University, Cambridge, Mass. 02138. (Material on the Kohlberg approach and information on the various research application projects.)

Guidance Associates, 757 Third Avenue, New York, N.Y. 10017. (Audio-visual materials oriented toward values questions.)

Journal of Moral Education, Pemberton Publishing Co., 88 Islington High Street, London, England.

National Humanistic Education Center, 110 Spring Street, Saratoga Springs, N.Y. 12866. (Materials and information on the values clarification approach.)

Ontario Institute for Studies in Education, 252 Bloor Street West, Toronto, Ontario, Canada. (Materials and reports on various research projects.)

Pennant Educational Materials, 4680 Alvarado Canyon Road, San Diego, Calif. 92120. (Extensive catalogue on values education materials.)

Public Education Religion Studies Center, Wright State University, Dayton, Ohio 45431.

Appendix

Moral Education's Muddled Mandate

Kevin Ryan and Michael G. Thompson

Members of Phi Delta Kappa are almost unanimous in thinking that an active program of moral education in the schools would be a helpful addition to the efforts of family and church to improve the moral development of children; however, they are widely divided as to what such a program should be. They underscore the primacy of the family in the moral life of the child; school rates only a close third in positive moral impact, following family and church. Kappans are deeply concerned about two major domestic and personal moral issues: rising crime and the decline of family life. They are substantially less concerned about international issues: warfare and world starvation. And while they think the former issues should be raised in schools in the primary grades, they would leave the latter to middle schools and high schools. Older members are both the most optimistic and the most pessimistic about the overall effectiveness of the schools as agents of moral education; younger members put more stress on their cognitive role. Finally, while Kappans tend to rate Americans as morally "about the same" as people in other countries,

Reprinted by permission from *Phi Delta Kappan* (June 1975), pp. 663-66.

they rate themselves as being very high both in moral behavior and in their ability to think about moral issues.

These are some of the results of a questionnaire on moral education mailed to a random sample of 1,000 members of Phi Delta Kappa on February 25, 1975. Some 561 members returned the seven-page instrument by the April 1 deadline. It probed a variety of issues, from the definition of "moral person" to religious affiliation to prescriptions for moral intervention in the schools. The answers point toward a feeling on the part of the membership that schools played a more effective role in the moral thinking and behavior of children twenty-five years ago than they do today, and suggest a clear recognition that the schools have a positive contribution to make in the moral development area.

Given seven definitions of a "moral person," a majority of respondents checked several (question 1). (The questionnaire is reprinted at the end of this appendix.) There was wide agreement that a moral person is one who "shows genuine concern about the rights and welfare of others" (97 percent) and "thinks clearly about issues of right and wrong" (89 percent). Interestingly, the two definitions that received the fewest checks were those relating to dominant societal sexual mores and societal expectations in general. Few Kappans see moral behavior as conformist behavior. Only a third believe society's rules concerning sex define a moral person.

When asked to rate the moral behavior of Americans in comparison to people in other nations (question 2), 18 percent rated it as somewhat better, 42 percent about the same, and 11 percent somewhat lower. A full quarter could not rate it. The respondents rated their own moral behavior highly. Seventy-three percent rated themselves in the top two categories on moral behavior and 88 percent rated themselves in the top two on moral reasoning. The 15 percent difference suggests an awareness of human limitation—e.g., "Do what I say, not what I do." That educators see themselves as being highly moral is noteworthy. While their responses suggest that they see themselves as potential moral leaders and clearly see the schools under their direction as having a strong mandate for developing active programs of moral education, there is no evidence that they think schools should become the dominant agents of moral education.

The association membership defers consistently to the family and church in matters of moral training (question 4). Eighty-two percent believe the family is either a very or somewhat positive moral force in the lives of children. When asked what should be the most important moral force in the lives of children, the consensus, almost unanimously (94 percent), was that the family should be (question 5). Only three Kappans thought the school should be the primary moral educator! (Chapter 4 gives some insight into how the question of "should be" might be answered in other societies, such as China and the U.S.S.R.) The church was seen as the second most powerful moral educator (75 percent), schools as third (68 percent).

A general distrust of government agencies was evident, as was a pronounced negative view of the mass media. Sixty-four percent of the respondents saw the mass media as having a negative effect on the moral life of children. Forty-nine percent saw government agencies as having a negative impact. (There is some question as to whether the respondents were thinking of the "moral model" aspect of government agencies or were focusing on the day-to-day contact of government with children. Perhaps it is simply Watergate backlash.) While the mass media are the most obvious villain, distrust of government goes even deeper. When the "neutral" category is added to the "negative" one, it is government (87 percent) which is seen overall as having the least positive moral impact. By contrast, 27 percent thought the mass media might be an effective moral educator. The only issue on which the sample was evenly divided was the impact of peers on the moral life of children. Fifty-three percent saw peers as having a positive moral impact, 46 percent as neutral or negative. The responses indicate that the child's friends should follow the family, church, and school in moral influence. It is interesting nonetheless that educators, whose primary professional responsibility is child development, are sharply divided on how children affect each other.

Kappans see the schools as having substantially less impact on the moral thinking and behavior of children than they did twenty-five years ago (questions 21 and 22). It is in the area of behavior that the schools are perceived as having less control than in years past (69 percent). A small but significant number of the sample (19 percent) seem to feel that the school's impact on moral thought has improved, even while its hold on behavior has diminished. Perhaps this is the mixed blessing of more open questioning by students of societal values.

When asked to indicate their overall view, the respondents were widely divided on the present impact of schools (question 8). Approximately half thought they were effective in helping children think about issues of right and wrong and half thought that the school's impact is on moral behavior. Still, almost a fifth of the respondents believe schools have little effect on either area. When the sample is broken down by age, differences appear. Specifically, younger educators stress the cognitive impact of the schools and are the least pessimistic (see table 1). Older Kappans were almost twice

Table 1
Age Differences in Views of School Influence

Age	Schools help both behavior and thinking	Schools help thinking	Schools help behavior	Schools do neither
0-35	16	38	29	17
36-50	19	33	30	18
51+	32	23	24	21

Significance level, .01

as likely to see the school as helping both the moral judgment and behavior of the child, but were very pessimistic about the school's moral influence.

Eighty-eight percent of the sample indicated that they think an active program of moral education in the schools is an important adjunct to family and church (question 11). Only 2 percent rejected out of hand the school's active participation in moral education. There is a clear mandate in the responses for the schools to intervene in the moral life of children, but no clear direction emerges. Of the five alternative approaches offered, only one was chosen by as much as a third of the sample (question 10); that was a program "where a child is helped to clarify his own values." All the options had significant support, however. Trends appeared in the choices according to the age of the respondents (see table 2). Those educators age thirty-five and below seemed to favor the "clarifying values" approach (43 percent); enthusiasm for this form of intervention is less pronounced among older educators. An opposite trend is found with respect to programs of service which help the child to behave in a moral way and programs in which the school is made into an exemplary just and

Table 2
Age Differences in Choices of Moral Education Approach

Age	Help children think about morals	Help children clarify own values	Program of service and experience	Make school a just community	Good solid liberal education
0-35	15	43	13	14	15
36-50	15	36	19	19	11
51+	11	23	31	21	14

Significance level, .001; Gamma +0.16

moral community. Only 13 percent of the younger members favored service programs while 31 percent of the older Kappans responded positively.

Kappans are in general agreement that the school's ability to affect the moral thinking and behavior of children is greatest when they are youngest. Sixty-three percent think that between the ages of five and nine the school has the most power to direct the moral thinking and behavior of children. (See chapters 12 and 20 for evidence that children are open to change, at least in their thinking, at later ages.)

What moral issues concern the PDK membership? Among the areas of greatest concern are domestic and personal issues: rising crime (75 percent), breakdown of family life (72 percent), political corruption (72 percent), and decline of personal honesty (70 percent). Not surprisingly, the same or closely related moral issues are the ones that the sample feels should be brought up at the earliest possible date in school, from kindergarten to fourth grade: respect for property (88 percent), lying and cheating (91 percent), and physically harming another (87 percent).

The two areas which generated the least concern overall were the decline of religion and changing sexual mores. A contradiction is suggested by the fact that while educators see the church as the second most important moral force in society, they were least concerned with the decline of religion. Either they do not see religion as being in decline, or for them its decline is not affecting its moral impact.

International issues are a source of moderate concern to Kappans, but that concern does not translate into curriculum action as readily as personal honesty, for example. International warfare, distribution of the world's wealth, and even duty to country are left for treatment in middle schools and high schools.

Many questions were answered similarly by people of different ages, experience, position, and religion. For example, views on the schools of twenty-five years ago were generally the same for educators of all ages and positions. However, on issues of concern, cross-tabulations revealed significant differences of opinion between different groups.

Older educators (over fifty-one) worry most about changing sexual mores. With the bulk of the respondents of all ages expressing moderate concern, approximately a third of the respondents under thirty-five years of age were not at all worried about sexual mores, while more than a third of those over fifty-one were greatly concerned (see table 3). Almost the identical pattern existed for concern

Table 3
Age Differences in Concern About Changing Sexual Mores

Age	Very great concern	Moderate concern	Not at all concerned
0-35	15	53	32
36-50	22	54	24
51+	38	46	16

Significance level, .001; Gamma −0.30

about the decline in religion. Principals and superintendents, as opposed to classroom teachers, were significantly more concerned about changes in the sexual realm.

Superintendents and principals, closely followed by classroom teachers, seem to worry most about the lack of respect for authority on the part of young people. Fifty-nine percent of the principals and superintendents rated it of great concern, while 47 percent of the elementary and secondary teachers did (see table 4). These figures are in striking contrast to the concerns checked by teachers and administrators in higher education. Only 25 percent thought it was a matter for significant worry; a slightly larger percentage of this higher education grouping (26 percent) were not at all concerned. The strength of the relationship between position and concern about

Table 4

Position Differences in Concern About Lack of Respect for Authority

Position	Very great concern	Moderate concern	Not at all concerned
Teachers and department chairmen	47	43	10
Principals and superintendents	59	38	3
College and university professors and administrators	24	50	26
All others	33	55	12

Significance level, .001; Gamma +0.25

lack of respect for authority grows stronger when the sample is divided by institutions (see table 5). As indicated by recent Gallup surveys, the American people are deeply concerned about school discipline. That concern is reflected in the responses here; however, judgments depend on educational role and institution.

Table 5

Institutional Affiliation Differences in Concern About Lack of Respect for Authority

Institution	Very great concern	Moderate concern	Not at all concerned
Public schools	50	44	6
Colleges and universities	24	51	25
All others	36	51	13

Significance level, .001; Gamma +0.34

Although there were numerous predictable relationships between religious affiliation and a number of variables (e.g., concern about the decline of religion, the place of church in moral training), one striking finding was the relationship between present religious status and concern about the family (see table 6). Agnostics and atheists are significantly less worried about the breakdown of family life than are the religiously affiliated; at the same time, there is little difference in level of concern among Protestants, Jews, and Catholics.

Table 6
Religious Affiliation Differences in Concern About the Breakdown of the Family

Religious affiliation	Very great concern	Moderate concern	Not at all concerned
Agnostic	35	59	6
Atheist	33	67	0
Catholic	80	20	0
Jewish	75	20	5
Protestant	75	20	5
Other	68	26	6

Significance level, .001; Gamma −0.23

Moral Education Questionnaire

(Numbers report percent response unless otherwise noted.)

1. What does the term "moral" mean to you? As an indication, please respond to each of the statements below. Check *Yes* those you believe essential to morality, *No* those not essential. (Note that no one statement is necessarily intended to define a "moral person" fully; you may consider some characteristics necessary but not sufficient, others neither necessary nor sufficient.) If dissatisfied with these statements, you may wish to frame *your own definition* in the space provided. But that should be *in addition to* filling in the blanks.

A person is moral who:

Yes	No	
65	35	Obeys the laws enacted and interpreted by government agencies.
71	29	Obeys the dictates of his own conscience.
89	11	Thinks clearly about issues of right and wrong.
37	63	Follows dominant societal mores governing sexual behavior.
97	3	Shows genuine concern about the rights and welfare of others.
50	50	Follows the rules of his church or closest reference group.
41	59	Does what is expected of him by his society.

(Respondents were given the option of providing their own definition.)

2. How would you rate the moral behavior of the average American in comparison with that of the average person in other countries?

Response	
2	American's morality extremely high
18	American's somewhat better
42	American's about the same
11	American's somewhat lower
2	American's much lower
25	Don't know how to rate it

N Missing = 13

3. Indicate your level of concern for each of the following moral issues. (Circle the appropriate number in each row.)

	Very greatly concerned	Moderately concerned	Not at all concerned	N missing
Political corruption	1 (72)	2 (27)	3 (1)	7
Breakdown of family life	1 (72)	2 (26)	3 (2)	8
International conflict and warfare	1 (46)	2 (50)	3 (4)	6
Changing sexual mores and sexual behavior	1 (26)	2 (51)	3 (23)	6
Rising crime rate	1 (75)	2 (24)	3 (1)	6
Decline of personal honesty	1 (70)	2 (26)	3 (1)	5
World poverty and starvation	1 (48)	2 (26)	3 (4)	7
Decline of religion	1 (26)	2 (49)	3 (3)	6
Lack of respect for authority among young people	1 (26)	2 (52)	3 (22)	8
Other (please specify) _____	1 (41)	2 (46)	3 (13)	9
	1 (96)	2 (4)	3 (0)	

4. How would you rate these institutions and groups in terms of their present impact on the moral thinking and behavior of children? (Circle one response in each row.)

	Very positive	Somewhat positive	Neutral	Somewhat negative	Very negative	N missing
Family	1 (31)	2 (51)	3 (10)	4 (7)	5 (1)	13
School	1 (9)	2 (59)	3 (21)	4 (10)	5 (1)	10
Church	1 (18)	2 (57)	3 (17)	4 (7)	5 (1)	9
Mass media	1 (13)	2 (14)	3 (9)	4 (49)	5 (15)	7
Child's friends	1 (23)	2 (30)	3 (25)	4 (21)	5 (1)	9
Government agencies	1 (2)	2 (11)	3 (30)	4 (40)	5 (9)	9

5. Now, how would you rank these institutional groups in terms of what *should* be their positive impact on the moral thinking and behavior of children? ("1" indicates the greatest impact and "6" the least impact.)

	1	2	3	4	5	6
Family	94	5	1	0	0	6
School	1	30	56	11	2	0
Church	3	51	18	13	12	3

Mass media	1	4	9	23	45	18
Child's friends	1	9	14	45	21	10
Government agencies	0	0	3	8	20	69

N Missing = 109

6. At what age level do you believe the school has the greatest impact on the moral *thinking* of children? (Check one.)

Response

63	5 to 9	10	14 to 18
19	10 to 13	8	All the same

N Missing = 8

7. At what age level do you believe the school has the greatest impact on the moral *behavior* of children? (Check one.)

Response

63	5 to 9	8	14 to 18
21	10 to 13	8	All the same

N Missing = 8

8. Which one of the following statements comes closest to expressing your own views? (Please check only one category.)

Response

23 Our schools help children to think about right and wrong and also help them to behave according to that thinking.

30 Schools help children think about right and wrong, but have little impact on the child's moral behavior.

28 At present schools help children behave normally, but do little to help them understand moral issues.

19 The schools have little impact on either the child's moral thought or behavior.

N Missing = 7

9. Which of the following moral issues should and should not be dealt with in the school, and at what grade level should they first be discussed? (Check the one inclusive grade level when the issue should be raised.)

	K to 4th	5th to 8th	9th to 12th	Should not be treated in schools	N missing
Theft and vandalism (respect for property)	88	11	1	0	31
Respect for duly constituted authorities	77	19	3	1	43

	K to 4th	5th to 8th	9th to 12th	Should not be treated in schools	N missing
Lying and cheating	91	7	1	1	34
Physically harming another	87	11	1	1	32
International wrongdoing and warfare	9	47	42	2	27
Violating someone's civil rights	28	47	24	1	34
Taking responsibility for one's own actions	67	28	5	0	34
Duty to country	32	37	25	6	39
Taking responsibility for the welfare of one's fellow man	37	31	28	4	33
Duty to family	67	18	7	8	42
Sexual mores and behavior	17	58	17	8	34
Distribution of the world's wealth	6	21	62	11	26

N Missing = 16

10. Granted, you've not been given enough information, but which of the five approaches described below do you feel would be most effective in a school program? (Check one.)

Response

14   A program helping children gain ability to think about moral issues

33   A program where a child is helped to clarify his own values

22   A program of service and experiences in which the child is helped to behave in a moral way

19   A program to make the school an exemplary just and moral community

12   A program of good, solid liberal education to develop careful thinking

N Missing = 16

11. Which one of the following is closest to your overall view on the issues of moral education?

Response

4   An active program of moral education in the schools would infringe on the role of the family and church.

88   An active program of moral education in the schools would be a helpful addition to the efforts of family and church to improve the moral development of children.

3   An active program of moral education in the schools would extend the influence of the school too far into the private lives of children.

2   An active program of moral education in the schools is simply out of the question.

3   Other (please specify) _____

(Questions 12 through 18 sought personal information: age, position, years of experience, level of education, religious training and denomination.)

19. How would you rate your own moral behavior?

Very high						Very low	N missing
1 (18)	2 (55)	3 (22)	4 (4)	5 (1)	6 (0)	7 (0)	6

20. How would you rate your own capacity for moral reasoning?

Very high						Very low	N missing
1 (34)	2 (54)	3 (11)	4 (1)	5 (0)	6 (0)	7 (0)	6

21. Do you think schools have more or less impact on moral *thinking* than they did 25 years ago?

More				Less	N missing
1 (3)	2 (16)	3 (21)	4 (40)	5 (20)	6

22. Do you think schools have more or less impact on moral *behavior* than they did 25 years ago?

More				Less	N missing
1 (2)	2 (9)	3 (20)	4 (44)	5 (25)	10

Index

Acting, 77-78, 97-98, 121-122
Activities, 80, 103-104
Adell, A. W., 137-138, 146, 151
Affective domain, 63-65
Affective education, 321-322
Affectivism, 314, 315-316, 319-322
Alschuler, A. S., 121, 125
Alston, B., 288, 289
Aspirations, 79, 100-101
Atkinson, R. F., 12, 19
Attitudes, 79, 99-100
Auden, W. H., 361, 369
Authority, 380-383
Avila, D. L., 120, 125

Baier, K., 25, 29, 153, 169
Baldwin, J. M., 177n
Bane, M. J., 349-369
Beck, C. M., 58, 221-234, 265, 272-273, 304, 305, 306, 349n, 399
Behavior modification, 317
Beliefs, 80
Benn, S. I., 356, 357, 369
Beyer, B. K., 291, 297n, 301, 302, 303, 304, 306

Blatt, M., 190-191, 195, 211, 219, 242, 259-262, 271, 273, 280, 287
Bloom, B. S., 120, 125
Botkin, P. T., 270, 273
Boyd, D., 259, 264, 273
Boyden, F., 213
Brandt, R. B., 16, 18, 19, 331, 347
Bronfenbrenner, U., 36, 43, 201-202, 219, 289, 313n, 329
Brown, G., 277, 286
Bruner, J., 253, 256, 273, 361, 369
Bull, N. J., 299, 306
Burke, E., 378

Canada, 221-234, 264-265
Carkhuff, R. R., 243, 266, 270, 273
Carr, D. B., 254, 273
China, 30-39, 42-43, 313n
Choosing, 76-77, 78, 81-84, 96-97, 120-121
Civic education: aims of, 182-195; research in, 187-189
Clarifying responses: criteria for, 87-88, 113; examples of, 104-112; list of, 90-98; purpose of, 113; topics for,

419

98-104, 112; as VC strategy, 86-115; valuing processes related to, 96-98

Cognitive development: fundamental ideas in, 253-259; future prospects for, 271-272; implementation of, 259-270; interactionism in, 257-259, 293; introduction to, 173-175; omissions in, 288-290; research on, 178, 298-300; reservations about, 291-307; review of programs using, 252-274; sequence in, 254-256, 292-293; structural organization of, 253-254, 292; theory of, 292-293; VC compared to, 185-187, 275-287

Cognitivism: curriculum of, 323-327; moral education related to, 313-329

Colby, A., 275-287

Combs, A. W., 120, 125

Communicating, 121

Connell, W. F., 30-43

Counseling skills, 241-244

Cremin, L., 236

Crittenden, B. S., 221, 233, 265, 273, 349n, 399

Culture: classroom, 49-50, 388; school, 52-53, 196-220, 229-233, 389; student, 51-52, 388

Curriculum: cognitive, 323-327; evaluation of, 260-261, 263-264, 296; formal, 45-48, 388; hidden, 48-53, 62-63, 197-199, 202-205, 229-233, 388-389; in moral education, 235-251, 260, 261, 262, 330, 333-347

Daitch, P., 144, 151

deSherbinin, P., 143, 147-148, 149-150, 151

Democracy, 193-194, 370-383

Development, moral: in democratic society, 370-383; family related to, 189-190; theory of, 238-239, 371-373

Developmental theory, 65-66

Developmentalism, 314, 316, 319-320

Dewey, J., 4, 10, 14, 146-147, 173, 176-177, 188, 194-195, 197, 206, 236, 252, 266, 292, 306, 399

DiStefano, A., 250, 251

Dilemmas, 179-180, 182, 190-191, 206-208, 216-219, 240-241, 260, 261, 262, 263, 301-303

Discussion, 190-191, 354-355

Dowell, R. C., 242, 250, 251

Dragunova, T. V., 38, 43

Dreeben, R., 197-198, 199-200, 203, 204, 205, 206, 219

Durkheim, E., 63, 197-198, 200-201, 202, 205, 206, 208, 219, 254, 273, 399

Education: authoritarian, 22-23; democratic, 20-23; goals of, 5-6; moral content of, 20-29; philosophies of, 13-15; pluralism of, 8

Ehrlichman, J., 324

Elfenbein, D., 178, 183, 195

Elkind, D., 266, 267-268, 273

Elkonin, D. B., 38, 43

Emotivism, 17-18

Engel, P., 185

England, 39-42

Erickson, V. L., 250, 251

Erikson, E. H., 266, 267, 273

Example, 35-36

Exhortation, 35

Existentialism, 15

Experience, 36-39

Feeling: values related to, 79-80; in valuing process, 120

Fenton, E., 191, 192, 194, 258, 273, 291, 296, 298-300, 302, 304, 306

Flavell, J. H., 270, 271, 273

Fletcher, J., 359, 369

Fox, R., 337, 347

Fraenkel, J. R., 291-307, 335-337, 347

Frankena, W. K., 25, 29, 165, 169

Friedenberg, E. Z., 197, 198-199, 203, 205, 210, 219

Fry, C. L., 270, 273

Galbraith, R. E., 301, 302, 303, 306

Gallup Poll Index, 7, 10

Goncharov, N. K., 22, 29

Gordon, T., 121, 125
Gray, F., 160*n*, 169
Greif, E. B., 291, 307
Griffen, A., 242, 251
Grimes, P., 250, 251
Guidance: moral education related to, 235-251, 265-270; rationale for, 236-237

Hampshire, S., 157*n*
Hare, R. M., 12, 19, 288, 358, 369
Harmin, M., 12, 19, 73, 75-115, 118, 124, 125, 135, 141-143, 147, 151-155, 158, 165, 166*n*, 169, 254, 274-277, 280, 283, 285-287, 305, 307, 334-335, 348, 399, 400
Hartshorne, H., 184, 195, 204, 219, 313, 329, 399
Hartwell, M., 144, 151
Harvard Social Studies Project, 351-355
Haynes, S., 250, 251
Heilbroner, R., 6-7, 10
Hentoff, N., 212, 219-220
Hickey, J., 192, 195, 259, 262-263, 273
Hobhouse, L., 177*n*
Hoffman, M. L., 289, 399
Holstein, C., 211, 220, 299, 306
Howe, L. W., 12, 19, 118, 125, 140, 151, 277, 281-282, 284, 285, 287, 400
Hunt, D. E., 138, 228, 233
Hunt, M. P., 258, 273, 303, 305, 306, 339-340, 347
Hurt, B. L., 250, 251

Idealism, 13-14
Indoctrination: defined, 56*n*; issue of, 55-58; as moral education method, 11-12, 17-18
Institutions: legitimacy of, 373-375; obligations to, 378-380; responsiveness of, 375-378, 379
Intellect, 61-62
Interests, 79, 102-103
Intervention, 65-66
Issues, identification of, 351-353

Jackins, H., 120, 125
Jackson, P. W., 196-197, 203-204, 220
Jacob, P. E., 365, 369
Jarvis, P. E., 270, 273
Jones, T. M., 301, 303, 306
Jones, V., 254, 273, 400
Jourard, S. M., 121, 125

Kairov, K. A., 31, 43
Kant, I., 182, 288
Kelley, E., 208-209, 220
Kenniston, K., 362, 369
King, M. L., Jr., 142, 165, 214, 298, 334
Kirschenbaum, H., 12, 19, 116-125, 140, 142, 146, 149, 151, 277, 280, 281, 282, 284, 285, 287, 399, 400
Klevan, A., 277, 287
Kneller, G. F., 13, 14, 15, 19
Kohlberg, L., 62-63, 65-67, 120, 123, 125, 138, 168*n*, 169, 173-226, 228, 233-234, 236, 238, 241, 242, 245, 251-307, 315, 316*n*, 320, 356-357, 359, 367, 369, 400
Kohlberg Test of Moral Maturity, 246, 249, 270
Kramer, R., 278, 287, 299, 307
Krebs, R., 181, 195
Kristol, I., 370-383
Kurtines, W., 291, 307

Lane, R. E., 361, 369
Lang, M., 277, 287
Lenin, N., 31
Liberal humanism, 373, 375
Lilge, F., 22, 29
Lippitt, R. O., 337-338, 347, 361-362, 369
Lockwood, A. L., 152-170, 241, 251, 256, 264, 273, 274, 330-348
Loevinger, J., 138, 269, 274
Loevinger Test of Ego Development, 246, 247-248, 249

McDougall, W., 177*n*
McIntyre, J., 121, 125
Mackie, P., 243, 251

Makarenko, A. S., 32, 400
Marcia, J. E., 270, 274
May, M., 184, 195, 204, 219, 313, 329, 399
Mayer, R., 66, 67, 168n, 169
Mayerson, C., 212, 220
Mehlinger, H., 342, 347
Meta-ethics, 16-19, 324-325
Metcalf, L. E., 258, 273, 303, 305, 306, 339-340, 347
Mischel, W., 288, 289, 298, 307
Moral atmosphere, 191-220
Moral character, 206-213
Moral dilemmas, 179-180, 182, 190-191, 206-208, 216-219, 240-241, 260-263, 301-303
Moral discussion, 190-191, 354-355
Moral education: affective considerations and, 63-65; aims of, 182-195; approaches to, 275-287; attitudes toward, 405-417; character education as, 184-185; cognitive approach to, 309-383; cognitive development as theory for, 304-306; cognitive-developmental approach to, 171-307; commitment in, 393-394; and community views, 389-390; confrontation in, 391-392; curriculum for, 235-251, 260, 261, 262, 330, 333-347; defined, 5; developing, 211-212; developmental considerations and, 65-66; direct approach to, 58-61; Durkheim's system of, 200-201; educational consequences of, 199-205; elementary school program for, 222-225; examination of, 387-390; failure of, 313-315; goals of, 283-284, 323, 390-394; group situation for, 365-367; and hidden curriculum, 48-53, 62-63, 197-199, 202-205, 229-233, 388-389; implementation of, 325-327; implications of, for schooling, 23-29; indirect approach to, 61-63; as indoctrination, 9; inevitability of, 44-54; inquiry in, 392-393; instructional issues in,

55-67; integrative approach to, 60-61; just schools as ends of, 213-214; knowledge in, 323-324; meta-ethics in, 16-19, 324-325; methods of, 11-13, 34-39; moral reasoning in, 324; national aims and methods of, 30-43; philosophical issues in, 11-19; planned, 189-195; and politics, 31; prison studies of, 262-264; process of, 323; programmatic approach to, 59-60; psychological assumptions in, 279-280; reasoning in, 349-369; relativism related to, 330-348; and schools, 3-10, 363-364; secondary school program for, 225-229, 239-246; time given to, 328; VC approach to, 71-170
Moral judgment, 179-181
Moral philosophy, 182-183
Moral point of view: acceptable, 344-347; in classroom, 57; in democratic education, 25-28; in VC, 164-167
Mosher, R. L., 58, 192, 194, 235-251, 265-272, 274
Myrdal, G., 157n

National Assessment of Educational Progress, 313, 324
Naturalism, 16-17
Neill, A. S., 204-205, 213, 220
Newberg, N., 321
Newcomb, T. M., 365, 369
Newmann, F. M., 168n, 169, 264, 305, 307, 340-342, 347, 351, 369
Nixon, R. M., 188, 327, 376

Objectivity, 41, 42-43
Oliver, D. W., 168n, 169, 258, 264, 274, 305, 307, 328, 340-341, 347, 348, 349-369
Ontario Institute for Studies in Education, 221-222, 264-265

Paolitto, D., 250, 251
Parilch, B., 190, 195

Parnes, S. J., 120, 125
Participation, social, 42-43
Patrick, J. J., 342, 347
Peer groups, 37-39, 388
Perry, R. B., 21-22, 23, 29
Peters, R. S., 25, 29, 199, 220, 288-290, 295, 356, 357, 369
Phi Delta Kappa, 5-6, 405-417
Piaget, J., 65, 138, 173-174, 177, 179, 195, 197, 206, 222, 252, 255, 256, 258-259, 261, 266, 267, 270, 278, 289, 292, 293, 307, 315, 400
Plato, 22, 173, 188
Pluralism, 326-328
Pragmatism, 14-15
Prescriptivism, 18-19
Prizing, 77, 78, 97
Public issues curriculum: and ethical thought, 355-357; moral education through, 349-351; problems with, 357-363; and relativism, 340-342
Purkey, W. W., 120, 125
Purpel, D., 3-10, 44-67, 387-395
Purposes, 78-79, 101-102

Quinton, A., 319, 329

Raths, J., 277, 287
Raths, L. E., 12, 19, 73, 77-115, 118-120, 124, 125, 135, 141-143, 146-148, 151-155, 158-166, 169, 254, 274-277, 280, 283, 285-287, 305, 307, 334-335, 348, 400
Rationalism: democratic education related to, 24-29; as moral education method, 12, 13, 14, 17, 18
Rawls, J., 182, 183, 195, 288
Realism, 13-14
Reasoning, 349-369
Reflective thinking, 339-340
Relativism: defined, 331; moral education related to, 330-348; pluralism related to, 326-328; roots of, 318-319; unacceptability of, 331-333; in VC, 123, 142-146, 166-169, 280-283, 334-335

Religion, 314-315, 326
Rest, J., 178, 195, 252-274, 292, 298, 300-301, 307
Rogers, C. R., 120, 125, 158-164, 169, 243, 250, 251, 266
Rokeach, M., 122, 125
Role playing, 64-65
Rustad, K., 250, 251
Ryan, K., 3-10, 44-67, 387-395, 405-417
Ryan, W., 233, 234

Scandinavia, 313n
Schaeffer, P., 249, 251
Schaible, L., 337, 347
Scharf, P., 192, 195, 263, 274
Scheffe Multiple Comparisons Test, 247, 248
Scheffler, I., 20-29
School: activities of, 50-51; atmosphere of, 52-53, 196-220, 229-233, 389; discipline in, 200; just, 192-194, 213-214; moral education and, 3-10, 363-364; as value transmitter, 203-204
Science Research Associates, 337-339
Scriven, M., 295, 305, 307, 313-329
Selman, R., 138, 259, 264, 274, 278-279, 287, 400
Shaver, J. P., 168n, 258, 264, 274, 305, 307, 328, 340, 348
Simon, S. B., 12, 19, 73, 77-115, 118, 124-135, 138, 140-155, 158, 165, 166n, 169, 222, 254, 275-287, 305, 307, 334-335, 348, 399, 400
Simpson, E. L., 291, 299, 307
Skinner, B. F., 289, 317, 320
Smith, M. B., 361, 369
Spears, H., 5-6, 10
Speicher, A., 280, 287
Spencer, H., 4
Sprinthall, N. A., 237, 241, 242, 250-252, 265-272, 274
Stages, moral: characteristics of, 177-178; in cognitive development, 176-180; defined, 215-216; develop-

ment of, 206-210; discussion related to, 359; reservations about, 294-296, 316; as structures of moral judgment, 179-180

Stewart, J. S., 136-151

Sugarman, B., 5, 10, 168n, 170, 258, 274, 400

Sullivan, E. V., 58, 221-234, 265, 273, 349n, 399, 400

Sullivan, P., 58, 235-251

Taba strategies, 335-337

Tabor, D., 121, 125

Teacher training, 232-233

Teachers, 212-213, 229-233, 260, 261-262, 296-297

Teaching skills, 244-246

Thinking, 120

Thompson, M. G., 405-417

Turiel, E., 168n, 169, 178, 195, 210, 220, 254, 259, 273

Turnbull, C., 294, 307

Union of Soviet Socialist Republics, 22, 31-39, 42-43, 200-202, 205, 208, 313n

United States, 39-42

Values clarification (VC): affective domain related to, 64; clarifying response for, 86-115; as client-centered therapy, 158-164; cognitive-development approach compared to, 185-187, 275-287; criticisms of, 136-170; in the curriculum, 58; defined, 122, 152-153; through discussion, 351-355; indoctrination vs., 126-135; introduction to, 71-74; issues in, 116-125; judgmental nature of, 141-142; as moral education method, 12, 15, 19; moral point of view in, 164-167; peer pressure in, 139-141; problems and contradictions of, 136-151; relativism of, 123, 142-146, 166-169, 280-283, 334-335; research on, 147; social context of, 117-118; strategies for, 129-134, 354; superficiality of, 137-139; theoretical base of, 123-124, 146-149; usefulness of, 126-128, 134-135; as value free, 122

Value judgments, 327-328

Values: accepted, 12-14, 15, 16-17, 18; defined, 75-78, 153-158; indicators of, 78-81, 98-104; moral distinguished from nonmoral, 330-331, 333-342, 343-344; personal nature of, 84-90; standards for, 333-342

Valuing, 76-78, 96-98, 118-122, 124

Veatch, H. B., 166, 170, 332, 348

Vivian, F., 17, 19

Wallace, G., 208

Watkins, J. W., 11-19, 56n

Wehlage, G., 330-348

Wellenberg, E. P., 254, 273

Wessler, R., 269, 274

West Virginia, values conflict in, 8, 326

White, R. K., 361-362, 369

White, R. W., 361, 369

Whyte, W. H., 39

Williams G., 323

Williams, N., 5, 10, 168n, 170, 258, 274, 298, 299, 307, 400

Williams, S., 298, 299, 307

Wilson, J., 5, 10, 12, 19, 168n, 170, 258, 274, 400

Wright, D., 299, 307

Wright, J. W., 270, 273

Yesipov, B. P., 22, 29